D1191098

PERSUASION

A Means of
Social Control

PRENTICE-HALL SPEECH SERIES

PERSUASION

A Means of Social Control

Winston Lamont BREMBECK

University of Wisconsin

William Smiley HOWELL

University of Minnesota

PRENTICE-HALL, INC.

Englewood Cliffs, N. J.

L.C. Cat. Card No.: 52-10155

First Printing ....November, 1952
Second Printing ....June, 1953
Third Printing ....May, 1955
Fourth Printing ....March, 1958
Fifth Printing ....June, 1959
Sixth Printing ....January, 1961
Seventh Printing ....January, 1962
Eighth Printing ....June, 1963

PRINTED IN THE UNITED STATES OF AMERICA

66108—C

To

NEVA

and

JESSIE

PREFACE

Modern living demands an understanding of persuasion. Urbanization and increased communication bring the individual into daily contacts with numerous people of his county, state, nation, and the world. He finds himself a consumer and producer of persuasion in an ever-expanding and increasingly competitive market place of ideas. To champion his own ideas and to evaluate critically those of others he must understand the principles and methods of the intricate science of influencing human behavior.

The authors assume that an adequate understanding of persuasion must rest upon knowledge of the relevant bases of human behavior rather than a descriptive study of techniques and appeals used by successful persuaders. The inductive approach of this book leads the reader in a search for the fundamental elements of human motivation from which the methodology of persuasion is derived. First, there is a consideration of the role of persuasion in modern society and suggestions for systematic observation of it. Next, the bodily and social bases of persuasion are discussed. Then the tools of the persuader—language and the psychological and logical forms in which it appears—are treated. The methods of applying knowledge of the bases and tools of persuasion to oral communication are presented in detail next in the book. Finally, the various approaches to evaluating persuasion are presented. These include a survey of the experimental studies, the tested devices for measuring audience response to persuasive stimuli, and discussion of ethical issues confronting the persuader.

All citizens who, as consumers of persuasion, desire to make careful appraisals of persuasion directed at them should find this book of value.

We are indebted to the many authors and publishers who have permitted us to quote from their writings and publications; this indebtedness is acknowledged elsewhere in this book. Sincere appreciation is expressed to Professor Robert T. Oliver, Chairman of the Department of Speech, Pennsylvania State College, for his encouraging leadership in developing persuasion as a field for college study. Special gratitude is extended to Professor Henry L. Ewbank, Department of Speech, University of Wisconsin, and to Dean James H. McBurney, School of Speech, Northwestern University, for reading the manuscript and for making many valuable suggestions for its improvement.

W.L.B.
W.S.H.

TABLE OF CONTENTS

Part V. Applying Persuasion to Speaking, 241

Part VI. Evaluating Persuasion, 393

PERSUASION

A Means of Social Control

Part I

INTRODUCING THE STUDY OF PERSUASION

Persuasion has been and will continue to be one of the chief levers of life. Today the density of competing persuasions is greater than ever before, making the study of persuasion not only necessary for the specializing few but also requisite for all who would live effectively in modern society.

The chapters of Part I remind us of the significance of persuasion in our daily lives and suggest an overall approach to be used in the study of its separate elements. It is hoped that together these introductory chapters will provide the reader with a clear orientation and a firm foundation for the study of the succeeding chapters.

Chapter I

PERSUASION IN MODERN MASS SOCIETY

I. Introduction

II. Persuasion—the Cementing Principle of Modern Civilization

III. Factors Determining the Role of Persuasion in Modern Democratic Societies

A. Leadership in Populous, Democratic Countries Dependent on Persuasion

1. Leadership in Government
2. Leadership in Business
3. Leadership in Personal-Social Relationships

B. Social Problems in a Democracy Often Resolved in Arena of Competing Persuasions

IV. An Understanding of Persuasion Requisite to Modern Living

A. Essential for a Personal Adjustment to Modern Life

B. Essential to the Perpetuation of Democracy

V. Summary

Readings and Exercises

Chapter I

PERSUASION IN MODERN MASS SOCIETY

Introduction

Two Chinese coolies were engaging in a heated argument. A stranger in the anxious crowd expressed his surprise that no blows were being struck. A Chinese friend replied, "The man who strikes first admits that his ideas have given out." This method of settling differences is one with which we in the United States, along with all other freedom-loving, democratic peoples agree. We believe that human differences should be settled by persuasion rather than by fists and carbines. We believe that the right to persuade is basic to democracy and that the collective opinions which result should rule us.

Democratic societies are composed of many diverse elements, but there is general acceptance of the basic principle that each group has the right to try to influence the others, and that both unsuccessful and successful competing persuasions shall be heard. When the Republicans sweep the country, for example, the Demo crats do not stage an armed insurrection, but abide by the Republican-controlled government, and at the same time, are allowed to begin a campaign to persuade the voter to place the Democrats in office at the next election. When the customer buys a Chevrolet instead of a Ford, the Ford dealer accepts his defeat and prepares even more carefully his sales talk for the competition with the Chevrolet dealer to "sell" the next prospective customer. Thus, through persuasion the political minority may become the majority, one cigarette may achieve the largest sale in its field, and a certain student organization may become the most influential on the campus. Freedom to persuade is an accepted principle of our democracy; the effective use of persuasion is becoming increasingly essential to success.

Today we find ourselves in a society where the competition for votes, customers, joiners, sympathizers, readers, contributors, and so on, is most intense. We live in a country with perhaps the greatest persuasion density in the world, and where the manufacture and manipulation of public opinion through persuasion is recognized as a legitimate and intricate science. To understand persuasion, then, is requisite to modern living. This book is an attempt to view realistically the role of persuasion in modern society and to help the reader understand its bases, methods, applications, and responsibilities.

Persuasion—the Cementing Principle of Modern Civilization

Persuaders and persuasions reflect the social milieu of their times. It is not only to man's physiological and psychological make-up that we must look, but also to the basic features of his society, if we are to explore the fountainheads of human motivation. Until the middle of the fifteenth century there was little freedom of public persuasion. The propagation of ideas was monopolized by the church and certain state officials. However, with the invention of printing, the Protestant Reformation, the Renaissance, the rise of business classes, the Industrial Revolution, and the discovery of new lands, came growing democratic ideas and the attendant belief in the right of freedom of persuasion for all. As democracy spread, as the vote was granted to an increasing number of people, and as advances were made in education and communication, free trade in persuasion came to be accepted as an essential factor in democratic societies.

The early American colonists carried on active campaigns of persuasion not only in the field of religion, but also in commerce, labor, and politics. Samuel Adams and his Committees of Correspondence, as well as the writings of Thomas Paine, helped prerevolutionary political progaganda assume significant proportions. Following the American Revolution, the arena of competing persuasions was enlarged by groups of varying interests. Socio-economic classes became more clearly defined and articulate. More recently the expansion of governmental agencies has added extensive systems of "public relations."

The advances of capital, labor, and agriculture have been made possible by intensified systems of public persuasion and governmental lobbying. Today there are approximately 10,000 commercial and industrial organizations in the United States, 1500 of which are interstate, national, or international in scope.[1] Most of these organizations have systems of persuasion on behalf of their special interests. Outside the fields of politics, business, labor, and agriculture, there are various racial, religious, professional, and other special-purpose organizations. Childs points out that "more than 500 national associations have headquarters in Washington and seek directly or indirectly to mold public opinion and public policy." [2]

But what happens to the individual whose mind is besieged by all these persuasions? Technological advance and increased industrialization have produced an urban culture. Today's individual has become a specialist living in a mass of grouped yet isolated city dwellers. Sociologists use the term *mass society* to describe our present social structure, and generally agree that individuals living under modern technology develop psychological characteristics which differ from those of our grandfathers who, together with friendly neighbors, cleared and tilled the land, and whose villages were small and personal. Young says that "Today, under urban conditions especially, we have a mass of isolated individuals, interdependent in all sorts of specialized and external ways, yet lacking any close sense of personal intimacy and emotional security, and often having no central unifying value or purpose. In a sense, modern urban culture has produced a crowd-minded society, with transitory contacts, emotional reactions, irrationality, and values quite different from those of more stable cultures." [3]

Today's individual is faced with more than the simple, local problems of the early American citizen. Urbanized life along with modern methods of communication have led the individual to form opinions on numerous problems extending from his home town to Washington, New York, London, Berlin, Tokyo, and Moscow. Modern society has become so complex, its agencies of control so remote, and its demands so numerous, that all too often we cannot

---

[1] H. L. Childs, *An Introduction to Public Opinion.* New York: John Wiley and Sons, Inc., 1940, p. 77.

[2] *Ibid.,* p. 78.

[3] K. Young, *Social Psychology.* New York: Appleton-Century-Crofts, Inc., 1945, p. 408.

know things as they *actually* are, but only as we are *told* they are. We do not know if our toothpaste actually is the best brand or if Representative Jones has done a good job in Washington. We must decide on the basis of what we are told.

As members of this mass society and in the midst of these numberless demands, we often become distraught, our sense of security lessened. Our quest for intimacy and security has led us to become a nation of "joiners." We grasp at the butterflies of political promises. We may follow one who will promise a chicken in every dinner-pail, a car in every garage, or an appealing old-age pension. Increased attendance at sports events, wrestling matches, all types of rallies and fewer but more violent mob actions are other evidences of the fact that modern man reflects the behavior of a crowd-minded society.

This, then, is the type of society in which we find ourselves. Succeeding chapters will give a more detailed account of this social structure. Since its complexity makes it impossible for us actually to *know* or *experience much of it directly,* we must depend on what we are told. Thus our thoughts and actions are to a great extent the products of the prevailing systems of persuasion. In this sense, persuasion may be said to be the cementing principle of modern society.

Factors Determining the Role of Persuasion in Modern Democratic Societies

We have seen that great masses of men live a pattern of life designed for them to a great extent by those who persuade. Let us examine more specifically some of the chief factors to which we may attribute the significant role played by persuasion in modern society.

LEADERSHIP IN POPULOUS, DEMOCRATIC COUNTRIES DEPENDENT ON PERSUASION

Methods of leadership vary with the type of society. Kings ruled by "divine right" for many centuries; their leadership was largely in the form of edicts, proclamations, and certain rigid institutions. Autocratic governments, though often having gained power through the channels of persuasion, have tended to maintain this power by force, violence, and impersonal bureaus. No matter what the specific form, leadership in autocratic nations is limited to the few who rule. The instruments of social control are not available for popular use. Public discussion and debate and public persuasion are not encouraged by autocratic governments. Democratic nations provide the right for each citizen to attempt leadership in the areas of his choice. Because our society is so populous and complex, the leader, or would-be leader, often cannot know or be known by those whom he would lead. He must persuade groups from the public platform and reach audiences in far places by "distant-contact" methods. These methods rely upon the major vehicles of persuasion—the radio, television, newspapers, motion pictures, magazines, books, pamphlets, parades, and so on. But whether it be by direct or distant-contact means, the aspirants to leadership must compete successfully with many others aspiring to the same position. This fact explains the rise of highly-skilled systems of propaganda in democratic leadership techniques.[4]

Today, therefore, political parties, business groups, unions, corporations, and numerous other special-interest groups resort to some form of persuasion to gain and maintain leadership.

The competition for leadership in the areas of government, business, and personal-social relations include the areas chiefly responsible for the development of the vast, skilled systems of modern persuasion. We shall consider them in this same order.

Leadership in Government. Democracy is government by popular discussion and representation. In the colonial days our forefathers gathered around the cracker-barrel in the local grocery or met in a small town hall to discuss their common problems and elect their leaders. Usually the leaders were known by every voter; the relationship between leader and follower was personal and direct. The "record" of the political candidate was common knowledge. There was little need for the aspiring leader to employ much persuasion in his own behalf. Today, however, the local town meeting has assumed national proportions, the radio and television have replaced the colonial town crier, and the problems of government are far more numerous and complex. When Plato concluded that

---

[4] The reader will note that the authors considered propaganda to be one form of persuasion. Definitions of propaganda and persuasion are given in Chapter II.

democracy, in the sense of direct rule by public opinion, was practical only in small communities, he did not foresee the development of our modern systems of communication. By radio, today's political leader can speak to 100 millions almost as effectively and conveniently as Patrick Henry delivered his famous speech to the Virginia convention.

But with all our developments in communication we note that the relationship between leader and people in our mass society is not personal and direct, but often quite impersonal and indirect. As Lippman says, "The real environment is altogether too big, too complex, and too fleeting for direct acquaintance." [5] The voter is confronted by huge political parties which are as distant and impersonal to him as modern industry, and the political issues often are complicated beyond his comprehension. As a result, the voter is forced to look to political parties, writers, and speakers for guidance. Certainly he has not been disappointed in this regard, for from all quarters have come those who seek to give him "the facts" about Senator So-and-so, and the "low-down" on the pilfering along the Potomac. The competition seeking his support often becomes so intense and conflicting that, like the old mountaineer, he finds "It's more simple just to always vote Democratic."

We live in a time when the struggle for political leadership is intense. For this reason vast, expert systems of popular information and persuasion have been developed, ranging in scope from the more obvious persuasion of the local ward heeler to the extensive, subtle system of propaganda directed by the national head of the party. Numerous special-interest groups participate in the arena of competing persuasions in attempts to influence party and public policies in ways helpful to their interests. If an individual desires political leadership, and if the minority is to become the majority, there must be a thorough understanding of, and skill in the manufacture and manipulation of public opinion. This means an understanding of persuasion in its broadest and deepest sense.

Leadership in Business. In our country, commercial persuasion has achieved a pervasiveness, skill, and organization probably unsurpassed by that of any other nation. The growth of advertising

---

[5] Walter Lippman, *Public Opinion.* New York: The Macmillan Company, 1931, p. 16.

and salesmanship seems to have paralleled the growth of the economic warfare carried on by an ever-increasing number of business competitors. To be successful, or even to survive, in the present-day business world, one must become skilled in the art of persuasion. Thus advertising and salesmanship have become standard courses of study in commercial training, and publicity agents and public-relations counselors now are among the most highly paid employees of large commercial concerns. During the years following 1920, there was an annual expenditure of from one billion to two billion dollars on advertising in the United States. In 1947 three billion was spent annually for *product* advertising, and industry aimed at an equal amount for ideological advertising in 1948 to "boost free enterprise." [6]

Using every available avenue and method of motivation, commercial organizations have developed systems of persuasion designed (a) to reap quick profits, (b) to establish a permanent good will, (c) to encourage investment and thus gain capital, and (d) to avoid ruinous competition. It was the persuasion of the advertisers which elevated the cigarette from its lowly estate as a "coffin nail" to a national necessity in peace and war; which made every lover fearful of B.O., and every baby "cry for Castoria," and every man with a lifted glass into a "man of distinction."

So today every potential customer is living in mental climates created by skillful craftsmen in the art of human motivation. As he walks along the streets, lights flicker the merchants' wares, barkers' cries besiege his ears, billboards grab his passing attention, and sky-writers exploit his upward glances. When he arrives at home, radio and television commercials run the whole gamut of devices to get him to buy, and the ads in his evening paper follow him from page to page. Whether the customer buys Chesterfields instead of Camels, or a Plymouth in preference to a Ford depends to a great extent upon the relative strength of the competing persuasions. There can be no denying that leadership in business is greatly dependent upon successful persuasion. These systems are vast and complex and will be considered in detail later.

Leadership in Personal-Social Relationships. In our concern with the important role persuasion plays in the achievement of leadership

[6] From a speech by Kalman B. Druck in "Editor and Publisher," September 13, 1947.

in such large areas as government and business, we must not overlook its significance to leadership in the more common and far more numerous personal-social situations. Many of us do not aspire to great leadership, but most of us do desire places of prominence in our local social groups. We belong to many and varied groups. We are members of a home, a church, a school, class, an art club, a language club, the Lions, Rotarians, Elks, Kiwanis Club, or Knights of Columbus, a bridge club, the international relations club, a labor union, a sports club, a forensic society, the Young Democratic club, and many more. It takes but a moment's reflection to realize the complexity of the social web we have woven about ourselves. Who among us has not found difficulty in making even the more simple adjustments to our increasingly complex social organizations, to say nothing of the problems involved in gaining places of leadership?

Both the need and desire for leadership in the many personal-social relationships have resulted in a growing demand for training in the direction of human thought and action. Books, booklets, and magazine articles on "winning friends and influencing people" have become best sellers. Churches, clubs, youth camps, personnel bureaus, and so on, have established their own leadership training courses. All these have recognized that adjustment to the social group which is of sufficient effectiveness to constitute leadership must necessarily make considerable use of the elements of persuasion.

SOCIAL PROBLEMS IN A DEMOCRACY OFTEN RESOLVED IN ARENA OF COMPETING PERSUASIONS

Modern mass society is a dynamic organization. Unlike the older, more stable societies, our society is constantly in a state of flux. Our fashions, customs, conventions and social ideologies are continually changing. Social problems are bound to be constantly arising and articulated in a nation where freedom of speech is guaranteed and where each group and class has the right to try to improve itself or to defend its position.

As social problems arise, they are usually talked into solution or oblivion. Ideally, public opinion formation in a democracy should follow the steps of the scientific method in the solution of social problems. That is, (1) a problem is posed, (2) analyzed, (3) hypotheses or possible solutions are considered, (4) a best solution is chosen and tested, and (5) a conclusion is drawn and acceptance of it is sought. Following the suggestions of John Dewey, Ewbank and Auer have shown the need for and methods of forming public opinion in such a rational manner.[7] These and other writers have recognized, however, that quite often the current procedures of resolving social problems are based on appeals to tradition, desires, prejudices, hatreds, and so on. So we have, on the one hand, the rational and more ideal formation of public opinion, while, on the other hand, we have opinion formed in ways which deviate from such a pattern. Students of human motivation should understand the part played by persuasion in each. To show these two procedures more clearly, a paralleled development is given below.

RATIONAL FORMATION OF PUBLIC OPINION

1. *Locating and Defining the Problem.*

Some problem begins to be defined by certain interested individuals or groups. A physical catastrophe such as a flood may pose the problem directly; the desire for a new community gymnasium may present and define the problem; rising prices may pose a very real problem to consumers; or a Pearl Harbor attack may raise the question of blame and begin an investigation.

Whatever the problem, those who pose it must define it; they must determine its precise nature and location so that it can be discussed efficiently.

2. *Analysis of the Problem.*

Here an exploration is made of the problem. How serious is it? Is now the time to discuss it? How many of us does it affect? These and other questions are asked in our talks to our neighbors, in news

POSSIBLE DEVIATIONS FROM THE RATIONAL PATTERN

1. In modern mass society, social problems tend to be defined in vague and general terms. Again the complexity of modern society does not lend itself to clearly defined issues and simple solutions. If the expert outlines the facts of the problem sufficiently to provide a basis for its rational consideration, the layman often is smothered in a pile of complex data. This fact offers some explanation of why the agitator or demagogue who simplifies the problem and offers an easy remedy is given more support than that extended to the expert.

Thus in modern society, accurate and rational location and definition of a social problem are very difficult.

2. Persuaders for special interests may, by appeals to special interests, desires, group prejudices, and so on, prevent an objective analysis of the problem. Those who stand to benefit or lose personally from the solution of the

[7] H. L. Ewbank and J. J. Auer, *Discussion and Debate.* New York: Appleton-Century-Crofts, Inc., 1941.

stories and editorials, in radio discussions and speeches. Investigations are made to discover facts about the problem. Ideally these investigations are made objectively and survey all the pertinent facts.

3. *Examination of Possible Solutions.*

Following the analysis of a problem, we look around for a possible solution. We examine various possibilities. The proponents of this or that solution begin to influence opinions. Radio and press, town hall and church discuss the proposed solutions. The number of proposals gradually becomes reduced and the opposing camps of opinion become more clearly defined.

In this step, investigative discussion usually grows into persuasive speaking in attempts to influence the direction of decision.

4. *Selection of the Best Solution.*

Here we have arrived at the place where a preferred solution is tested in the crucible of debate. We examine its pros and cons. Some attempt to analyze the proposal carefully and objectively, organizing evidence to support each point at issue. Others choose to win the debate for their side by appealing to our needs, our desires, and our prejudices.

In democratic organizations, a vote is taken to determine the winner, be it in political office, in a congressional debate over a bill, or in some local, community problem.

problem may develop active systems of persuasion in an attempt to analyze the problem only from their particular point of view. Investigations are sometimes deliberately confused by special interests; censorship of certain facts may distort the analysis of the problem.

3. Special interest groups are very active during this stage of public opinion formation. Each group is attempting to win assent for its proposed solution. Industrial managers may contend that prosperity can come only through more production, and more production only by more rigid labor legislation. Contractors will favor a new gymnasium as the answer to the juvenile delinquency problem of the community.

The systems of persuasion used by the special-interest group may prevent the rational consideration of all the possible solutions, and focus attention on personal rather than the common welfare.

4. In the heat of public debate on a question of national concern, the use of irrational language, of slogans, stereotypes and legends comes in. Deepseated emotionalized values are not readily changed by rational considerations.

Skillful systems of propaganda, appealing to the old traditions and sentiments, may cause the direction of public debate to move toward a very irrational solution of a social problem.

5. *Gaining Acceptance of the Chosen Solution.*

In Step Number 4 usually a consensus is gained; seldom is there unanimous agreement. The majority may continue to legitimate its position by persuasion designed to get an ever-increasing acceptance of the winning proposal. The authors of a bill which has become law may continue to justify its existence; the political leader may continue a system of public relations "to keep himself in office"; or the proponents of the new gymnasium may conduct many community functions in the newly built building to enlist greater support.

5. Here the minority may continue to oppose in the hope that the majority opinion may be overthrown. Vast systems of propaganda may be established to render the majority legislation ineffective.

On occasion, revolutionary groups attempt to arise at this point, defying the opinion of representative democracy and seeking to overthrow by force and violence that which they opposed earlier in a losing battle of persuasion.

A classic and interesting example of the manner in which both the rational and non-rational patterns of public opinion may operate is found in the history of the prohibition movement in the United States. Throughout early American history isolated attempts were made to arouse public opinion to the evils of drink. At first the problem was posed by only a few. Preachers and such lay crusaders as Francis E. Willard aroused public discussion. Those personally engaged in the liquor industry attempted to minimize the problem. After 1900 the Anti-Saloon League became an organization which voiced the opinions of an ever-increasing number of "Dry" sympathizers. Working through many churches, the League held numerous discussions regarding possible solutions to this problem. It was decided that the mere teaching of temperance was not enough, but that prohibition laws must be established and enforced. Then the Drys began chasing "John Barley-corn" in earnest. Their persuasion was centered first on getting local option laws and next on statewide prohibition laws. When it was realized that a wet state was a reckless partner to be next to a dry state, the persuasion was focused on Congress and national prohibition.

The United States Brewers' Association began realizing the weakness of their own methods of persuasion and the strength of their opponents' when in 1913 the Drys succeeded in gaining passage of the Webb-Kenyon bill. In 1916 a Congress favorable to the submission of a national prohibition amendment was elected, and in 1917 the Eighteenth Amendment to the Constitution was submitted to the states for ratification. In 1919 the necessary three-fourths of the states ratified the amendment. The majority persuasion kept at work, so that by 1922, forty-six states had joined the prevailing opinion which some years before had only been the advocacy of a few who felt a problem existed and needed a solution.

But we today know the story does not end here, for in our time we have seen very dramatically how a minority can persuade its way back into majority rule. In the late 1920's and early 1930's, the "Brewers' Big Wagon" began to roll again, and in 1933 the sneaking customer of the speak-easy became a legal, respectable citizen.

Some have said that this simply demonstrates the fickleness of the public mind. Such an observation, however, misses the points illustrated most—namely, that public opinion is derived both rationally and irrationally, and that propaganda and other forms of modern persuasion have brought new elements into the traditional and ideal steps of public opinion formation.

An Understanding of Persuasion Requisite to Modern Living

One conclusion cannot help but be drawn from our discussion thus far: an understanding of the basic principles and methods of persuasion is no longer an academic luxury for the many, or a necessity only for the specializing few: *It is requisite for all.* It is necessary for personal adjustment to modern living and for the perpetuation of our democratic way of life.

ESSENTIAL FOR A PERSONAL ADJUSTMENT TO MODERN LIFE

We have seen how persuasion is necessary if one desires leadership in government, business, and personal-social relationships. Most of us, however, are more commonly concerned with a personally simple, rational adjustment to this booming, buzzing world in which we find ourselves. The popularity of "peace of mind" books and articles testifies to our sense of insecurity, our quest for warmth and kinship with the world about us. A brief glance at some of the causes for this feeling may be helpful.

Our search for these causes brings us again to the complicated, highly urbanized and competitive society of which we have already spoken. As was suggested earlier, today the citizen seldom sees the political candidate, a fellow not of his own personal choosing, but the choice of a large, impersonal party machine. His boss at the factory is some abstract figure representing a large, powerful industrial enterprise. Even his labor union has become a powerful organization which often does not consult, but dictates when and where he shall work. When he goes to buy a new suit, he is important only as one more customer. Inept propagandists have "hoodwinked" him into distrust of all propaganda. The repetition of appealing slogans, the singing commercials, and his fear of dandruff, gingivitis, halitosis, and five o'clock shadow have left him in a state of emotional confusion and mental numbness. Too often all this has produced within the individual a very real sense of insignificance. He sees himself merely as a rather unimportant cog in a large, impersonal machine. Fear and insecurity often result.

Adjustment to this situation cannot be made by flight from it. Training in "resistance to propaganda" is not the answer. To become cynical about everything which "smells like propaganda" serves only to perpetuate and intensify the problem. The answer lies in understanding democracy as a science wherein the free exchange of persuasion is an essential part of that continual "sifting and winnowing" by which alone the common good may be found. Such understanding of the role and methods of persuasion should reduce one's sense of futility and insecurity, and usher the individual into a positive relationship with the ongoing social processes about him.

Happily there are signs that we are awakening to this need. The consumer's movement in the United States has given rise to organizations designed to help the consumer understand the essential nature of advertising, and to revive a sense of criticality and significance in buying. Some colleges and universities are conducting courses in leadership and public opinion, modern merchandising, salesmanship, argumentation and persuasion. Most of these courses emphasize that as individuals we are more often consumers than producers of persuasion, and that, therefore, we must not only know how to persuade, but also be able to analyze in terms of our own welfare the persuasion used on us.

For these reasons, we believe that a thorough, commonsense understanding of persuasion is a necessity to each individual in his personal adjustment to modern society.

ESSENTIAL TO THE PERPETUATION OF DEMOCRACY

Since in a democracy it is assumed that each responsible citizen shall play a part in the formulation of public policies, it follows that each citizen must appreciate and understand the methods of their formulation. If, as was described above, the citizen, in his lack of understanding of the role and methods of persuasion, develops a sense of futility and personal insignificance, he is unprepared to be a helpful citizen. Rather, he is a fit victim for the clever demagogue who makes him feel important and who replaces his feeling of uncertainty with a "positive mission that will save the world." Or he may become just an automaton conformist to the prevailing policies, offering no suggestion whatsoever for the improvement of the general welfare. In either event, democracy has lost in him one more chance for its survival. Our generation has seen very vividly, we trust, the result of democracies whose citizens were politically immature, inexperienced in the methods of self-government.

We must remember that propagandists are working more often for special interests than for the good of all, and that democracy must tolerate propaganda or persuasion against itself. Powerful lobbies influence legislation for their private gains, and foreign governments may seek to destroy our democracy through skillful persuasion. Here, again, it is clear that every responsible citizen must be able to evaluate all persuasion directed at him in terms of what is good for the general welfare.

One important point remains. If the democratic theory is to work, the competition for public favor must be open to all entries on an equal basis. This means that the channels and instruments for spreading persuasion should be available to all. When control of these channels of communication begins to become centralized in the hands of a few, we have less democracy and a warning regarding the future of democracy itself. Already we see these warnings. Many groups cannot compete financially with more powerful propaganda organizations in hiring the radio, television, press, and motion picture to market their persuasion.

Summary

We have contended that each citizen must understand persuasion as an integral part of our way of life. For him to conclude that all propaganda is fraud and lies which must be stopped by rigid censorship and the curtailing of freedom of speech, is only to begin losing democracy itself. Cynicism and distrust must be replaced by acceptance and understanding. The hope of democracy lies not only in the continual rise of persuaders who will champion its cause, but also in the constant, courageous, and careful auditing of all systems of persuasion.

Readings

1. Lang, William C., "Public Address as a Force in History," *Quarterly Journal of Speech* (February, 1951), XXXVII: 31–34.

2. McBurney, James H., "The Plight of the Conservative in Public Discussion," *Quarterly Journal of Speech* (April, 1950), XXXVI: 164–168.

3. Miller, Clyde R., *The Process of Persuasion.* New York: Crown Publishers, Inc., 1946, Ch. I, "It'll Never Replace the Horse."

4. Oliver, Robert T., *Persuasive Speaking.* New York: Longmans, Green & Co. Inc., 1950, Ch. I, "How Persuasion Occurs."

5. Smith, Charles W., Jr., *Public Opinion in a Democracy.* New York: Prentice-Hall, Inc., 1942, Ch. I, "The People Rule."

Exercises

1. Prepare and deliver a speech on "A Day as a Persuadee." In preparation for this speech make a list of all attempts to persuade you during the course of a single day. Try to account for the attempts which succeeded and those which failed.

2. Prepare and deliver a speech on "A Day as a Persuader." In preparation for this speech make a list of all your attempts to persuade others. Try to account for your failures and successes.

3. Write a 500-word paper on the place of persuasion in the government of your fraternity, sorority, dormitory, or private rooming house.

4. Prepare and deliver a 5-minute informational speech on one of the following topics:

   a. The role of persuasion in a democracy
   b. Persuasion in business
   c. Persuasion in personal-social relations
   d. How persuaders may interfere with the rational formation of public opinion.

5. Make a list of the things persuaders have done which you disliked and a list of the things you liked. What lessons do these lists teach you about effective persuasion?

Chapter II

AN APPROACH TO THE STUDY OF PERSUASION

I. Introduction

II. The Derived Motive Approach to the Study of Persuasion

III. Definitions of Persuasion, Argumentation, and Propaganda

IV. Application of the Inductive Method to the Study of Persuasion

V. The Process of Persuasion

- A. Gaining and Maintaining Attention
- B. Arousing Desires Useful to the Persuader's Purpose
- C. Demonstrating How These Desires Can Be Satisfied by Acceptance of the Persuader's Proposition
- D. Producing the Specific Response Desired

VI. Summary

Readings and Exercises

Chapter II

AN APPROACH TO THE STUDY OF PERSUASION

Introduction

In Chapter I a general survey was made of the place of persuasion in modern society. The question confronting us now is: How shall we study contemporary persuasion?

In our estimation, the study of persuasion should begin with (1) some knowledge of the derivation of human motives, (2) a clearly defined terminology, (3) a view of the educational methods most useful in the study of persuasion, and (4) knowledge of the steps in the process of persuasion. With this information in mind, the reader should be equipped with an approach helpful in his study of the remainder of the book.

The Derived Motive Approach to the Study of Persuasion

As has been emphasized, we have entered an era characterized by a carefully planned and intensive struggle for the control of human thought and conduct. Simple lists of "persuasive devices" or "sure-fire appeals" cannot provide the necessary understanding. Certainly many of the short-cut approaches to the complex subject of human motivation fail to provide social leadership and wealth, to say nothing of their failure to provide basic information.

Likewise, long academic lists of human motives are apt to fall into the error made by those who earlier sought to explain all behavior in terms of instincts—namely, the fallacy of giving a name to an act as an explanation of it. To say that a man cheated and lied in achieving his office because of a strong mastery motive does not explain why he desired the mastery. To say men are motivated by rivalry, greed, and pride does not account for the fact that elsewhere men are motivated by a sense of co-operation, generosity, and humility. Certainly the soldiers of World War II found that the Japanese, the German, the Italian, and the Chamorron on Saipan did not behave according to a common list of motives nor in identical degree to any one motive. Thus it should be clear that the approaches alluded to generally supply only descriptive, non-explanatory treatments, and that motivational categories are useful only if we know *how the motives are derived.*

A valid approach to the study of persuasion must account both for the rise of motives as impelling forces in human life and for the divergencies of motivation among people of different cultural climates. In sum, it must equip the aspiring persuader with a sufficient knowledge of the *bases of persuasion* so that, no matter in what social situation he may find himself, he can, as Aristotle suggested, "find the available means of persuasion." Admittedly, this is a big order and one which cannot be completely filled by the study of one book and in the space of one semester. The nature and nurture of human behavior present at once a field for broad and continuous study.

All members of the race have approximately the same biological and physiological heritage and, consequently, have the same basic wants or needs—i.e., the need for oxygen, liquids, food, rest, bodily eliminations, sexual satisfaction, and protection against bodily harm by cold, heat, tissue injury, and so on. No matter what the degree of personal sophistication, the individual must seek satisfaction for these "physiological imperatives." So in our quest for an understanding of the development of human motives, and the wants and desires upon which they are based, we must always keep in mind the elementary biological drives that impel the organism to various forms of activity.

Watson, Dashiell, Shaffer, and others have observed that an infant's reaction to physical overstimulation involves widespread and profound visceral changes which are described as *emotions.* As Shaffer indicates, "at a very early age loud noises, loss of support, restraint, rough handling, and pain are reacted to as overstimulating. As the child develops, many other stimuli become conditioned arousers of the same emotional tension. The substitute stimulus arouses an emotional response which is a visceral tension and this acts as a drive to activity. Emotional reactions serve as a connecting link between external and internal stimuli."[1] Those stimulations which have given pleasure—petting, fondling, and stroking—are said to give rise to the *love* emotion; those which are forms of restraint of bodily movement produce the *rage* emotion; while those which produce bodily pain result in the *fear* emotion.

Thus the child has not only a set of physical drives, but also soon develops emotional tensions (love, rage, fear) as a result of bodily stimulation. In infancy these basic drives and emotions can be expressed without much interference. As the youngster gets older, however, he finds these must be carried out according to the dictates of society—its conventions, customs, mores, and laws. He arrives on a stage where the scene already is set and the play in progress. What formerly was a biological self now must take on a social dimension, for at every turn the individual is dependent on others for the satisfaction of his wants. The *socialized being* must develop ways and means of satisfying these drives within a social framework. It is in this connection that *motives* are formed. Socially acceptable *subsistence motives* are developed to provide food, drink, shelter and other bodily needs. The sex drive becomes hidden in many social niceties and/or sublimations. Rage emotion assumes the approved forms of *mastery,* and fear causes us to *conform* to the group. As man becomes more socialized, his system of motives becomes more complex. Thus motives are drives that have been modified through the ordinary processes of learning. They constitute the springs of human response.

In summary, this approach suggests that a basic understanding of motivation can be achieved only by a consideration of the manner in which physiological drives become overlaid with social and cultural effects. Such a study will reveal not only the persuasive elements operative within one's own society, but also provide a method for determining systems of motivation at work in other social structures.

Definitions of Persuasion, Argumentation, and Propaganda

In developing an approach to the study of persuasion, some discussion of the terms *persuasion, argumentation,* and *propaganda* is

[1] L. F. Shaffer, *The Psychology of Adjustment.* Boston: Houghton Mifflin Company, 1936, p. 97.

necessary. These good words have been lead astray by loose usage among laymen and by technical differences among professionals. As a result, to some *persuasion* means the method of influencing conduct by appeals primarily addressed to the emotions, while *argumentation* is, essentially, influencing people by means of fact and logic. Others consider any verbal method of motivating people as persuasion, while still others call this argumentation.

Propaganda has come to be viewed as having a moral dimension; there is "good" and "bad" propaganda. Some go so far as to consider all propaganda bad and are like the elderly lady who "drops everything which looks like propaganda into the waste basket." At least one writer conceives of *persuasion* as operating only in face-to-face situations and upon one person or small group, whereas *propaganda* is a mass phenomenon influencing many people in extended situations.[2] In this view, *persuasion* is merely a supplementary method, one of the hand-maidens of the propagandist.

These few remarks are sufficient to indicate that some agreement upon these terms is necessary before we proceed further in the development of our study. This, we believe, can be done simply, and in obedience to the facts of human behavior. In Part I of the present chapter and at length in Part III of the book, it is pointed out that the dominant basis of human belief and action is *desire* as expressed through an elaborate and often subconscious system of *motives.* Although psychologists disagree among themselves on many points of their subject matter, they demonstrate convincing agreement on the point that desire is a basic consideration in tackling the problem of human behavior. Long a careful student of persuasion, Brigance suggests that "human nature does not respond, or at least very seldom responds, to purely logical or "rational" motives, for down within us all, below the surface, is a maze of subconscious motives that buffet our powers of reason to and fro like a wave-tossed ship." [3] *When man does use reason or demands of others facts and logical reasoning, he does so because such a procedure serves some basic desire or motive.*

The term selected to include the over-all process of symbolically

---

[2] L. W. Doob, *Propaganda—Its Psychology and Technique.* New York: Henry Holt and Company, 1935, p. 146.

[3] W. N. Brigance, *Speech Composition.* New York: F. S. Crofts and Company, 1939, p. 134.

directing behavior should be one which fits these basic facts. Of the terms in use today, we believe the term *persuasion,* by common and critical usage, comes nearest to meeting these requirements. It is defined as *the conscious attempt to modify thought and action by manipulating the motives of men toward predetermined ends.*

Depending on the motives operative within the persuadee (s) and the urgency of the situation, persuasion may employ (1) a system of emotional appeals, (2) a maximum of fact and logical reasoning, or (3) varying combinations of (1) and (2). In any given case, the persuader's analysis of his purpose, audience, occasion and himself must determine the methods of persuasion. The process of persuasion which seeks its response predominantly by means of evidence and logical reasoning, and in a less immediate manner may be called *argumentation.* When persuasion is designed for great masses of people in non-face-to-face situations, it may use such vehicles as social organizations, newspapers, the radio, television, motion pictures, the stage, bill boards, rumors, parades, and so forth. Used in this manner and with its purposes either revealed or concealed, persuasion may be called *propaganda.*

Persuasion as a means of social control is often supplemented by discussion in the investigation of problems common to a group. Discussion involves the co-operative deliberation of interested participants, usually under the direction of a leader. Ideally discussion is free of the intentional advocacy of the persuader.

Application of the Inductive Method to the Study of Persuasion

In regard to the problem of correlating experience with classroom study, Judd points out that "every adult encounters in his mature life problems which are very different from those to which he was introduced in textbooks. If a pupil learns not only how to solve textbook problems, but how to extract from his school experiences methods of analyzing situations and applying ideas to new situations, he will carry over into his mature life, powers of progressive organization which are of first order importance." [4]

Certainly teachers and students of persuasion must be especially concerned with the pedagogical procedures suggested by Professor

---

[4] Charles H. Judd, *Educational Psychology.* Boston: Houghton Mifflin Company, 1939, p. 498.

Judd. If we are to discover plots motivating the actors in various scenes of this dynamic human drama, we must never lose sight of the actors themselves. To attempt to learn about human behavior solely from *reading about it* has many limitations. Even the most vivid description of a persuasive event is a poor substitute for being there in person. Something is lost in translating human acts into words. Symbolic records and interpretations of what people do are valuable, but they must be supplemented wherever possible by observation and participation. Where these have been neglected, the following disadvantages result:

1. Little immediate need for knowledge exists to stimulate study.
2. Subject matter tends to seem remote, unreal, and uninteresting.
3. Text illustrations are not as concrete as "living illustrations."
4. Text materials are frequently set in social situations outside the student's experience.
5. Limitation to symbolic source materials does not utilize the important aptitude for social learning possessed by many students.
6. There is the danger of taking attractive short-cuts to the explanation of human behavior.

Making active use of the persuasion going on about us substantially reduces each of these disadvantages. Practice in observing persuasion increases awareness of persuasive stimuli. It helps to identify subtle techniques and indications of response to persuasion that could not be detected previously. The authors' experiences indicate that the collection, reporting, and careful interpretation of these instances of persuasion should be a major project in any course in argumentation or persuasion. Therefore, in the study of persuasion we recommend the use of inductive methods, by which a student, in an advised and systematic manner, collects from his environment those illustrative materials which provide provocative bases from which subsequently are derived interpretations and principles of human behavior. Thus a theory of persuasion emerges as a direct and realistic consequence of the experiences of the student.

In the following chapter we suggest principles and methods of investigating persuasion at work.

The Process of Persuasion

Before the reader proceeds to a study of the specific elements of persuasion, it is well to understand the general steps or stages that make up its basic process. Then, keeping these in mind, the small segments of the total process (treated in the succeeding chapters), can be fitted more readily into the total pattern. Our purpose here, therefore, is not to present a detailed account of the process of persuasion, but merely to sketch its broad outlines sufficiently to provide orientation for further study and practice.

An analysis of the basic process of persuasion reveals four general steps or stages which may occur in the following order: (A) Gain and maintain attention; (B) arouse desires useful to the persuader's purpose; (C) demonstrate how these desires can be satisfied by acceptance of the persuader's proposition; and (D) produce the specific response desired. These steps are often telescoped and interrelated.

GAINING AND MAINTAINING ATTENTION [5]

Persuasion begins by gaining the attention of others. Without attention persuasion cannot take place. If we are to be influenced by the message of the orator, the evangelist, the debater, the magazine or billboard advertisement, our attention must be captured *first*. It not only must be gained, but also it must be maintained, if the remaining steps of the process are to be taken.

AROUSING DESIRES USEFUL TO THE PERSUADER'S PURPOSE [6]

After our attention is gained and while it is maintained, the persuader must arouse those desires of ours which can supply the motive power propelling us toward the goal he seeks. This implies both a knowledge of the bases of human wants or desires and of methods of appropriating them for predetermined ends. "Persuasion flows from the headspring of dynamic inner urges, drives, or wants. Attention is merely its channel of flow, not its springhead. We are creatures of desire, moving onward always toward the satisfaction of material, intellectual, emotional, spiritual,

---

[5] See Chapter XIV for a detailed discussion of attention.

[6] The chapters of Part III discuss this point in detail.

or aesthetic wants. Desires stamp the matrix of human beliefs. They largely determine judgment." [7]

DEMONSTRATING HOW THESE DESIRES CAN BE SATISFIED BY ACCEPTANCE OF THE PERSUADER'S PROPOSITION [8]

If desires are to supply the impelling power to persuasion, the persuader must be able to show that what he proposes can satisfy one or more human wants. This presents at once a task of considerable magnitude, for our desires are woven into an intricate fabric which often seems to defy analysis. To present a proposition which can satisfy certain basic desires without at the same time conflicting with other desires requires careful preparation.

PRODUCING THE SPECIFIC RESPONSE DESIRED [9]

Successful persuasion begins with and perseveres in gaining some clearly defined and specific purpose or goal. A definite response is sought from the persuadee. Steps A, B, and C work toward this end. In fact, at the close of step C the persuadee may be so motivated that immediately he proceeds to give the desired response. On many occasions, however, he cannot provide the desired response without some specific directions. He may need to sign appropriate papers, see the proper real estate agent, or be given the specific procedure for donating blood to the local blood bank. Properly given, specific directions can be very important. Much persuasion fails because this step is not carefully worked out.

In addition, and still more difficult to guarantee, is the response that is desired at some future date. An October speech may seek a vote in November; a potential customer, now financially unable to buy a good car, needs to be kept persuaded that he should buy a Cadillac; the persuasion designed to get a promising high-school athlete to play for the Wisconsin Badgers or the Minnesota Gophers next fall needs a re-enforcement which will produce the desired response several months hence. In these instances of *delayed action* the persuader is seeking a *precurrent* response, a response which

---

[7] W. N. Brigance, *Speech Composition.* New York: Appleton-Century-Crofts, Inc., 1939, p. 136.

[8] See Chapter XX for further discussion of this point.

[9] See Chapter XX for further discussion of this point.

prepares the hearer for a delayed final, or *consummatory,* action. When this type of response is sought, the persuader must buttress his appeals with enough strength to withstand other subsequent and contrary persuasions and carry the hearer at last to the desired action.

Summary

In this chapter we have attempted to provide the student with a practical and realistic approach to the study of persuasion. The reader has been urged to seek the headsprings of human motivation and not to be content with hasty, inadequate approaches to this vital study. Some definitions have been given as aids to study, and the inductive method has been offered as a useful plan of study. The process of persuasion has been outlined in the hope that it will provide the reader with a helpful synthesis and frame of reference as he proceeds to study the many separate aspects of persuasion.

Readings

1. Brigance, W. N., *Speech Composition.* New York: F. S. Crofts and Company, 1939, pp. 135–139, "The Three Steps in Persuasion."
2. Lund, F. H., "The Psychology of Belief," *Journal of Abnormal and Social Psychology* (1925), XX: 194–195.
3. Rowell, E. Z., "Prolegomena to Argumentation," *Quarterly Journal of Speech* (1932), XVIII: 1–13, 224–248, 381–405, 585–606.
4. Shaffer, L. F., *The Psychology of Adjustment.* Boston: Houghton Mifflin Company, 1936, pp. 100–108.
5. Zelko, Harold P., "Do We Persuade, Argue, or Convince?" *Quarterly Journal of Speech* (October, 1939), XXV: 385–392.

Exercises

1. Write a paper on the topic, "The Derivation of Human Motives." Use reading reference No. 4 above to help you.

2. Compare the author's definition of persuasion with that of Doob referred to in footnote 2 on page 23.

3. List five examples of persuasion that may be labeled *argumentation* and five examples that may be called *propaganda.*

4. Prepare and deliver a five-minute persuasive speech which exemplifies clearly the steps in the process of persuasion.

5. Select a printed persuasive speech. Prepare a written analysis of its use of the steps in the process of persuasion.

Part II

INVESTIGATING PERSUASION AT WORK

An understanding of persuasion cannot be gained simply by reading about it. Reading must be supplemented by the study of persuasion in action. The actual process of persuasion often has so many subtle aspects that it can escape the untrained eye and ear. Part II provides suggestions for the critical study of persuasion. By becoming a sensitive observer of persuasion early in the course the student will be better equipped to understand and apply the principles and methods as they are presented.

Chapter III

OBSERVING PERSUASION IN ACTION

I. Introduction

II. General Suggestions for the Study of Living Persuasion

A. Be Reluctant to Assign Motives

B. Beware of Formulas

C. Be Sensitive to Obstacles to Accurate Observation

1. Obstacles to objective observation found within the environment of persuasion
2. Obstacles to objective observation originating within the observer

III. Selecting Examples of Persuasion for Study

IV. Writing up Observed Persuasion

V. Summary

Readings and Exercises

Chapter III

OBSERVING PERSUASION IN ACTION

Introduction

We noted in Chapter II that the observation of persuasion going on around us can contribute to our understanding of the process of persuasion. Obviously, inductive methods are needed to guide our observations, our reporting of what we have observed, and the interpreting of our reports.

In our quest for human motives at work we have three sources of information:

1. What people say they *should* do.
2. What people *say* they do.
3. What people *do.*

None of these can be neglected if we are to develop a useful picture of persuasion. First observations of all three can be very confusing. As you suspect, they do not always agree. It is perhaps regrettable, but people are not always consistent. It is not uncommon for us to verbalize one pattern of conduct and act out another.

We suggest that you consider the third source of information as most significant. What people *do* is probably of greater importance to us than what people *say* they do or what they say they *should* do! For instance, the effectiveness of our moral and ethical traditions can be tested only if we have some rather complete notions of how people in our twentieth-century civilization *actually* behave.

Starting with analysis of simple efforts of "personal persuasion" is easy, interesting, and more practical than starting with persuasive events of broad social significance. The process of "talking" Dad into giving you permission to use the car in the evening, the salesman's effort to sell the co-ed a dress of the very latest style, the professor's attempt to motivate his class in the direction of the reserve shelf in the library are all raw materials for your storehouse of information. Many methods of persuasion can be discovered at work in the everyday social and business contacts of every person who reads this book.

Basic motives are not buried as deeply in personal examples as in cases of large-scale persuasion. If you are involved, simple introspection will reveal connections otherwise difficult to determine. People you know will be helpful in describing their methods and responses, even their motives, if they admit them and know what they are. All this helps to develop sensitivity to subtle skills of persuasion essential to the observation of such mass operations as a political campaign or the public relations program of a large industrial concern.

General Suggestions for the Study of Living Persuasion

BE RELUCTANT TO ASSIGN MOTIVES

In the study of any unit of persuasion there is a strong temptation to assert, "He (or she) did that because . . . ." At the beginning we must recognize that guesswork will not reveal the human motives prompting any given act. The assembling of accurate data, and their cautious interpretation according to known principles of human behavior, are the minimum essentials for establishing a *probability* that any given motive is the true motive for the observed action. (Note: *Probability* rather than *certainty*).

It is difficult to over-emphasize the dangers of giving unsupported personal opinion the weight of factual evidence in recording and analyzing examples of persuasion. The desires, prejudices, opinions, and moral code of the observer lead him to "read in" things that actually are not there.

In order to avoid "assigning motives" as much as possible, it is convenient to apply the standards of the scientific method to the observation of persuasion. This means that we should record only what we see or hear or check up on through the help of reliable authority. Placing the area of mental speculation "out-of-bounds" is admittedly a severe limitation, but one which reduces the probable error of the results of our observations.

BEWARE OF FORMULAS

This advice is an attempt to be realistic. We admit that persuasion is complicated and we remind ourselves that we are not going to solve, once and for all, the riddle of human conduct. Proceeding logically, we can assume that any conclusions we reach about persuasion, through observation, will probably be tentative in nature and subject to subsequent examination and revision when more evidence is in.

It is disturbing to many people (probably most) that social problems have no objectively verifiable answers. Also, our contemporary culture inspires in us a "digest complex." We want our ideas done up in neat and compact packages. We want simple, direct explanations of why the United Nations is not working satisfactorily or why prices are going up, preferably presented to us in a list of not more than three clean-cut items. We resist the fact that human events just are not that simple by accepting over-simplifications as adequate explanations. In short, we are looking for *certainty*, something simple and direct that we can grasp and say, "Ah, this is *it*!"

Plenty of simple formulas for quick success in persuasion are available. Here is an example of such a pattern, listing the "six principles" of persuasion:

1. Don't try to do all the talking yourself!
2. Don't interrupt your opponent!
3. Avoid any argumentative attitude that is belligerently positive!
4. In the first half of an argument, inquire rather than attack!
5. Restate clearly and fairly in your own words the gist of each argument your opponent advances—as soon as he advances it!
6. Identify your *main* argumentative attack with one key issue. Then stick to that issue. Don't digress! [1]

Each of the six items is a useful bit of advice *if particular conditions are such that it applies.* But an attempt to use these "principles" to interpret what happens in any case of observed persuasion will reveal some of the fundamental inadequacies of simple formulas.

---

[1] R. C. Borden and A. C. Busse, *How to Win A Sales Argument.* New York: Harper and Brothers, 1926, p. 114.

Probably the authors of this sequence would not contend that the repertoire of the persuader is limited to these half-dozen techniques. However, the fact that such an implication results from titles like "The principles of ———" or "How to ———" makes pitfalls that ensnare many sincere beginning students.

If you understand and accept the fact that there are no easy answers or universal explanations of persuasion, you may not be alarmed when you find *almost* identical cases of persuasion with drastically differing results. If your study of persuasion is a quest for certainty, you will be disappointed when probabilities result. Therefore, when you are confronted by a probability you should never say, "*Only* a probability," but, "Eureka! a *probability*." It is *something,* where before there was virtually *nothing*. And think of the areas of social confusion where not even low-grade probabilities can be found!

Understand, too, that uncertainty need increase neither discomfort nor indecision. We recommend as food for thought this quotation from Stevenson:

> The demand for a final proof springs less from hopes than from fears. When the basic nature of a subject is poorly understood, one must conceal his insecurity, from himself as much as from others, by consoling pretenses. It is only when the subject develops that an inquirer can recognize, without losing confidence, that his conclusions may meet with intelligent opposition, or that they may require the correction of further experience and reflection. And in those admissions there need be no lack of conviction—no general skepticism that ends in inactivity. There need be only that temper of mind, which abiding firmly by the conclusions that seem at the time most trustworthy, is still sensitive to the fact that living questions are too rich in their complexity to be answered by a formula.[2]

BE SENSITIVE TO OBSTACLES TO ACCURATE OBSERVATION

Simple recognition of the fact that it is difficult to attain objectivity in recording observed events helps to improve the accuracy of such reporting. Some analysis of specific stumbling blocks on the path to impartial observation enables the reporter to identify and, to some extent, to isolate many potential sources of error.

---

[2] Charles L. Stevenson, *Ethics and Language.* New Haven: Yale University Press, 1944, p. 336.

1. *Obstacles to objective observation originating outside of the observer.*

a. Within the source of the persuasive appeal may be hidden forces that "slant" your observation. Perhaps the speaker represents an organization hostile to your interests or the news commentary you are reading is found in a newspaper whose editorial policy is in total accord with your own opinions.

b. The *occasion* itself may contain misleading elements which should be identified and discounted. Homecoming weekend with its associated sentiments may enhance a persuasive appeal for funds for you as observer.

c. The *physical setting* often restricts observation by placing the observer where he is uncomfortable and perhaps cannot see or hear all that goes on, or by supplying stimuli to which the observer reacts emotionally. Clever use of symbols in the setting to stir patriotism or other group loyalty should be noted. In informal persuasion, manipulation of the setting is often a major part of the persuasive appeal. Wouldn't you make sure that your father is comfortable amid congenial surroundings before asking his permission to attend the next out-of-town football game? If you are being persuaded, be particularly critical of the elements in the setting, and note carefully all evidences of planning.

d. Within the persuasive *appeal* may be items which seem significant to you, but may not be important to someone else. Reference to your hobby or incidental mention of your pet peeve may cause you to generalize from your own reaction that others are responding as you are. You cannot be sure unless they show it clearly. So—discount heavily emotional surges within yourself.

e. Many *"accidental" items* develop which, although they are not an intended part of the persuasive process, make objective observation difficult. For example: A dog fight outside an open window, a defective public address system, the conversation of your immediate companions, and a crying baby. Before you estimate the effect of such annoyance look for evidence of the extent of distraction in the entire audience. Again—do not generalize from your own response!

2. *Obstacles to objective observation originating within the observer.*

a. It is a good plan to estimate your *physical condition* and its probable effect on the quality of observation. A thumping headache or upset stomach can cause you to distort or miss details, and reduce the total accuracy of impressions.

b. Closely correlated to physical condition is *mental adjustment* at the time of observation. The psychological repercussions of recent stresses in your life lower your ability to concentrate on other matters. For example, the breaking up of a romance commonly causes maladjustment sufficient to affect study and all mental tasks requiring sustained application. Try to compensate for such a recognized condition by making unusual efforts to focus totally on the observation.

c. Your *network of opinions, attitudes, sentiments, stereotypes, and prejudices* is an ever-present menace to objectivity. All of us have these agents of bias in rather stable form. We probably could not change them if we wanted to. We can aim at a clear definition of our feelings toward the topic of persuasion, and an estimation of effects those feelings may produce on observation and subsequent reporting. We can "lean over backward" to take in the point of view of the opposition as well as our own. But if you are a good Republican or Democrat it will require penetrating analysis and strong discipline if you are to give unprejudiced attention to a speaker representing the Socialist Party.

d. Predominantly irrational *personal preferences* can throw the observation process out of focus. If, for example, you "just don't like" a certain type of person, then you will have to be extremely careful to avoid error in reporting persuasion involving anyone in that category. Many a job has been lost because the applicant wore a tie the prospective employer did not like, or perhaps a heavy perfume, too much lipstick, or a crew haircut. Such snap judgments blind us to good points of the individuals concerned. Forcing ourselves to ignore the items which disturb our personal preferences is necessary if we are to get past them to examine pertinent data in the case.

e. Your *habits of thinking* may hinder or help your observation of persuasion. If your normal pattern of problem solving is a quick jump-to-a-decision, follow-a-hunch process, then a conscious and methodical slow-down is indicated. Suspending judgment may be for you a painful process, but practice it nevertheless. Available data must be accumulated before any interpretation is made because often just one little item, overlooked, will change an entire hypothesis. If you are of a habitually cautious, reserved, slow-to-decide mentality, fine! Your willingness to accumulate evidence and to study it before making up your mind will help you avoid many mistakes of premature generalization.

The listed obstacles to objectivity can be overcome by recognizing them frankly and openly, and attempting to adjust to them. *List* as many obstacles as you can in an observed instance, *describe* each obstacle impersonally, *decide* how each obstacle would probably "slant" your reporting and its subsequent interpretation, and *correct* for each obstacle by double-checking your report to eliminate all evidences of distortion.

In summary, the reader is reminded that the quality of the final persuasion case study is dependent upon effective observation. You must be alert. Let no apparently insignificant item escape your notice. Remember, many persuasion cues must be subtle, if they are to be effective. Watch people's faces, note vocal inflections, study choice and arrangement of words. Examine physical surroundings to determine how these fit into the persuasion picture. Ask yourself concerning every item, "Has this been planned to help the process of persuasion?"

Now, firmly resolved to resist the temptation to assign motives hastily, to beware of simple "formula" explanations, and to recognize and conquer the many obstacles to objectivity in observation study of persuasion, we turn to the problem of locating suitable examples of persuasion at work.

Selecting Examples of Persuasion for Study

As you might suspect, the prerequisite to fruitful observation of persuasion at work is the intelligent, discriminating selection of samples for analysis. We will try in this section to set up specific guideposts to help you in planning your observations.

How do you locate possible examples? We suggest, first, that you attempt to identify, in your environment, *all situations in which it is useful to a person or group to guide others to a predetermined conclusion or course of action.* Remember always to look carefully, for much of the more effective persuasion is subtle, and, in many cases, is deliberately concealed. Some excellent illustrations of persuasion turn up where you least expect to find them.

Any case selected for analysis should be sufficiently complete to justify studying it.

It should have a clear-cut, identifiable purpose.

The persuader should recognize his goal.

The persuader should make systematic efforts to achieve his purpose, though he may not be conscious of using any system of persuasion.

Select simple, personal examples of persuasion first, then move along to those of gradually increasing complexity. Select cases which you can observe personally. Your collection of examples in the aggregate should constitute the best possible representative sampling of the varied persuasive situations you can observe. Here are suggestions to help broaden the base of your observations.

Select a sample or two from your contacts with each of the social groups in your experience.

Choose examples of persuasion of varying scope, from person-to-person incidents and small audience situations to examples of mass persuasion.

Use examples from every medium of communication—informal speech, formal speech, radio, television, newspapers, magazines, and so on.

Get examples representing a variety of schools of thought such as divergent political beliefs, conflicting private interests, and different religious faiths.

Consider the source of persuasion in each case; be sure that persuasion originating in organizations and persuasion originating in individuals are both represented.

Sample both amateur and professional efforts to persuade.

Here are topics for study which constitute a sampling of contemporary persuasive activities.

1. Renting an apartment.
2. Selling an unwanted record player.
3. Obtaining church pledges.
4. How a pretty girl sold magazines.
5. Securing co-operation of a student group in staging a college homecoming.
6. Persuading G.I.'s to sign up for life insurance at port of embarkation.
7. Rushing a prospective fraternity man.
8. An appeal for careful driving from The National Safety Council.
9. Persuasion used in commercials on the Longines Symphonette Program.
10. A broadcast by Radio Moscow.
11. Securing contributions for a civic theatre from a luncheon club of businessmen.
12. A candidate's election-eve appeal on the radio.
13. A Gerald L. K. Smith letter to "Christian Americans."
14. Persuasion in a series of British Library of Information releases.
15. Persuading an employer to hire members of minority groups.
16. Use of the sample ballot to get votes in the recent election.
17. Night advertising devices in your college town.
18. Persuading people to enroll in the Dale Carnegie course.
19. A National Association of Manufacturers' radio program.
20. An American Federation of Labor television program.

Writing up Observed Persuasion

Record every item you notice which seems to have been planned to help the process of persuasion. Do not trust your memory; things happen fast and details evaporate with the lapse of time. Brief notes suffice to call items to mind if the report is prepared soon after the observation, though, of course, note-taking is sometimes impossible. Then the making of a record of events immediately after the observation becomes doubly important.

You will start writing up a persuasion "case" with a page or two of notes, a memory of supplementary details, and a set of responses to the experience. Your immediate problem is to produce an accurate resume of the sequence of events.

The linguistic ideal in the writing you will do is the use of "report language." The purpose of "report language" is to control the effects of our emotional responses on the reporting of the observation. "Report language" is the most objective, fairest, most unbiased word usage we are able to command. It enables the reader or listener to respond primarily to the factual content of the communication. It consciously avoids all indefinite and emotional terms, phrases, and figures of speech. You can not eliminate emotional tone completely from your reporting, but you can cut down its "percentage content."

Editing the first draft helps a lot. Many words and phrases will be found that "trigger" conditioned emotional responses. Throw them out and replace them with less emotional, more precise language.

Here is a pattern which can be followed in recording each observed instance of persuasion. Complete sentence outline form is suggested as a convenient and economical method of carrying out this plan. In the interest of encouraging systematic and uniform reporting, and of making it possible to file interesting cases for future reference, it is suggested that this form be mimeographed and used for all reports on observed persuasion.

RECORDED OBSERVATION OF PERSUASION

Case # ——— Name ————

I. Topic
II. Specific purpose of persuader
III. Occasion

IV. Persuader(s)

V. Persuadee(s)

VI. Items of persuasion

List elements of persuasion in the *setting* first, then significant details of what happened in chronological order. Use reverse side of sheet if more space is needed. *Underline* items which seem to be of key significance.

VII. Response to Persuasive Effort (Use back of sheet if necessary)

A. Observed:

B. Estimated:

Summary

You are ready to select cases for study, to observe them systematically, and to write up objective and accurate reports of them. Since you are primarily interested in how people behave, you should pay most attention to what people *do,* rather than what they *say* they do, or what they say they *should* do. The appendix contains students' reports of persuasion they have observed. Perhaps you can benefit from their experience, and equal or improve upon their reporting techniques.

Readings

The following readings are examples of persuasive speaking which contain units of persuasion suitable for study.

1. Baird, A. C., ed., *Representative American Speeches: 1948–1949.* New York: The H. W. Wilson Company, 1949, pp. 155–164.

2. Glasgow, Geo. M., *Dynamic Public Speaking.* New York: Harper and Brothers, 1950, pp. 279–309.

3. McBurney, J. H., O'Neill, James and G. E. Mills, *Argumentation and Debate.* New York: The Macmillan Company, 1951, Appendix B, pp. 314–332.

4. Oliver, Robert T., *Persuasive Speaking.* New York: Longmans, Green & Co. Inc., 1950, Appendix I, pp. 229–240.

5. Sandford, W. P. and W. H. Yeager, *Principles of Effective Speaking.* New York: The Ronald Press Company, 1950, pp. 466–526.

Exercises

1. Study the student-written case histories of persuasion in the Appendix. Which is the best written? The most informative? Explain your choices.

2. Which of these student-written case histories makes the best use of "report language"? Locate specific violations of "report language" and explain why you classify them thus.

3. Observe and write up an example of an instance of persuasion in each of these categories: (a) Primary group relations, (b) small speaker to audience persuasion, and (c) persuasion via one of the mass media of communication. Use the "Recorded Observation of Persuasion" form and follow the instruction in this chapter.

4. Present your most interesting case study from exercise #3 to the class in the form of a five-minute speech, and lead a brief discussion on the topic of its interpretation.

5. Prepare and present a four- to five-minute speech on the topic: "An Example Illustrating that Simple Formulas Cannot Explain Persuasion."

Part III

EXAMINING THE BASES OF PERSUASION

Principles and methods of persuasion must rest securely on a knowledge of the bases of human behavior. Part III first reviews the earlier attempts at seeking the sources of persuasion and then proceeds to an exploration of those bases which are the headsprings of human action. These include our bodily and social needs, our attitudes, sentiments and stereotypes, and the part played by reasoned discourse in persuasion.

A careful study of the bases of persuasion is necessary to any thorough understanding of materials presented in the succeeding parts of the book.

Chapter IV

THE SEARCH FOR THE SOURCES OF PERSUASION

I. Introduction

II. Early Theories of Human Nature

A. Philosophic Theories

1. Platonic versus Aristotelian Views
2. Hedonism
3. Early Religious Theories
4. Machiavellianism
5. Rationalism
6. The Racial Determinists

B. Typological Theories

1. Hippocrates
2. The Character Writers
3. Kretschmer's Morphological Types
4. Thomas and Znaniecki's Sociological Types
5. Jung's Psychological Types

III. Modern Psychological Theories of Motivation

A. Psychoanalysis
B. The Instinct Theorists
C. Behaviorism
D. Social-Interactionism

IV. Modern Rhetorical Theories of Persuasion

A. Phillips
B. Winans
C. Brigance

V. Motivational Categories are Non-Explanatory

VI. Summary and Conclusions

Readings and Exercises

Chapter IV

THE SEARCH FOR THE SOURCES OF PERSUASION

Introduction

From the beginning of history no subject has been more fascinating to people than other people. The skilled and unskilled observers of every age have watched the "passing parade" and have asked themselves the greatest $64 question: Why do people behave as they do? What makes them "tick"? We must attempt to answer this persistent question in terms of available information if we are to seek the foundations of human persuasion. To search for the sources of persuasion is to seek the foundations of human behavior.

There are many and varied examples of our attempts to answer this intriguing question: Men have concluded that, "You can't trust a blonde," "Artists are temperamental," "Our behavior is written in the stars," "There will always be wars because man has a pugnacious instinct"; the list contains innumerable answers to the human riddle. But a truly adequate explanation only now is beginning to emerge from skilled observers of the past and present.

The inability to provide an adequate explanation of why people behave as they do did not deter enterprising persuaders, largely through trial and error, from developing skill in manipulating men in desired directions. Over three thousand years ago Egyptian wise men suggested principles for dealing with others. The courtesans, the politicians, and the traders of every age have developed skills in recognizing human motives and appropriating them for useful ends. The advertisers were among the early persuaders: The earliest advertisement on record, written on a sheet of papyrus paper from Thebes and advocating the return of a runaway slave, is dated about 3000 B.C., and advertisements of gladiatorial contests and baths have been found by excavators on the walls of old Pompeii.

These early evidences of persuasion have been followed by ever-increasing attempts at persuasion, until today, as was mentioned in Chapter I, we have numerous craftsmen highly competent in manipulating the motives of men. Our lack has not been those who *try* to persuade, but rather scientists skilled in the analysis of the foundations of human behavior, men who can seek out the true fountainheads of human conduct and thus provide reliable bases for the critical study of persuasion. We believe that students of persuasion in modern society need such preparation if they are to be adequate to the day in which they live.

Certain of the great thinkers of the past have contributed much to our understanding of human motivation. The course we shall take in our search for the bases of persuasion will become clearer if we consider again, briefly, the principles which guided the early thinkers in their quest for a theory of human behavior.

Early Theories of Human Nature

PHILOSOPHIC THEORIES

Platonic versus Aristotelian Views.[1] These two great philosophers differed in their views regarding the origins of human behavior. Plato saw individual conduct more as a reflection of the society in which the person was reared. To him the reasons for human behavior were to be found largely in the character of society. Aristotle, however, took the view that society essentially is a resultant of the "nature" of the individual. Thus in his *Rhetoric,* Aristotle was able to suggest with considerable certainty the fixed ends of human action, to outline in precise order the emotions of man, to categorize people into age groups and to suggest the behavior characteristics according to these groups.

The schools of thought started by these two philosophers still persist, with the adherents of one school looking more to the structure of society and its many influences to explain why we act as we do, and the proponents of the other belief trying to establish the fact that there are fixed, innate patterns by which man lives and which determine the essential character of his society.

It should be clear that if a student of persuasion were to follow

[1] See R. T. La Piere, and P. R. Farnsworth, *Social Psychology.* New York: McGraw-Hill Book Co., Inc., 1936, pp. 6, 7.

the Aristotelian view much of his time would be spent seeking to know these fixed desires and action tendencies of man. On the other hand, those who follow the opposing view must become more ardent students of society. They must be able to detect the emergence of new, sometimes differing, social motives among the various peoples of the world by observing critically the social matrix from which these motives are derived.

Hedonism. The traditional doctrine of psychological hedonism has long been a general theory of human motivation. Early hedonism was started among the Greeks and contended that people "naturally" do those things which are pleasing to them and avoid the displeasing experiences. This early *pleasure-pain theory* did describe behavior under certain conditions, but it erred in assuming that it is "natural" for men to do some things and equally "natural" for them to avoid doing other things. Today we believe that much of our behavior is *socially,* rather than *naturally,* determined. We know that experiences which may be pleasurable to us as human animals may be painful to us as socialized human beings. The early hedonists found it difficult to explain why some people voluntarily submit to sacrifice, pain, and suffering and yet actually seem to enjoy it.

More modern hedonists tend to relax the "natural" explanation of the early hedonists and point out that it is natural for man to respond only in certain generalized ways and that most of his ways, although socially determined, are in the direction of the increase of personal pleasure and the avoidance of displeasure. Critics of this more modern view suggest that the categories of pleasantness and unpleasantness do not constitute an adequate explanation of the causes of human conduct, but rather are merely the dynamic interplay of motives which require a different and less narrow theory of explanation.

We agree with the technical point raised by these critics of modern hedonism. The theory is too limited. Nonetheless, we should add that *in a general sense* humans tend to seek that which gives physical pleasure and to avoid the discomforts of life. This fact is of use to the student of persuasion and is discussed at length in Chapter V.

Early Religious Theories. Medieval theologians postulated that man's behavior was due not to nature but to God. When it was discovered that some people behaved in ways not acceptable to the church, it was reasoned that such conduct was motivated by an opposing force—Satan. Man, it was contended, had the right of choice as to whom he would serve. This was sometimes called the "free-will" theory.

Another early religious answer to the human riddle was the "doctrine of original sin," a doctrine still accepted by many people today. This theory holds that from birth man is possessed of degrading influences and that his individual behavior and his society are direct evidences of this fact.

Critics of these early religious theories of human nature point out that these attempts at single postulates designed to explain man's nature and modes of conduct tend to neglect the important influences of training and socialization on the motive structure of the individual.

Persuaders who have based their persuasion on these theories have been successful chiefly among those who are willing to grant the doctrinal assumptions involved.

Machiavellianism. Niccolo Machiavelli was an adviser to Italian princes and, according to some writers, the father of chauvinistic political theory. In defiance of the free will doctrine of the medieval theologians, he asserted that man is by nature a bad creature, and that he has no choice in the matter. Therefore, Machiavelli advised the princes that if men are not to do evil they must be persuaded to do good by wily political leadership, and thus tricked into thinking they are gaining their evil ends. In *The Prince* (1513), Machiavelli records the various strategems which politicians may use to gain their goals. This book was one of the earliest manuals of political craftsmanship.

If we were to adopt Machiavelli's theory of the debased nature of man, then our persuasion to get men to do good would necessarily employ deceptive methods.

Rationalism.[2] Bacon, and later Hobbes, Locke, Berkeley, Hume, and others, repudiated the earlier explanations of human behavior and declared that human *experience* is the source. Out of this early scientific movement arose another, and rather unfortunate, theory

---

[2] For a detailed and interesting discussion of rationalism see W. E. H. Lecky, *History of the Rise and Influence of the Spirit of Rationalism in Europe.* New York: D. Appleton and Company, 1914.

of the origin of human behavior which stated that man, through experience, gathers data and then decides on some course of action suggested by the observed facts. Man is held to be an extremely rational fact-finding machine. Irrationality is explained as being a result of inadequate factual information. Thus, if an individual knows all the facts he can be depended on to behave in accordance with them.

From this it could be concluded that all a persuader needs to do is to present the facts and the persuadees can be expected to respond rationally.

Critics of this theory have pointed out that here we have nothing more than a revival of the free-will theory of the medieval theologians, with rationality substituted for God and irrationality playing Satan. The critics assert further that man is not consistently propelled by the power of facts, but that he frequently acts upon the promptings of desire. The defendants also are asked how they will reconcile the fact that what is considered rational conduct in one society may not be so regarded in another.

We have seen here that the theory of *rationalism* fails to provide an adequate explanation of the sources of human behavior. It is probably true that modern man is demanding more rational appeals in his persuasion, but the explanation, as we shall see later, is not to be found in an innately rational conduct.

The Racial Determinists. Closely allied to the theory of rationalism is the theory that by the slow process of biological selection the more rational members of the race tend to survive. This leads to social or racial groupings and to the assertion that some groups are more rational than others. Some protagonists have concluded that certain races are biologically inferior and therefore incapable of as much rationality as others. This belief has led dictators to proclaim that their people are destined to rule all others and, as Adolf Hitler demonstrated, this persuasion can achieve certain successes.

Modern science, however, has repudiated the theory of racial determinism as valid or sufficient explanation of human conduct.

TYPOLOGICAL THEORIES

To the list of those who have advanced notable answers to the great question of the origins of human behavior and thus of the sources of persuasion must be added the names of those who have believed that individuals can be categorized or typed as to behavior. They have asked: Are there not differing physical and personality structures among people which allow them to be divided into types?

Since to "type" people is a favorite pastime of gossips and a hazard in the path of the persuader, it is well that we review briefly some of the more worthy attempts at explaining behavior by descriptive traits and types.

Hippocrates. Five centuries before the Christian era Hippocrates and other Greeks introduced the concept of personality types by dividing people on the basis of physiological differences. The body, they pointed out, contained four fluids or "humors"—yellow bile, black bile, phlegm, and blood—and these humors influenced the behavior of the individual.

The dominance of one fluid over the others determined a person's reaction tendencies or disposition. In discussing this theory, Young points out that there were thus four different temperaments which might develop, depending on which fluid was dominant: "(1) *choleric* (from *choler,* meaning yellow bile), characterized by irascible, hot-tempered make-up; (2) *melancholic* (from *melas* and *choler,* meaning black bile), marked by a depressed, sad, and gloomy outlook on life; (3) *phlegmatic* (from *phlegm,* meaning mucus), indicated by sluggish, apathetic disposition; and (4) *sanguine* (from *sanguis,* meaning blood), characterized by the cheerful, hopeful, or even ardent nature." [3]

Even though the physiology of the Greeks has been discarded, their early theories regarding physiological types have influenced subsequent thinking on personality and human behavior. Persuaders who have followed these theories have sought first to know the "type" of the persuadee and then to fit their persuasion to this type.

The Character Writers. A pupil of Aristotle, Theophrastus, founded "characterology," a literary description of personality types. Sargent points out that "he described, skillfully and with striking examples of behavior, thirty extreme types of persons, such as the penurious man, the boor, the flatterer, or the loquacious man. Two

---

[3] K. Young, *Personality and Problems of Adjustment.* New York: Appleton-Century-Crofts, Inc., 1940, pp. 302, 303.

thousand years later character writing was resumed by the Frenchman Jean De La Bruyere and by numerous English writers, among them Ben Jonson, Joseph Addison, Richard Steele, and Samuel Butler. Character writers have generally shown much psychological insight, though they seldom have probed deep enough to uncover the real origins of behavior."[4] The student of persuasion must understand more basic facts regarding human conduct than have been presented by character writers if he is to seek out the springs of human response.

Kretschmer's Morphological Types. Certain other scientists believed that the shape of the body or the physique of a person is an index of his personality, that bodily traits and behavior characteristics are causally related. Among the best-known theories in this area is that advanced by Kretschmer in 1925 after his study of mental patients in a hospital in Germany. He concluded there are three rather distinct physical types: (1) The *asthenic* type, characterized by a lean, narrowly built frame, poor blood, inadequate skin secretion, narrow shoulders, long, thin arms with delicately shaped hands, a long narrow chest, thick stomach, and angular face; (2) the *athletic* type, characterized by strong development of the skeleton and the muscles, firm and healthy skin, broad shoulders, thick chest, muscled abdomen, trunk tapering toward mid-section, narrow pelvis, tapering and shapely legs, muscular arms, firm face and jaw, and short, snubby nose; and (3) the *pyknic* type, which does not reach its highest development until middle age and is characterized by a rounded figure, fatness about the trunk, a deep, vaulted chest which tends to broaden out toward the lower part of the body, soft and round limbs, and rounded shoulders pushed slightly forward.

Kretschmer was not content to classify people morphologically, but related physical traits to particular psychological traits. Thus the asthenic and athletic types fell chiefly into the category of schizophrenics, and pyknics into the manic-depressive group. The *schizothymes* tend to be unsocial, reserved, eccentric, timid, shy, sensitive, nervous, irritable, and interested in nature and books, while the *cyclothymes* are inclined to be sociable, friendly, good-natured, genial, cheerful, jolly and, on occasion, easily depressed and soft-hearted.

---

[4] S. S. Sargent, *The Basic Teachings of the Great Psychologists.* New York: Doubleday & Company, Inc., 1944, p. 137.

Although Kretschmer's research and theory have caused much debate, it cannot be denied that here is a provocative attempt at seeking the bases of human behavior. This research prompted other scientists to attempt verification of Kretschmer's findings and challenged still others to seek the explanation of behavior in the functions of certain endocrine glands.

Thomas and Znaniecki's Sociological Types.[5] While some were seeking the answer to behavior and personality in terms of physical traits, others were exploring the possibility of classifying people in terms of their social roles, which led to the concept of *social types* in use among sociologists today. Thomas and Znaniecki are among the best known researchers in this area, by virtue of their study of the Polish peasant in Europe and in America. As a result of social influences, assert these writers, three types of character are developed: (1) The *Philistine,* or practical man, who has a strong wish for security and safety; (2) the *Bohemian,* who tends toward new experience, flightiness, and pleasurable pursuits; and (3) the *Creative* man, who is relatively stable yet possesses the capacity for changing his attitudes and desires in terms of some goal of a creative nature such as may be found in art, religion, mechanical invention, politics, and economics.

The concept of sociological types encouraged other researchers to enter the field. By bringing out into more clear relief the relationship between the social order and the individual's behavior patterns, these studies have shed much light on the sources of human motivation.

Jung's Psychological Types.[6] Probably the best known theory of psychological types is the *introvert* and *extrovert* classification advanced by Jung (1922). The *introvert* is said to focus his attention on himself and creates an inner, subjective world, while the *extrovert* is chiefly interested in the world outside himself. Jung did not suggest that all people should be classified as either introverts or extroverts, but he did contend that everyone has tendencies toward both introversion and extroversion, and that one generally predominates. These major classifications are also divided into the sub-classes of

---

[5] See W. I. Thomas and F. Znaniecki, *The Polish Peasant in Europe and America.* 2 vols. Boston: Badger, 1918–1920.

[6] See C. G. Jung, *Psychological Types.* New York: Harcourt, Brace and Company, 1922.

thinking, feeling, sensation, and intuition. Thus we have the extroverted thinking type, the extroverted feeling type, and so on.

We agree with the many critics of Jung's theory that certain social conditions surrounding a person can produce one or the other of these personality traits, but to say that these traits lie inevitably within the *natural* make-up of a person seems to go beyond the facts.

Here again the student of persuasion can see the dangers of hasty classifications of people, and also can learn the possible personality traits which can emerge under given social training. Certainly the persuader cannot be oblivious to the facts which go to make up personality traits.

We trust the above examples of "typing" people are sufficient to indicate the nature of the attempts to seek explanations of human conduct. Psychologists have learned the hazards of type theories, the dangers which come from our tendency to pigeonhole people in this or that category. While acknowledging the usefulness of the type theories, they now tend to regard types as extreme forms of personality traits or as very generalized divisions, and point out that the concepts are yet too roughly drawn to warrant generalization about them or prediction of human behavior in terms of them.

It is obvious, then, that the persuader should be warned against hastily classifying possible persuadees.

Modern Psychological Theories of Motivation

All persuaders have sought the help of the psychologist and social psychologist, for human behavior is their chief concern. Here again, therefore, it will be profitable if we review briefly a few of the theories of human motivation advanced by certain psychologists, always keeping in mind that to know what dictates human action necessitates knowing the fundamentals of human behavior.

PSYCHOANALYSIS

While developing psychoanalysis in an attempt to cure neurotic patients, Dr. Sigmund Freud of Vienna (1900) worked out his theory of human motivation. According to him, each person has a fundamental drive called the *libido,* which, broadly speaking, is a sexual drive. The complete self of a person was divided into three parts: (1) The *Id,* characterized by man's more primitive animal nature; (2) the *Ego,* which is our "rational self" and which strives to control the basic urges of the Id; and (3) the *Super-Ego,* which is that part of a person in charge of the moral ideas and ideals. The *Super-Ego* and the *Id* are thus in constant conflict, a conflict resolved successfully in the normal person but unsuccessfully in the abnormal personality.

Here we have each human personality being divided into differing sections or faculties. Psychoanalysis, and the "faculty psychologies" which divided the individual into various faculties—such as intellectual, emotional, and volitional—have given rise to certain popular misconceptions. We have heard of "appeals to our better selves," and "appeals to our rational selves." Oftentimes such appeals are in order, but the reasons for their referents are not to be found in fixed compartmentalizations of personality structure. Nonetheless, psychoanalysis has sensitized all of us to the psychic states which can beset man; it has awakened us to that complex labyrinth which is the mind of man.

THE INSTINCT THEORISTS

In a revival of the theory regarding man's fixed, innate nature, certain psychologists around 1900 theorized that man behaves according to a set of instincts. Chief among these advocates was William McDougall,[7] who interpreted all behavior, even social behavior, as a manifestation of certain innate impulses. To McDougall certain conduct in man such as flight, pugnacity, curiosity, mating, food-getting, acquisitiveness, sneezing, and so on are all instincts. William James held that man has more instincts than any other animal, and compiled his own list of instincts. Later Thorndike added more instincts to the growing lists, preferring to call them simply "unlearned" behavior.

Some writers in other fields began to use the term. Thorstein Veblen wrote *The Instinct of Workmanship;* a sociologist, Wilfred Trotter, wrote *Instincts of the Herd in Peace and War;* and Ordway Tead, a personnel specialist, wrote *Instincts in Industry.*

So great was the rush into the instinct camp that Bernard (1924) [8] found in a survey of approximately 400 authors that the term in-

---

[7] William McDougall, *An Introduction to Social Psychology.* London: Methuen, 1908.

[8] L. L. Bernard, *Instinct: a Study in Social Psychology.* New York: Henry Holt and Company, 1924.

stinct had been applied to almost 6,000 different urges and activities of man.

In addition to Bernard, Dunlap, Watson, and Woodworth began to overthrow the instinct theory. Later anthropologists helped the overthrow by showing how many of the so-called instincts are not innate in the race, but are learned behaviors. It was shown for instance, that the "instinctive love for one's own children" does not exist among the Murray Islanders, where there is indifference to real parentage and where children often do not know their true parents. The instinctivists found it difficult to explain the "maternal" and "fighting" instincts when confronted with societies where the fathers, not the mothers, rear the children and with societies where fighting is unknown.

Thus gradually it became clear that the explanation of human behavior and the fountainheads of persuasion had to be sought elsewhere. In spite of the rejection of the instinct theory by many scientists, the influence of the theory still persists and shows itself frequently in "sure-fire" lists of appeals to instincts for the salesman, and in our everyday conversation when we lack a better explanation of why our neighbor's youngster is so "disgustingly mean."

Almost the only known drives found in all normal members of the race are the drives which seek to care for our physical wants—food, freedom from injury, shelter, drink, sex, and air. These, as we shall see in Chapter V, play a major part in the social motives to which persuaders appeal.

BEHAVIORISM

Behaviorism is linked most with its chief proponent, John B. Watson. Watson (1924) questioned the tenets taken by many earlier psychologists that human behavior can be explained in terms of consciousness, mental states, the will, instincts, and imagery determined by means of introspection. He held that human conduct can be explained in terms of stimulus and response, and, therefore, he rejected instincts and all hereditary mental traits and emphasized the role of environment and training in the formation of the behavior patterns of the child and adult.

Although many have disagreed with Watson on this or that specific point, it is generally agreed that he ushered in an era of more objective ways of studying behavior. The student of persuasion is indebted to the behaviorists for suggesting that the fountainheads of human desires are not to be found in some mystical, innate force, but to a great extent within the cultural environment in which the individual lives.

SOCIAL-INTERACTIONISM

The increase in objective methods of study and the focus on training and environment as the sources of human behavior stimulated many psychologists and sociologists who set out to provide more adequate answers to our age-old question. If human behavior is not based on instinct, then its foundations must be sought elsewhere. Physiological psychologists began to emphasize the motivation power of hunger, thirst, sex, and other physiological needs, and introduced the term "drives" to indicate the energy or force which seeks their satisfaction.

It was soon found, however, that the term "drives" was not able to describe all aspects of human motivation, that humans do not live long on a strictly physiological level, and that there are other urges such as social approval, conformity, and so on which apparently are of social origin. In fact, it was found that even the manner in which the physical needs were satisfied was dictated by social customs, mores, conventions, and laws. These socially determined urges were called "motives."

Names like Baldwin (1897, 1911), Cooley (1909), Dewey (1922, 1925), G. H. Mead (1934), Thomas (1918, 1923), Park and Burgess (1924), E. Faris (1937), K. Young (1940), and others are among the ranks of those who consider human personality and conduct to be fundamentally a social-cultural product, a dynamic structure which constantly reflects the social-cultural influences of a given place and time. We believe it is not a misinterpretation of these writers to say that, according to this theory, a student of persuasion must understand this dynamic quality of human nature if he is to be able to analyze the motives of a given audience at a given time and place.

Since the theory developed in the following chapters is based fundamentally on the work of the writers mentioned above and their colleagues in this area, we have reserved until later in this volume a more specific and detailed discussion of how the persuader can find the available means of persuasion within a given group.

Modern Rhetorical Theories of Persuasion

Students of speech have depended largely on the philosophers, the psychologists, the social psychologists, and the sociologists for the raw material out of which they have constructed their own theories of persuasion. They have not been as actively interested in the search for the sources and the bases of persuasion as might be desired. Nonetheless, we must not neglect to give credit to a few who have joined in this search and who have formed the background of modern theory of persuasion. To review briefly several of the chief contributions by writers in the field of speech will help the reader see in its proper continuity this brief history of the search for the sources of persuasion, and will serve to delineate more clearly the theory to be developed in the succeeding chapters.

PHILLIPS

Phillips was among the earliest speech writers of the modern period [9] to incorporate the findings of modern psychology.[10] He emphasized the fact that to arouse men to action persuasion must consider mankind's desires or "impelling motives," and he defined these impelling motives as man's spiritual, intellectual, moral, and material wants. Wants were classified as self-preservation, property, power, reputation, affections, sentiments, and tastes.

Thus it is clear that Phillips believed the sources of persuasion were to be found in neither the shape of the human body nor some set of unchangeable instincts, but in man's basic desires or motives. He did not explain the origin or variation of these motives among different peoples, but simply discussed the above classifications as relatively certain and fixed, as were the classifications of Aristotle. Many succeeding writers in the field of speech either have borrowed directly, or modified slightly, this original list of motives suggested by Phillips.

---

[9] A review of the works of the classical writers in speech would be outside the scope and purposes of this book. The modern writers cited draw upon classical sources.

[10] A. E. Phillips, *Effective Speaking.* Chicago: The Newton Company, 1924.

WINANS [11]

Another writer in the field of speech is Winans, a writer and teacher of great influence. He pioneered in the attempt to actually define the *technique* of persuasion, and to place the processes of persuasion upon a clearly defined psychological foundation. Winans rested his theory essentially on the psychology of William James, the psychology that "what holds attention determines action." [12] Thus Winans defined persuasion as the "process of inducing others to give fair, favorable, or undivided attention to propositions." He points out that ideas which "arouse emotions" hold attention, and that the most evident way to fix attention is by awakening desire for the end sought; an effective desire we call a motive. Apparently considering an analysis of motives to be unnecessary for students of public speaking, Winans adopts the list given earlier by Phillips. He does not believe that persuasion should depend solely on the use of appeals to motives or emotions, however, but points out that logical argument may be necessary to induce belief.

Thus the two writers agree on the basic ingredients of persuasion, but Winans changes the *process* of persuasion by emphasizing the psychology of attention.

BRIGANCE

With great respect for the pioneering work of Winans, Brigance suggests that more recent psychological research provides a better insight into the nature of persuasion.[13] This point Brigance supports by indicating that whereas James and Winans viewed persuasion as a *mental* process, "the generally accepted view today, however, is that persuasion takes place, not on an intellectual, but rather on a motor level." [14] He points out further that even though the psychologists are often divided on technical points, they present a convincing agreement on the fact that the dominant basis for human belief and action is *desire.*

---

[11] See James A. Winans, *Public Speaking.* New York: The Century Company, 1917.

[12] See William James, *Psychology, Briefer Course.* New York: Henry Holt and Company, 1892.

[13] W. N. Brigance, "Can We Re-Define the James-Winans Theory of Persuasion?", *Quarterly Journal of Speech* (February, 1935), XXI: 19–26.

[14] *Ibid.,* p. 21.

Brigance's study, therefore, compelled him to redefine Winans' theory of persuasion and to state his own definitions of persuasion as follows:

1. When the aim is to rouse from indifference, to inspire, or to stimulate lagging enthusiasm and faiths, *persuasion is a process vitalizing old desires, purposes, or ideals.*
2. When the aim is to secure the acceptance of new beliefs or courses of action, *persuasion is a process of substituting new desires, purposes, or ideals for old ones.*[15]

Brigance has been instrumental in focusing attention on the facts of modern psychological literature with respect to the process of persuasion.

Motivational Categories are Non-Explanatory

As we have seen, modern psychological research has led to the emphasis upon *desire* and the focus on human *motives.* Contemporary writers in speech have based their treatments of persuasion largely upon this or that list of motives. As this is being written, there are quite a few lists of human motives in existence, and the total number is mounting in attempts to meet the growing complexity of the persuader's problem. But the important fact is that motivational categories are merely descriptive; they do not provide the necessary understanding of human motivation. "In using motivational terms," warn La Piere and Farnsworth, "we must be careful to avoid the conventional assumption that giving a name to an act provides us with an explanation of it. To say that a man committed murder because he wanted money or because he was jealous of his wife immediately brings up the question of why he wanted money and took this way of obtaining it, or why he was jealous of his wife and took this way of expressing it." [16]

In short, *naming is not explaining.* We believe that if the persuader in modern mass society is to be successful, he must not only be able to name his tools, but also be able to explain their derivation and, if need be, to create new ones to appeal to the complex and ever-changing wants and desires of modern man.

---

[15] W. N. Brigance, *Speech Composition.* New York: Appleton-Century-Crofts, Inc., 1939, p. 139.

[16] La Piere and Farnsworth, *op. cit.,* p. 250.

Summary and Conclusions

We have assumed in this chapter that the true goal in any thorough study of persuasion is to explain insofar as is possible the sources of persuasion by a study of the foundations of human nature. We reviewed briefly some of the paths man has taken in his search for the sources of human motivation and we saw that he has "ridden off in all directions." At first, great philosophers stood back and philosophized about man; these men often were long on insight but short on experimental evidence. Too often early theories of human nature sought to explain this complex structure with some simple, single postulate. The "innateness," the "mysticism," and the "fixity" of human behavior dominated the thinking of many writers for many centuries. Others believed that people fell into "natural types," which could be determined by physical structure, body chemistry, social or psychological traits, and that these types would demonstrate certain predictable behavior patterns. But the human riddle still persisted.

More recently we have come to believe that the individual comes onto life's stage where the scene already is set and the play in progress, and that to play his role in this great drama he must satisfy certain physical and social desires or wants.

The question confronting us now is, Have the writers of the past gone far enough to help us reach our goal? We believe one more step is necessary. They have told us *what* motives and *what* desires we have and have provided lists of motives and desires for us to use in persuading an audience. But the reliance on a rather standardized, simple list of motive appeals is no longer adequate. At best, such approaches are "reductionist"—describing behavior only under simple and few conditions in a society where the conditions of behavior are neither simple nor few. Then, too, the old argument that "human nature never changes" no longer can be used to defend a standardized set of motives. In attempts to recognize the increasing number and complexity of man's motives, some textbooks in both speech and psychology have attempted to solve the problem by simply adding additional and more discriminative motivational categories. These treatments, we believe, are helpful to a degree, yet if such practice persists our lists of human motives will soon assume the embarrassing proportions of man's instincts listed by earlier psychologists.

It seems to us, therefore, that we have come to the time when a persuader must know more than a *set of motives* and the imputation of them to an audience; he should know *how* and *why* motives are derived and thus be able *to find for himself* the motives operative within his audience. Only then will he be able to "find the available means of persuasion" as Aristotle suggested so long ago.

We now are ready to consider the bases of persuasion in the light of modern psychological research.

Readings

1. Brigance, W. N., "The Genetic Approach to Persuasion," *Quarterly Journal of Speech* (June, 1931), XVII: 329–339.
2. Brigance, W. N., "Can We Re-Define the James-Winans Theory of Persuasion?" *Quarterly Journal of Speech* (February, 1935), XXI: 19–26.
3. Winans, James A., *Public Speaking* (Rev. ed.). New York: The Century Company, 1917, pp. 185–200.
4. Woolbert, Charles H., "Persuasion: Principles and Methods," *Quarterly Journal of Public Speaking* (1919), V: 12–25, 101–119, 212–238.
5. Young, Kimball, *Personality and Problems of Adjustment.* New York: F. S. Crofts and Company, 1940, Ch. XIII, "Types of Personality."

Exercises

1. Prepare and deliver a five-minute speech on "The Importance of Understanding Human Nature."

2. Prepare and deliver a five-minute speech on "Some Popular Ways of Explaining Why People Behave As They Do."

3. Prepare and deliver a ten-minute speech on one of the following topics:
   a. The Philosophic Theories Regarding Human Nature
   b. The Typological Theories Regarding Human Nature
   c. The Instinct Theory Regarding Human Nature
   d. The Behavioristic Explanation of Human Nature

4. Write a 500-word paper summarizing Brigance's article: "Can We Re-Define the James-Winans Theory of Persuasion?" See reading reference No. 2.

5. Write a 300-word paper summarizing Brigance's article: "A Genetic Approach to Persuasion." See reading reference No. 1.

Chapter V

THE BODILY BASES OF PERSUASION

Chapter V

THE BODILY BASES OF PERSUASION

Introduction

Our review of the searches for the headsprings of human motivation was closed by suggesting that human nature is not absolutely fixed, and that it is not so simple as to be explained in such single, universal terms as types or instincts. Today we believe there is much nurture in man's nature, and that both nature and nurture work together in producing individuals of many and varying wants, desires, or motives. Even though today's emphasis is on human desires or human motives, however, we still must account for their derivation and nature if we are to establish the bases of persuasion.

In beginning the development of the bases of persuasion we should recall that there are certain helpful common denominators within all people, from which vantage points we may observe the growth and differentiation of human motives. Chief among these, of course, is the fact that all members of the race have approximately the same biological and physiological heritage and, consequently, have essentially the same basic physical wants—i.e., need for oxygen, food, rest, sexual satisfaction, and protection from bodily harm. These basic physical needs are some of the foundation stones upon which any theory of persuasion must rest. They account for much human motivation and, as such, often form the basis for successful persuasion.

The "primary sources of motivation," states Lund, "are very much the same in humans as in animals. They center about physical comforts and the attainment of elemental and biological needs. These sources of motivation are always fundamental, and are the means through which the secondary and derived motives are established."[1] Oliver points out that "It is perfectly evident that

---

[1] F. H. Lund, *Emotions*. New York: The Ronald Press Company, 1939, p. 265.

much human activity is designed to achieve the greatest possible degree of bodily comfort. We try to eat when hungry, sleep when drowsy, rest when tired. More than this, we labor, plan, and economize in order to have funds to carry us into the mountains or to the seashore so we can be cool during the hot season. We mortgage weeks of our time to pay for a new heating system to keep us warm in winter. We are creatures of the body to a very considerable extent. In many respects, our tissues rule our minds."[2]

For years the successful salesman has taken his prospective buyer out to a big, satisfying steak dinner before bringing up the matter of buying that new refrigerator or signing on the dotted line for more insurance. A large percentage of the lobbyists' budget frequently goes for such purposes. "You just can't sell anything but food to a man with an empty stomach," has been heard by all of us. And this common sense statement points to a very real fact, one of which all persuaders should be aware: *Man is basically a biological organism and, as such, is like the lower animals.*

No matter what the degree of personal sophistication, in whatever cultural setting, man somehow will serve his basic biological needs. Who has not read of or witnessed the tragic scenes in war devastated areas where a mere piece of stale bread was of sufficient persuasive appeal to permit various types of personal degradation? Who can soon forget the neglect of certain of the finer human motives as some housewives shoved, elbowed, and cheated their way into getting some of the "limited" food items during wartime rationing? What court has not seen men trade freedom for food?

Granting, then, the significance of bodily needs in any system of persuasion, it is important that we consider each of these biological imperatives from the point of view of the persuader. To those who think such a specific consideration is laboring an obvious point, let it be said that much everyday persuasion fails because the would-be persuaders either are unable or unwilling to recognize and utilize the existing physical drives of the persuadees. Thus to be sensitized to the specific strengths and the interrelationships of these basic drives must be one of the first lessons in the training of the persuader.

---

[2] R. T. Oliver, *The Psychology of Persuasive Speech.* New York: Longmans Green & Co., Inc., 1942, pp. 139, 140.

In preparation for this discussion, we first should distinguish between the terms *drive* and *motive*. Frequently these terms are used interchangeably. One person may speak of another's *drive* toward social prestige; others may speak of the *motive* to gain social prestige. The present writers are aware, too, that psychologists tend to differ in their definitions of these terms. For our purposes it is useful to define *drive* as *any persistent stimulus (usually internal) that produces some sort of activity of the organism until the stimulus ceases to be effective. Motive,* on the other hand, *is the term we shall apply to the learned behavior which has become associated with the release of the tension produced by the drive.* Thus, for example, the rhythmic contractions of the stomach may arouse a persistent tension or drive known as hunger. This *drive* may be reduced or completely stopped by certain subsistence *motives* the person has developed and which lead to the reduction of the *drive.*

Now we are ready to look at these physical drives of ours and to see how they form an important part of the bases of persuasion. In general, we have followed the classification of drives as outlined by Shaffer in his excellent writing on motivation.[3]

Drives Related to Internal Stimuli

HUNGER AND THIRST

Animal psychology has given us much of the available experimental evidence regarding the strength of these and other physical drives. By using variously fed animals in "obstruction boxes," experimenters have accumulated much evidence to support the fact that hunger and thirst are strong drives. Experiments on human subjects have shown how these drives are *drives to activity.* Sociologists and criminologists have pointed out the ends to which man will go to satisfy these basic drives. In "polite society" he develops *cultured* motives, the satisfaction of which keep him fed. During times of crisis when food and drink may not be easily accessible, he may work twice as hard, lie, cheat, connive, and even kill, for food or drink. Mohandas Ghandi once observed, "God Himself dare not appear to a hungry man except in the form of bread."

Writing in the New York *Herald Tribune,* Mac R. Johnson told of riding on a Japanese train with liberated World War II prisoners.

---

[3] See L. F. Shaffer, *The Psychology of Adjustment.* Boston: Houghton Mifflin Company, 1936, Ch. IV.

> Their minds wandered as they told their stories. They knew this and apologized. One said: "I guess I got a rice mind. I forget things." He meant that so intense had been their thoughts of food that events sometimes made little impression and they forgot them.
>
> As each month passed in the prison camps they had talked less of the homes and civilized life they had known, and spoke more and more of food and how to get it. The few times that the Japanese distributed Red Cross boxes had made the greatest impression on the men, and they had talked of the biscuits, canned meat and butter the packages contained.[4]

Just how much wood a man will chop or how many of his possessions he will give up for a meal depends on the strength of these drives at a given time. Jacob persuaded the hungry Esau to part with his entire birthright for a mess of pottage. But of one thing the persuader may be sure: *Human behavior everywhere is basically modified to assure the continuing satisfaction of the hunger and thirst drives.* If you would persuade, keep this in mind.

SEX

The sex drive is second in strength only to hunger and thirst as a basic drive. In humans it develops more slowly than other drives and does not express itself in definite patterns of response until later in life. In youth sex characteristically manifests itself in general irritability and in increased and diffused activity. The sexual behavior beyond the basic tensions and urge to activity involves social learning. Since in civilized man the satisfaction of the sex drive is thwarted by more social conventions than is perhaps any other drive, man develops many substitute stimuli and substitute responses. The directions and manners in which these manifest themselves are discussed in the following chapter under "sex motives."

TEMPERATURE REGULATION

All living organisms operate with greatest efficiency and satisfaction within a certain and usually narrow range of temperature. For years educators have sought to apply this fact by carefully regulating the temperature in the classrooms. Business houses of all types—theaters, restaurants, department stores, and so on—are

---

[4] C. R. Miller, *The Process of Persuasion.* New York: The Crown Publishers, Inc., 1946, p. 25.

becoming more aware of the relationship between temperature regulation and successful salesmanship. An "air-conditioned" sign may be more effective in getting you into the restaurant than a sign suggesting "mincemeat pie just like mother used to make"; and to mention the great amounts of money spent each year on clothing, housing, and travel to assure bodily comfort is an obvious point.

These facts are re-emphasized here because this basic drive of the organism for a comfortable temperature is all too often neglected by the speaker who foolishly thinks that the "power of his persuasion alone will hold his audience." He neglects to consider the possible operation of a *more basic persuasion* which may, and often does, take the listener out the door or put him to sleep.

REST FROM FATIGUE—SLEEP

The degree of fatigue of the persuadee can never be ignored with profit, for here again a basic organic need is involved. Although little is known of the physiological basis of the response called sleep, experience has taught us much regarding the strength of the drive for rest and sleep. Recall the instances where soldiers on guard duty have been willing to risk losing life itself for "just a wink of sleep." The saleslady who first invites her prospective customer to "go freshen up a bit in our new lounge" has the right idea; she is recognizing a fundamental fact.

ELIMINATIVE TENSIONS

The excretory products of the organism produce tensions which result in unrest and bodily discomfort. Each of us has experienced a time when these basic tensions or drives have overridden all other motives and desires. Like the reduction of most physiological tensions, the reduction of the eliminative tensions generally is met in certain socially determined ways. But, socially accepted or not, this drive will be served.

Some Drives Related to External Stimuli

BODY INJURY

One learns early in life that any known stimulus causing injury or complete destruction to any tissue of the body acts as a drive. We avoid any overstimulation of the cutaneous receptors, be the stimulus one that causes a cut, bruise, burn, loud sound, bright light, strong taste, or unpleasant odor. With learning, protection of the body from harms of external origin becomes one of the constant concerns of every individual. In fact, this concern oftentimes becomes so great during periods of physical danger that we develop definite anxieties and, on occasion, complex psychic disturbances. Combat soldiers, torn between the drive for physical safety and the fear of social disapprobation if they appear cowardly, frequently are cases in point.

Any system of persuasion must take into account the storehouse of persistent "avoidance reactions" each individual has developed to maintain physical well-being.

EMOTIONAL TENSIONS

If our discussion of the physiological bases of persuasion is to be complete, we must give a consideration to the much-discussed topic of *emotion.* Even though it is true that our basic emotional tensions soon become overlaid with many social-cultural influences, and thus are of greatest concern to us in their social setting (as we shall see in Chapter VI), we must not neglect the physiological bases of emotion and how emotions may be viewed as drives.

At an early age the youngster reacts to loud noises, restraint, loss of support, pain, and rough physical treatment as overstimulation. And, as Shaffer points out, "Reaction to overstimulation always involves the profound visceral changes which have already been described as those of excited emotion. A great turmoil is set up which constitutes a visceral tension." [5] Dockeray supports this view:

> . . . it seems apparent that one of the natural developments during emotional behavior would be the creation of tensions in many places in the body. Physiologically, these tensions would be indiscernible from those that are part of many drives. We may expect, therefore, that the organism will persist in certain forms of activity until the tensions are relieved. Emotion thus serves the same function as a drive. Emotions are tensions that generally increase activity. Usually, this activity persists until the tension is removed. Thus learning becomes associated with emotion in

---

[5] Shaffer, *op. cit.*, p. 97.

> the same sense that it is related to the satisfaction of the tissue conditions that we called *drives*.[6]

Studies by Cannon [7] revealed that the internal or physiological conditions during emotion include acceleration of heart beat, irregular breathing, inhibition of the movements of the stomach and intestines, contraction of the visceral blood vessels, and the erection of hairs on the body surface.

Thus far we have seen that emotional reactions are connecting links between external and internal stimuli. As Cannon suggests, emotions represent increased and repeated efforts of the organism to make satisfactory adjustments to its environment. We also have seen that, physiologically, emotion is characterized by rather widespread and diffused visceral and somatic changes in the body, and that these conditions set up body tensions similar to drives and, like other tensions, need means of reduction. Now let us proceed to the specific primary emotional states.

Early writers in the field of emotion compiled long lists of separate emotions. Like the long lists of instincts, the number of emotions went beyond scientific control. More recent writers in the field of psychology have tended to study emotion more carefully and have recognized that many of the emotions listed by earlier writers are really mixtures of emotional and intellectual experiences, all considerably modified through training. The Behaviorist, John B. Watson,[8] was a pioneer in the study of emotions and his study tended to influence subsequent work. He contended there are only three distinct emotional states in infant behavior—fear, rage, and love or sex. The fear response is elicited by loud sounds and loss of support, said Watson, and the rage response results from restraint of movement. Love or sex is stimulated by stroking or patting of sensitive zones of the body. Watson demonstrated that emotional responses are acquired, thus challenging those who contended that certain stimuli were native arousers of given emotions.

More recent studies, summarized by the following statement by Lund, in turn have challenged the early studies of Watson:

---

[6] F. C. Dockeray, *Psychology*. New York: Prentice-Hall, Inc., 1945, p. 184.

[7] W. B. Cannon, *Bodily Changes in Pain, Hunger, Fear and Rage* (2nd ed.). New York: Appleton-Century-Crofts, Inc., 1929.

[8] John B. Watson, *Psychology from the Standpoint of a Behaviorist* (2nd ed.). Philadelphia: J. B. Lippincott Company, 1924.

> As to the overt features of infant emotionality, Watson's early studies indicated a fairly high degree of differentiation. More recent accounts have stressed the absence of differentiation. Sherman found that observers were unable to distinguish, with any degree of consistency, different types of emotional response when their stimuli were excluded from observation. Bridges and Shirley note that at birth the emotional conduct of the infant is in the nature of "general excitement," which later becomes differentiated into "distress" and "delight" or into "pleasant" and "unpleasant" forms of behavior. . . .[9]

It appears that, physiologically, emotions present pretty much the same undifferentiated pattern. As the infant attempts to adjust itself for greatest bodily comfort, more specific, learned behaviors come into use. In this manner the differentiation of emotions takes place. Shaffer makes this point clear.

> Rather early in life the child learns to differentiate between situations that are best met by combating them and situations that require running away. Some responses which involve emotion and struggling become stereotyped early in the individual's experience and the rage response is formed. Other overstimulating situations become connected to emotion plus withdrawing, constituting fear. Rage, then, is excited emotion plus learned struggling movements. Fear is excited emotion with the addition of learned avoidance movements.[10]

And the love emotion is similarly conditioned.

Of what importance, then, is this consideration of the physiological basis and early differentiation of human emotions? First, it should be clear that here again we have explored one of the chief sources of human motivation, for, as we shall see in the succeeding chapters, many important motives serve our basic emotions. We have seen that emotions which serve as adjustment devices to environment are really much like the tensions of our physical drives and, similarly, cause the individual to seek satisfaction through the reduction of the tension. Thus the infant begins life not only with the drives of hunger, thirst, sex, and so on, but also soon develops a set of primary emotions, chief of which are rage, fear, and love.

The manner in which these emotions are expressed (or the manner in which these tensions are reduced), is of prime importance to the

---

[9] Lund, *op. cit.*, p. 242.
[10] Shaffer, *op. cit.*, p. 45.

persuader. Individuals will express these differently because the social group surrounding the person dictates to a great extent the acceptable channels of tension reduction through its conventions, customs, and laws. Here the *motives* designed to take care of our physical drives and emotional tensions are formed.

The Interrelationship of Drives

A persuader must remember that bodily conditions are so delicately balanced and interdependent that a change in one organic factor likely will produce changes in another. Thus one cannot depend always on one drive being the strongest, or, indeed, being operative at all.

Experiments on animals have shown that deprivation of water brings about a reduction of the hunger drive.[11] The sexual drive is weakened by prolonged hunger. In an experiment by Miles,[12] twenty-four young men lived under a restricted diet with an energy content of approximately two-thirds to one-half of their supposed caloric requirement. Personal interviews given during this time of lowered nutrition disclosed a weakening of the sex drive. The men showed less desire to associate with the opposite sex, and less desire for dances and other social affairs. No one man reported increased sex desire concurrent with the lowered nutritional level.

An emotional tension may cause a man to "forget all about his sore finger or his empty stomach." No one can forget the classic example of the Crusades where the dwarfish, emaciated persuader, Peter the Hermit, so emotionalized his listeners to "hear nothing but the groans of the Cross" that their heightened suggestibility often eclipsed the more basic considerations of providing for such drives as hunger, thirst, and general bodily care. As a result, thousands died in that tragic march toward Jerusalem. In our own time we have seen members of religious cults, while in a state of extreme emotional tension, "abuse the body happily." Still other illustrations could be added by each reader.

One further fact should be noted: The relative dominance or

---

[11] F. A. Moss, "Study of Animal Drives," *Journal of Experimental Psychology* (1924), VII: 165–185.

[12] W. R. Miles, "The Sex Expressions of Men Living on a Lowered Nutritional Level," *Journal of Nervous and Mental Disorders* (1919), XLIX: 209–224.

strength of our drives is largely dependent upon the specific set of circumstances operative at a given time. Undoubtedly this fact can explain the variations in the results of experiments designed to determine the comparative strengths of drives. Probably there is no immutable hierarchy of drives.

Although experimental findings in this area are few and not sufficiently conclusive to justify either extensive discussion or definite conclusions, a brief review of several experiments will serve to indicate the variations in their results and, at the same time, their general agreements regarding the primary strength of our physiological drives.

Starch [13] prepared a list of forty-four motives for action and had them rated by seventy-four men and women. Each rater was instructed, "Ask yourself in connection with each one how important it is in determining your own actions from day to day." The "motives" were rated on a scale from 1 to 10. Table I gives the ratings of the forty-four biological and social drives.

TABLE I

The Rated Strength of Biological and Social Drives

Motives	*Per Cent*	*Motives*	*Per Cent*
Appetite-hunger	9.2	Respect for Deity	7.1
Love of offspring	9.1	Sympathy for others	7.0
Health	9.0	Protection of others	7.0
Sex Attraction	8.9	Domesticity	7.0
Parental affection	8.9	Social distinction	6.9
Ambition	8.6	Devotion to others	6.8
Pleasure	8.6	Hospitality	6.6
Bodily comfort	8.4	Warmth	6.5
Possession	8.4	Imitation	6.5
Approval by others	8.0	Courtesy	6.5
Gregariousness	7.9	Play-sport	6.5
Taste	7.8	Managing others	6.4
Personal appearance	7.8	Coolness	6.2
Safety	7.8	Fear-caution	6.2
Cleanliness	7.7	Physical activity	6.0
Rest-sleep	7.7	Manipulation	6.0
Home comfort	7.5	Construction	6.0
Economy	7.5	Style	5.8
Curiosity	7.5	Humor	5.8
Efficiency	7.3	Amusement	5.8
Competition	7.3	Shyness	4.2
Cooperation	7.1	Teasing	2.6

[13] D. Starch, *Principles of Advertising*. Chicago: Shaw and Sons, 1923, p. 273.

An experiment by Hollingworth [14] had fifty different advertising appeals ranked by the subjects according to their "persuasiveness, that is, according to the degree to which they make you desire the article or convince you of its merits." The appeals which ranked from first to tenth place were as follows: Health, cleanliness, scientific, time saved, appetizing, efficiency, safety, durability, quality, and modernity.

Using the same fifty appeals as employed by Hollingworth, Adams [15] secured evaluations of the appeals from a sample of sixty persons of both sexes and found considerable agreement with the findings of Hollingworth. The ten top-ranking appeals were: Durability, sanitary, efficient, appetizing, time saved, value, scientific, ambition, family affection, safety, and evolution.

Poffenberger,[16] in a more carefully prepared study, classified the various appeals under twelve headings based on the actual advertising copy and then subsumed all the data of Hollingworth and Adams under these twelve categories. When this was done, the following rank order was achieved: Appetite, family affection, protection, sympathy, health, economy, recommendation, activity-sport, conformity-fashion, superiority-ambition, group spirit, and beauty-attractiveness.

As was mentioned earlier, the results of these studies are not in consistent agreement, but the general agreement relative to the motivational strength of those primary drives which seek to keep the body in a state of well-being seems unmistakable.

Summary and Conclusions

We have seen that our physiological drives—hunger, thirst, temperature regulation, rest from fatigue, eliminative tensions, sex, avoidance of bodily harm, and emotional tensions—provide the first level or underlying foundation of our behavior. As such, these are basic considerations in a theory of persuasion. A speaker must be able to utilize and adapt the physiological drives of his

---

[14] H. S. Hollingworth, "Judgments of Persuasiveness," *Psychological Review* (1911), XVIII: 234–256.

[15] H. F. Adams, *Advertising and Its Mental Laws*. New York: The Macmillan Company, 1921, p. 130 ff.

[16] A. T. Poffenberger, *Psychology in Advertising*. New York: McGraw-Hill Book Co., Inc., 1932, p. 95.

hearers to his own purposes. A hungry audience or one with still other physical discomforts may be more easily aroused by the leader who demands more pay, more food, and more physical comforts for his listeners.

If drives useful to the persuader are not operative, the persuader may arouse them by his verbal imagery. Who has not heard the radio commercials that attempt this by "mellow-mouthed" words about those "creamy, crispy, crunchy tid-bits that melt in your mouth"? Using the same method of persuasion but on a somewhat different level, the advocates of the Marshall Plan for giving aid to Europe after World War II went to great lengths to get us to "feel how it must be to have one slice of bread a day and a pinch of meat once a week."

In the following chapter we shall see how man develops social motives which he uses to reduce the basic physiological and emotional tensions we have been discussing.

Readings

1. Dockeray, F. C., *Psychology*. New York: Prentice-Hall, Inc., 1945, Ch. VI, "Physiological Basis of Motives."

2. Shaffer, L. F., *The Psychology of Adjustment*. Boston: Houghton Mifflin Company, 1936, pp. 40–53, "Emotion."

3. Valentine, W. L., *Experimental Foundations of General Psychology*. New York: Farrar and Rinehart, Inc., 1941, Ch. IX, "Drives and Motives."

4. Young, Kimball, *Social Psychology*. New York: F. S. Crofts and Company, 1945, Ch. IV, "Drives and Emotions."

5. Young, P. T., *Motivation of Behavior*. New York: John Wiley and Sons, Inc., 1936, Ch. III, "Animal Drives."

Exercises

1. Prepare and deliver a five-minute persuasive speech which relies on appeals to one of the following drives for its motivating power:

a. Hunger
b. Rest from fatigue
c. Satisfactory temperature regulation
d. Freedom from body injury from external sources.

2. Clip from a newspaper or magazine an advertisement which bases its persuasion on one or more of the human wants discussed in this chapter. Discuss this advertisement with your class.

3. Make a list of the things you did during the course of a single day which primarily were done to satisfy one or more of the basic bodily needs. Would you say the bodily needs are important considerations in the study of persuasion?

4. Prepare and deliver a ten-minute informational speech on one of the following topics:

   a. Emotional Tensions as Drives
   b. The Interrelationship of Drives

5. Prepare and deliver a five-minute persuasive speech which relies for its motivating power on appeals to one of our basic emotions.

Chapter VI

THE SOCIAL BASES OF PERSUASION

I. Introduction

II. The Elusiveness and Complexity of Motives

III. Dependence of the Individual Upon the Group

IV. The Elaboration of Physical Drives into Social Motives

V. General Classifications of Motives

A. Subsistence Motives

B. Social Approval Motives

C. Conformity Motives

D. Mastery Motives

E. Sex Motives

F. Mixed Motives

G. Habits as Motives

VI. Summary and Conclusions

Readings and Exercises

Chapter VI

THE SOCIAL BASES OF PERSUASION

Introduction

In Chapter V we explored the bodily bases of persuasion. We discovered that each infant at birth has a set of physical drives and that soon after birth a set of primary emotional tensions is developed—love, rage, fear—in attempts to adjust to the environment. In short, we found that the infant is not a miniature man with all of the adult's social motives only to a lesser degree. Rather, he is an unsocialized being with basic physical drives but without social motives.

We know, of course, that the infant does not long continue to live on a strictly biological level, but that soon (and for some parents much too soon), he develops *social motives.* These not only serve to take care of his physical wants but also help to develop for him a social selfhood. These socially-determined motives increase in both number and complexity as the child grows older, until by adulthood the persuader finds it extremely difficult to discover the specific motivational key that will release the springs of response within that individual.

Let us look at these motives closely, trace their derivation and development, and observe the part they play in persuasion.

The Elusiveness and Complexity of Motives

To attempt to handle motives is like trying to pick up quicksilver; the substance is elusive and uncertain. It is extremely difficult to determine with accuracy the motives of others by observation. The individual himself often is at a loss to understand his own motives. Ask a man the simple question of why he works and he will come back quickly with the retort that he must live.

When pressed further, he will begin to recount the values of living, his duty to family, friends, country, and so on. But these are often rationalizations, reasons assigned with a view to their social implications—i.e., how they will "sound" to others. Whether these "reasons" are operative may be open to question.

Then, too, motives sometimes seem fickle and shifting to us. What man has not been disturbed at the "fleeting fancies of women," and who has not at one time or another accused someone of being "as changeable as the weather"? What we enjoy today we may reject tomorrow. Katie the co-ed may be "too busy with her school work" to go out with Jake, the common sophomore, but later that night she may manage to find time to sneak away for "two precious hours" with the senior president. Mrs. Hopeful's "splitting headache" may keep her from accepting an invitation to tea with Mrs. Nobody, but her headache is sufficiently mild to allow her to go for a ride into the country with Mrs. Plushpurse. The salesman's prospect may see no use for insurance until it is mentioned that the family's social rival has such a policy.

Man is a product of both his own structure and his environment. The fact that these two contributors to behavior are infinitely complex means that men themselves will differ. Not only will they differ among themselves but also there often will be contradictions within the individual himself. So it is that he may be both greedy and philanthropic, competitive and co-operative. All this means that at various times and places, and in differing situations, motives work in varying strengths and combinations to serve the basic drives and primary desires of the individual. Like an iceberg, the hidden portion of our motives often far outweighs the surface appearances.

We have given this brief discussion of the dynamic interplay of motives prior to a more detailed consideration of each of them for a very good reason. In order for the student of persuasion to understand clearly these foundations of human response *(motives)*, it is necessary to consider each class of motives separately, as though it occurs in isolation, even though actually it does not. We caution the reader to keep in mind that life does not always present a simple pattern of motivation. Rather, as one writer puts it, "each day becomes either a theater in which many motives work together in playing their roles in the drama of our lives or is a prize ring where motives compete, singly and in teams, for supremacy in the direction of our life patterns." [1]

Dependence of the Individual Upon the Group

We must remember that survival is dependent upon some degree of co-operation between each man and his fellows, regardless of the cultural pattern. Social psychologist Young provides explanation of this fact when he states that

> . . . everywhere the human being begins his basic adaptation in a state of dependency on other members of his species, specifically on his kinship group, especially on his mother or, in relatively few instances, a mother substitute. While the satisfaction of his needs for oxygen, sleep, and elimination are at the outset biologically individual, his need for food is satisfied only by *social* means—that is, through the interposition of another member of his species, the mother or other adult. So, too, his general bodily requirements for protection against pain, cold, heat, and other noxious stimuli are, in the earliest period at least, satisfied only by the assistance or cooperation of others. Also much of the basic learning involves early socialization of responses to the need for elimination, rest and sleep, and other basic needs or wants. Later, the matured sexual drives can be satisfied only by interaction. In short, though we need not posit a social or gregarious instinct or drive, the universal setting of survival is a *social act* . . .[2]

A brief reflection on the part of the reader will confirm what the statements above suggest. At almost every turn we are dependent on others for the satisfaction of this or that drive or desire. In order to secure this help, satisfactions must occur in socially accepted ways. Early in life we learn that there are certain *expectations* made of us by those about us and if we are to maintain the approval of the group, upon which our survival depends, we must meet these expectations favorably. As youngsters, we learned that those about us would make only slight adjustments to us. The social scene was already "set"; we were expected to conform to its conventions, customs, mores, and laws. If we "acted acceptably" our physical and social satisfactions were assured.

Thus we see that the satisfactions of our physiological drives be-

---

[1] F. C. Dockeray, *Psychology*. New York: Prentice-Hall, Inc., 1945, p. 143.

[2] K. Young, *Social Psychology*. New York: Appleton-Century-Crofts, Inc., 1944, p. 42.

come associated with social objects and, as a result, these objects achieve great significance. *So it is that of all the objects which acquire the power to act as substitute satisfactions, the approving individual is the most important.* Here we see the birth of the motive of social approval.

This dependence upon the group results in such a craving for continued social approval that isolation becomes one of the most severe punishments. For the prisoner to be placed in a multiple cell is bad enough, but to be cast into the "isolation cell" is maddening. To be banished from his native country to the lonely island of Elba was Napoleon's greatest hardship, and elderly Marshal Petain experienced a similar fate on an isolated island off the coast of France.

The persuader must keep in mind not only the dependence of every individual upon the group, but he must keep in mind the companion fact, suggested earlier, that each group has a *set of expectations* which it applies to each member of the group. Thus it is necessary that the persuader know the expectations which must be met if a person is to gain group approval and its help in satisfying his drives and desires. When the persuader knows these "expected" things, he can link what he wants with the achieving of that which is socially expected and hence desired by the persuadee.

To know these sources of persuasion, the persuader must keep in mind that the individual may be dependent on and thus seeking approval from various groups and on differing levels. One person's desire to be considered "just a good American" may be dominant; another may wish first of all to be a good Lutheran. Still others are at one time seeking national approval and local approvals, be they in the Kiwanis Club, Rotarians, college class, or elsewhere.

Differing social groups have differing codes of expectation. For social approval in our society a man may have to conduct himself differently than he would if he were in another society. In our own country, salesman Charles Atlas, the muscle builder, may appeal to successful physical rivalry to get boys to buy his correspondence course, but it is not likely that the youths in the Kwakiutl tribe of the Canadian Pacific region would be impressed by the Atlas advertising, for they are not expected to settle their differences by fighting, which to them is unknown. Our "success courses" would have little or no appeal to the Zuni Indians who, as Ruth Benedict found, frown on a person who seeks prestige and power over others. Otto Klineberg, a social psychologist, found the accurate testing of the intelligence of many Indian tribes impossible because the members of the tribes could not seem to grasp the idea of *competing* with their fellows in achieving a high score. The call to arms has no appeal to a pacifist. The appeal to competition and to the acquisition of personal property is not persuasive to a member of those social groups who live a communal life where all gains are common gains and where property is shared by all.

World War II American soldiers found that the persuasive appeals given the Japanese soldiers to defend their homeland and emperor seemed to result in virtual fanaticism on the part of the warriors; the Kamakaze suicide pilots could hardly be understood by the GI's. Yet when one recalls the rigidly organized Japanese society with its basic codes of complete obedience to patriarchal authority and submergence of personal desires to the good of the larger group and the imperial family, and when we add the additional fact that this intense in-group feeling with its submerged individualistic impulses allows for intense hostility toward the out-groups, we can begin to understand the motive structure of the Japanese soldier. Strength and force against the out-group are to him the "male" principles, and sympathy, compromise, and democratic procedures are "female" weaknesses.[3] The Nazi, too, was found to possess unusual motivation; his devotion to der Fuhrer also seemed fanatical. Hitler had succeeded in transferring the rebellion of many against their insecurities and deprivations to a revolt against institutions, the Jews, and foreign powers. Thus appeals to violence, strength, and force against the "enemies of National Socialism" were responded to favorably by "good Nazis."

Examples might be multiplied on both local and national levels to indicate the differing *sets of expectations* in differing societies and the concern the individuals have within these groups for the group's approval because of their dependence upon the group for survival. It is up to the persuader to understand the "persuasion climate" in which the persuadee seeks to satisfy his basic drives.

---

[3] See "The Way of the Subjects," quoted in O. D. Tolischus, *Tokyo Record.* New York: Reynal and Hitchcock, Inc., 1943.

The Elaboration of Physical Drives into Social Motives

Since the individual is dependent on others to a very great extent for the satisfaction (reduction), of the basic drives necessary to his survival, we would expect him to develop, out of social learning, types of behavior which would provide ways and means of gaining these satisfactions. And this is precisely what takes place. Beginning early in infancy, we develop a set of *action tendencies* or *motives* which move us in the direction of these satisfactions. When a persuader appeals effectively to any of these tendencies we are aroused to action.

These social motives become the forces which impel us to varying behaviors. They cause one to join a labor union, another to refuse to join; they cause one student to join one fraternity instead of another, and to skip one class, but attend another. Now let us turn to a different level. On one occasion a man commits a murder and is hanged for it; on another occasion a man kills another and we reward him with a medal. The act of slaying is the same in both cases as to method and result. What, then, makes the difference? *Motives.* In the first instance the killing served society's interests (our collective desires) best to hang the murderer; in the second case it served our motives best to give social approval to the murder.

General Classifications of Motives

SUBSISTENCE MOTIVES

Foremost are the motives man develops to care for his organic needs, motives which will lead to the provision of food, drink, and bodily protection. In fact, most of the motives to be discussed do not arise independently of bodily states. Our subsistence motives include our major *economic motives.* These have been given various names, such as the *profit motive, our acquisitive wants, desire for property, the work motive, motive of self-preservation, health and safety motives,* and our *material mindedness.*

No matter what the name, it must be clear that man has developed many motives which lead him to the satisfaction of his basic needs. The power of these subsistence motives is in evidence all about us. They drive men into the remote areas of the earth to pan for gold; they compel others to sweat from early morning until late at night in harvest fields and in factories; still others may spend long, lonely hours at sea in search of new markets and profits in other hemispheres; and we must not neglect to observe those who will cheat, lie, enslave, and even kill for food and drink or the money to procure these essentials.

Money has become the substitute stimulus for our subsistence satisfactions and has achieved an almost ruinous status. "Tap a man's pocketbook and you strike a gusher in the field of human motivation."

The study of economics presents a detailed account of subsistence motives, outlining the principles and policies by which these motives can be served best for both society and the individual. Our purpose here is to indicate the power of these motives in persuasion.

SOCIAL APPROVAL MOTIVES

In our discussion of the dependence of the individual upon the group we stated that of all the objects which acquire the power to act as substitute satisfactions, the approving individual is the most important. This fact suggests the basic explanation of the rise of one of our strongest sets of motives—*the social approval motives.* We constantly seek the approval of others within the home, the neighborhood gang, the school, the church, the lodge, the sorority, the state, and the nation. "No more fiendish punishment," says William James, "could be devised, were such a thing physically possible, than that one should be turned loose in society and remain unnoticed by all members thereof. If no one turned round when we entered, answered when we spoke, or minded what we did, but if every person we met 'cut us dead,' and acted as if we were non-existent things, a kind of rage and impotent despair would ere long well up in us, from which the cruelest bodily tortures would be a relief; for these would make us feel that, however bad might be our plight, we had not sunk to such a depth as to be unworthy of attention at all." [4]

During wartime the motive of social approval has driven some men to wear the uniform of their country's armed forces illegally.

---

[4] William James, *Principles of Psychology*. New York: Henry Holt and Company, 1890, I: 293–294.

And what military commander has not observed the persuasive power of medals and ribbons, tokens of public approval? Men are slaves to such, said Napoleon.

Psychological experimentation has shown that students working in groups tend to do more work than when alone. Industries have found the same result among piece workers. And who of us can ignore the effect of what "people will say" on the selection of our dress, our house architecture, our social clubs, our college or university. Students of church history know how the martyrs actually welcomed the flames which consumed them, motivated at least in part by the approval of a certain select group and by the thought that "hereafter whole generations will rise up and call us blessed."

If the persuader can show that by doing as he suggests the persuadee will participate to a greater degree in social approval, he has used an appeal difficult for any of us to ignore. Persuaders dealing in the state affairs of Wisconsin make the appeal that "others are looking to this great progressive state to continue to lead in progressivism and what I am suggesting will assure this confidence." In the famous Loeb-Leopold case, Clarence Darrow attempted to motivate the judge by showing that the type of sentence he (Darrow) was recommending had the approval of the people as evidenced by previous legal examples. Who has not heard the political orator ask in imploring tones, "What will the coming generations say of the history we are now writing?"

CONFORMITY MOTIVES

Closely allied with our social approval motives are our motives to conform. Whereas our desire for social approval operates positively, causing us to seek approval, the motive to conform operates negatively, causing us to avoid blame and disapproval for non-conformity. There are times when we rebel against the social codes of conduct set for us, occasions when we would prefer to seek satisfactions of our drives in our own way. In fact, our newspapers carry stories of these attempts every day. For the most part, however, we conform to avoid punishment. Certain psychologists believe that our motives to conform are developed from the *fear* emotion conditioned in infancy. The child finds that punishment of various kinds (usually physical) follows non-conformity. This fear of blame, physical punishment, and other forms of social disapproval leads us to conduct ourselves in a manner so that we "belong." We bow to the force of customs, conventions, mores, folkways, rituals, and laws.

Experimentation has indicated that when given a choice to go along with majority or expert opinion we generally are influenced more by the majority or general public opinion, thus conforming to the larger group. These motives to conform constitute the underlying premises of such books as Trotter's *Instincts of the Herd in Peace and War,* LeBon's *The Crowd,* and Conway's *The Crowd in Peace and War.* Some writers have called this action tendency the "gregarious instinct." Speech writers, also, have given this general motive various other names, such as the motive *to belong, to live up to expectations,* the *imitation motive,* and *submission motive,* and so on.

Allport[5] posited what he called the J-Curve Hypothesis to express our tendency to conform. He noted that the normal bell-shaped curve did not apply when conformity behavior is being graphed, but that most social behavior is so similar as to be plotted on a virtually straight line with the few non-conformists causing the line to curve off into a J shape. Our tendency toward fads and fashions is evidence of this same motive at work.

Try wearing a derby on your campus awhile if you doubt the pressure of this motive. Recall, too, the embarrassment you experienced when you had to wear that large bandage over one eye, or that "awful looking stuff" over the sore on your cheek. Sometime, secretly, ask a judge of an oratorical contest how he felt when he learned that the other four judges had given first place to the orator he had ranked fifth.

All types of political persuaders have made us feel keenly sensitive regarding what a "good American should do." The Senator cries, "It's un-American; it defies the flag." The sales clerk parrots almost automatically, "This is what *they're* wearing this year." The preacher exhorts, "It's un-Christian." The commercial advertiser urges, "Smoke the cigarette that *millions* smoke." The bobby-soxer tells her mother, "Everybody's doing it." The campaigner shouts, "It's the will of the majority," the propagandist pleads, "Get on the bandwagon," and the party promoter contends

[5] F. H. Allport, "The J-Curve Hypothesis of Conforming Behavior," *Journal of Social Psychology* (1934), V: 141–183.

that his candidate is, "Just one of the many plain folks which make up this great country of ours." The adjustment psychologist suggests to his students in calm academic tones, "For the greatest *comfort* never be the first to start the new nor the last to discard the old."

As previously noted, social approval and conformity motives are closely related, so much so that an act of "meeting expectations" usually has some ingredients of each. We can term these the "Social Pressure Motives" and represent their interaction by a continuum.

Social Pressure Motive Continuum

Conformity 100%	50%	0% Conformity
Social Approval 0%	50%	100% Social Approval

The motivation behind any act of "doing what others do" will fall at some spot on the continuum. Usually positive rewards (approval) supplement fear (conformity) motivation and vice versa. Probably most social pressure motivation is a blend of this sort, and most behavior in this category evolves from motivations clustering around the mid-portion of the continuum.

One further note of clarification—a particular act that illustrates adherence to conventional social practice may, in one individual, be predominately a result of fear motivation, while the same act in the case of another person may be predominately motivated by the desire for social approval. The individual plus the act plus the particular context all determine the relative proportion of the two social pressure motives.

MASTERY MOTIVES

Like the conformity motives, it is believed that mastery motives are derived essentially from emotional tensions aroused early in life. As was indicated earlier, the restraints of the child develop a primary emotion termed *rage,* which later he finds must be expressed in socially accepted ways. Thus this rage behavior manifests itself in motives *to excel, to rival, to compete, to dominate, to lead, to gain prestige, to seek authority,* and so on. In short, we find satisfaction for the rage emotion (reduction of this basic emotional tension) in various forms of mastery, which become more refined and sophisticated as social learning increases.

The mastery motives operate on all levels and in varying degrees of intensity. To say "He's a big boy now" often is sufficient to move a youngster to the desired behavior, just as "Deutschland Uber Alles" has demonstrated its effectiveness in appealing to a collective desire for mastery. In between these extremes are hosts of examples of mastery motives at work—the salesman getting the Smiths to "keep up with the Joneses" by buying a new Packard, the Hollywood hopeful buying make-up used by Lana Turner, the Badgers defeating the Golden Gophers on the gridiron, the Independents defeating the Greek Letter societies in a campus election, the college debater getting higher grades than the All-American, a certain college building a larger stadium than a rival institution, the Methodists getting more new members than any other denomination, and General Electric declaring profits greater than those of Western Electric.

When we lose or fail to achieve the capacity for successful masteries, we may achieve them vicariously. We may *identify* ourselves with the master by "sitting at the speaker's table," living the part of the hero in the movie, or by being "intimately acquainted" with the President.

Man's mastery motives have caused him to do much of the world's work, and have caused him to make peace and to make war.

SEX MOTIVES

"Love is what makes the world go round." We have heard it many times. And this everyday observation has much truth in it if we refer to its power to propel people in many directions and into many forms of behavior.

The sex drive is, as we stated earlier, a glandular and physiological one. Animals satisfy this drive in a direct manner, but man has erected about it many social barriers which prevent its direct satisfaction. We control its expression by many customs, mores, laws, and economic restrictions. If the reader wishes to regain the feel of the power of social mores relative to sex behavior, he should reread Hawthorne's *The Scarlet Letter.* The fact that this strong drive is thwarted has served to draw much attention to it and has given rise to numerous substitute stimuli and substitute responses. According to Shaffer, "By learning processes, chiefly verbal in nature, the presence of persons of the opposite sex, pictures, books, articles of clothing, in fact an innumerable inventory of objects and events become sexual stimuli. Many substitute tension-reducing activities such as games, sports, dancing and even more remote reactions become in a broad sense sexually adjustive." [6]

Just as many objects and events present a complex pattern of sexual stimuli, so we develop a complex set of sex motives which direct us into behaviors bringing about satisfactions (either directly or in substitute forms) of the basic sex drive. Sometimes the most perceiving psychiatrist is confounded in his attempts to unravel the web of sexual motivation within his patient. Then, too, we tend to build up whole systems of emotional response around our love objects, which give these objects or people unpredictable strength as stimuli. These systems of emotional response are called *sentiments,* and they are of sufficient importance in persuasion to be treated separately in the succeeding chapter.

The persuader's problem in the use of appeals to sex motives is both easy and difficult. It is easy in that the sex motives are strong and universal, and therefore susceptible to appeal at all times. It is difficult in that appeals to the finer love motives as found in varying degrees of sophistication and sublimation in conjugal, parental, filial love, and as expressed in various forms of art and humanitarianism, require much prior thought if they are to be effective.

The overwhelming role of sex in our civilization has caused every type of persuader to appeal to it. The average persuader usually has relied upon the standard appeals to physical attractiveness, to the possibility of a happy married life, to the various virtues approved by the opposite sex, be they manliness, social grace, or the various prestige positions of our society. To follow the advertising antics of the salesmen of perfume is interesting recreation. Note a few of their sales appeals—"sensuous as the beat of tom-toms," ". . . not too innocent," ". . . such stuff as dreams are made of," "as mischievous as a sidelong glance," ". . . to be utterly

---

[6] L. F. Shaffer, *The Psychology of Adjustment.* Boston: Houghton Mifflin Company, 1936, pp. 105, 106.

devastating," and on ad nauseam. The soap advertisers provide similar recreation; "the skin you love to touch," "no lonely evenings for this blonde," and "may he kiss you with his eyes open?" The dominant appeal is clear. Appeals to sex motives are used in advertising more widely than any other motive appeal. Such appeals also play a major role in all other areas of persuasion.

MIXED MOTIVES

The motivational categories we have discussed thus far are, admittedly, quite arbitrary. We have discussed them as such because they at least approach what might be called "pure" motives, if indeed there are such. There are additional motives, however, which may be said to be derived or elaborated from more than one drive or emotional tension. Take, for instance, the need for *security* as discussed by sociologist W. I. Thomas. Security, as a motive, surely owes part of its derivation to our physiological needs, but we must not forget, too, that it is a mark of achievement, of mastery, of social approval, of prestige to have gained *security* in our society. In all likelihood this motive is born of more than one need—a mixed motive.

The *acquisitive wants* of man—savings, property, and so on—do, as we suggested earlier, guarantee to a great extent the satisfaction of our physiological needs. Beyond a certain point amassed wealth takes on a social dimension; it serves our desire for mastery, for prestige, social reputation, and sometimes sex. Consider, too, the matter of *parental love*. Even though the first foundations of such love are found in nursing and fondling of the child, the social approval factors soon come in and as some children find out, the mastery motives may find expression. *Adventure* is frequently listed as a motive and here again we have a mixed motive. Physiological satisfactions (thrills) are gained, but the thrills would not be half so enjoyable if you could not tell others about this brave adventure. The adventurer frequently is avoiding certain painful conformities, and anticipating new situations which will bring about more satisfaction. The test pilot of the latest jet fighter gains in mastery and social approval, to say nothing of the financial rewards.

Creativeness also has been listed as a motive. A man may spend months carving a small ship inside a bottle. A lady may spend a similar amount of time crocheting a fancy bedspread or weaving a colorful tapestry. Why? The rewards again are not singular. To say "I made this myself" has the obvious social rewards of recognition and approval. Thus, in addition to the economic value created, desires for mastery are rewarded.

These examples are sufficient to indicate the nature of mixed motives which are combinations of motives.

HABITS AS MOTIVES

By repeated actions humans acquire certain ways or mechanisms which serve the motives in bringing about the desired responses. The animal's instincts are fixed and definite; his behavior can be predicted. The bird's instincts, too, are quite fixed, and each instinct results in the same type of response behavior as witnessed in nest-building, maternal behavior, and so on. But man's motives cannot be predicted to result in identical behaviors. After living awhile, however, man, both by accident and planned training, does develop set ways of achieving the satisfactions impelled by the existing motives. These *habits,* these mechanisms or ways of ordering our satisfactions, seem to operate as motives. As Woodworth once pointed out, "the mechanism furnishes its own drive."

When the salesman went to sell the farmer his first tractor, he needed not only to appeal to the economic and prestige motives, but he also needed to overcome the farmer's, "We've always done it this way," or, "They'll never take the place of the good old horse." Who has not seen a small fit of rage result when the man of the house comes to enjoy the satisfactions of his evening paper, his pipe, and warm slippers only to find the parts of the paper strung over the house, his pipe out of the rack, and one slipper too far under the bed to be reached?

Often the persuader must show the persuadee that the proposed satisfactions can be achieved through tried, tested, *habituated* means which fit into his "orderly life."

Summary and Conclusions

During the course of this chapter we have considered those elements of psychology and social psychology which provide an understanding of the derivation and development of human motives. The purpose has been to help the student identify those bases of persuasion found in man's social motives.

We noted that the individual's dependence on the group has caused him to develop motives and mechanisms which see to it that his physical and social needs are met in socially accepted ways. We have seen, too, that this process of adjusting one's individual needs to the environment results in many and varying motives.

It should be re-emphasized that motives seldom operate singly. Frequently many strong motives may be the determiners of a single act. The dynamic interplay of human motives presents for the student of persuasion a challenging study, one which he must continue to pursue as new light is brought to the subject. The final chapter on human motives will not be written until the final page of human history is penned.

Readings

1. Allport, F. H., "The J-Curve Hypothesis of Conforming Behavior," *Journal of Social Psychology* (1934), V: 141–183.
2. Oliver, Robert T., *The Psychology of Persuasive Speech*. New York: Longmans, Green & Co., Inc., 1942, Ch. III, "The Influence of Social Consciousness."
3. Phillips, A. E., *Effective Speaking*. Chicago: The Newton Company, 1908, Ch. V, "Action and the Impelling Motives."
4. Ruch, F. L., *Psychology and Life*. New York: Scott, Foresman and Company, 1937, pp. 277–286.
5. Thomson, J. K., *The Springs of Human Action*. New York: D. Appleton and Company, 1927, Ch. XXII, "Economic Motives."

Exercises

1. Write a 500-word paper on the topic, "How physical drives give rise to social motives."

2. Analyze your own motives in (a) coming to this school, (b) joining a certain student organization, (c) selecting your particular vocation, or (d) dressing as you do. What motives seem to be quite strong in directing your conduct?

3. Prepare a six-minute persuasive speech which has one of the following as its chief appeal:

a. Appeal to wealth
b. Appeal to social approval
c. Appeal to conformity

d. Appeal to mastery
e. Appeal to sex motives
f. Appeal to security
g. Appeal to adventure
h. Appeal to creativeness

4. Bring three persuasive advertisements to class and be prepared to analyze the motive appeals used in each.

5. Select a printed persuasive speech and write a 500-word analysis of the motive appeals used by the speaker or writer.

Chapter VII

ATTITUDES, SENTIMENTS, AND STEREOTYPES IN PERSUASION

I. Introduction

II. Attitudes

A. General Nature of Attitudes

B. Definition of Attitude

C. Classification of Attitudes

1. Central and Segmental Attitudes
2. General and Specific Attitudes
3. Dominant and Latent Attitudes
4. Positive and Negative Attitudes
5. Private and Public Attitudes
6. Attitudes and Opinions

D. Attitudes and Persuasion

1. People with Like Attitudes
2. Attitudes the Result of Learning and Experience
3. Dominant Attitudes
4. Verbal Expression of Attitudes
5. Influence of Majority Opinions

III. Sentiments

A. General Nature of Sentiments

B. Sentiment of Self-Regard

C. Sentiments and Persuasion

IV. Stereotypes

A. Rise and Operation of Stereotypes

B. Relation of Stereotypes to Attitudes and Sentiments

C. Stereotypes and Persuasion

1. Objectivity in Personal Stereotypes
2. Recognition of "Loaded Words"
3. Cautious Approach for Modifying Prejudices

V. Summary and Conclusions

Readings and Exercises

Chapter VII

ATTITUDES, SENTIMENTS, AND STEREOTYPES IN PERSUASION

Introduction

In continuing our examination of the bases of persuasion, we must probe into certain other forces which exert strong directive influences on human conduct. Through the normal processes of learning and experience we tend to build up systems of anticipatory response in relation to certain objects, ideas, events, and people. These organizations of reaction tendencies constitute important bases of persuasion. We refer to *attitudes, sentiments,* and *mental stereotypes.*

Attitudes

GENERAL NATURE OF ATTITUDES

"How was I to know he had that attitude toward salesmen?" grumbled the novice as he picked himself and his brushes off the front steps. "What you are shouts so loud that I cannot hear what you say," remarked Emerson in a statement that indicates vividly the influence of attitudes on our appraisal of those about us. "Choose ideas that fit in with your hearer's attitudes toward you and your subject," suggests the teacher of public speaking.

What are attitudes? What is their origin? What role do they play in persuasion?

Let us suppose that when you were in primary school your first grade teacher caused you physical discomfort by not allowing you to visit the rest room as often as was necessary. Then, too, she may have punished you for being late to school by ridiculing you before the entire class. On still another occasion she may have given you so much work to do that you had no time to play in the class ball game against the second graders. Still other unpleasant situations may have been caused by this and other teachers. As a result of this series of thwartings of your physical drives and social motives you developed a given predisposition, reaction tendency, or *attitude* in relation to schoolteachers. The formation of this attitude might be shown schematically, where the various stimulus situations (S1, S2, S3, S4), produced the unpleasant responses (R1, R2, R3, R4), which in turn combined or organized themselves into a generalized response R or *attitude* toward teachers.

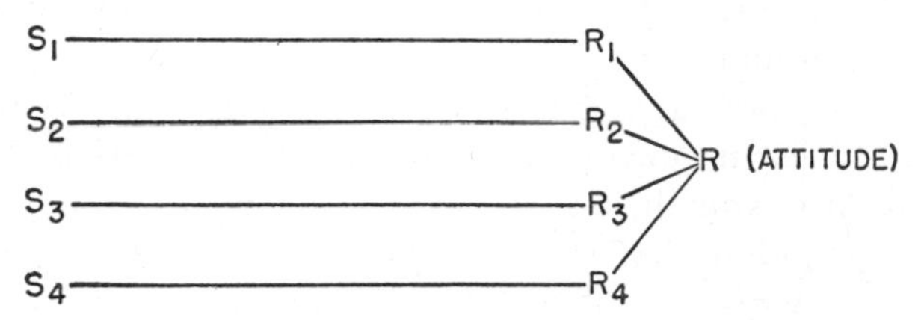

Thus through the accumulation of experiences we form many of our attitudes. Not all, however, are formed in this manner. A single, dramatic, intense emotional experience may be sufficient to result in some relatively permanent attitude. What reader can not trace certain attitudes to some intense emotional experience during childhood? Some of our attitudes may be "ready-made" attitudes, having been formed through the imitation of parents, friends, teachers, and so on. Many attitudes are handed down from generation to generation by this means.

So it is that we develop a large reservoir of attitudes or systems of anticipatory response which predispose us toward certain ideas, images, people, and objects, and which form many of the bases of belief. Thus we develop attitudes toward spinach, John Doakes, cigar smokers, politicians, old maids, sororities, doctors, preachers, and so on. Whole societies, as a result of generations of experiences, develop attitudes which are handed down from one generation to another, and we gain attitudes about kings, dictators, negroes, Jews, imperialism, laissez-faire, Protestantism, Catholicism, Canada, Mexico, marriage, and death.

DEFINITION OF ATTITUDE

Kimball Young's definition includes the salient points. "An attitude may be defined as a learned and more or less generalized and effective tendency or predisposition to respond in a rather persistent and characteristic manner, usually positively or negatively (for or against) in reference to some situation, idea, value, material object or class of such objects, or person or group of persons." [1]

Certain specific facts regarding the nature of attitudes should be of help in understanding the role of attitudes in persuasion. From what we have said thus far it must be clear that attitudes are usually associated with external objects, ideas, images, and values. In addition, we must keep in mind that attitudes are preconditions of human behavior; they are incipient and preparatory rather than overt and consummatory. Attitudes are more numerous, more personal, and more varying than motives. They may be regarded as *modi operandi* in human behavior rather than as original sources of motivation. Nonetheless, the association of attitudes with our feelings or emotions has caused certain writers to ascribe to attitudes not only *directive* power but *driving* power. In any event, it is agreed that attitudes are of major importance in the process of persuasion.

CLASSIFICATION OF ATTITUDES

By classifying attitudes one may gain further understanding of their organization. Doob [2] and Allport [3] provide very helpful classifications.

Central and Segmental Attitudes. Those attitudes which govern the more enduring and consistent aspects of human behavior are called *central attitudes.* Such attitudes might be concerned with the home, church, or school. Those attitudes which regulate only a small part of a person's conduct may be called *segmental attitudes.* The isolationist may have only a segmental attitude toward world federal government or the United Nations.

General and Specific Attitudes. Attitudes which regulate behavior in a wide variety of situations and which tend to control the individual's other attitudes might be called *general attitudes.*

---

[1] K. Young, *Social Psychology.* New York: Appleton-Century-Crofts, Inc., 1944, p. 122.

[2] L. W. Doob, *Propaganda.* New York: Henry Holt and Company, 1935, Ch. IV.

[3] G. W. Allport, "Attitudes," pp. 798 ff. of Carl Murchison, ed., *A Handbook of Social Psychology.* Worcester, Mass.: Clark University Press, 1935.

Those which direct human behavior only in certain specific situations are called *specific attitudes.*

Dominant and Latent Attitudes. The attitude which is exerting its tension at a given moment is a *dominant attitude,* and, accordingly, the remaining attitudes of the individual may be said to be *latent attitudes.* It is perhaps an obvious point to suggest that a persuader must be most vitally concerned with the dominant attitudes of his audience, though, of course, the latent attitudes may be back-stage properties for use to advantage or disadvantage.

Positive and Negative Attitudes. It is generally agreed that attitudes can be rated quantitatively or on an "intensity scale." That is, our attitudes are usually "for" or "against" some object, idea, or person, or somewhere on a scale between these two extremes. The preparation and use of "attitude scales" as aids in determining the attitudes of people will be discussed later.

Private and Public Attitudes. William James once highlighted the conflict between these two types of attitudes by telling the story of the magistrate who, in sentencing a prisoner, said, "As a man, I pity you, but as an official I must show you no mercy." Our *public attitudes* are formed to suit the social situation about us, and we are quite free to express these attitudes. On the other hand, we are reluctant to disclose our *private attitudes.* In fact, such attitudes as a rule can be learned only through some indirect means and after a long and very personal acquaintance with an individual.

Attitudes and Opinions. Many laymen and some psychologists consider these terms synonymous. We are using the term *attitude* to refer to those forms of inner life which prepare us for responses to the ideas, objects, and people about us, and which give direction to our behavior. An *opinion,* on the other hand, is considered an expressed or verbalized attitude which may or may not correspond to the attitude that is supposed to be expressed. An opinion might be called a *public attitude* in terms of Allport's classification given above. Our opinions generally are subject to social pressures; they serve various social motives. Therefore, an opinion may not be a reliable index to a person's true attitude. Doob makes this point vivid in the following manner: "A., who actually has an unfavorable attitude toward B., is asked by C. to express his opinion of B. A. explains that B. is trustworthy, good-natured, and docile, descriptions which are quite misleading in respect to A.'s real attitude toward B. These opinions, therefore, are not merely functions of A.'s real attitude toward B., but also of A.'s attitude toward C. For A. must have some rather specific attitude toward C. which makes him distort what he actually thinks about B. If A. possesses a different attitude toward D., on the other hand, his description of B. may be more in accord with the attitude which actually motivates his behavior toward the latter."[4]

Viewing opinions and attitudes in this light, it is clear that to determine people's real attitudes relative to a given topic is a very difficult task, and, as was pointed out in Chapter III, can be learned better from what people do, the real direction of their behavior, than from what they say, that is, from their opinions. Social scientists have been attempting to measure attitudes and opinions by various types of attitude scales and opinion polls. Although these instruments need much refining, as was demonstrated by the pollsters' predictions of the presidential campaign of 1948, they nonetheless are becoming very helpful in learning to predict reaction tendencies and in serving as helpful means in controlling human behavior. We shall discuss these instruments of attitude and opinion measurement in Chapters XVII and XXIII.

ATTITUDES AND PERSUASION

If attitudes are significant influences in the course of human behavior, then it follows that a persuader must apply himself to a study of them. He must be able to determine their existence and strength in those he wishes to persuade and to enlist these attitudes in the service of the ends he seeks. Admittedly this is a large order but a very necessary one. Certain basic facts regarding the nature of attitudes, when applied to the task of the persuader, make this task easier.

People with Like Attitudes. People having like attitudes tend to congregate together. "Birds of a feather flock together." Many organizations exist solely for the perpetuation and promotion of certain prescribed attitudes. Thus we have the No-Tobacco League, the Humane Society, The Society for the Prevention of War, the Na-

---

[4] Leonard W. Doob, *Propaganda.* New York: Henry Holt and Company, 1935, p. 35.

tional Association of Manufacturers, The Friends of the Public Schools, and so on. Some audiences, of course, are heterogeneous, and to assume an extensive system of like attitudes would be unfruitful if, indeed, not disastrous.

Attitudes the Result of Learning and Experience. As has been pointed out, attitudes are not as fixed as are our basic drives, but are the results of learning and experience. Thus a persuader may create or build up attitudes useful to him. Oftentimes persuasion is not just the process of finding and utilizing the attitudes already present within a persuadee, but takes the form of building up new attitudes and using them at the proper time and in an effective manner. When World War II orders prevented the production of civilian cars, the Ford Motor Company (and other such companies) continued to build up favorable attitudes toward their company and cars by a vast system of advertising, pointing out their patriotic efforts and suggesting, "There is a Ford in Your Future." Commercial organizations are constantly watching for the opportunity to build attitudes favorable to their company and product. Today we are besieged by radio programs designed to do this. Some companies give free travel and other helps to the blind, others give young artists a chance to break into radio or stage, and still others bring together families whose meager resources would not have permitted extensive travel, make mothers "Queen for a Day," and provide luxuries for men in uniform.

A persuader cannot ignore the advantages which can be gained by building up attitudes favorable to his purposes.

Dominant Attitudes. People generally act in accordance with their dominant attitudes. Again, this fact helps simplify the task of the persuader. Oftentimes it is not necessary to determine the many, interrelated attitudes of the person to be persuaded; to discover and utilize his dominant attitudes may be sufficient. In this connection it should be remembered, however, that attitudes vary under differing conditions. In fact, on occasion attitudes are subject to sharp variations. A persuader cannot reason, therefore, that because an attitude is dominant at a certain time and under certain conditions it will therefore be dominant at other times and under other conditions.

Verbal Expression of Attitudes. As was stated earlier, a verbalized attitude is an opinion or socialized expression of an attitude. An opinion may or may not reflect a true attitude because of the influence of social pressures and desires. After our opinions are registered publicly, we are reluctant to change them lest we appear to be an unreliable person "who is always changing his mind." We do not wish to seem "wishy-washy"; we do not wish to admit being influenced by others. Then, too, the expression of an opinion tends to establish the attitude more clearly and firmly in our minds, rendering it less subject to change. In a study by Doob, 52 per cent of the students who actually had changed their attitudes as shown by tests would admit that this change had taken place.[5] Our Congressmen know how difficult it is to change the attitudes of a colleague if he has already "gone on record" as having an attitude contrary to that desired by the persuader.

These facts must be remembered by the persuader. If his persuasion is running counter to the expressed opinions of his customer, the salesman has three alternatives: (1) To change to an approach which does not conflict with the persuadee's opinions; (2) to present such a powerful appeal that it overcomes the conflicting opinions; or (3) to prepare a way in which the customer can "gracefully" change his opinions. This latter alternative may take the form of pointing out that what the salesman is trying to sell is really in line with certain other and more worthy opinions of the customer.

Finally, the persuader should decrease the opportunities for the verbal expression of attitudes unfavorable to his purposes and increase the opportunities for the oral expression of attitudes favorable to his ends. The cigarette companies which have the studio audiences verbalize in chorus the merits of their product recognize the value of this idea.

Influence of Majority Opinions. Attitudes tend to be influenced by majority opinion to a greater extent than by expert opinion. In matters pertaining to speech and to morality, Moore [6] found that college students changed their opinions to conform to those of the majority. In another study, Marple [7] found that his subjects were

---

[5] Leonard W. Doob, "Some Factors Determining Change in Attitude," *Journal of Abnormal and Social Psychology* (October, 1940), 35: 549–565.

[6] H. T. Moore, "The Comparative Influence of Majority and Expert Opinion," *American Journal of Psychology* (January, 1940), 32: 16–20.

[7] C. H. Marple, "The Comparative Susceptibility of Three Age Levels to the Suggestion of Group vs. Expert Opinion," *Journal of Social Psychology* (May, 1933), 4: 176–186.

influenced by both majority and expert opinion on social and political issues, but the influence of group opinion was greater than that of the expert.

Although the persuader should not forget to quote authoritative or expert opinion in support of his case, he should keep in mind the influence of majority opinion in changing people's attitudes.

The place of attitudes in a theory of persuasion will be made clearer by considering the nature and functions of sentiments and stereotypes.

Sentiments

GENERAL NATURE OF SENTIMENTS

Persuaders of every age and station have experienced the power of sentiments in the direction of human lives. The strength of the sentiments we attach to national symbols was appropriated to advantage by Rouget de Lisle, author of "La Marseillaise," when he was arraigned before a French jury on a capital charge. "Frenchmen!" he pleaded, "hear my defense; I am guilty, but I am the author of 'La Marseillaise!'" Those present began singing the anthem while the author was set free. When Old Glory was bravely placed at the peak of Mt. Surabachi during World War II it not only inspired the troops nearby, but Americans and Allies everywhere thrilled to the picture and the story and were motivated to a greater war effort. Everyone has seen violent behavior result from slighting remarks about one's mother, university, state, fraternity, Christmas, Santa Claus, and so on. A moment's reflection can bring to the mind of any reader many dynamic positive and negative sentiments.

To the English psychologists, Shand and McDougall, must go much of the credit for the development of the concept of *sentiment,* even though a part of their discussion of sentiments might be classified under our discussion of attitudes. They point out that sentiments are emotional dispositions which tend to become organized around various objects and classes of objects. Shaffer helps to clarify the concept by suggesting that,

> . . . sentiments are not pure emotions or motives because they cannot exist apart from relationship to some person or object, and because this object may call forth different emotional behavior at

> different times, which behavior is still consistent with the sentiment. The person to whom the love sentiment is attached calls forth love emotion and adient motivation when he is present, fear when he is in danger, rage when he is threatened. The hated person or object elicits fear or rage or both when he is present, rage when he succeeds and joy when he is overthrown.[8]

Thus sentiments are learned forms of behavior and, as the reader already has guessed, are very much like attitudes. In fact, we conceive of *a sentiment as being only a special case of an attitude.* Many of our "prejudices" are sentiments. When a sentiment operates pathologically we call it a *complex.*

Through the ordinary experiences of living the individual develops numerous sentiments in connection with the objects and persons about him. Like attitudes, the number of possible sentiments is inexhaustible and presents at once a sobering job of analysis for the persuader. Fortunately, however, such sentiments as loyalties, patriotism, religiousness, parental, filial, and other love sentiments are quite general and, as a rule, are reliable aids to persuasion.

THE SENTIMENT OF SELF-REGARD

One of the most important sentiments to be understood by the persuader is the *sentiment of self-regard.* While the individual is developing sentiments toward other people and objects he is also organizing a sentiment in relation to himself. Shaffer goes so far as to state that it is the interacting pattern of all of the fundamental motives of the individual. "The most useful meaning of the sentiment of self-regard is as the interaction of the conditioned emotional motives. The mastery, social approval, submission and love motives do not act separately, but with mutual modifications. The whole of these motives, which is something different from the summation of the motives taken separately, is the self-motive or sentiment of self-regard." [9]

As youngsters we learned to see things in relation to the satisfaction of our basic drives; we were egocentric in most situations. As adults we still tend to show our egocentricity, only perhaps in more "cultivated ways." We attempt to gain objectivity, but psy-

---

[8] L. F. Shaffer, *The Psychology of Adjustment.* Boston: Houghton Mifflin Company, 1936, p. 109.

[9] *Ibid.,* p. 110.

chologists and experience tell us we still retain a generous amount of self-regard, a sentiment which influences our behavior in all areas of living.

SENTIMENTS AND PERSUASION

The need for the persuader to understand and be able to appropriate for his own use the existing sentiments within others is surely clear. He must understand the sentiments which people relate to other people and objects as well as the sentiment they develop about themselves. It may be helpful, however, to add certain specific hints and illustrations regarding the use of sentiments in persuasion.

The sentiment of most concern to the persuader is the sentiment of self-regard, for, as was stated above, it is the interacting pattern of all the fundamental motives of the individual. The strength of this sentiment varies among individuals. Some have succeeded in considerable self-effacement, particularly those who lose themselves in great causes. The great masses of people, however, still worship before that inner shrine of self, and they who violate its sanctity have lost their power to influence. One of the most common manifestations of this sentiment can be observed when a person's name is mispronounced, misspelled, or completely forgotten. The first lesson a salesman learns is to get the full name of the potential customer and to give the name its proper pronunciation, for errors in this regard have lost many sales. Just to see one's name in print or to hear it broadcast provides a certain thrill. On the desk where this is being written is a large, attractive blotter which carries no writing save the name of the present writer along with his complete academic title. This was sent by an insurance agent who understands the role of the sentiment of self-regard in persuasion. Many sales are clinched by pointing out that your name will be engraved in gold letters on the product.

Many of the "easy, quick methods to sales effectiveness" are nothing more than a list of simple rules to follow in giving the customer a feeling of personal worth or self-respect. Psychologists writing in the area of "dealing with people" frequently point out very helpful suggestions in this regard. For instance, one writer makes the following recommendations: [10]

---

[10] W. White, *The Psychology of Dealing with People.* New York: The Macmillan Company, 1941, Ch. I.

—Crediting another with already knowing what one says.
—Crediting another with having suggested what one advocates.
—Presenting ideas as being related to views or acts of another or his ancestors.
—Stimulating another to self-expression of one's idea.

The list might be continued, but the above examples are sufficient to indicate the ways in which a persuader may utilize the persuadee's sentiment of self-regard.

Theodore Roosevelt was reputed to be a master at devising means of appropriating the other fellow's self-motive to great political advantage. Webb and Morgan state Roosevelt's method in the following passage:

> Across the banquet table, Theodore Roosevelt sees a cluster of strange faces. They belong to Republicans whose names begin with "T."
>
> These men know Roosevelt, of course—but coldly, from a distance. Of every one, before the banquet ends, he wishes to make a devoted follower.
>
> Just back from Africa, Roosevelt is in Omaha on his first campaign trip with the 1912 election ahead.
>
> And for these strangers at banquets, he is prepared. He has a plan that hinges on asking a single question.
>
> "After cross-cover introductions," writes Dr. Victor Rosewater, who sat beside him, "Colonel Roosevelt bent closer and said to me quietly, 'Tell me, Rosewater, something about these fellows in front of me.' Complying, I gave him a brief characterization of each."
>
> Now Theodore is ready to fascinate these men whom he has never seen before. It is easy. He has learned what each one is proud of, what he has done, what he likes.
>
> Here, from behind the scenes, we see Roosevelt's "genius in personal contacts" at work.
>
> "Possessed of this information," continues Dr. Rosewater, "Colonel Roosevelt immediately had topics of conversation to fit every one of his table companions."
>
> In order to win these strangers, Roosevelt has taken the trouble to post himself ahead of time about their affairs. So he is able to start them talking about themselves—able to make known his *interest* in *them*. Each of these men will leave the table delighted and impressed.
>
> With Roosevelt this strategy was a fixed habit. At the White House, says Isaac Marcosson, the noted journalist, he "found out everything about a man before that man came to see him. . . .

Most people are vain, and nothing flatters their vanity more than to realize that facts about them are known and not forgotten." [11]

At times the sentiment of self-regard may stand in actual opposition to the motives served by wealth, property, and so on when they are operating at the expense of the self-regarding sentiment. Ruch reports an experience by Walter Dill Scott which illustrates this point very well.

Walter Dill Scott, now President of Northwestern University, reported an experience showing the role of sentiment in determining the behavior of a group of employees in a labor dispute. At a certain time the workers in the men's clothing industry in Chicago were discontented because of various conditions in that industry. To reduce this discontent, most of the employers announced pay increases of ten per cent. Company X, however, did not increase wages, but posted a notice on the bulletin board promising a "special extra pay envelope" to all workers who would remain loyal until a certain date. This offer failed to change the attitude of the workers. A few weeks after the notice was posted, the president of Company X *bought* $34,000 worth of Liberty Bonds, which were distributed among the workers. The workers still showed no appreciation of the gift. When the special pay bonus was given, the workers expressed active discontent. The president was so completely unable to understand this situation that he called in a local labor leader, and also requested the services of Dr. Scott as a consulting psychologist. The following conversation took place between the president of Company X and the labor leader.

PRESIDENT X: "I can't understand the lack of appreciation of my men. I gave them $34,000 worth of Liberty Bonds and a special extra pay envelope of a full week's wages. The union agreement has now put all the firms on an equal wage basis. Although I did not increase wages 10 per cent for the period preceding the union agreement I have given my men more than any other company by the extra pay envelope and the Liberty Bonds. I can't see what more they want."

LABOR LEADER: "Yes, Mr. X, you have done all you say, and your people are not contented as the people are at the other houses. They wanted the 10 per cent and felt that they had deserved it."

PRESIDENT X: "No, I did not give them the 10 per cent, but I did give the extra pay envelope and the Liberty Bonds, which amounted to much more than the 10 per cent."

---

[11] E. T. Webb and J. J. B. Morgan, *Strategy in Handling People*. Chicago: Boulton, Pierce and Company, 1931, pp. 13, 14. Reprinted by permission of the publishers, Doubleday & Company, Inc. (Garden City Books Division). Copyright 1930 by Elizabeth J. Webb.

LABOR LEADER: "Yes, I have figured it up and you gave them in extra pay and bonds somewhat over $10,000 more than they would have received by the increase they asked. But that is not what they wanted. They do not want the gift of the extra pay envelope and of the bonds but they do want the 10 per cent even if it is less than the extra pay and the bonds. I believe they would be willing to refund the $34,000 worth of bonds if you would give them $24,000 in what they regarded as earned wages."

PRESIDENT X: "Very well, I will gladly make the exchange for I shall thereby gain $10,000."

LABOR LEADER: "I think the discontent will be greatly reduced by the exchange. I will take it up with the people at once."

The proposition was presented to the workers and was accepted enthusiastically, even though it entailed a recognized monetary loss of $10,000. However, it soothed their offended pride and left them happy.

The president had reasoned something like this:

Major Premise: All that wage earners want is more money.

Minor Premise: The extra bonuses and bonds come to more than ten per cent.

Conclusion: Therefore, the workers prefer the bonds and bonuses.

On the other hand, the experienced leader of working people knew his followers. He knew that they were as much influenced by pride and self-respect as they were by money. Mere money was not enough to compensate the workers for the loss of feeling of personal worth which was engendered by the note of charity introduced by their employer's scheme. They felt that they earned more money than they were getting. They wanted the extra money to come as honestly earned wages and not as a tip given to a servant or as alms to a beggar.[12]

If you would persuade, be mindful of the specialized attitudes—sentiments—which exert such a powerful, though often irrational, influence upon people.

Stereotypes

Few of us have the time, interest, or opportunity to know our environment and those about us accurately. In fact, it is virtually impossible in a single lifetime to know much more than a small segment of mankind's activities. Nonetheless, this lack of under-

---

[12] F. L. Ruch, *Psychology and Life*. New York: Scott, Foresman and Company, 1937, pp. 288–290, as adapted from Walter Dill Scott, "Changes in Some of Our Conceptions and Practices of Personnel," *Psychological Review* (March, 1920), XXVII: 2, p. 86–88.

standing of the larger world about us does not stop us from forming a "system of thought" about it. Walter Lippmann has pointed out that these "systems of thought" or "pictures in our heads" are really incomplete reflections of economic, political, and social reality. To these he attached the term *stereotypes.* He explained this concept by stating that stereotypes

> are an ordered, more or less consistent picture of the world, to which our habits, our tastes, our capacities, our comforts and our hopes have adjusted themselves. They may not be a complete picture of the world, but they are a picture of a possible world to which we are adapted. In that world people and things have their well-known places, and do certain expected things. We feel at home there. We fit in. We are members. We know the way around. There we find the charm of the familiar, the normal, the dependable; its grooves and shapes are where we are accustomed to find them. And though we have abandoned much that might have tempted us before we creased ourselves into that mould, once we are firmly in, it fits as snugly as an old shoe.[13]

RISE AND OPERATION OF STEREOTYPES

Stereotypes grow out of our everyday contact with people and events or with verbal and pictorial communications about them. In short, they arise out of our social milieu. You and I tend to accept the stereotypes handed down to us.

In childhood we are exposed to stereotypes which reflect the status of our families, their economic, political, and religious views, and the views they hold of the community, state, and nations. By the time we are old enough to participate socially with others our relations with them have been predetermined to a great extent by the stereotypes or the "mental pictures" we have been given of them in advance. As we grow older, whether we are educated or not, we tend not only to maintain the stereotypes we were exposed to as youths, but also to add new ones in our attempts to complete our picture of our world. So it is that we develop stereotypes of "foreigner," "bootlegger," "politician," "senator," "preacher," "democracy," "conservative," "liberal," "fascist," "communist," "Japanese," "German," "Britons," "Yankees," "Indians," "Scotsmen," "red-heads," "Catholics," "Prot-

---

[13] Walter Lippmann, *Public Opinion.* New York: The Macmillan Company, 1922, p. 95.

estants," "Jews," "Americanism," "professors," "poets," "bankers," "farmers," and so on. We are at ease in *this world,* for it is easier to be guided by this simplified though not necessarily accurate interpretation of events.

RELATION OF STEREOTYPES TO ATTITUDES AND SENTIMENTS

We have seen that an *attitude* is a reaction tendency or a predisposition to respond in a characteristic manner in reference to situations involving ideas, values, people, and events, and that they are related to our emotional behavior. A *sentiment* was described as a specialized attitude. *Stereotypes* give meaning to the situations from which attitudes spring by representing the knowledge which we imagine we possess. Doob considers a stereotype as "one of the internal responses—knowledge—which evokes an attitude. It is the attitude which has drive value and thus produces action. Stereotype, like knowledge, is an end product of learning and usually represents a form of simplified knowledge." [14] Young helps in clarifying the distinction by suggesting that "the attitude, or action tendency, is illustrated by the like-or-dislike, for-or-against, approve-or-disapprove element, and, of course, always points to some overt response or habit. This linkage is equally obvious in those meanings in which stereotypes are involved. The stereotype, like a sound idea, then, is the imaginal core—carried chiefly in words or visual images—from which attitude and action spring. The function of the stereotype is to give meaning to the situation—that is, to delimit behavior with reference to it; it defines the situation in terms of acts, potential or actual." [15]

Thus we see that functionally attitude, sentiment, and stereotype are inextricably intertwined. From the "pictures in our minds" or stereotyped knowledge of the events and people about us—in short, *our world*—we form *attitudes* and *sentiments* which emotionally relate us (for or against) to the events, values, ideas, and persons of this world, and predispose us to certain actions. It is on the basis of stereotypes, then, that most of our attitudes are formed.

---

[14] L. W. Doob, *Public Opinion and Propaganda.* New York: Henry Holt and Company, 1948, pp. 201, 202.

[15] Kimball Young, *Social Psychology.* New York: Appleton-Century-Crofts, Inc., 1944, pp. 190, 191.

The function of stereotypes will be made clearer by a brief review of several studies. The classic study of the effect of stereotypes on human judgment was made by Rice. He asked 141 Dartmouth undergraduates and, later, members of the Norwich, Vermont, Grange to look at unidentified portraits of nine persons: (1) Edward Herriot, Premier of France; (2) James Duncan, Vice-President of the American Federation of Labor; (3) Leonid Krassin, First Ambassador of the Soviet Government at Paris; (4) Joseph W. McIntosh, Deputy Comptroller of Currency; (5) Martin H. Glynn, Governor of New York; (6) Max Agel, arrested as a bootlegger; (7) Charles M. Schwab, Chairman of the United States Steel Corporation; (8) Howard Heinz, manufacturer of food products; and (9) Senator George W. Pepper of Pennsylvania. The pictures were numbered from 1 to 9. The subjects were told that the pictures included an alleged bootlegger, a labor leader, a European Premier, a United States Senator, a Bolshevik, an editor-politician, two manufacturers, and one financier. Each subject was to identify these individuals by number. Even though the correct judgments were double the number which might be expected by chance, the results with respect to certain individuals demonstrated how judgments can be influenced by stereotypes. The table on page 112 gives the judgments of the students.

The judgments of the Grange members tended to confirm the results. It is clear that Senator Pepper did not fit the senatorial stereotype of the students, for he was identified as labor leader, Bolshevik, financier, editor-politician and manufacturer as often as, or more often than, senator. As another example, note that the correct identifications of Soviet Envoy Krassin were fewer than the incorrect. He had been shown dressed in a wing collar, wearing a Van Dyke beard and mustache. Apparently he was too distinguished looking to fit the popular stereotype of a Bolshevik. Had Krassin been wearing a beaver cap and a long, heavy, snow-flecked overcoat the vote would have been different. Take, on the other hand, Mr. Agel, the alleged bootlegger, who was shown in a heavy overcoat with upturned collar, a cap, shell-rimmed spectacles and a cigar held firmly between his teeth. He must have fitted quite accurately into the bootlegger stereotype of the students, for he received the largest number of correct identifications.

Person Pictured	Number identifying person as:									Identifications which would be correct if one guessed
	Premier	Labor Leader	Bolshevik	Financier	Editor-Politician	Bootlegger	Manufacturer	Senator	Total	
Premier Herriot	54	11	55	2	3	4	4	..	133	15
Labor Leader Duncan	29	25	15	13	14	1	30	9	136	15
Soviet Envoy Krassin	31	..	9	15	11	..	16	59	141	16
Financier McIntosh	7	20	14	15	16	24	33	8	137	15
Editor-Governor Glynn	6	20	5	21	31	2	33	14	132	15
Bootlegger (alleged) Agel	1	6	9	4	11	86	18	2	137	15
Manufacturer Schwab	1	14	4	18	20	2	56	21	136	15
Manufacturer Heinz	5	19	6	31	16	6	46	10	139	15
Senator Pepper	..	22	15	16	19	11	35	15	133	15

Rice also asked his subjects to rate each person shown in the photographs as to intelligence and craftiness. In preparation for this, he divided the students into three groups: (1) Those in the first group were permitted to believe that their original judgments in identifying the person were correct; (2) those in the second group were given different but still inaccurate identifications of the persons pictured; and (3) the third group was informed of the true identities. The judgments made regarding the two traits were definitely biased by the supposed identity of the persons photographed. In other words, the students' judgments were influenced by the stereotypes connected with the man's supposed position.[16]

Hartmann conducted a study designed to observe the influence of such stereotyped terms as liberalism, conservatism, socialism, fascism, and communism. Using 107 farmers, shopkeepers, miners, laborers, housewives, and women clerks as his subjects, he gave an attitude scale dealing with liberal political reforms. The test showed that the group as a whole was quite favorable to such collectivistic or socialistic policies as public ownership of national resources and industry and extensive legal provision for social security. Later, however, when these policies were pointed out as reflecting socialistic or communistic principles, most of the subjects took either opposite or more conservative positions. As Hartmann pointed out, two-thirds of the subjects would refuse a public school license to a teacher who believed in socialism, more than three-fourths were opposed to state ownership of land, and three-fifths had no desire to be affiliated with a socialist party. This study demonstrated that many of the subjects wanted certain socialistic changes but they did not want them "labeled that way."[17]

Menefee conducted an experiment very similar to that of Hartmann. Nearly a third of his subjects opposed certain statements they had originally endorsed when these statements were labeled "fascist," "communist," or "radical."[18] In another and some-

---

[16] S. A. Rice, "Stereotypes: A Source of Error in Judging Human Character," *Journal of Personnel Research* (1926), 2: 268–287.

[17] G. W. Hartmann, "The Contradictions Between the Feeling Tone of Political Party Names and Public Response to Their Platforms," *Journal of Social Psychology* (1936), 7: 336–355.

[18] S. C. Menefee, "The Effect of Stereotyped Words on Political Judgments," *American Sociological Review* (1936), 1: 614–621.

what similar experiment, Stagner presented his subjects with a series of arguments on economic and political questions taken from German fascist materials. The results revealed that 73 per cent of his subjects disapproved of the arguments, yet, when the same statements were included in another questionnaire but were not labeled fascist, the subjects indicated a sharp rise in the amount of agreement with the arguments.[19]

Racial stereotypes are of primary concern to the persuader. Katz and Braly secured a list of eighty-four trait names of ten races or nationalities by asking a sample of college students to write down the adjectives which they believed characterized these races. This list of eighty-four traits was then given to another sample of a hundred students, asking them to select the five most typical traits for each of the ten nationalities. The results of the study demonstrated that, for the most part, the experimental subjects reflected the stereotypes common to the general public. For instance, three-fourths regarded the Germans as very scientifically minded, and four-fifths considered the Jews shrewd and the Negroes superstitious. Half of the students regarded the Italians as artistic and the Americans as industrious. Slightly more than half believed the Turks to be cruel. The judgments of the students were more stereotyped in regard to Negroes, Jews, and Germans than they were to Japanese, Chinese, and Turks.[20]

These studies provide the reader with some reliable data regarding the influence of stereotypes. We must keep in mind, of course, that most of these studies used college students as subjects. Investigations of the stereotypes used by a more heterogeneous, adult population outside the classroom are to be desired.

STEREOTYPES AND PERSUASION

Although we have already indicated, both directly and indirectly, the role stereotypes play in the direction of human conduct, a few specific suggestions to the persuader may be helpful.

Objectivity in Personal Stereotypes. One of the first points to be remembered by the student of persuasion is that he, too, is carrying a large complement of stereotypes, as well as attitudes

---

[19] R. Stagner, "Fascist Attitudes: An Exploratory Study," *Journal of Social Psychology* (1936), 7: 309–319.

[20] D. Katz and K. Braly, "Racial Stereotypes of 100 College Students," *Journal of Abnormal and Social Psychology* (1933), 28: 280–290.

and sentiments, and is subject to their influence. As a consumer of persuasion, one must be aware of the stereotypes, the "pictures," in his own mind if he is to give critical evaluation to the persuasion used to influence him. As a producer of persuasion, one must also acquire an objective, critical view of his own system of stereotypes if he is to attempt, in a deliberate manner, to change, avoid or appropriate to his advantage the stereotyped thinking of others. To reduce the influence of stereotypes requires, first of all, a broadening of one's background by the greatest variety of educational experiences. It is important to understand the importance and practice of accurate language habits, cultivate the habit of considering all available data before drawing even a tentative conclusion, and examine the *will to believe,* which leads to the hiding place of many prejudices and other stereotypes. In short, an open and critical mind is essential in becoming sensitized to personal stereotypes and being able to influence those who are taking easy residence in the stereotyped world they have created for themselves.

Recognition of "Loaded Words." Remember that our stereotypes usually are identified and influenced by words having strong emotional overtones. These "loaded words" become the harbingers of our stereotypes as well as our attitudes and sentiments; their usage, therefore, influences us for or against the cause of a persuader. In an often-used quotation, Joseph Conrad said: "He who wants to persuade should put his trust not in the right argument, but in the right word. Give me the right word and the right accent, and I will move the world." In *The Tyranny of Words,* Stuart Chase points out vividly the power of our stereotyped words, the words which describe *our pictures* of the universe. Mock and Larson discuss the role of such words in winning World War I in *Words That Won the War.* The Office of War Information during World War II was kept busy trying to outdo Herr Goebbels in selecting persuasive words. Each war produces its "yes-and-no-response words," words which are linked favorably or unfavorably with our basic stereotypes. We built "Victory" ships; our "first line of defense" became many things. To announce an "orderly retreat" took some of the sting out of defeat. To know the retreat was "orderly" was not so bad; it seemed to rest more easily in "the eternal fitness of things."

To announce a program of "taxation for unemployment insurance" meets with a negative response because of our taxation stereotype, but to announce a program of "social security" receives our vote. Political leaders are constantly attempting to link their new programs to some old stereotype with which we have been living comfortably for many years.

Pitkin wished to find out the reactions of people to eighty often-used "loaded words." He presented this list of words to 600 subjects (100 high school students, 200 university underclassmen, 200 university upperclassmen, and 100 adults), and asked them to mark their responses to the words—"A" for favorable, "U" for unfavorable, and "X" for neutral or when the word-stimulus was either received without emotional concern or the person responding was confused or doubtful about what response was aroused by the word. The table below gives the total responses of all the groups in terms of percentages.

Studies in Loaded Words [21]

The Total Responses of all the Groups in Terms of Per Cent

	A	U	X		A	U	X
1. despotism	6.7	85.	8.3	24. logical	83.2	2.8	14.
2. corruption	6.1	89.	4.	25. traitor	6.8	89.5	3.7
3. betrayal	5.8	89.7	.5	26. foul	6.3	89.9	3.8
4. amiable	91.5	1.8	6.7	27. freedom	94.	.2	5.8
5. sacred trust	81.7	6.3	12.	28. democracy	87.2	3.2	9.6
6. noble	95.	2.5	2.5	29. Mussolini	27.	40.2	32.8
7. genius	90.2	1.8	8.	30. majestic	86.4	1.3	12.3
8. scholarly	82.8	6.	11.2	31. slums	4.3	87.7	8.
9. heresy	5.7	71.7	22.6	32. realism	60.8	5.4	33.8
10. tyranny	5.5	87.7	6.8	33. jailbird	2.5	86.7	10.8
11. tight-wad	3.5	90.7	5.8	34. nigger	3.3	77.4	19.3
12. autocratic	9.2	68.3	22.5	35. negro	40.3	23.2	36.5
13. radical	14.2	65.3	20.5	36. wench	5.	78.7	16.3
14. the grind	6.5	76.5	17.	37. atheist	13.2	55.3	31.5
15. sheik	11.5	68.9	19.6	38. plebeian	20.2	36.8	43.
16. Bolshevik	5.2	81.	13.8	39. brawny	59.	13.	28.
17. miser	3.8	90.	6.2	40. communism	13.5	56.5	30.
18. blue-law	8.3	66.	25.7	41. anarchist	6.	80.3	13.7
19. generous	97.	.7	2.3	42. old fogy	5.	82.	13.
20. idealism	87.7	4.	8.3	43. coward	4.	92.	4.
21. flapper	16.3	50.8	32.9	44. gossip	3.5	90.2	6.3
22. pedagogue	16.8	36.7	46.5	45. mother	98.8	.2	1.
23. square-deal	90.5	3.2	6.3	46. comrade	97.7	.3	2.

[21] W. M. Pitkin, *A Study of Loaded Words.* (Unpublished M.A. thesis, University of Wisconsin, 1931.)

	A	U	X		A	U	X
47. stench	4.	81.	15.	64. wishy-washy	2.	86.5	11.5
48. collegiate	43.7	24.	32.3	65. snoopy	2.5	93.	4.5
49. broad-minded	89.8	2.3	7.9	66. asinine	5.7	76.5	17.8
50. Phi Beta	55.5	9.2	35.3	67. moron	4.3	82.2	13.5
51. treacherous	7.5	87.	5.5	68. slapstick	5.8	70.8	23.4
52. Pollyanna	32.2	31.7	36.1	69. unbiased	68.	11.8	20.2
53. jazz	36.3	33.	30.7	70. crony	31.2	44.2	24.6
54. straightforward	93.9	2.3	3.8	71. smirk	4.5	81.2	14.3
55. abnormal	12.5	58.3	29.2	72. smile	97.	.2	2.8
56. diplomat	72.3	6.7	21.	73. quitter	4.2	91.3	4.5
57. frenzy	10.3	60.5	29.2	74. upright	92.9	1.8	5.3
58. dead past	8.7	40.8	50.5	75. sweetie	28.3	51.7	20.
59. heretic	8.2	65.2	26.6	76. Mencken	18.	23.5	58.5
60. hash	13.2	63.2	23.6	77. hackneyed	4.	69.2	26.8
61. propaganda	10.3	64.4	25.3	78. imperialism	18.2	59.	22.8
62. evangelist	24.5	43.5	32.	79. atrocities	5.7	73.3	21.
63. jingoist	5.5	46.8	47.7	80. heroic	92.5	3.3	4.2

The student of persuasion should practice detecting stereotypes in the speeches he hears and in the editorials he reads. He should become perceptive of the rhetorical uses of stereotypes by all types of persuaders.

Cautious Approach for Modifying Prejudices. Finally, the persuader should remember that he cannot hope for success if what he suggests tends to upset too abruptly the hearer's preconceived or stereotyped patterns of thought. To do this would seem, as Lippmann warned, "like an attack upon the foundations of the universe. It is an attack upon the foundations of *our* universe, and, where big things are at stake, we do not readily admit there is any distinction between *our* universe and *the* universe." [22] The writer recalls an acquaintance whose fundamentalist view of the Bible will allow but one interpretation of Biblical literature. Even to suggest another rocks the very foundations of his faith. So he rebels violently at any new interpretations or applications of religious theory.

The "Divine Right of Kings" certainly was one of the strongest and, for the kings, most useful stereotyped constructs of all history, and it took generations of time and much bloodshed to change it. American history shows similar illustrations. After taking many years to construct the stereotype of "no entangling alliances," we found that the appeal of the League of Nations was not sufficient to overcome the power of our "isolation" stereotype. The women of

[22] Lippmann, *op. cit.,* p. 95.

America know how strong a stereotype can be; they are still battling "woman's place is in the home."

These illustrations of the stubbornness of stereotypes suggests that only as a last resort should a persuader attack them head-on. We believe the persuader has the greatest chance of success if he will take one of the following approaches: (a) Link the idea or action he recommends with some existing stereotype in the hearer's mind; (b) if (a) does not appear possible, then avoid open conflict with an existing stereotype by discussing the idea on other grounds; (c) if the persuader can neither appropriate nor avoid existing stereotypes to advantage, then there is left the challenge of constructing a new stereotype servant to the persuader's purpose.

Summary and Conclusions

In this chapter we have explored other bases of persuasion. In addition to the physical drives and social motives discussed in earlier chapters, we found that through experience and imitation man builds up systems of anticipatory response in relation to the objects, events, and people about him. We saw that these attitudes, sentiments, and stereotypes also play significant roles in human motivation. We said that each of us has his own limited and often inaccurate view of the world and events, and that *this world*—this set of stereotypes—is *our world,* and we will respond favorably to any word or set of words which fits into this world, just as we will rebel against anything which tends to destroy this world and thus our peace of mind. The persuader was encouraged to learn the stereotypes of the persuadee and to learn to adapt his appeals to them.

In terms of this stereotyped world—this pseudo-knowledge—the individual makes evaluations of ideas, objects, events, and persons in terms of his personal desires. Thus he develops a large repertoire of *attitudes* which predispose him for or against these ideas, objects, events, and persons. These reaction tendencies—attitudes—also are of prime importance to the student of persuasion, for they dictate the direction of our behavior. Frequently, because of unusual emotional adience or avoidance of certain objects or persons, we establish a more highly emotionalized relationship with these objects or persons. These *sentiments* are said to be special cases of attitudes and to have unusual influence in human conduct.

Stereotypes, attitudes, and sentiments are the chief foundation stones of human behavior. On these are built our hopes, our fears, our loves, and our hates. Respect these and you will be given a fair hearing; disregard them and your persuasion will fail.

Readings

1. Cantril, Hadley, "General and Specific Attitudes," *Psychological Monographs* (1932), XLII: No. 192.

2. Dashiell, J. F., *Fundamentals of Objective Psychology.* Boston: Houghton Mifflin Company, 1928, pp. 252–254. "The Organization of Sentiments as Motives."

3. Lippmann, Walter, *Public Opinion.* New York: The Macmillan Company, 1922, Part III, "Stereotypes."

4. Oliver, Robert T., *The Psychology of Persuasive Speech.* New York: Longmans, Green and Company, 1942, Ch. II, "The Influence of Self-Interest."

5. Young, Kimball, *Social Psychology.* New York: Appleton-Century-Crofts, Inc., 1945, Ch. IX, "Stereotypes, Myths, and Ideologies."

Exercises

1. Prepare and deliver an informational speech on *one* of the following topics. Use the reading references above to help you prepare the speech.

   a. The Formation of Attitudes
   b. The Classifications of Attitudes
   c. The Use of Attitudes in Persuasion
   d. The Use of Sentiments in Persuasion
   e. The Nature of Stereotypes
   f. The Use of Stereotypes in Persuasion

2. Analyze your own system of stereotypes in such areas as politics, business, education, religion, race, and so on. What role have these stereotypes played in your responses to the persuasion directed at you?

3. Prepare a 600-word written analysis of a political speech's use of "loaded words."

4. Prepare and deliver one of the five-minute persuasive speeches suggested below:

   a. A speech designed to change a dominant attitude known to exist in the minds of the class members.
   b. A speech which depends chiefly upon appeals to the sentiment of self-regard.
   c. A speech which depends chiefly upon appeals to patriotism or other loyalties.

5. Make a study of the advertisements of some commercial organization which are designed to build favorable attitudes toward the company.

Chapter VIII

REASONED DISCOURSE IN PERSUASION

I. Introduction

II. Definition of Reasoned Discourse

III. The Rise of Reasoned Discourse

IV. The Importance of Reasoned Discourse

V. Reasoned Discourse as a Motive Appeal

VI. Some Advantages of Reasoned Discourse

A. Universal Appeal

B. Contrast to Emotional Appeals

C. Enduring Nature

D. "Burden of Proof"

E. Reducing Conflict

F. Supplement to Emotional Appeals

VII. Summary

Readings and Exercises

Chapter VIII

REASONED DISCOURSE IN PERSUASION

Introduction

Physical and socio-psychological elements do not complete the foundation materials for the study of persuasion. Man takes great pride in the fact that, to some extent at least, he is undeniably a rational animal. The role of reason in the development of complex twentieth-century cultures has been a large one. It is not surprising that appeals to our critical faculties are important influences in contemporary persuasion.

We are interested at this point in systematic, purposeful reasoning in verbal communications to persuade. We term messages in this category "reasoned discourse." This chapter assesses our receptivity (or lack of it) to reasoned discourse persuasion.

Since persuasion is basically a means of appealing to the motives of men we will concern ourselves here with the utility of reasoned discourse as a method of reaching and touching off these springs of response. Is it possible to appeal to a man's wants by urging him to think critically? Is rational, suspended judgment involved in the satisfaction of basic desires? To what extent, if any, are reasoned and emotive appeals incompatible? All these questions demand answers if we are to determine the "persuasiveness" of reasoned discourse.

Definition of Reasoned Discourse

The essence of reasoned discourse is found in two definitions, one of reasoning and the other of reasoned discourse. Black defines reasoning as ". . . the use of possible truths as evidence in support of other possible truths."[1] He adds, "reasoning is an

[1] Max Black, *Critical Thinking.* New York: Prentice-Hall, Inc., 1946, p. 4.

attempt to pass from certain items of information (or possible truths) to others for which they are evidence."[2] O'Neill and McBurney apply a similar concept of reasoning to written and oral communication, "by reasoned discourse we mean that language which groups known truths and accepted premises in relationships which will cause readers or hearers to accept new truths or conclusions. These relationships may be such as to prove the conclusion, imply its truth, or merely motivate its acceptance. In any case, it is a dynamic process which generates new ideas and conclusions from existing facts and beliefs. As such, it is to be distinguished from pure narrative discourse, descriptive discourse, and other rhetorical forms which present more or less static pictures of existing facts and conditions."[3]

Thus, reasoned discourse is a particular application of language and is identifiable. It is designed specifically and purposively to reveal the logical process upon which the persuader's conclusion rests. It demonstrates to listener, or reader, the evidence upon which the thought structure is based, and by implication submits it to scrutiny. Use of reasoned discourse says, in effect, "Here is the path by which I reach a certain conclusion; will you check it carefully to see whether or not I am right?"

Woolbert[4] in 1918 stated that systems of logic run through, in fact serve as bases for, all persuasive communication. However, he develops the thesis that much of this application of logic is at the "subconscious" level; hence is concealed. His subconscious and partly conscious uses of logic, however, would be excluded from the area we have assigned to reasoned discourse. The persuasive stimuli we are talking about as reasoned discourse are directed toward producing in the individual listener or reader a conscious and somewhat painstaking intellectual judgment to be contrasted to less deliberate and less conscious "hair-trigger" responses from many so-called "emotional" appeals.

---

[2] *Ibid.*, p. 9.

[3] James M. O'Neill and James H. McBurney, *The Working Principles of Argument*. New York: The Macmillan Company, 1932, pp. 2, 3.

[4] Charles H. Woolbert, "The Place of Logic in a System of Persuasion," *Quarterly Journal of Speech Education* (January, 1918), IV: No. 1.

The Rise of Reasoned Discourse

"However much people in general tend to believe what they want to believe, to be emotional and even irrational at times, it is well to remember that their survival in a semi-hostile environment over millions of years has been due in part to that cunning contrivance of nature called the brain, the critical functions of which are not easily lulled to sleep by persuasive devices." [5]

This comment on the role of critical thinking in the development of the human race and our modern cultures reminds us that much of man's progress has been due to rational judgments rather than emotionalized thinking to achieve solutions for his problems. Automatic responses are limited to learned habit patterns. Progress, by definition, demands rearrangement and systematic modification of previous knowledge. Modern technology is a highly systematic use of reasoning to solve human problems in one area of endeavor. Reasoned discourse is the application of those same principles to communication. It is not surprising that in a culture idealizing the sciences, we have attempts to apply the standards of scientific experiment to our uses of language. Then, too, reasoning occupies an important role in persuasive communications because it is a vital ingredient in the making of decisions, and persuasion concerns itself with helping people make decisions. We members of the human race have learned the hard way that it pays to be sensible. Not too long ago critical thinking was necessary for survival of the individual in his day-to-day living. The cave-man who interpreted his environment according to his experiences and objective observations outlived his friend who relied on "hunches." Today we fortunately are seldom faced with the necessity of outwitting the threat of violent death. But we know very well indeed that it is necessary on many occasions to follow the dictates of our good judgment even to the point of doing things we would much prefer not to do. We scrimp for years to save money for a remote retirement, for example. People who exhibit behavior of this sort demonstrate the power of facts and reason to change human beliefs and conduct.

---

[5] Lester Thonssen and Howard Gilkinson, *Basic Training in Speech.* Boston: D. C. Heath and Company, 1947, p. 490.

The Importance of Reasoned Discourse

Analyzing irrational human behavior has been a popular theme of writers in persuasion in recent years. The idea of man's conduct being a resultant of forces exerted by blind desire has proved to be provocative. It has lead to a quest for "push buttons" which would control those forces. Some interesting points of view result from the application of findings of modern psychology to persuasion. Brigance summarizes the persuasive power of appeals to the intellect: "It is not sufficient just to 'know the subject' or to 'give the facts' or even to 'prove the case,' supremely important as are knowledge of facts and proof." [6]

At first glance this statement might seem to minimize the role of reasoning in the persuasion process, but Brigance contends that reasoning is highly important.

> Where do reasoning and argument enter the picture? Do they play an important part in human behavior? They do indeed. Obviously most people desire to know the truth, to detect chicanery, to avoid gullibility, and to live in the main a rational life. To satisfy such desires intelligent people must resort to reason. Furthermore even if we dislike reasoning things out because the exertion is too great (and that is why many people do not think on everyday problems), nevertheless when we get in a jam and must find a way out we resort to reasoning. *Reason, in other words, is the instrument for solving our problems, for satisfying our desires, for climbing upward toward the higher values of life.* Argument (which is simply reason set forth in print or speech), then, has a fundamental place in this scheme of things. To be sure we cannot argue someone into wanting something he does not want, but we can through argument enable ourselves and others to solve problems and to advance toward attaining the desires. In short, we can show people how to get what they want.[7]

This is a clarification of the supplementary nature of reason and desire. If we understand it thoroughly, statements like "no appeal to reason that is not also an appeal to a want is ever effective," are no indictment of the persuasive power of reason. Rather, they suggest that reasoning about the wants of human beings is a thoroughly practical way to achieve desired ends. Brigance re-

---

[6] William N. Brigance, *Speech Composition.* New York: Appleton-Century-Crofts, Inc., 1937, p. 134.

[7] *Ibid.*, p. 140.

states this relationship: *"The effective argument must motivate human wants and arguments which merely appeal to 'human reason' without touching human wants will be ineffective."* [8]

Considerable confusion among students of persuasion has come about through the consideration of appeal to reason and appeal to desire as distinct and separate entities. Some argue that one should and can be used to the exclusion of the other. But the practical persuader cannot choose to persuade either "logically" or "psychologically" as all his utterances have *both* logical and psychological aspects. He can emphasize one of these means of motivation but the attempt to eliminate one or the other reveals a failure to understand the nature of their interaction.

Reasoned argument has certain social values in a democracy. Those who believe that we should increase the amount of reasoning in our persuasive efforts say that the results from reasoned discourse are better for society, that is, they have greater *social utility* than do the results from other types of persuasion. This point is stressed by Ewbank and Auer: ". . . we believe that decisions based upon the consideration of evidence and arguments are likely to be better than those made under the spell of overpowering emotion. Our government is founded on this belief. Our whole system of legislative delays was designed to give time for the gathering of evidence and the sober second thought that renders less effective the crowd compellor who sways audiences simply by playing on their hopes and fears." [9]

Now that we have considered the integration of reason and desire in practical persuasion, we might logically ask ourselves, "What do we know of the role of reason in determining beliefs and actions of the individual?" We submit that to the date of this writing very little is known. Research experiments involving reasoned discourse generally compare the effectiveness of "logical" and "emotional" appeals. This reminds us of the concept which we asserted to be fallacious, assuming that "reason" appeals and "emotion" appeals are separate. What many of these studies appear to have measured is the difference between results of persuasion using vivid imagery, and the results of persuasion from which vivid

---

[8] *Ibid.*, p. 182.

[9] Henry Lee Ewbank and J. Jeffery Auer, *Discussion and Debate.* New York: Appleton-Century-Crofts, Inc., 1941, p. 259.

and visual imagery is excluded. Apparently the experimenters attempted to remove rhetorical "glamour" from the stimuli which they chose to label as reasoned argument. In their "emotional" appeals they certainly did not succeed in abolishing all logical structure. Obvious and striking signposts of formal logic were eliminated. But in each of these "emotional" appeals, it is usually easy to brief the logical structure of the argument presented. Hence, the experimental "emotional" appeals consisted, actually, of a logical framework overlaid with human interest, and vivid and colorful imagery. Then we compared results from reasoned discourse, with all possible factors of interest removed, with the results from reasoned discourse plus vivid imagery. It is significant that differences in these results have been very small. Repeatedly experimenters have concluded that the unadorned reasoned appeal is "as good as" the "dressed-up" version of the argument.

Reasoned Discourse as a Motive Appeal

If we view the above analysis in the framework of our definition of persuasion (controlling behavior by manipulating human motives), we see that reasoned discourse may be viewed as a motive appeal. Derived motives determine much of the behavior of the individual. Controlling this motive-behavior is the goal of persuasion and reasoned discourse has been seen to be a means for effecting that control. Therefore, we submit that a sound justification for using reasoned argument in persuasion is its motivating power.

O'Neill and McBurney [10] suggest this interpretation when they isolate "associating desire with the proposition" as a key problem in persuasion. They specify four methods: (1) By suggestion, (2) by rationalization, (3) by open explication, and (4) by demonstration. Methods three and four can be classified as reasoned discourse. Number two, rationalization, assumes the form of reasoned discourse, and only suggestion circumvents the logical basis of the argument. All four of these techniques, however, are designed to accomplish the association of desire within the persuadee with the goal of the persuader. Therefore it seems useful to study reasoned discourse as a motive appeal.

---

[10] James M. O'Neill and James H. McBurney, *The Working Principles of Argument*. New York: The Macmillan Company, 1932, pp. 204, 205.

Some Advantages of Reasoned Discourse

UNIVERSAL APPEAL

Our culture has taught us to react favorably to reason. We reject flights of fantasy and fabrication as though they are immoral. In contrast, conservative argument seems to be associated in our minds with honesty, poise, confident sincerity. The very act of citing evidence impresses us favorably. Somehow the truth which we are willing to grant to known facts is transferred to the proposition linked to these facts. One implication of these tendencies is crystallized in a popular bit of advice to salesmen and speakers—"understatement is stronger than overstatement." We tend to believe an argument which is conservatively stated. When the persuader suspends judgment by saying, "Well, this seems probably to be the case," we are somehow disarmed and we tend to accept his conclusion. In many cases we go beyond it, forming more definite conclusions of our own.

Apparently reasoned discourse also has unique prestige values. People have high regard for "horse sense," brains, problem-solving ability, ability to suspend judgment, and insistence upon sound evidence as a prerequisite to decision. Our democratic form of government and Anglo-American jurisprudence have encouraged widespread respect for evidence and its systematic interpretation. Scientific advance and wide acceptance of scientific method in modern industry, plus the transfer of laboratory principles to education, have helped create the stereotype of "the educated man" as a thorough, methodical problem-solver. This inclusion of reasoning power at the heart of our "educated man" concept is termed by some authors the "idealization of the rational."

One of the results of the homage we pay to the person who thinks effectively is an aspect of our sentiment of self-regard; we like to think of ourselves as deliberate, critical, reasoning beings. Thonssen and Gilkinson discuss influence of this sentiment on reaction to persuasion:

> Reactions of indignation to low level persuasive appeals and rejection of them are not uncommon. The basic cause of this type of reaction is the inherent desire in most people to regard themselves as rational beings, capable of thinking a thing through for themselves. The speaker who employs low-level persuasion

> says to his listeners in effect, "You are a dumb lot, and I propose to win your acceptance of my proposal by suggestion and stereotyped appeals." The listeners may, depending upon the circumstances, resent the implication profoundly.[11]

Or, conversely, reasoned discourse is a method which protects the persuader from "insulting the intelligence" of his audience!

Of course, the practical necessity of critical thinking in discharging the duties of citizenship keeps the member of a democratic society alert to the business of problem-solving. Choices between contradictory arguments, evidence, and appeals must be made. Free and competing persuasions result in greater respect for reasoned discourse than is found among the citizens of countries where monopoly propaganda dominates the national scene.

CONTRAST TO EMOTIONAL APPEALS

Perhaps you have heard a speaker who relied on reasoning follow a speaker who relied on unsound emotionalized appeals. Actually or by implication he said to his audience, "Let's sit back and look over the facts of the situation. Let's consider them objectively and see just exactly what their significance may be." That, if done simply and sincerely, can be effective, because of its striking contrast. We mentioned that our consciences bother us a bit when we indulge in flights of fancy. Similarly when we "go along for the ride" with a highly emotionalized speech we do not feel quite right about it. Somewhere inside of us there is a censor who continually reminds us that there are items of evidence and reasoning to be considered which we may be overlooking. The highly emotionalized speaker may be so effective that he causes us to forget the censor; the reasonable speaker reminds us of the values of sound evidence and valid reasoning.

Perhaps our modern audience will not always *spontaneously* demand the facts, but the good persuader has little difficulty in reminding them of the importance of considering these vital items. Such a reminder is increased in effectiveness if it appears in contrast to persuasion lacking in reasoning and factual materials.

---

[11] Lester Thonssen and Howard Gilkinson, *Basic Training in Speech.* Boston: D. C. Heath and Company, 1947, pp. 493, 494.

ENDURING NATURE

The enduring effect of reasoned discourse cannot be proved experimentally at present. This judgment is based upon an analysis of reasoned discourse; its effect probably endures because its completeness enables it to stand by itself. A logically sound, well-worded argument continues to exist until it is logically refuted.

A student of persuasion provided an interesting testimonial concerning this attribute of reasoned discourse. He explained that when he began his study of persuasion he had little faith in the powers of reasoned discourse to persuade. He preferred to place his faith in visual imagery, human interest, and dramatic devices. At the conclusion of the unit on the application of logic to persuasion he made approximately this statement: "I am amazed to find that when you advance primarily emotional appeal you have to keep 'pushing' it all the time, but if you do a good job of building a logical argument you can sit back and relax; it will stand by itself."

This student's observation would seem to be verified by the experiences of others. Persuaders of the past have found that a good reason tends to be remembered long after impulses based on emotion have been forgotten.

"BURDEN OF PROOF"

First, let us define "burden of proof." This term, taken from formal debate, means simply the obligation to give adequate reasons for change of belief or action. The person who has the burden of proof must show not only what is wrong, but also indicate the direction of the change that should be taken. This is a significant burden.

A unit of reasoned discourse makes severe demands of anyone who would disagree because it cannot be adequately answered by assertion or innuendo. Because this argument accepts rigorous standards of evidence and reasoning, these standards are inferentially applied to any opponent. He is challenged to demonstrate equal or superior evidence and reasoning. In this sense a burden of proof is thrown on the opposition through proper use of reasoned discourse.

REDUCING CONFLICT

You and I feel "high pressure" competing persuasions impinging upon us from all directions. We are urged in the language of dynamic action to do this and that and the other thing immediately without taking time out for deliberation.

The categorical nature of advertising and political appeals make compromise within them impossible. For example, when the Democrats agree that "the Democratic administration has great integrity" and the Republicans assert that "the Democratic administration is the most corrupt in our history" the citizen being indoctrinated with these conclusions is understandably confused. Apparently this circumstance comes about because politicians and advertisers want their statements as strong as possible, and thus make them unconditional and admit of no exceptions. But because Mr. Citizen is incapable of believing that "so and so" is *black and white,* totally and at the same time, he is resentful. In advertising and politics approximately equally strong demands in opposite directions are as extreme as is this example.

As the media of mass communication intensify the campaigns of advertising and other propaganda, the need for a means of resolving contradictions increases. We have at present some agencies which sell the service of resolving conflicts produced by conflicting claims devoted to the discovery and propagation of reliable information about nationally advertised products. These agencies testify to the unreliability of advertising claims, a conclusion we might reach by a simple examination of their extreme and conflicting nature.

Political oratory typically makes no attempt to avoid conflicting claims, unreasonable black and white assertions, and deliberate contradiction of contrary views without any explanation of that contradiction. Probably this popular form of political persuasion is not effective in helping people make up their minds on important issues. Since citizens are subjected to approximately equal forces of propaganda from at least the two major parties, and since opposing claims typically conflict diametrically, we would expect exasperation rather than decision to be the outcome.

A study of public opinion poll findings reveals to some extent the results of political oratory. One essential question to be answered is, "Have campaigns changed votes?" Vote changing through political campaigning is analyzed and commented upon by Gallup and Lydgate, public opinion specialists:

> Presidential campaigns proceed according to conventional but essentially false theories about voting behavior. There are seven of these theories and they have never been seriously challenged, yet when they are examined in the light of modern public opinion research there is good reason to question every one of them.
>
> The seven theories are (1) that party platforms influence voters; (2) that Presidential campaigns change votes; (3) that speeches are a great factor in changing the minds of voters; (4) that getting a prominent national figure or organization to endorse a candidate will swing blocks of votes; (5) that political machines decide elections; (6) that special efforts must be made to appeal to women voters because of the woman's viewpoint in politics and (7) the bandwagon theory, which is that all voters will rush to climb on the bandwagon of the supposed winner.[12]

Gallup and Lydgate supply public opinion poll data indicating that these theories have little basis in fact. They conclude that the lack of effect of political speaking must indicate that something is wrong with the method. They suggest that probably the political "stump speaker" is going about his job in an inefficient manner. They even suggest the direction that change for improvement might take:

> Maybe campaigns would influence people more if they were not fought on such incredibly low planes. Candidates abandon all pretense of sportsmanship, fairness or intelligence, they set-up straw men and knock them over, they call the opponents blackguards and liars and then try to outlie them in attempting to bribe minority groups with promises. Is it surprising that we voters don't fall for this vituperation and doubletalk?[13]

We prefer to believe what we are told, but the fact that we try to be rational imposes the requirement that we have a *reason* for every change in belief and action. This accounts in part for the prevalence of rationalization in our modern society. We are continually in quest of good and sufficient reasons to justify our conduct

---

[12] George Gallup and William A. Lydgate, "Do Campaigns *Really* Change Votes?" *The Saturday Evening Post* (July 3, 1948), 221: 1, p. 23.

[13] *Ibid.*, p. 101.

and beliefs to ourselves and to others. This great search for good reasons is further proof of the fundamental respect we have for reasoned discourse.

It is a popular fallacy that the reasoning associated with rationalization is necessarily unsound, possibly resulting from attempts to assign a moral dimension to it. True enough, it *may* be poor thinking, but on the other hand there is nothing in the process of rationalization which is dependent upon the quality of the reflective thinking entering into it. If your rationalizing deceives yourself and others, your reasoning is defective. The better the thought structure of rationalization the better it serves the needs of the individual. Figuring out a network of good reasons to support any premeditated course of action can be a praiseworthy activity, and one which is subject to all the rigors of logical discipline. It is possible to apply to rationalization the criteria of reasoned discourse.

The speaker who supplies rationalization to his audience as a method of resolving their conflicts may use valid or invalid forms of support. He has a moral obligation to supply only sound reasoning based on revealed premises. Otherwise he will be indulging in misrepresentation and deception. But the *form* of rationalization demands that the speaker go to considerable pains to *appear* to be logical. When such is the case, as Higgins points out, "It is usually easier, and better, really to be logical than simply to appear to be." [14]

SUPPLEMENT TO EMOTIONAL APPEALS

A reasoned decision often is necessary to the implementation of an emotionalized appeal. Unless common ground of agreement is achieved, further development of the persuader's appeal is often stymied.

Actually, two steps are frequently necessary in accomplishing conviction: First, the creation or intensification of a desire for the proposition, and second, the removal of obstacles in the way of attaining it. Once the desire to do something has been established by the persuader, reasoned discourse is useful in clearing away

---

[14] Howard H. Higgins, *Influencing Behavior Through Speech.* Boston: Expression Company, 1930, p. 143.

obstacles to action. Those obstacles are usually objections of practicality. Reasoned discourse is by nature suited to answering those practical questions that come up in the persuadee's mind such as "Will it work?" "What am I going to do about problems which may arise if I adopt this selected course of action?" and so forth. Reasoned discourse alone can lead to the conclusion that no significant reasons remain to make the suggested action undesirable. Attaining this conclusion is a practical necessity for the persuader. This conclusion can facilitate the desired belief or action response.

Collins [15] explored the supplemental action of reasoned and emotional appeals in an experiment comparing audience ratings of the relative effectiveness of four speeches. Varied audiences of college students all rated the speech containing a series of logical arguments each followed by a short emotional appeal as most effective. Other arrangements, with extended emotional appeal, extended rational appeal, and long rational appeal followed by an extended emotional appeal, were rated as less effective. The Collins experiment suggests that efficient persuasion might well blend reasoned discourse with emotionalized appeals.

Summary

In this chapter we have discussed the nature of reasoned discourse and its place in persuasion. In evaluating the strengths of a reasoned discourse appeal we found that its conservative and reasonable nature is illustrated by the popularly accepted maxim, "Understatement is stronger than overstatement." Reasoned discourse seems strong when it is used as a deliberate contrast to highly emotionalized argument. When we compared reasoned discourse to persuasive stimuli designed to arouse emotional response we found that its effect probably persists longer, because a logical structure stands until adequately refuted.

In our culture reasoned discourse has unique prestige values. Important in contributing to this prestige are the scientific method, modern technology, and the fact that education has for many years identified the methods of reasoned discourse with our stereotype of "the educated man." Our democratic form of government, by

---

[15] G. R. Collins, "The Relative Effectiveness of the Condensed and Extended Emotional Appeal," *Quarterly Journal of Speech* (June, 1924), X: 3, pp. 221–230.

virtue of its reliance upon an informed citizenry making intelligent decisions, places emphasis upon the patterns of reflective thought and the communication of information through methods of reasoned discourse.

We found that reasoned discourse has a job to perform to relieve confusion produced by "high pressure" competing persuasions. We noted advertising and political propaganda as two sources of conflicting stimuli. Aid in reconciling conflicting claims is needed, and reasoned discourse offers a means of reducing such conflicts.

Finally, we noted that reasoned discourse is an effective supplement to other appeals to motives. Where persuasion is a two-step process—first, the creation or reinforcement of desire for the persuader's goal, and second, an overcoming of obstacles to it—reasoned discourse is uniquely suited to dealing with the obstacles, chief of which are usually objections of practicality.

Readings

1. Black, Max, *Critical Thinking.* New York: Prentice-Hall, Inc., 1946, Ch. 1.
2. Baird, A. Craig, *Argumentation, Discussion, and Debate.* New York: McGraw-Hill Book Co., Inc., 1950, Ch. 1.
3. McBurney, J. H., O'Neill, J. M., and Glen Mills, *Argumentation and Debate.* New York: The Macmillan Co., 1951, pp. 1–17.
4. Oliver, Robert, *Persuasive Speaking.* New York: Longmans, Green & Co., Inc., 1950, Ch. VI.
5. Thonssen, L., and Baird, A. C., *Speech Criticism.* New York: The Ronald Press Company, 1948, Ch. 22.

Exercises

1. Report orally on one of the above readings. What claims does it make for reasoned discourse?

2. Find a unit of argumentative writing that you would classify as effective reasoned discourse. What elements contribute to its *persuasive* qualities?

3. Find a unit of persuasion that is highly colored and emotional. Word the central proposition and attempt to outline the underlying logical structure (much of this may be implied).

4. Discuss: When is man a rational animal?

5. Discuss: Would society benefit if propagandists could use only reasoned discourse?

Part IV

IDENTIFYING AND INTERPRETING THE TOOLS OF PERSUASION

To influence others the persuader must rely on the tools of persuasion. Chapter IX discusses the basic tool—language. To increase persuasiveness, language is often presented in psychological and logical techniques or forms, as discussed in Chapters X, XI, and XII.

To evaluate persuasion critically the persuadee must be able to identify and interpret the tools used in the persuasion which is directed at him. To build effective persuasion, the persuader must know how to use the tools necessary to expert craftsmanship.

Chapter IX

THE LANGUAGE OF PERSUASION

I. Introduction

II. The Semantic Approach to Language Analysis

III. "Signal" and "Symbol" Responses

- A. Sources of Connotative Meaning
  1. Slanting
  2. Figures of Speech
  3. Euphemisms
  4. Two-Valued Orientation
- B. Encouraging "Symbol" Responses to Language
  1. Conscious Modification of Reaction Patterns
  2. Use of "Report" Language
  3. Compensation for the Changing Nature of Words
     - a. Contexts; their Influences
     - b. "Indexing" our Words

IV. Summary

Readings and Exercises

Chapter IX

THE LANGUAGE OF PERSUASION

Introduction

Justice Oliver Wendell Holmes had insight into the complexities of language usage as well as respect for the power of language. He made the following comment concerning the continuous variation of word meaning: "A word is not a crystal transparent and unchanged; it is the skin of a living thought and may vary greatly in color and content according to the circumstances at the time in which it is used."

Examples of language adapted to time and circumstances are all about us. We find a real estate salesman talking to the prospective purchaser of a house. He is saying, "Prices are not going up, it is just the value of the dollar going down!" We suspect that the comfort the purchaser derives from these soothing syllables comes more from the words so carefully chosen by the salesman than from the reality they describe. Another example is a barber shop which has an unusual sign in its window—an impressive sign, with old English letters on bordered glass: "Hair Cutting as an Art." Possibly the special feeling of expert tonsorial skill comes from a clever combination of words rather than any superiority in the quality of haircuts here dispensed.

It should be clear by now that while words cannot change events, they can alter perceptibly the impact of circumstances on people. Elmer Wheeler, an expert in the use of words to persuade, stated his beliefs about this power of words in the following manner:

> Not long ago I was taking a plane trip. The hostess announced "We're heading into a thunder storm—hook your safety belts." You could feel the tension mount. A short while later, I had another encounter with rough weather in the air. But

this time the hostess said, "May I fasten your seat belt? You'll be more comfortable in the weather ahead of us." What a difference her choice of words made in our morale.

Every day we meet people who think in terms of "thunder storms" and "safety belts," whose words always spotlight the worst. And in contrast, how refreshing it is to meet those whose words call attention to the best.

As Emerson said, "No man has a prosperity so high or firm, but that two or three words can dishearten it; and there is no calamity which right words will not begin to redress."

Ali Baba had no monopoly on the use of magic words. All of us may use "words of magic" every day to unlock the treasure troves of life. Our words not only influence those around us —they have an unmistakable influence upon us too. Many of our frustrations are caused by not using the right words to define situations. I remember when my Grandpa Stroble lost his savings in a bank failure. He insisted he was "ruined." "Of course we are not ruined," said Grandma. "Nothing has happened to us, we have merely lost a lot of money." Grandpa slept soundly that night. A new definition of the circumstances had robbed it of its power to get him down.

Confidence, faith, courage, happiness—even security—are in the final analysis, states of mind which we experience within ourselves. These states of mind are determined by the thoughts that we think. And since we think with words, it is clear that old Syrus' cryptic saying is unalterably true. The "words we live by" do shape our lives.[1]

It is amusing, and educational as well, to experiment with describing the same pattern of life facts with different words. Bennett Cerf describes a game based on this experiment. He credits it to Bertrand Russell and calls it the game of conjugating "irregular" verbs. Here are a few from his collection.

From Hugh B. Scott: "I love life. Aren't you rather burning the candle at both ends, old man? He's a dissipated wreck."

From George Tener: "I slave. You keep yourself occupied. He has an excellent secretary."

From Barbara Hoseld: "I like the opposite sex. You go for anything in a pair of pants. She'll need a whole chapter to herself in the next Kinsey Report."

From Pamela Harnett: "I like gayety. You are boisterous. He is a roughneck."

From Ina Bestal: "I look young. You are well preserved. She must have had her face lifted."

---

[1] Wheeler, Elmer, "Magic Words," *This Week Magazine* (August 15, 1948), p. 2.

From E. N. Davenport: "I dine innocently with my friend's husband. You run the risk of being talked about. She carries on with every married man in town."

From J. Whitington: "I am stimulated by talking to successful people. You are a celebrity chaser. He is a snob."

From Baynard Kendrick: "I am a careful historian. You are a good researcher. He is a dirty plagiarist." [2]

Mr. Cerf mentions also the game of "paradoxical phrases." These phrases contradict themselves, he explains, but nevertheless have been accepted and are widely used. He lists the following self-contradictory examples which he credits to Katherine Porter: "Light housekeeping, free love, honest prejudice, civilized warfare." [3]

Language exists to transmit meaning. We have been looking at examples in which the choice of words modifies that meaning. This fact is evidence that language in current use often is a low-fidelity mechanism for communication. We will not tolerate distortion in our radios and phonographs, although in language we must continually contend with it and sometimes with systematic and intentional distortion. Certainly it would seem that the time is ripe for us to turn to *scholars* of language for any help that they can give in improving precision of language.

A trend toward serious inventory of current language has appeared in recent years. For example, the 1948 political campaign focused attention on the language of politics. Much helpful criticism came as a result. Here is a commentary on the language of political conventions and other examples of campaign persuasion:

> But redundancy and equivocation are not confined to speeches. The whole language of present day politics is infested with sloppiness and insincerity.
>
> Extravagant claims are the debased coinage of so-called political leaders. A hundred times during and after this convention the public will be told things it will not believe—things the speakers know will not be believed.
>
> The eternal question is whether the ones who do the talking are deluding themselves. They are not dumbbells because they have held power by the most astute methods for many years. They cannot mean what they say.
>
> That of course raises an ethical question. Is politics a pro-

---

[2] Cerf, Bennett, "Trade Winds," *Saturday Review of Literature* (September 4, 1948), XXXI: 36, p. 4.

[3] *Ibid.*, p. 5.

> fession in which truthfulness is not a virtue? Is there a moral law in politics essentially unlike that which prevails elsewhere?
>
> These are considerations which might well be in the minds of citizens as they listen to the Philadelphia Story this week.[4]

There is more to language than meets the eye or ear and we might add that frequently language usage seems a good example of a "blooming, buzzing confusion." We are aware of the need for tools of language analysis in planning or analyzing persuasion; let us see what these are and how they are used.

The Semantic Approach to Language Analysis

Writers in semantics (the science of language usage) offer many helpful suggestions to help us in language analysis. Language inaccuracies, they say, are traceable to two characteristics of symbolic communication. First, the word is only a representation of something else, and second, a limited number of words must represent an infinite number of "life facts." The term "life facts" may be strange to you; it is roughly translatable as things and circumstances which surround us. Objects and events in the world, past or present, which are verifiable are "life facts."

Concerning the first of these sources of error, Lee writes:

> Starting with facts and opinions, the analyst will have to see that statements of fact are not life facts. In old fashioned terms, noumena are not phenomena. Language acts to represent both words and non-verbal life facts; the relationship is the same as that between a map and the territory. It would then follow because life and nature are complex, that any discussion of human affairs must leave out some details and that conclusions cannot encompass "all" of any life fact.[5]

This introduces the process of *abstracting*. It indicates what our common sense would tell us if we thought about it—that when we use a word to designate even a single object it cannot call to mind all the details of that object. If we say the word "desk" to another person, meaning a particular desk with which we are both familiar,

---

[4] Raymond Moley, "Our Political Language Is Insincere and Sloppy," *Minneopolis Star* (July 12, 1948), p. 12. Reprinted by special permission of the *Minneapolis Star and Tribune* and The Associated Newspapers, Inc.

[5] Irving J. Lee, *Language Habits in Human Affairs.* New York: Harper and Brothers, 1941, p. xxiii.

we can rely upon the memory of the other person to supply all but a few of the obvious details of that particular desk. This process of transmitting an incomplete (possibly adequate) picture is the process of abstracting. We can see how abstracting becomes still more vague when we use a word to designate a class of objects—for example, the word "desk" to refer to the category of desks. Because all kinds of desks are included we cannot expect several people to whom we are talking to have identical or even similar images in their minds in response to the word "desk." More details are lost, impressions are more general than when the word "desk" was used to refer to a single object, and more *abstracting* takes place.

The problem of abstraction is complicated by our second basic shortcoming of language, the limited number of words we have available. Common sense will again tell us that if we have a limited number of words and an infinite number of things which they must represent, any given word will have to be used to mean not one but several things. Our minds rebel at the idea that a word has many meanings. We prefer to think that a word stands always and forever for a given value or a fixed quantity. This results in what Hayakawa terms the "one word, one meaning fallacy." He believes that the tendency to assume that a word has but one meaning causes much sloppy thinking and mental confusion. He offers a remedy:

> Such an impasse is avoided when we start with a new premise altogether—one of the premises upon which modern linguistic thought is based; namely, that no word ever has exactly the same meaning twice. The extent to which this premise fits the facts can be demonstrated in a number of ways. First, if we accept the proposition that the context of an utterance determines its meaning, it becomes apparent that since no two contexts are ever exactly the same, no two meanings can ever be exactly the same.[6]

We know now that the word is only a group of letters or a sequence of noises and must not be confused with the pattern of life facts it designates. This fact implies inevitably the process of abstraction or loss of life facts in any symbolic communication. We remember that the limited number of words we have necessarily leads to the conclusion that no word has exactly the same meaning twice. Hence

---

[6] S. I. Hayakawa, *Language in Action.* New York: Harcourt, Brace and Company, 1946, p. 49.

we resolve not to be surprised when we find an old faithful word assuming the role of a stranger under the influence of its context. We suspect that the more abstract the term the more variable will be its meaning. Words standing for large classes of objects lose a great many details and consequently have a tendency to mean "all things to all men."

When conversation bogs down because it has become unclear we can resort to the helpful question, "What do you mean?" Frequently the asking of this question, not once but several times, forces a speaker to clear up confusions and to become more specific and, therefore more intelligible. Norman Thomas voiced the response of many thinking citizens when he wrote:

> It is a sign of hope in our democracy when the people begin insistently to ask:
>
> "Just what do you mean by that high sounding declaration? What will you do to carry it out?
>
> "How many tons of oratory will equal an ounce of effective performance in halting the inflationary price rise, or giving us the houses we so desperately need, or winning the peace without which all our hopes are dust and ashes?" [7]

High level abstractions (terms conveying little specific information) are difficult to define. It is helpful if we define them always in a particular unit of communication. In other words we suggest that it is perfectly proper to stipulate a definition for a special purpose. We must recognize that it is ordinarily impossible to be comprehensive. We must use a sampling technique. We must use examples of what we mean which are as concrete and unmistakable as possible. By listening to a variety of well-chosen examples we can secure meaningful definitions of even abstract and general terms.

At the moment a word badly in need of definition is "Communism." Here is an example of an effort to define that term.

What Is Communism—What Is not Communism

There are three current forms of communism: Voluntary Communism, Marxian Communism, Soviet Communism. The Marxian and Soviet varieties are frequently intermixed.

The voluntary communist freely gives up his rights of private ownership of property and self determination of activity. Volun-

---

[7] Norman Thomas, "G.O.P. Full of Complacent Assurance," *Minneapolis Star* (June 23, 1948), p. 8.

tary communism has been practiced for centuries by small numbers of people chiefly in religious organizations.

The Marxian Communist is a follower of the doctrine of Karl Marx. He denies the existence of God, believes in world revolution and dictatorship of the proletariat. He looks to an ideal, future state in which each person works to the limit of his capabilities and receives in return only his material needs under a system in which there is no government as such.

The Soviet Communist believes that the government of Soviet Russia is the most vital force in the world today and wishes to spread its influence abroad by the establishment of puppet dictatorships subservient to Soviet Russia. Under the name of communism the Soviet followers in Russia and abroad practice a system based on expediency, which is far removed from Marxian communism but equally as objectionable in its deification of the state and its leaders, denial of human rights and subjugation of peoples.

"What is not communism?"

In general everything that does not come under the definitions of voluntary, Marxian or Soviet communism is not communism.

It is not communism to advocate better treatment of individuals, classes, groups, races or nations.

It is not communism to preach or practice brotherhood of man and the equality of races, creeds and colors.

It is not communism to demand better wages for workers.

It is not communism to attack abuses of power or functions in high or low places, in government or industry.

It is not communism to demand equitable distribution of money, food, land.

It is not communism to seek access to education for all persons.

It is not communism to criticize restrictions on the right to work or to advance within a chosen field.

It is not communism for employees—or for employers—to organize for collective bargaining purposes with respect to hours, wages and working conditions.

It is not communism for employees to strike or employers to suspend operation.

It is not communism to maintain that everyone has right to "Life, Liberty and the Pursuit of Happiness." [8]

Suppose Mr. Quigley had decided, as do many columnists, to define communism by adding abstractions. He might then have said, "Communism is a *way of life which we despise.* It is *foreign*

---

[8] Martin Quigley, Jr., "What Is Communism?" *Motion Picture Herald* (October 4, 1947), p. 25.

totally to our *democratic concept*." His relative contribution to general understanding of the facts of communism (as he saw them) would have been smaller than the contribution of the above article. Why? Because there are a great many ideologies other than communism which are foreign to our democratic ideals. By being more abstract Mr. Quigley would have increased opportunity for error. His decision to go in the direction of concreteness and cite specific elements that are and are not communism at least provides points on which our minds can meet. Each additional example increases the area of understanding.

Not all concepts can or should be defined. Much persuasion occurs in the form of figurative language which relies for its persuasive power upon colorful images. Such imagery may vary in terms of the experience of the auditor or reader without doing damage to the communication. In these instances the writer or speaker is aiming at an emotional response rather than the faithful transmission of the idea. We suggest as an example of figurative language which defies definition a Norman Thomas description of the National Democratic Convention in 1948: "The effect is that of a carnival in a morgue lined with unburied hopes."

I think you will agree that any literal attempt to define what Mr. Thomas meant by these words would be not only futile expenditure of energy but would spoil a rather effective unit of emotional communication. In this, as in many other cases of figurative language, attempt at definition amounts to misinterpretation of the communication.

What do we mean by definition? Simply, definition is an explanation for somebody of what the speaker or writer is talking about. It is necessarily an expansion of the term which supplies some of the details lost in the process of abstracting. How do we go about making a definition? That is one of the central problems in the study of semantics. Here in diagrammatic form is one approach to its solution.

Levels of abstraction at which you can tell somebody about a teaspoon.

Personal possession
Household necessity
Item of hardware
Kitchen utensil
Spoon

Teaspoon
Silver teaspoon
Sterling silver teaspoon
Spoon No. 1 (word selects an object we both remember)
Picture of Spoon No. 1
Model of Spoon No. 1
Object—Spoon No. 1—Hold it up for examination

In answer to the question, "What do you mean, teaspoon?" the lower levels of the above list are meaningful. To say it another way, if we select symbols relatively low on the list we are doing less abstracting (losing fewer details) than if we choose the words relatively high on the list. We can go still further in reducing misunderstanding or possibility for error in communication if we *get below* words altogether. A picture of Spoon No. 1 is less subject to communicative error than the most descriptive terminology. A model of Spoon No. 1 adds a third dimension, further reducing opportunity for distortion. Of course, the best means of communicating accurately what is meant by "this particular teaspoon" is to resort to inspection of the object. Hold up Spoon No. 1 for examination and the people talking about it will have an almost perfect meeting of minds on the subject of their conversation.

The reason why the words "sterling silver teaspoon" represent more precise communication than "spoon" is not difficult to determine. There are fewer sterling silver teaspoons than there are spoons. Every category in these levels of abstraction contains the lower categories and many more besides. Thus, words near the bottom of the list stand for fewer "things" than the words higher on the scale. By the time we get to the top of the list we have "catch-all" words which stand for so many objects that their meanings are obscure unless the context in which they occur is definitive. We can draw a moral from this study of levels of abstraction: Using specific, "low-level" words contributes to precision of communication because they stand for fewer things and thus reduce opportunity for misunderstanding.

"Levels of abstraction" is a useful tool of language analysis for improving the precision of communication. Operating at low levels of abstraction approaches life facts. Hence, definition is, ideally, progression to lower levels of abstraction. This helps us surmount the obstacle of communication by a limited number of symbols.

"Signal" and "Symbol" Responses

Human beings respond to stimuli in two different ways. Ordinarily, any single response has ingredients of both. The two methods of responding are "Signal Response" and "Symbol Response."

Signal responses are immediate, unthinking, largely automatic. They are uncritical. *Symbol responses* are to some degree deliberate and discriminating. They modify reaction tendencies to harmonize with the immediate environment and may be said to be made "in context."

An example will clarify the nature of the difference between symbolic and signal responses. A chimpanzee, according to Hayakawa, was taught to drive an automobile. He handled mechanical operations competently. When he came to a stop light he would stop if the light turned red. When the light turned green he would start the car. There was one significant difference, however, between his driving and the driving of a skilled human. When the light turned green the chimpanzee would start the car whether or not the way before him was obstructed. If a large truck were in front of him and the light turned green the chimpanzee would drive right ahead. To him the light meant not "go ahead if such seems feasible" but it meant "go ahead!" He did no interpreting of the signal in terms of his surroundings. His response was automatic and uncritical, exemplifying the pattern of the signal response. Symbolic behavior in this circumstance is, quite obviously, looking around, surveying the situation, and starting the car when the light turns green *only if* the environment is suited to the indicated action.

The contents of communications which produce these two types of response are called *connotation* and *denotation.* To the extent that communication produces "Signal" response it has connotative meaning. To the extent that the response produced is "symbolic" in nature, the communication has denotative meaning.

The difference between connotative and denotative meanings and the nature of signal and symbol response are important concepts to the student of language. Much of language analysis is oriented around identifying elements which are connotative and produce signal responses and those which are denotative and are conducive to symbol responses. Nevertheless, one must not expect to find signal and symbol responses in isolation or connotative meanings separate from denotative meanings. If we were to graph the qualities of response we might say that all communications fall upon a continuum in something approximating a bell-shaped curve. A great many units of communication are near the center of the continuum where we have almost equal amounts of connotative and denotative meaning. Hence response would be mixed signal and symbol in character. As we move to the extremes we have fewer communications. Pure *signal response* is seldom achieved by meaningful language, and pure *symbol response* probably only if at all in the language of science or mathematics.

CONTINUUM FOR CLASSIFYING THE CONTENT OF
UNITS OF COMMUNICATION

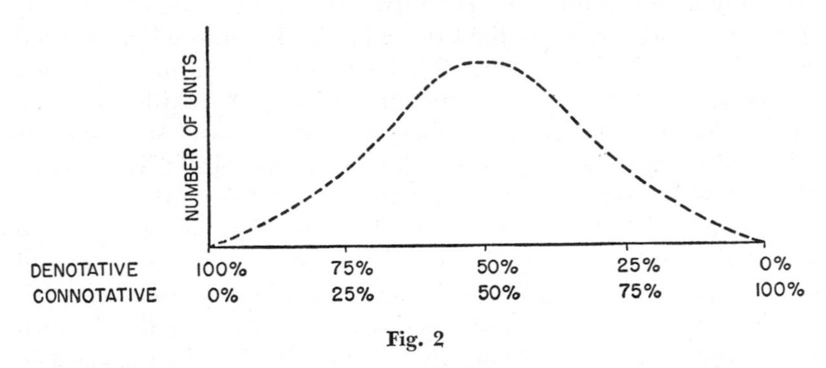

Fig. 2

Any unit of communication (message) cannot be labeled either "connotative" or "denotative." To be accurate we must say this communication "tends to be more denotative than connotative." The above continuum makes this "mixture" relationship visual. It should be possible arbitrarily to assign a unit of communication to a point on the scale. A person might say, "My reaction to this message is about fifty-fifty, half symbolic and half signal response. Hence for me it contains approximately equal amounts of connotative and denotative content." It may appear that denotative meaning and symbolic response are always to be preferred to signal response. Such is not the case. There are examples in which signal response to language is to be desired, and in which any symbolic response is a hindrance to the process of communication. Here the purpose of the communication is to produce an immediate and uncomplicated physical response. In its simplest form it might be illustrated by the verbal command "duck" on the field of battle.

Instruction in dancing, automobile driving, and airplane flying are other cases in point. One of the most recent and interesting contributions to our thinking about the utility of signal response comes from a new system of flight instruction that eliminates symbolic response from the communication process.

> Holcombe's new instruction system is based on elimination of in-flight talk. All instructions are transmitted by buzzers contained inside the student's helmet. A buzz on the front of the helmet means "up," on the back of the helmet means "down," and on the right or left means "fly away from the impulse signal." . . .
>
> A signal from the front push button to the student's forehead buzzer brings back, nose up, pressure on the stick. A rear button signal to the back of the student's head brings forward pressure on the stick. Beginners are conditioned to response to side signals with both stick and rudder. These reactions are natural, away from the impulse signal.
>
> The buzzer stimuli on the student's head are both auditory and tactual—both sound and vibration. He hears them and he feels them. Although it is not necessary the tone of the buzzers can be different for ease of identification and for variations in stick pressures. In pilot models used so far the front buzzer is louder than the others, emphasizing back pressure on the stick to flare the airplane on landings.
>
> The student takes off, turns and lands on these four signals without any talk. He learns that varying tone and duration of signal call for varying travel of the controls and varying durations of application. Combination signals may be used but they are not even mentioned before solo. The elimination of in-flight talk is important in this primary training system. Here are Holcombe's reasons why. With the buzzer system:
>
> There is no time lost while the instructor turns his ideas into words and sentences. The student's reaction to the buzzer is automatic.
>
> No lag results from inadequate exposition by the instructor. Some instructors are less fluent than others.
>
> There is no transfer of emotions through voices raised in

disgust or fatigue. The signal can't shout or call names. It is impersonal.[9]

The moral of this story might be that it is foolish to rely upon language when there is a more direct means of communication. Holcombe demonstrated the values of going below the verbal levels into the world of physical objects. His solution to a particular problem in communication was to seek the lowest satisfactory level of abstraction. In doing this he increased his communicative efficiency as we do when we select the concrete word in preference to a higher level abstraction.

SOURCES OF CONNOTATIVE MEANING

We now describe and illustrate categories of communicative units which evoke signal responses. The following five classifications overlap, but as a group include most of the recognized ways of implementing so-called "emotional" appeals in persuasion.

Slanting. Slanting consists of selecting descriptive methods to encourage acceptance or rejection. Commonly, it is "loading the dice" in language. A comparison of two descriptions of the same strike provides an example.

LAWLESSNESS RETURNS WITH IMPORTED C.I.O. GOONS

Respect for law and order means little or nothing to C.I.O. strike leaders in South St. Paul.

Wednesday a large mob of C.I.O. strikers and "imported" Goons brought a return of lawlessness to this community. This mass mob denied Swift and Company employees their right, under Minnesota law, to enter and leave our plant.

In an effort to call a halt to these Goon tactics, Swift and Company asked for an injunction in the Dakota County District Court. This injunction was issued by the court on Wednesday. The injunction specifically forbids the C.I.O. Union, its members and officers, from interfering with the right of our employees to enter and leave the plant and intimidating any employees or using force or violence against any employee.[10]

The same circumstances were described later by the C.I.O. as follows:

---

[9] Blaine Stubblefield, "Push-Button Instructor," *Flying Magazine* (July, 1949), 45: 1, pp. 42, 73.

[10] Swift & Co. Advertisement, "Lawlessness Returns with Imported C.I.O. Goons," *Minneapolis Star* (May 13, 1948), p. 9.

A MESSAGE TO MINNESOTA CITIZENS FROM C.I.O.
PACKINGHOUSE WORKERS

We striking packinghouse workers, 6500 of us with our families, are today fighting with our backs to the wall. Governor Youngdahl has called out the Minnesota National Guard to use bayonets on us people in South St. Paul.

The Wall Street packinghouse monopoly that helped smash O.P.A. and drove meat prices up and are today reaping a tremendous profit at your expense are being served by this action of the Governor. These people who own Swift, Armour, Wilson, and Cudahy are not Minnesota citizens. They don't spend their huge profits in the Minneapolis grocery stores. They don't help support doctors, they don't buy furniture in our local furniture stores. They grab up Minnesota wealth and take it out east where they come from. We spend our money here.

LOW WAGES

Two-thirds of us before the strike earned less than one dollar ten cents an hour. We have families to support. We are not asking for enough money to drive big cars or to have summer homes. We just want enough to clothe our kids and feed our families, and be able to go to a church and help support it, the things of that nature. We think our kids deserve a decent education. That's what we are fighting for.[11]

Attempts to achieve acceptance and rejection by choice of words can be found in the above slanted excerpts. The small proportion of factual information these two samples of opinionated prose have in common could be rewritten in neutral language so that the facts of the matter would have first prominence. If we succeeded in rewriting the factual content in that objective fashion the language could be called "report" language. The kind of language we do have in these advertisements is aptly described by the adjective "loaded." "Loaded words" are those which carry connotative meaning in addition to their denotation. Positive loading and negative loading are terms indicating whether the connotative adulterate tends to produce acceptance or rejection. The following headline illustrates extreme "loading" of language: "Patent Medicine Men seek Passage of Law Making Frauds Easier; Three Press Lords Support Measure." [12]

---

[11] C.I.O. Advertisement, *Minneapolis Star* (May 19, 1948), p. 20.

[12] George Seldes, "Patent Medicine Men Seek Passage of Law Making Frauds Easier; 3 Press Lords Support Measure," *In Fact* (January 26, 1948), p. 1.

Careful reading of the text under this headline reveals that manufacturers of pharmaceutical products were attempting to support legislation which would free them from certain restrictions of the Federal Trade Commission and that three publishers had gone on record as favoring the proposed change. The reader can practice intentional loading or slanting by rewriting the headline to encourage acceptance rather than rejection. A shift from *negatively* loaded to *positively* loaded language will do the trick.

Figures of Speech. A wonderfully varied source of connotative communication is found in figurative language. Similes, metaphors, and analogies lend clarification and attention value to communication. Part of the power of figurative communication lies in its visual imagery. Any language usage which produces clear-cut mental pictures is to some extent figurative. We like familiar pictures resulting from figures of speech, and, therefore, they constitute useful tools for the persuader.

Editorials are good sources for the study of figurative language in persuasion. The following sample develops its message through *metaphorical* argument.

THE WISE THRUSH

Everyone knows what the ostrich did with his head and the pile of sand. But no one has asked what was in that sand. The ostrich was trying to escape desert wide dangers (and obligations) by shutting his eyes to them—but perhaps not just for security. There is more to the story. He had come from a four year hungry and thirsty journey. And there was a mound and in it probably a hidden spring or some store of succulent roots, or whatever big greedy birds like ostriches eat (high prices, monopolies, easy money). He was tired of watching the horizon and running himself ragged for the welfare of the flock. So he shoved in his big bill, forgot the dust storm still far away, and gobbled at whatever he found there. This is not the African ostrich, remember, but the American—habitat Maine to California, scattered individuals everywhere, but a strong tendency to form blocs. Can best be studied in Washington, where sentinel birds collect around the feeding stations. Not much can be done about the ostrich except to dig him up and expose his beady eyes which are much more indicative of what he is after than his deceptive and prosperous tail feathers.[13]

---

[13] Henry Seidel Canby, "The Wise Thrush," *The Saturday Review of Literature* (July 13, 1946), XXIX: 28, p. 12.

Canby continues in this editorial by explaining that he really is talking about the American citizen and his problems of living in a world dominated by a "cold war." We suspect that most readers had come to that conclusion before he revealed it. But by his taking the trouble to specify what he was talking about metaphorically he illustrated a precaution which is wise when figurative language is used. The fact that figurative expressions are distant from life facts increases variation in responses among different individuals. To guarantee that your auditor is not misreading your intent with drastic results you can insure a proper interpretation, as did Mr. Canby. To be sure, it weakens the impact of the figure to some extent, but that may be a necessary compromise.

Personification results from our tendency to endow familiar objects with human characteristics. All of us have heard ardent motorists refer affectionately to their automobiles much as though they were people. A few years ago the sinking of the U. S. cruiser Salt Lake City was reported in a manner providing a good example of personification.

> The end came at 1:52 p.m. (Pacific Daylight Time) Tuesday after five hours of intermittent bombardment with everything 15 ships and scores of planes had to offer.
>
> The famous old sway-back fighting ship went down without protest—almost gracefully—as if she welcomed death under fire to desecration in a junk yard.
>
> She rolled over and hid her grotesquely twisted mast and other wounds in the kindly sea. Her stern rose and then she slid beneath the waves, bow first.
>
> Her grave is in the great depths 130 miles off the southern California coast. She went down in 2000 fathoms, more than two miles of water, where no diver can ever disturb her.
>
> Admiral C. D. Ramsey, Commander of the Pacific fleet who witnessed the sinking said: "In general the functioning of material was excellent. The Salt Lake City, a grand veteran of war and peace, has completed her last service. A final well done. As the Salt Lake City went down, Navy committal services were held on the submarine tender Nereus standing off a couple of miles." [14]

Though the concept of a ship consenting to die does not make sense, perhaps, it is, nevertheless, undeniably appealing. The hold-

---

[14] Norman Bell, "Sea Hides Wounds as Torpedoes Send Cruiser to Pacific Grave," A.P. story in *St. Paul Dispatch* (May 26, 1948), p. 1.

ing of "committal services" for a structure of steel and other inanimate materials indicates the prevalence and general acceptance of personification.

A variety of figures enlivens and dramatizes argument. Here are other figurative language usages to suggest ways of increasing your repertoire of verbal imagery.

Allusion: Metaphor referring to a well-known incident—"the ghost of the coalition returned like the ghost of Banquo."

Apostrophe: Absent addressed as though present and the inanimate as if intelligent and present—"Come to the bridal chamber Death," and, "Alma Mater, we love thee."

Antithesis: Things mutually opposed—"Better to reign in hell than serve in heaven."

Synecdoche: The name of a part denotes the whole or the name of the whole denotes a part—"Give us this day our daily bread" (meaning sustenance generally), or "the new world of television."

Simile: A likeness is pointed out in things otherwise unlike—"the tobacco habit settles upon one like a vampire and sucks his blood."

Figurative Analogy: A simile in which the identity is one of *principle,* and commonly of greater complexity than the usual simile:

"I think a politician might well remember that, while it's true that people don't shoot Santa Claus, they finally did plug Jesse James. I hope our politicians right now will be very careful not to slap more taxes on the U.S.A. I'd go back and read what finally happened to Jesse James."

"Communism is like a colony of ants."

"We must not try to patent the process by which Americans are made, or we will get an assembly-line product."

"Propaganda is a blitzkrieg of incendiary bombs."

Hyperbole: Intentional exaggeration is used to make a point—"The referees didn't let either team touch the ball during the first half."

"Minnesota opened holes in the Nebraska line as big as Grand Canyon on visitor's day."

"Socialism means to control the American family—to control the father, control the mother, control the child. That means the end."

Understatement: Reversed hyperbole, the drawing of a conclusion so extremely conservative in nature that it offers striking contrast to the expected conclusion. An example is the comment of a neighbor after two members of a religious "whipping cult" had been beaten to death, "Now, I'm certainly in favor of religious freedom, but this is, perhaps, going too far."

To test your understanding of these figures, classify this example from a wartime speech of Franklin D. Roosevelt: "We started punching and are still punching. We have driven the enemy into his corner."

Persuasive applications of figurative language are of dual purpose, to enliven and make vivid the communication and to convince persuadees to accept or reject concepts involved. Figures of speech can be infinitely varied and hence offer a challenge to the ingenuity of the persuader. Cleverness in the use of figurative language can "pay off" on a large scale.

Euphemisms. Euphemisms are language devices chosen because they are more socially acceptable than their synonyms. Usually a euphemism is an avoidance of direct communication. The euphemistic circumlocution is illustrated when, in talking about the death of a friend, we say he "went to his last reward" instead of saying "he died." Society demands rather peremptorily that certain words in our vocabularies be suppressed and their euphemistic equivalents used in polite communication.

A good exercise in detecting and compiling lists of euphemistic terms is to analyze conversations to locate the terms representing slightly inaccurate avoidance of blunt words that are not considered genteel. You will be surprised at the length of the list you can build in a short time. You might attempt to account for the historical development of their social unacceptability.

Two-Valued Orientation. The small number of words available compared to an infinity of circumstances to be described plus a naturally understandable desire to simplify complex social phenomena result in a source of language distortion termed "two-valued orientation."

We tend to describe people in extremes as saints or sinners, as good or bad, intelligent or stupid, handsome or homely, intriguing or stodgy. Inaccuracy comes about because of our failure to recognize a middle ground. In these examples we are talking in terms of *blacks* and *whites* and ignoring the more numerous *shades* of *grey*. Certainly most of us are intelligent in some things and tend toward stupidity in others. In some ways we are moral and in some situations we may be less than moral. The two-valued orientation of language, by placing objects described in extreme stereotyped categories, tends to introduce distortion and destroy precision of communication.

Political speakers long ago incorporated two-valued orientation into their repertoire of persuasive techniques. It lends itself particularly to arguments for preservation of the status quo in preference to a change suggested by the opposition. Herbert Hoover, speaking to the Republican National Convention in 1936, used such an appeal. "There are some principles that cannot be compromised. Either we shall have a society based upon ordered liberty and the initiative of the individual, or we shall have a planned society that means dictation no matter what you call it or who does it. There is no half way ground."

Current controversy over Communism produces many examples of two-valued orientation. An individual is never patriotic to a degree! He is *either* patriotic or subversive. Adolph Menjou in testifying before the House Un-American Activities Committee cited many Hollywood writers as "Communists." Movie producers were fundamentally different. "He emphasized that he does not consider any movie producers to be Communists. On the contrary, he said, they are 'patriotic Americans.' "[15]

The truly fortunate people are those who shifted from writing to producing movies prior to Menjou's testimony.

An amusing example of two-valued orientation appeared in campaign literature supporting the candidacy of a John Simmons for Mayor of Minneapolis in the 1949 elections. The four-page tabloid size folder supplying reasons for voting for Simmons has a three frame cartoon strip at the top of the first page. In the strip we have the voter in quest of information conversing with a source who has the situation well in hand. The inquiring voter says, "Me vote for Simmons, why should I? Who's for him?" Answer from informant, "Why, professional men, working men, business men,

---

15 "Hollywood Full of Communists, Menjou Charges," *Minneapolis Star* (October 21, 1947), p. 1.

parents, home owners. . . ." The inquirer continues, "And who's against him?" Replies the informer, "Oh, people who want special favors, communists. . . ." That makes up the inquirer's mind once and for all, and in the final frame he is shown smacking fist in palm in final decision and saying "Okay, that settles it. I'm for Simmons!" [16]

Colorful, extreme language characterizes two-valued orientation. Moderate, tentative language is characteristic of multi-valued orientation. A careful avoidance of over-statement and a conscientious effort to recognize middle ground will do much to break our habits of two-valued orientation.

ENCOURAGING "SYMBOL" RESPONSES TO LANGUAGE

It follows that because symbol responses are more discriminating they usually are more desirable than are signal responses to the same language. Certainly from the point of view of the person being persuaded symbol responses are to be desired. Improvement in critical response to language can be made in any individual by encouraging increased symbolic response to words. How can a person do this? Here are specific suggestions.

Conscious Modification of Reaction Patterns. Suppose the cheerful voice of the radio announcer says "The thermometer now reads 97 degrees." A signal response might well be increased sensation of human misery and lowered patience with those around us. Symbolic behavior can evaluate that signal tendency and recognize it. Simply realizing that the radio announcement did not change the temperature in the room mitigates the signal response. One symbolic response to this same stimulus might be, "Better not play tennis today, it isn't safe at my age."

Understanding the nature of symbol and signal responses makes it possible for us to practice the detection and modification of "signal" elements. Semanticists believe that with no other aid beyond this understanding and the will to improve, the individual can evolve into a measurably more rational human being.

Use of "Report" Language. Under *Slanting* we mentioned "report language," the conscious avoidance of slanting. Not using

---

[16] "Here's Why John Simmons will be a Good Mayor of Minneapolis," Simmons for Mayor Volunteer Committee, 85 S. 10th St., Minneapolis, Minnesota, 1949, page 1.

heavily loaded words helps increase denotative meaning of our communications and encourages symbol responses. In case a communication confuses you, rewrite it in report language. This process is frequently necessary as a preliminary to evaluation of the content of a message. Sometimes, too, we can make progress by consciously translating some of our own "purple prose" to less loaded synonyms before utterance.

Compensation for the Changing Nature of Words

Study the Influence of Contexts on Word Meaning. Whenever a word is used there are influences which determine important shades of meaning that make this particular usage unique. The elements preceding and following the word are perhaps most important in determining its meaning. Non-verbal influences include the nature of the source, the knowledge and prejudices of the persuadee, and attendant circumstances. Truly, no word has the same meaning twice. Recognition of these elements as influences in changing and determining word meaning should make us more cautious. We should be less willing to assume that our listener or reader understands precisely what we mean when we use a word. Appreciation of these influences dramatizes the need for clear definitions of key terms.

Mentally Indexing our Words. Language understanding can be increased by the use of the numerical sub-script. This is a little number after a key term in a particular usage to indicate that it has one meaning, the particular one determined by that context. As Hayakawa phrased it succinctly, Cow_1 is not Cow_2. This device of linking numbers with words reminds us that words can stand for many things, but that in this case one word means one particular thing. The habit of inserting little numbers after confusing words at least guarantees that we remain aware of multiple meanings.

Summary

It is necessary to understand the basic ingredients of language communication if the student is to become competent in analyzing or constructing persuasive messages.

Two characteristics of language are at the root of our linguistic difficulties: First, the fact that the word is only a representation of something else, and second, the fact that while we have only a limited number of words they must represent an infinite number of facts. To overcome difficulties we examined one aid provided by the semanticists, the concept of *levels of abstraction.* Definitions seem to be most helpful when lower levels of abstraction are reached. A word at a low level of abstraction can represent relatively fewer "life facts" than another word we might use at a higher level. Hence the opportunity for misunderstanding is reduced.

Examination of the responses made to units of language reveals that a fundamental distinction separates "signal" and "symbol" responses. The signal response occurs in the form of automatic and relatively uncritical reaction. Symbol response takes a little more time, is critical, and involves consideration not only of the stimulus but also of the context. A distinction paralleling this one of response was made in language meaning; to the extent that a communication produces "signal" response it has connotative meaning, and to the extent that it produces "symbol" response we say it has denotative content. Four sources of connotative meaning in popular language usage are slanting, figures of speech, euphemisms, and two-valued orientation. In most thoughtful communication increasing the amount of symbol response is desirable. We considered report language, the influence of context on word meaning, and the process of "indexing." Conscious effort to remember these distinctions will help to increase the precision of communication in persuasion.

Readings

1. Flesch, Rudolf, *The Art of Plain Talk.* New York: Harper and Brothers, 1946.
2. ——————, *The Art of Readable Writing.* New York: Harper and Brothers, 1949.
3. Hayakawa, S. I., *Language in Thought and Action.* New York: Harcourt, Brace and Company, 1949, Ch. 7.
4. Johnson, Wendell, *People in Quandaries.* New York: Harper and Brothers, 1946, Chaps. VIII, IX, X, XII.
5. Lee, Irving J., *Language Habits in Human Affairs.* New York: Harper and Brothers, 1941, Chaps. VI, VII, VIII, IX.

Exercises

1. Rewrite the Norman Bell account of the sinking of the U.S. cruiser Salt Lake City in strict "report language."

2. Find an editorial that uses terms in the upper levels of abstraction. Select a few key paragraphs and try re-writing them at the lower levels. Can this be done without changing the original meaning? Discuss the difficulties of converting abstractions to concrete instances.

3. Report to the class on the "two-valued orientation" used in cigarette advertising, and its relative reliance on "signal" and "symbol" responses.

4. Look for "euphemisms" on the editorial page of your daily newspaper. Replace any you find with the more blunt and accurate terms and analyze probable effects on readers.

5. What are the advantages and disadvantages of an extensive use of figurative language in persuasive speaking? Give specific examples to illustrate each.

Chapter X

THE PSYCHOLOGICAL FORMS OF PERSUASION

Chapter X

THE PSYCHOLOGICAL FORMS OF PERSUASION

Introduction

Just as logical appeals to the persuadee's reason may take various forms, as are discussed in Chapters XI and XII, so the psychological appeals or the appeals to the persuadee's emotions, motives, or desires may use various forms or appear in various effective settings. These are such a vital, inherent part of the process of persuasion as to be of prime concern to both the producer and consumer of persuasion. The form in which appeals are made may open or close entries into that inner shrine where dwell the sincere motives of men. The persuader must know how to gain access into this inner shrine of ours; the persuadee must know the methods of the persuader's appeals if he is to appraise critically those methods operative in arousing his desires and directing his motives.

We review below those forms which are in common use today. The list is not exhaustive. The reader should be on the lookout for new forms or techniques as the avenues to the minds of men continue to become more crowded with persuaders.

The forms of persuasion reveal the purposes and ethical standards of the persuaders. But forms or methods of one sort or another are employed by all manipulators of human motives. As Miller states in discussing the "devices" of the persuaders:

> They are employed by persuaders and propagandists who may be honest or dishonest, sincere or insincere, humanitarians or demagogues, scientists or charlatans, unselfish saints who build great religions of brotherhood or scoundrels who will ruin a man or nation to satisfy their avarice and vanity.
>
> They reveal the emphasis of decent men and the slanting of "stuffed shirts," "phonys," charlatans, demagogues.

They reflect the factors of distortion of the various channels of communication which are also the channels of persuasion: press, radio, cinema, church, school, Chamber of Commerce, labor union, grange, patriotic society, political party, government.[1]

Suggestion and Persuasion

Who has not experienced and watched others respond to the promptings of suggestion? It might have been a quick "yes" to a friend's "Have a cigarette?" or to the filling station attendant's "Fill 'er up?" or, again, it may have been your vain attempt to shrug off "Better Buy Buick" or "Vote Democratic." What reader, being familiar with the savage ecstasy of the historic Crusades, has not reflected on the power of mass suggestion? And the extreme form of suggestion—hypnosis—has been a curious phenomenon to people for many generations.

If the reader will reflect for a moment, he will realize that he is acting upon suggestion at almost every turn. Much, if not most, persuasion employs forms and methods which operate according to the laws of suggestion. It is important, therefore, that we precede our discussion of the specific methods or forms of persuasion by a brief review of the nature and laws of suggestion. Suggestion, as a general psychological method, will be found operative in various degrees in those specific forms or techniques discussed later in the chapter.

THE NATURE OF SUGGESTION

There is no uniform view among psychologists as to the complete nature of suggestion. The area of agreement is enlarging, however, and experimentation continues to throw light on disputed points. An analysis of suggestion must begin, of course, with the fact that an individual being affected by suggestion is responding to some stimulus or set of stimuli (stimulus-situation). The nature of the response will depend on the individual's internal condition —his physical wants, ideas, images, attitudes, and sentiments—and on the nature of the external stimulus (or stimuli) producing the response. In short, the response results from the perception of the stimulus and from the existing attitudes of the persuadee.

---

[1] Clyde R. Miller, *The Process of Persuasion.* New York: Crown Publishers, Inc., 1946, p. 146.

In a definition helpful to a persuader, Doob states that "suggestion results from the manipulation of stimulus-situations in such a way that, through the consequent arousal of pre-existing, related attitudes there occurs within the mental field a new integration which would not have occurred under different stimulus situations." [2] And "non-suggestion occurs when people merely perceive stimulus-situations and when the changes that take place within them as a result of the perception are independent of the attitudes that are aroused." [3]

Young defines suggestion "as a form of symbol-communication by words, pictures, or some similar medium inducing acceptance of the symbol without any self-evident or logical ground for its acceptance. However, suggestion is not a special mechanism, any more than is imitation. The acceptance (or rejection) of the proposition or symbol is determined by the stimulus and the internal conditions operating together. In this sense suggestibility is a phase of anticipatory activity which may either directly or indirectly affect conduct. The process of suggestion short-circuits logical analysis, inhibits critical restraint, and leads at once to the desired conclusion." [4] Young states further that "since we are moved far more effectively by emotions and feelings than by rational ideas, the most far-reaching effects of suggestion are produced by appeals to those emotionalized images, sentiments, and attitudes which rest upon previous conditioning." [5] "Not sociality, not rationality," says Sidis, "but suggestibility is what characterizes the average specimen of humanity, for *man is a suggestible animal*." [6]

It should be clear from the above statements that pre-existing attitudes and the proper manipulation of stimulus-situations are of major importance in suggestion and that suggestion tends to short-circuit the more critical and logical considerations of the problem.

---

[2] Leonard W. Doob, *Propaganda: Its Psychology and Technique*. New York: Henry Holt and Company, 1935, p. 54.

[3] *Ibid.*, p. 55.

[4] Kimball Young, *Social Psychology*. New York: Appleton-Century-Crofts, Inc., 1944, p. 110.

[5] *Ibid.*, p. 110.

[6] Boris Sidis, *The Psychology of Suggestion*. New York: D. Appleton and Company, 1921, p. 17.

THE TYPES OF SUGGESTION

When the focus is on its psychological aspects, suggestion may be classified as *ideomotor suggestion, prestige suggestion,* or *auto-suggestion.* When the approach is concerned with the direction of suggestion, one may classify suggestion as *direct, indirect, positive, negative,* or *counter-suggestion.*

Ideomotor Suggestion. We find this at the sensory-perceptual level. Ideas have an impulsive, dynamic nature, and when one enters the mind it tends to result in some action unless stopped by some competing idea. If you have been around where lice were reported, you may have felt an itching sensation, even though you may not have been host to any of the unwelcome bugs. All of us have seen the effects of repeatedly telling a perfectly healthy person that he or she looks sick. If you begin a college course with the idea that it will be boring, it has a good chance of turning out so.

The ouija board operates on this principle. The persons around the board place their fingers on the movable member and ask ouija a question. While "concentrating" on the problem and knowing that "yes" would be a very desirable answer to the question, the players involuntarily push toward the "yes" corner. Clairvoyants make use of the same principle, watching or tactually noting closely the involuntary muscular contractions of the subject.

Illustrations of ideomotor suggestion are all about us. The persuader will do well to ponder the usefulness of such a principle.

Prestige Suggestion. Persuaders of all varieties use the appeal of a great name. The soap manufacturers may get a Hollywood star to underwrite the merits of their product; the teacher may seek to gain acceptance for his concept by relating it to the work of some noted authority, and the preacher may motivate others to live better lives by reminding them of great men of the past.

Great orators and others in positions of authority owe at least some of their power over others to their ability to arouse submissive attitudes. Prestige suggestion has been increased by such means as publicity and by elevated speaking rostrums which place the hearer in a submissive relationship to the speaker.

This type of suggestion is very strong. When the prestige is achieved through genuine merit it can help persuasion. When it rests upon artificially created bases, it may be successful but it rests, indeed, on precarious and questionable foundations.

Auto-Suggestion. This type is a matter of selling ourselves something. Here the individual directs his own thought and action. Auto-suggestion often has its start in prestige suggestion, but proceeds on its own. A classic example is the belief people showed in Emile Coué, a French popular psychologist, who championed the theory that people could cure themselves of worry, mild illnesses, and anxieties by repeating over and over to themselves, "Day by day, in every way, I am getting better and better." The well-known song "Great Day," by Vincent Youmans, makes use of the same principle when it suggests that "When you're down and out Lift up your head and shout There's gonna be a Great Day." *

In sum, persuasion here takes the form of helping others persuade themselves.

Direct Suggestion. This enables the individual to perceive the suggestor's immediate aim, for it comes in an explicit, straight-forward manner. It says "Buy war bonds," "See America first," "Let's put an end to the pilfering along the Potomac," "Drive safely, for the life you save may be your own," and so on. Usually couched in "loaded words," the direct suggestion generally seeks acceptance in a more immediate manner than does the more lengthy logical considerations of courses of action or grounds for belief.

Indirect Suggestion. Because its aim is difficult to detect, this is more subtle than direct suggestion. It is used by persuaders who, for one reason or another, wish their purposes to be concealed. The indirect suggestion of Shakespeare's villain Iago in Othello is a classic example. At no time did Iago let Othello, the suggestible Moor, know that his purpose was to ruin Othello by getting him to slay his beautiful wife, Desdemona. Iago, knowing of Othello's pre-existing attitudes of jealousy, gradually and cleverly manipulated the stimulus-situations in such a way as to get Othello to suspect his innocent wife of unfaithfulness and, as a result, to murder her.

Oliver gives some helpful hints regarding the use of direct and indirect suggestion: [7]

---

* "Great Day," lyrics by William Rose and Edward Eliscu, music by Vincent Youmans. Copyright 1929 MILLER MUSIC CORPORATION and Vincent Youmans, Inc. Used by special permission.

[7] Robert T. Oliver, *The Psychology of Persuasive Speech.* New York: Longmans, Green and Company, 1942, pp. 234, 235.

Direct Suggestion	*Indirect Suggestion*
Use when the audience is polarized.	Use when the audience is mentally alert.
Use when the audience feels itself inferior to the speaker intellectually or in other ways.	Use when the audience feels itself equal or superior to the speaker intellectually or in other ways.
Use when the speaker's prestige is high.	Use when the speaker's prestige is comparatively low.
Use when addressing youthful auditors.	Use when addressing adults.
Use when some immediate, definite, precise form of action is required.	Use when the aim is to create an attitude or belief which may lead to future action.
Use when the speaker is completely master of the speech situation.	Use when the speaker is comparatively unskilled.

Positive Suggestion. To state or phrase a suggestion affirmatively is to use *positive suggestion.* Generally, suggestion is strongest at its "positive pole." "Thou shalt" is coming to be considered more effective than "Thou shalt not." The mother who says, "Willie, you will come home immediately after school today," is a wise lady, but the mother who says, "Johnny, don't go skating after school today, but come right home," is likely to see Johnny coming home late, for she has planted within his mind a competing and negative idea which he must overcome before he can come home.

Negative Suggestion. This kind is designed to get the persuadee to avoid some act or belief. Campaigners for better health, public safety, and so on, often use negative suggestion. In general, negative suggestion is not as effective as positive suggestion. The negative element or aspect of the suggestion may not remain as long or as vivid as the positive element in a suggestion. The negative aspect may actually invite its opposite. To read "Do not open until Christmas" on a package may make it all the more difficult to desist.

Negative suggestion also suffers from the lack of a constructive decisiveness. In this regard it has value to the agitator and reformer who is more clear on what he is against than on what he is for.

The persuader should rely chiefly on positive suggestion. Negative suggestion should be used with great care and then perhaps only in combination with positive suggestion.

Counter Suggestion. A positive or negative suggestion is used in the hope of receiving an opposite response. We know there are those who are "contra-suggestible," that is, contrary souls who can be relied upon to do just the opposite of what is suggested. To tell the boy, "You aren't big enough to help get the hay into the barn" may be the very technique needed to get him to help do a tiring job. To tell the stubborn parent that his son is probably not capable of college work may be the way to get the father to send his boy to the best college in the country. And to tell the freshman, uninterested in fraternities, that he "Doesn't have what it takes to get in a fraternity," may send him forth full steam ahead in his goal to pledge the best fraternity in Greek row.

The persuader must keep in mind one basic fact when he is tempted to use counter-suggestion: If it does not succeed, he has reaped the opposite of what he desired.

THE LAWS OF SUGGESTION

Having studied briefly the nature and classifications of suggestion, it should be helpful now to consider some general rules or laws which seem to characterize the function of suggestion. The reader will note the relationship of these laws to the points discussed above. Hollingworth has formulated seven laws of suggestion which include the chief rules governing suggestion.

> 1. The strength of a suggestion depends in part on the degree to which it seems to be of spontaneous origin, an act of the individual's own initiative. Arrogance and domination are at once and instinctively resented and resisted. The more indirect the suggestion, the more it can be made to be an original determination or plan or conclusion on the part of the listener, the greater its dynamic power.
>
> 2. Within the limits of the law just indicated, the dynamic power of a suggestion will be the greater, the more forcefully and vividly it is presented. This is especially true when the suggested act is in harmony with the pre-established habits and tendencies. When the suggestion violates life-long habits and instincts, attempts to be forceful and vigorous usually lapse into arrogance and thereby defeat their own purpose.
>
> 3. It is more effective to suggest the desired response directly than it is to argue against a response that is not desired. Suggestion is most active at its positive pole, and the negative suggestion tends to defeat its own purpose. The Old Covenant with its

"Thou Shalt Not" was readily displaced by the New Covenant with its simple, positive "Thou Shalt."

4. The action power of a suggestion varies directly with the prestige of its source. The more we revere a speaker, for any reason whatsoever, the greater confidence we tend to place in anything he may say, and the more prone we are to imitate him and to adopt his suggestions, even when they are unsupported by sufficient reasons.

5. The strength of a suggestion will be determined in part by the degree of internal resistance it encounters. That suggestion will be most effective which can call to its aid or appropriate the dynamic force of some other impulse that is already active or latent. Suggestions to violate life-long habits, firmly fixed moral feelings, and sacred relationships are impotent, even during the pronounced suggestibility of the hypnotic trance.

6. The strength of a suggestion varies with the frequency with which it is met. But mere mechanical repetition avails little unless the repeated suggestion is attended to with interest. Experiment shows that repetition of advertising appeals is twice as effective when the form, style, and expression is varied, with constant theme, as when exact duplication of previous appeals is used. Repetition accompanied by sufficient variety to lend interest but with sufficient uniformity to acquire a constant meaning, produces a genuine cumulative effect.

7. In appealing over the short circuit for a specific line of action, no interference, substitute, rival idea, or opposing action should be suggested. Such an idea merely impedes the action power of the first suggestion, by inviting comparison and thus involves deliberate choice and hesitation.[8]

SUGGESTIBILITY

Thus far we have been concerned with suggestion as a stimulus and how this stimulus may be made to arouse desired responses. We turn now to the persuadee. Is he suggestible? To answer this, the persuader must know the facts of suggestibility. Usually suggestibility is considered to be a trait of personality. Actually many factors play a part in creating suggestibility.

External Conditions. Such items as prestige-bearing statements, bright colors, pleasant and rhythmic tunes, temperature, architectural design, and the amount of social facilitation all make for suggestibility. The physical setting of the speech can weaken or

---

[8] H. L. Hollingworth, *The Psychology of the Audience.* New York: American Book Company, 1935, pp. 142–144.

strengthen the persuasion. This is discussed later under the heading "The Atmosphere Effect."

Internal Conditions. Those internal conditions favoring suggestibility are fatigue, prejudices, emotional disturbances giving rise to uncontrolled associations, anxieties of all sorts (as in time of war), lack of organized knowledge, sex (women and girls are slightly more suggestible than men and boys), narcotics and intoxicants, age (suggestibility tends to decrease as age increases), and intelligence (those of low intelligence tend to be more suggestible than those of high intelligence).

But even though individuals may differ as to the *degree* of suggestibility, *all are suggestible.* It remains for the persuader to so prepare the stimulus-situations in terms of the persuadee's pre-existing attitudes, ideas, and sentiments that the desired response is achieved.

The Psychological Forms of Persuasion

THE ATMOSPHERE EFFECT

The setting in which the persuasive speech is to be made is of considerable importance. If the audience is to be rendered suggestible to a desired end, all surrounding stimuli of the occasion and place must be favorable; stimuli that offer competing ideas and distractions must be eliminated. This may include favorable advance publicity and an effective introduction of the speaker. The speaker's physical position in relation to the audience should give him dominance. The visual symbols in the room should be appropriate. Flags on patriotic occasions play a significant role. The bunting, flags, slogan-banners, music, pictures of party greats, and so on all help in political conventions. The salesman who rents a luxurious hotel suite for his day of interviews with wealthy clients has the right idea, just as does the antique dealer who houses his antiques in a building characterized by period architectural design.

Many of us have witnessed the failure of an otherwise impressive speech because of a squeaky door, uncomfortable seats, "stuffy" air conditions, poor acoustics, or improper lighting. Odors, too, have their effect in the work of suggestion.

Commercial houses and speakers are becoming increasingly aware of the role proper environmental factors play in persuasion and often go to considerable expense to prepare conducive "atmospheres."

THE "TOGETHER DEVICE" [9]

To get hearers to become more aware of each other's responses and thus to create greater uniformity of response—a more polarized audience—the persuader can have the audience members do things together. To do this it is quite important first to have the hearers seated shoulder-to-shoulder. It is difficult to create a psychological crowd out of a small audience scattered throughout a large auditorium.

Persuaders of all types use the "Together Device." The grand old hymn or responsive reading the preacher calls for helps create a favorable unity. An appropriate song can melt individual differences into a more unified chorus of belief. The "show of hands" approach in seeking answers to questions regarding religious or political status, residence, beliefs on common enemies, and so on, of the audience has been found helpful in uniting an audience.

Dictators have used such devices as "Heil Hitler," the "Goose Step" and the "Sieg Heil" salute. In 1934 Reich Minister of the Interior, Dr. Frick, in a letter to the Deutscher Industrie—und Handelstag, enlisted the co-operation of the "roof" organization of trade and industry in giving the German salute more nation-wide application. Said Dr. Frick, "It is a task of popular enlightenment to introduce the German salute among all sections of the German people as the expression of national solidarity." [10]

The "Together Device" also tends to give the illusion of universality, whether it be by a mass parade or by saying to the customer: "This is what *they* are wearing this season."

Churches, fraternities and many other organizations use rituals of various kinds to help create group solidarity. In fact, all movements which seek some common denominator of the beliefs and actions of people rely upon "Together Devices." As Miller points out, "History is largely the record of the successes and failures of the 'Together Device.' The record is seen in the spread of various religions; the rise and fall of feudalism; the Reformation; the

---

[9] This term is used by Clyde R. Miller in *Process of Persuasion.* New York: Crown Publishers, Inc., 1946.

[10] *Hamburger Fremdenblatt,* No. 34, February 4, 1934 (Evening Edition).

rise of capitalism, fascism and communism; the scientific concept; public health movements such as those to fight infantile paralysis and tuberculosis." [11]

COMMON GROUND

"When Pat went to Mike and said, 'Let's talk over our differences,' the wiser Mike replied, 'No, let's talk over our agreements.' Mike's method was likely to lead to a settlement; Pat's to a fight." [12]

To minimize disagreements and to emphasize the area of agreement between persuadee and persuader has always been effective practice. One of the persuader's first tasks is to discover this *common ground.* Each of us has witnessed heated arguments which were dispelled when it was discovered that the disputants were actually in agreement but were arguing because the initial statements were not clear enough to expose the common ground that actually existed.

If the persuader gives the impression of a feeling of superiority, we rebel immediately; if he evidences a "calculated" tolerance of our views, we may question his sincerity; but if he strikes a true common ground and genuinely develops his persuasion in terms of it, we will trust him.

Common grounds may be found in our interests, feelings, and beliefs. To find these areas of commonalty implies an accurate analysis of the audience beliefs, attitudes, ideas, and interests.[13] Knowing these, the persuader can proceed to establish that common ground useful to his purposes.

Most of the master persuaders have demonstrated ability in this regard. Christ's common-ground approach came largely in parables —parables of the fishermen, the husbandmen of the vineyards, and the shepherds of the flocks. Henry Ward Beecher was failing in his early preaching until a review of the sermons of the apostles gave him the key to his later greatness.

> And I studied the sermons until I got this idea: That the apostles were accustomed first to feel for a ground on which the people and they stood together; a common ground where they

---

[11] Miller, *op. cit.,* p. 214.

[12] James A. Winans, *Public Speaking* (Rev. ed.). New York: Appleton-Century-Crofts, Inc., 1917, p. 263.

[13] See Chapter XVII for a detailed discussion of this point.

could meet. Then they heaped up a large number of the particulars of knowledge that belonged to everybody; and when they got that knowledge, which everybody would admit, placed in a proper form before their minds, then they brought it to bear upon them with all their excited heart and feeling. That was the first definite idea of taking aim that I had in my mind.

"Now," said I, "I will make a sermon so" . . . First I sketched out the things we all know . . . And in that way I went on with my "you all knows," until I had about forty of them. When I got through with that, I turned round and brought it to bear upon them with all my might; and there were seventeen men awakened under that sermon. I never felt so triumphant in my life. I cried all the way home. I said to myself: "Now I know how to preach." [14]

Theodore Roosevelt always made a special effort to know in advance the interests, feelings, and beliefs of potential supporters and developed his speech in these terms. In World War II Winston Churchill helped, in no small measure, to hold an empire together by appeals to the great common heritage of all Englishmen of courage and culture in this "their finest hour." In a masterful stroke of persuasion, Franklin Delano Roosevelt created the "Fireside Chats" to talk over our common problems.

To strike a common ground, many persuaders have used the "plain folks" device of appearing as just "one of the boys." The Congressman up for re-election may get into some overalls and ride the prize bull at the county fair, or be photographed milking a cow out on his farm. The homely suspenders worn by a canvassing candidate usually are doing more than just holding up his trousers. The lawyer, dressed in a very ordinary suit, may make references to his own "life on the farm" as he attempts to persuade the rural jurors.

On the other hand, the salesman who is working among members of the "exclusive set" may rent a large and new car, keep meticulously dressed and brush up on all social graces. In short, he, too, is attempting to appear to "belong" to this social situation.

As is apparent, the applications of the common ground method are many and varied; some are sincerely conceived and others nothing more than artifice. The perceptive persuadee can discover the

---

[14] Henry Ward Beecher, *Yale Lectures on Preaching.* Chicago: The Pilgrim Press, 1902, p. 11.

difference. Genuine common bonds based sincerely on common interests, emotions or beliefs, are strong and would appear to be ethical means of persuasion.

RATIONALIZATION

Rationalization is a way of protecting our sentiment of self-regard. It assigns logical, intelligent "reasons" for opinions and conducts which are really non-rational. People don't want to appear irrational to others, so they gain facility in justifying, logically, their behavior. The older and more intelligent we are the more proficient and subtle we become in this matter. Such a procedure soothes our consciences and often protects us from facing the disconcerting reality of some very selfish and socially unapproved desires and behaviors.

We may rationalize *before* or *after* the act. Of course, you won't be guilty of such behavior, so watch your room mate start rationalizing his attendance at the Junior Prom next week, even though he (or she) has two important examinations the following morning. Or, as an example of after-the-fact rationalization, listen to him (or her) justify missing that twenty inch putt or going into debt for that new car.

A persuader can use rationalization in the following ways:

(1) If the persuadee already has a desire for your product or for any other course of action or belief, then persuasion becomes the process of helping the individual justify the desired end or, in short, of helping the person rationalize.

(2) A second use is suggested by Ewbank and Auer ". . . we may use rationalization as a "short circuit" appeal in persuading others to accept conclusions we have reached on a rational basis. . . . The purpose, of course, is to present via the "short circuit" approach what cannot, for reasons of time, perhaps, be presented in detail. And the persuader may feel himself ethically justified in using a non-rational technique to gain acceptance of a conclusion which he himself has reached on a rational basis." [15] (See Chapter XX for further discussion of this point.)

---

[15] H. L. Ewbank and J. J. Auer, *Discussion and Debate* (2nd Ed.). New York: Appleton-Century-Crofts, Inc., 1951, p. 47.

REPETITION

As was pointed out earlier, the strength of a suggestion varies with the frequency with which it is met. Repetition serves to clarify and to hold attention to an idea until it becomes a part of us. It may appear in two forms: (1) The repetition may use the same words (exact repetition), or (2) the same idea may be stated in different words (restatement).

The use of the slogan is the most familiar example of the first form. Who does not know the products referred to in the following? "The Breakfast of Champions," "Ask the man who owns one," "From Contented Cows," "LS/MFT." In the political area we have seen the effect of "The Divine Right of Kings," "No Entangling Alliances," "Don't Switch Horses in Mid-stream," and "Government of the people, by the people and for the people." No persuader in modern times understood the effectiveness of repetition more than did Adolf Hitler. "Tell a people a thing often enough and they will, ere long, believe it to be true," was Hitler's motto.

> Hitler, either by design or because of his lack of creativeness, hit upon an elementary electioneering truth and has adhered to it ever since. He knows that an uneducated political public wants endless repetition of a few trite phrases; and he has kept on parroting certain fixed phrases for over fifteen years. A brainier man would have wearied of this role of human gramophone, but, even today, every speech of Hitler's is mainly composed of the same old generalizations, the same old denunciations, the same old form of patriotism.[16]

In a study of the American agitator, Lowenthal and Guterman made an examination of a series of agitational speeches and writings and found "unmistakable similarity of their content and tone." There were recurrent motifs, the "constants of agitation."[17]

The effectiveness of continued repetition was tested on September 21, 1943—War Bond Day for the Columbia Broadcasting System. During a span of eighteen hours—8 a.m. to 2 a.m.—Kate Smith spoke from one to two minutes at repeated intervals. Her audi-

---

[16] Stephen H. Roberts, *The House that Hitler Built.* New York: Harper and Brothers, 1938, p. 15.

[17] Leo Lowenthal and Norbert Guterman, *Prophets of Deceit.* New York: Harper and Brothers, 1949, p. 5.

ence was estimated at between twenty-one to twenty-three million listeners. On sixty-five different occasions throughout the eighteen-hour persuasion marathon, Miss Smith asked (in various ways) her hearers to buy war bonds. Her repeated slogan—"Will you buy a bond?"—was mentioned by listeners more often than any other part of the content of her broadcasts. This slogan was combined with a variety of appeals. During this extraordinary example of mass persuasion Kate Smith sold thirty-nine million dollars worth of bonds.

In a study of this example of mass persuasion, Merton and others observe that "*Repetition with variation* of appeals proved an important element in the process of persuasion. Smith's broadcasts aimed at one and the same goal, but each was unique. The effect, therefore, was not one of mere reiteration. And the goal, in this instance, was an act which the listener was expected to perform. Each new entreaty sought out a new *vulnerability* in some listeners." [18] This study is discussed further in Chapter XXII.

Jersild [19] found that the most effective form of emphasis in public speaking is repetition to the extent of three or more presentations, but that the benefit arising from repetition "does not increase in proportion to the number of added repetitions."

In closing this discussion of *repetition,* the reader is encouraged to re-read Hollingworth's sixth law of suggestion quoted earlier in the chapter.

PRESTIGE

"Whatever has been a ruling power in the world," says LeBon, "whether it be ideas or men, has in the main enforced its authority by means of that irresistible force expressed by the word 'prestige.' " [20]

You will recall that one of the laws of suggestion stated that the motivational power of a suggestion varies directly with the prestige of its source. The prestige of a persuader, whether natural or acquired, long has been recognized as playing an important role

---

[18] Robert K. Merton and others, *Mass Persuasion.* New York: Harper and Brothers, 1946, p. 36.

[19] A. T. Jersild, "Modes of Emphasis in Public Speaking," *Journal of Applied Psychology* (December, 1928), 12: 611–622.

[20] Gustav LeBon, *The Crowd* (14th Impression). London: T. Fisher Unwin, 1922, p. 147.

in persuasion. If the persuader is known by us ("an old friend of the family" or a "solid citizen") we are much more ready to accept his suggestions.

When the speaker is not known, he must constantly be alert to the creation of a favorable reputation. Individuals and large corporations who cannot do this alone hire able "public relations" agents whose job is to build prestige for their clients. This has become a thriving profession in modern society where impersonal relations are so widespread. Public relations men create favorable prestige for political candidates, corporations, products of all sorts, universities, enterprises, and movements of many types. Publicist Ivy Lee changed John D. Rockefeller's reputation from a greedy, rather scheming individual to a kindly, religious, and generous human benefactor.

In sum, to support one's arguments by relating them to "prestige" names is usually helpful. The beginning salesman soon learns the value of mentioning that a respected neighbor or civic leader uses his product.

THE SCAPEGOAT

The *scapegoat* is a target used by individuals or groups for the absorption of tensions of one sort or another. Persuaders of dubious ethical standards have become proficient in directing people's pent-up emotional energies at scapegoat targets, thus giving the appearance of helping solve the problem at hand but actually only supplying targets for aggressive feelings aroused by the problem.

Christ became the scapegoat of certain special interests of his day; the Christians were convenient scapegoats for Nero's failure; Hitler charged the problems of Germany to the Jews, the Treaty of Versailles, and the "bolshevik" menace. *Never* was national Socialism at fault. This appeal to hatred and prejudices hit a peak in the German Lord Haw-Haw's broadcasts to England during World War II. Winston Churchill was his special target. Churchill became "Winnie in Wonderland," "the evil old wretch." "Roly, Poly, Windsy Churchill," and "this mean corrupt little man," while the rulers of England became "the degenerates of Downing Street," "these fat and pompous plutocrats," and "the apostles of Mammon."

In our own country the Wall Street bankers, the New Dealers, the Catholics, the Jews, and the "foreigners" among us have been among the chief scapegoats.

Most "name calling" is done to arouse hatred and to focus aggressiveness on a convenient, external target. As individuals, most of us find scapegoats when they are needed; it is so much easier and more ego-protecting than actually facing the situation squarely and solving it.

Ambitious demagogues and professional agitators are among the most frequent users of this form of persuasion. Their method should be exposed and condemned.

THE BIG LIE

In our extremely complex society, in complicated, unverifiable situations in international affairs, the use of the outright lie is possible. Under some conditions the liar may have just as much advantage as the honest man. Nazi propagandists were said to have operated on the theory that "the bigger the lie, the more easily it is believed, that its very fantastic nature makes it more creditable."

Flagrant dishonesty in advertising is more rare now. However, before the passage of the Pure Food and Drug Acts, a considerable number of large falsifications were exposed. Nonetheless, the reader and listener still have to beware of the unnamed "expert," sweeping claims of many kinds, and undocumented statistics.

Since the "big lie" technique is not easy to detect, everyone should be alert to the symptoms of its presence and ready to expose such fraud. It is regrettable that the ethical standards of some persuaders permit such procedures. Such unprincipled men usually use for carrying their lies media which cannot be readily checked, like whispering campaigns, leaflets, and unverified "reports" which are smuggled into the columns of various newspapers.

THE STRATEGY OF TERROR

Each generation seems to have a few persuaders in high and low places who chafe under the more tedious process of change through peaceful persuasion, yet who are sufficiently sensitive to social pressures not to engage in a complete system of force. As a result, they use a combination of force and symbolic persuasion to achieve their ends. On an international scale we have the "atrocity stories" based on just enough fact to increase the effectiveness of printed and broadcast propaganda. During World War II we saw atrocity propaganda backfire; it was found that atrocity stories tended to *increase* the resistance of the enemy and to beget other atrocities. Therefore the nations at war began to emphasize the "kind treatment" given prisoners of war. This was a much wiser procedure.

In our day we see a new emphasis on another use of the strategy of terror. We are seeing "warfare waged psychologically" in contrast to "psychological warfare."[21] Hitler used this type of terror strategy from 1936 to 1941, and Soviet Russia used it after World War II. This type of warfare (sometimes referred to as a war of nerves), with its surprise attacks and ever-threatening nature, does not have military victory as its goal, but victory through the attendant confusion, the panic, and the demoralizing effect it has on the enemy. This same method is used by those who incite riots, foster rebellious parades, mass demonstrations, and other panic-producing displays of force. The "strong arm" man in the third ward, the occasional disappearance of "uncooperative" businessmen who will not pay "protection" money, and the note threatening kidnaping if a sum is not paid are all cases in point. More subtle uses of the strategy of terror are unfounded accusations leveled against office holders. Common among these is the treason charge.[22]

These examples use the strategy of terror and its appeals to fear as the basic ingredients of the persuasion. This technique seeks to lessen resistance and to gain acceptance by creating anxieties, panic, hysteria, confusion, dissension, and futility. Such tactics represent the lowest and most reprehensible form of motivation and should be eliminated wherever and whenever possible.

---

[21] For an excellent treatment of these concepts see Paul M. A. Linebarger, *Psychological Warfare.* Washington: Infantry Journal Press, 1948, Ch. III.

[22] See W. S. Howell, "The Persuasive Utility of the Treason Charge," *The Gavel* (May, 1950), XXXII: 76, 77, 86.

WORD MANIPULATIONS [23]

Word manipulations are considered last because, having studied the other forms, the reader is in a position to see how the manipulations of words can and do operate in conjunction with all the other forms or techniques mentioned above.

"He who wants to persuade," said Joseph Conrad, "should put his trust not in the right argument, but in the right word. . . . Give me the right word and the right accent and I will move the world." And Joseph Conrad was right, indeed, for the right manipulation of words has been moving people since the beginning of human speech. Miller tells this interesting story:

> Clarence Darrow, the famous criminal lawyer, once told me of his early boyhood in Ohio and how he "read law" under a country attorney with a local reputation for unusual success in swaying juries. "Once," said Darrow, "he was trying a libel suit. He was attorney for the plaintiff. The defendant was a newspaper editor. Libel suits are hard to win and yet my friend won his suit.
>
> "Congratulating him later on the favorable verdict the jury had rendered, I said to him, 'Sir, if you don't mind my raising the point, I was puzzled by your pronunciation of the word "libelous." You kept pronouncing it throughout the trial as though it were spelled "libeelious." You do know, of course, that that is not how it is pronounced.'
>
> "'Certainly I know,' was his answer. 'And also I knew what I was doing when I pronounced it "libeelious." You see, "libelous" correctly pronounced has a dry, technical, colorless sound, but when pronounced "libeelious" it sounds frightfully evil and wicked. I know the men on that jury. I have grown up with some of them. I know how they feel about evil, wicked things and I knew just what response that evil-sounding word would evoke. Well, it worked all right. We won.'" [24]

Words which have been used in the heat and fire of daily crises take on "loaded" meanings; they elicit "yes" or "no" responses from us. Compare such words as "mother," "home," "hearth," "heaven," "godly," "decent," and "American" with "rascal," "devil-

---

[23] The reader should review Chapter IX, *The Language of Persuasion,* and the section on *Stereotypes* in Chapter VII, *Attitudes, Sentiments and Stereotypes in Persuasion.*

[24] Miller, *op. cit.,* page 119–120.

ish," "communist," "tyranny," "dictator," "conniving," "liar," and "decadent."

Such words, when fitted into our system of stereotypes, carry effective motivating power and can "move or change the world." Evidences of effective word manipulation are all about us. "The Divine Right of Kings" (mentioned earlier) was a masterpiece of word manipulation if not of political integrity. To label a congressional bill's purpose as "taxation for unemployment insurance" goes against our "taxation" stereotype and causes us to rebel, but call it "Social Security" and we vote for it. We built "victory" ships during World War II. The sting of the defeat of the British at Dunkirk was lessened by calling it a "glorious retreat" and a "miraculous escape." Our "arsenal for democracy" helped motivate full production, and the American's respect for the British was increased when we were told Britain was the "citadel of freedom" in the dark days after Dunkirk. The "lend-lease" bill's name certainly helped in overcoming an almost natural opposition to giving up war materials to other countries.

The persuadee must be alert to the types of word manipulations used on him and should be able to assess their justification. The persuader must, within ethical limits, decide what trigger-words are needed to release the response he desires from his audience.

The "Devices" of the Institute for Propaganda Analysis

In 1937 the Institute for Propaganda Analysis in the United States began; it ceased functioning shortly before this country entered World War II. Financed to a great extent by philanthropist Edward A. Filene, sponsored and directed by various individuals attached to academic institutions, and operated largely by journalists, this organization sought to help our citizens in the analysis of propaganda. Most of the time the Institute analyzed propaganda in terms of seven "devices." These devices or forms of persuasion were found to be helpful and, as a result, became well known among analysts of all types of persuasion. It is fitting, therefore, to include the Institute's own summary of these techniques.[25]

> *Name Calling*—giving an idea a bad label—is used to make us reject and condemn the idea without examining the evidence.

[25] Alfred McClung Lee and Elizabeth Briant Lee (eds.), *The Fine Art of Propaganda.* New York: Harcourt, Brace and Company, 1939, pp. 23, 24.

Glittering Generality—associating something with a "virtue word"—is used to make us accept and approve the thing without examining the evidence.

Transfer carries the authority, sanction, and prestige of something respected and revered over to something else in order to make the latter acceptable; or it carries authority, sanction, and disapproval to cause us to reject and disapprove something the propagandist would have us reject and disapprove.

Testimonial consists in having some respected or hated person say that a given idea or program or product or person is good or bad.

Plain Folks is the method by which a speaker attempts to convince the audience that he and his ideas are good because they are "of the people," the "plain folks."

Card Stacking involves the selection and use of facts or falsehoods, ilustrations or distractions, and logical or illogical statements in order to give the best or the worst possible case for an idea, program, person, or product.

Band Wagon has as its theme, "Everybody—at least all of us—is doing it"; with it, the propagandist attempts to convince us that all members of a group to which we belong are accepting his program and that we *must therefore* follow our crowd and "jump on the band wagon."

Summary and Conclusions

In this chapter we have discussed those forms, methods, or techniques in which the persuasion addressed primarily to the psychological elements may appear. Both the persuader and persuadee have been shown the strength, weaknesses, and ethical dimensions of these methods. That these forms or methods become, in actual practice, an inherent part of the persuasion should be clear.

It was pointed out that the psychology of suggestion plays a vital role in the operation of the methods themselves, and that a student of persuasion needs to understand the nature, types, and laws of suggestion if he is to grasp a more complete understanding of the operation of the psychological forms of persuasion.

The forms which were discussed include those in greatest use today. These include the methods of all types of persuaders. The reader has been urged to evaluate not only the strengths and limitations of each method but also its ethical considerations. In the persuasion density in which we live we are caught almost constantly in the web of some psychological form of persuasion. These often are so common or so subtle that they escape detection.

Readings

1. Doob, Leonard W., *Propaganda; its Psychology and Technique.* New York: Henry Holt and Company, 1935, Chapter V, "Suggestion, Prestige and Social Change."
2. Fried, Edrita, "Techniques of Persuasion," in Childs, H. L., and Whitton, J. B., *Propaganda By Short Wave.* Princeton: Princeton University Press, 1943, pp. 263–301.
3. Miller, C. W., *The Process of Persuasion.* New York: Crown Publishers, Inc., 1946, Part II, "Persuasion Methods."
4. Oliver, R. T., *The Psychology of Persuasive Speech.* New York: Longmans, Green and Co., Inc., 1942, Ch. VIII, "Suggestion."
5. Taylor, Edmond, *The Strategy of Terror.* Boston: Houghton Mifflin Company, 1940.

Exercises

1. Clip several advertisements from newspapers and magazines. Analyze for your class the types of suggestion used in the advertisements.

2. Select some propaganda organization for study. Write an 800 word paper on the organization's use of the psychological forms of persuasion.

3. Go to hear a political speech on your campus. Observe the speaker's use of the psychological forms of persuasion. Report your analysis of the speech to your class.

4. Prepare and present a six-minute persuasive speech which uses one or more of the following forms of persuasion:

a. The Atmosphere Effect
b. The Together Device
c. Common Ground
d. Rationalization
e. Repetition
f. Prestige
g. Word manipulations

5. Write a 300 word paper on "Ethical Considerations in the Use of the Psychological Forms of Persuasion."

Chapter XI

THE LOGICAL TECHNIQUES OF PERSUASION

Part I: Argument by Statistics, Circumstantial Detail, Comparison, and Analogy

Chapter XI

THE LOGICAL TECHNIQUES OF PERSUASION—PART I

Introduction

Reasoned argument is aimed at influencing the listener or reader to suspend judgment and look for the facts before making up his mind. The student should be able to (1) classify and interpret reasoned discourse arguments which he encounters in written and spoken language, and (2) prepare valid and persuasive reasoned discourse argument for use in his own persuasive efforts. Wherever forms of reasoned discourse have been simplified, mention will be made of specific sources which will provide additional information.

The Nature and Uses of Evidence in Reasoned Discourse

The possible truths which lead through reasoning to the discovery and acceptance of other possible truths (conclusions) constitute the raw materials of reasoned discourse, or *evidence*. The manner in which those truths are used is termed *reasoning*. Consequently, the complete process of composing reasoned discourse consists of utilizing information (evidence) in a manner such that conclusions become justified.

What constitutes evidence? Ewbank and Auer make a useful distinction. "All evidence is based upon matters of fact. Evidence comes chiefly from two sources, observations of facts and opinions about facts. So in terms of their sources we will discuss two types of evidence: (1) Evidence of fact, and (2) evidence of opinion."[1]

Evidence, then, is seen to be the basic "construction material"

[1] H. L. Ewbank and J. J. Auer, *Discussion and Debate.* New York: Appleton-Century-Crofts, Inc., 1941, p. 117.

on which reasoned argument is based. It is used in two forms, fact evidence and opinion evidence. Can we distinguish reliably between these forms? We consider fact evidence to be evidence that is verifiable. It is a reporting of some reality in a fashion such that both the reporting and the existence of information cited can be "checked up on." If a bit of evidence is *fact* evidence it can be validated. If we possess such evidence a person arguing against us may challenge the use or interpretation made of that evidence, but he will be unable to challenge the evidence itself.

The category of evidence of opinion is a wide one. It ranges from the inexpert and non-experimental opinions to the most expert and carefully supported judgments. For example, at one time or another we all are advised to adapt our behavior to some maxim or other. If we are inclined to postpone action we are told that "a stitch in time saves nine." If we are inclined to act hastily, we are told that "haste makes waste." We are advised that ferocious dogs will not bite little children, that men who are unpleasant at the office are henpecked at home, that there are no Irish on the Notre Dame football team, that captains always go down with their ships, and so on. These popular beliefs are perhaps the weakest type of opinion evidence and constitute, really, no evidence at all.

Closely related to the totally non-experimental social maxim is the broad generalization of many political speakers. We are told that price control will result in a police state, that raising taxes will destroy free enterprise, and that grass will grow in the streets if the other party is elected to office. The speaker who uses such strong positive assertions is benefiting from the resemblance of those statements to the maxims which we tend to accept. He probably hopes to sound so definite and sure of the truth of his absolute statement that we will accept it without question.

The great danger connected with this type of opinion evidence is the possibility that the assertion will be accepted as a fact. Indeed, that often seems to be the intention of the person resorting to such assertions. As an example of a bit of evidence of opinion that may masquerade as a fact we have a statement by Representative Charles Halleck of Indiana made shortly after President Truman had called a special session of Congress in the summer of 1948. "It cannot be denied that Mr. Truman in calling the session sought political advantage at whatever expense to the country rather than sane, sensible legislation to be worked out in a spirit of harmony and cooperation for the good of the country."[2]

Note that this statement records as a *fact* that President Truman convened Congress for selfish political purposes rather than the obtaining of legislation for the good of the United States. Note, too, how the statement is strengthened by use of the words "It cannot be denied." How do we go about examining this statement before we classify it as fact or opinion? We suggest two simple questions as a criterion of classification: "Can he prove it?" and "How?" Perhaps, after you have asked yourselves these questions, you will agree that the words "It cannot be denied" should be replaced by the words "It cannot be proved." Consequently this can be classed as pure evidence of opinion. We must rely then upon the judgment of Representative Halleck, deciding for ourselves the weight we wish to assign to his speculation.

Opinion evidence has a factual aspect. What Representative Halleck said *cannot be proved,* but that he *did say it* is a *fact.* "That all men are created equal" is debatable; "that many people believe that all men are created equal" is verifiable.

If the items of factual evidence apply directly to the argument at hand their impact is considerable. Many times a simple listing of items of factual evidence constitutes its own argument. If the evidence is comprehensive and verified to the satisfaction of the audience the conclusion is often so clearly implied that it need not be stated. As an example, here is a commentary on education in New York City.

> The other day a kid offered to bet me a quarter that the population of New York City is four million. I told the tot it was closer to eight million and asked him where he got his information. He told me that that was the figure that his geography book gave him.
>
> I asked the child some questions about American History; he knew all the answers up to Teddy Roosevelt; that was as far as his history book went, he said.
>
> I went around the next day and took a look at his school. Only a few of the rooms were equipped with electrical outlets, the walls hadn't been painted in almost twenty years.
>
> For six hundred kids there was one faucet for drinking and washing.
>
> The paper towel container was empty and there wasn't any

---

[2] Rep. Chas. Halleck, N.B.C. Radio Speech, July 28, 1948.

soap. One of the teachers told me the city budget didn't provide for such luxuries.

When I got home I phoned Mrs. Richard Rogers, the composer's wife. "The last time we met," I said, "you kept bending my ear about our school system, what's the name of that organization you are working with?" Dorothy told me it was the Public Education Association, a voluntary group trying to improve the New York school system.

I asked the association for some facts and figures. Well I almost wish I hadn't. They made me ashamed of the town I am always bragging about.

There is a building up in Harlem that used to be a prison twenty-five years ago. The police department decided it was unsafe and abandoned it.

Today it is called Public School 125.

The school kids eat their lunches in the cells.

The wealthiest city in the world hasn't even bothered to remove the bars.

P.S. 86 erected in 1889 has a seating capacity of 2059. It's a 6B school, kids 5 to 12.

To get to a lavatory the youngsters have to go down to the basement through an unheated passage.

The lavatories have no flushing facilities and there isn't a sink in the entire building.

P.S. 16 in Brooklyn has its toilets in the yard. Ditto for P.S. 127 in Manhattan and double ditto for 26 other schools.

P.S. 195 is a wooden structure heated by coal stove with overhead pipes.

The heat isn't turned on until the kids arrive and until the first hour of the day the temperature is often as low as 40 degrees. By modern standards 287 of our schools attended by 150,000 children are fire traps. P.S. 58 has exits on only one side of the building.

21 of our schools in New York were built before Lee surrendered to Grant.

According to the education experts New York needs 9,000 more classrooms and 10,000 more teachers.

And about 600 assorted doctors, nurses and mental hygienists.

Not to mention modern textbooks, workshops, gyms, musical instruments and some decent furniture. . . . A modern battleship costs $100,000,000.00. That much spent on a lot of young minds might eliminate the need for that battleship.

We are spending six percent of our national income for booze and smokes but only one and one-half percent to teach our kids to think straight.[3]

---

[3] Billy Rose, "Pitching Horseshoes," *Minneapolis Star* (December 30, 1947), p. 11.

Do you agree that a simple listing of selected facts can be strong persuasion?

Now let us turn our attention to the other uses of evidence. The acquisition of factual and opinion evidence leads usually to these questions (1) "Do the facts make sense?" (2) "Does this knowledge fall into any meaningful pattern?" and (3) "What can we conclude?" "Rules of the game" are needed to help us answer these vital questions. Hence the need for systematic patterns of interpreting evidence. The role of *logic* in reasoned discourse is to supply the necessary tested, definite rules.

There are two general cautions concerning the interpretation of evidence. First is an error of omission, having evidence and failing to make the most of it. This is somewhat rare and is found commonly in sincere but argumentatively unskilled utterance. It is totally unnecessary since the most important prerequisite of sound argument (good evidence) is available. We must be ever mindful of the need for continual scrutiny of the evidence we have. We must continually ask ourselves "Does this evidence justify relevant conclusions other than the ones I am making, or conclusions of greater definiteness than the ones I have formulated?" When a person is thinking in a planned pattern it is easy to miss significance of evidence in a related area.

A second common error in the interpretation of evidence is that of over-generalizing. This danger consists in argumentatively going beyond one's visible means of support. This is more popular and prevalent than understating evidence. Argumentative zeal and enthusiasm lead naturally to the drawing of absolute conclusions. We have a strong tendency to cite some evidence and without regard to its limitations draw the conclusion we desire. This over-generalizing is so tied up with the tendency to believe what we want to believe that it is difficult to avoid. It can be controlled, however, if we watch for it carefully and remind ourselves that conservatively stated conclusions are more convincing, as we noted in Chapter VIII.

The Reciprocal Relationship of Evidence and Reasoning

Consider the correlative nature of factual material and the associated reasoning in this quotation taken from a message by President Truman to a special session of Congress.

> The cost of living is now higher than ever before in our history.
>
> Prices are already so high that last year more than one-fourth of the families of this country were forced to spend more than they earned.
>
> At the same time industrial prices which affect all business and employment are rising fast. Large price increases have recently been announced by industries that set the pace for the whole economy.
>
> The rise in industrial prices is just as important in the long run as the high cost of living; it is already squeezing the independent businessman. It threatens to destroy a fair balance between industry and agriculture. It can end only in catastrophe if allowed to continue.
>
> Positive action by this government is long overdue. It must be taken now.
>
> I therefore urge the Congress to take strong positive action to control inflation.[4]

In the preceding passage it is difficult to separate facts and reasoning. They all blend in a unit of argument to *establish* a *probability* that the stated conclusion is true. While it is possible to separate the steps in the reasoning process from the factual information supplied, such separation distorts significance of facts and reasoning to a considerable extent. Evaluation of an argument seems to require simultaneous consideration of both information and related thinking processes.

Facts are of significance only as they are used by the persuader. They become members of a particular argumentative structure. This resulting pattern or form suggests criteria which assess the worth of the facts used. These facts in turn dictate appropriateness, even correctness, of the form. In argument, reasoning and evidence are truly inseparable.

Just as the principles governing the building of a bridge are in terms of materials to be used, so too, logical reasoning assumes the presence of sound, pertinent evidence of a type appropriate to the particular logical form. In practical argument evidence is always an integral part of the reasoning process. It becomes a prime determiner of the soundness of the reasoning taking place. The nine methods of strengthening a contention, discussed below, illustrate the integration of these materials of persuasion.

---

[4] H. Truman, "Message to Congress," *Minneapolis Morning Tribune* (July 28, 1948), p. 7.

The Methods of Supporting a Contention

Sound use of various forms will be described and illustrated, as will common fallacies in the application of each type of reasoned discourse. Consideration of evidence suitable to each category of argument will accompany the analysis of the structure of that type of argument.

Because the terms "induction" and "deduction" are widely used in materials pertaining to reasoned discourse, we should define these and call the student's attention to the fact that our classifications of argument are based on a continuum leading from induction to deduction. Briefly, induction may be defined as the process of drawing a conclusion from the examination of specific data. Deduction in a sense reverses this process. It begins with the acceptance of a general statement and applies it to a specific instance. The reciprocal relationship of these processes is evident. Commonly both induction and deduction are involved in any argumentative discourse. Normally any extended argument involves both the citing of specific instances and the drawing of conclusions from them—a process of induction. Then the conclusions reached through induction are applied to particular cases—a deductive process. The nine methods of strengthening a contention are arranged in a progression from largely induction to predominantly deduction. Argument from statistics is primarily inductive. Arguments of generalization and authority mix induction and deduction, and the argument by category, last in the list, is a pure deductive method.

All readers and especially those who have taken courses in logic may have a tendency to interpret premises in these different forms of argument in an absolute sense. We would urge that the concept of probability be kept in mind since it underlies all of these arguments and is important particularly to realistic application of the deductive forms. The concept of probability simply recognizes that in social problems there is no absolute certainty. We can never say that any statistic or available pattern of factual information is the whole story. We can cite only the evidence we have and say that it seems to be representative of the complete picture. Hence we may accept it as an accurate statement of the state of affairs until we have more evidence available. But because we can have only a partial picture we are forced to acknowledge its tentative nature.

The truth of any premise in the areas of relationship of man with man is, then, only *probable.* The concept of probability suggests that we are dealing in social argument with norms of human conduct. Individual exceptions to our premises are to be expected. The absolute and all inclusive definiteness of premises sometimes occurring in formal logic is not encountered in practical argument.

The effect of this concept of probability upon the evaluation and construction of argument is profound. The test of good argument becomes not "Is the conclusion proved beyond the shadow of doubt?" but rather "Does this conclusion seem to follow reasonably from the evidence given?" Limitation of our learning about human affairs dictates that our decisions must be based on probabilities.

Castell describes this notion of probability in logical reasoning as follows:

> . . . . It can be said that the probability attaching to any hypothesis increases in proportion to the number and range of facts for which it accounts: It becomes more probable as more facts of a certain kind converge on it. The notion of probability is thus strictly a relative one. No hypothesis has any probability in itself, only in relation to the facts for which it accounts. To say that one hypothesis is inherently more probable than another is meaningless. Probable always means in relation to such and such evidence, hence, if the evidence changes the probability changes.[5]

ARGUMENT FROM STATISTICS

Argument from statistics involves the drawing of conclusion from *numerical* evidence. An hypothesis is made which "accounts for" some quantitative measure of circumstances. For example, we can formulate an hypothesis about the range of intelligence quotients of college students if we know the results of intelligence tests administered to large numbers of them from representative institutions.

It is said that one can prove anything with figures. We suppose that statement derives from fallacies which occur commonly in statistical arguments. Let us begin with analysis of three of those

---

[5] Albury Castell, *A College Logic.* New York: The Macmillan Company, 1935, p. 189.

pitfalls found in reasoning based on statistics. Later we will suggest tests of statistical argument.

Undocumented Statistical Assertions

> You, too, can sell "Ice Boxes to Eskimos."
>
> Here is a shortcut to sales success that carries a money-back GUARANTEE!
>
> The rich rewards of "Super-Salesmanship" are definitely within the grasp of any average man. America's great salesmen (such as Luckman, $300,000 a year head of Lever Bros.) were not born so much better than others, but followed a METHOD OF SELLING that is infinitely greater.
>
> As is true of perfection in everything, Super-Selling is simple. A famous sales psychologist, now on the staff of a great university, concentrated Super-Selling into a brief, basic formula. A former member of the faculty of another great university tested that formula thousands of times in actual daily sales work of all kinds. More than 2,000 well-known business firms have bought and used the sales training courses he developed.
>
> Clients of his have made records like these: A Minnesota firm increased sales almost 400% in one year against the fierce competition of giant corporations. Another increased advertising returns 800% per dollar. A sales correspondent increased mail returns 100%. A $20-a-week-clerk became a successful sales manager in 20 months. A man of 35 with no success behind him, became a nationally-known sales executive in 2½ years. They succeeded because they had been taught to use the only true "Super-Salesmanship." The man who taught them, is, we believe, the greatest teacher of salesmanship in America. We are fortunate to have persuaded him to teach a special evening class this winter; exclusive with this school. Tuition is $85.00; refunded cheerfully to anyone who upon completion is not convinced he has received the world's best sales training, far better than any he could secure elsewhere.
>
> Super-Salesmanship can add $2,000 to $20,000 a year to your income for the rest of your life; not only in selling goods, but in selling yourself, giving you influence over others, securing promotions and in social and civic affairs as well. Classes now forming. Write, call or phone for full information about this GUARANTEED course.[6]

First, there is an underlying assumption we must grant before the statistical items become meaningful. We must concede that in

---

[6] Advertisement of the American Business College, Minneapolis. *Minneapolis Morning Tribune* (December 1, 1947), p. 8.

every business success cited the cause of achievement was the application of the method taught by this particular course. At no point in the advertisement is this mentioned specifically. The ad admits of no other influence. If the $20-a-week clerk became a successful sales manager in twenty months we are asked to believe that his use of this course material accounted totally for his advance. We are asked to accept the assumption that nothing other than this business training entered into the self-improvement of the man of thirty-five with no success behind him, who became nationally known as a sales executive in two and one-half years. The corporations which increased their business in the past year or two apparently were not affected by the general bettering of business conditions throughout industry. Any increase in business they had is assumed to be due to their use of principles and techniques taught in the course. Of course, Mr. Luckman at $300,000 a year did not attain that income and his high position in industry because of any native ability. We are asked to believe that he attained his position because he followed the sales techniques taught in this course. It seems probable that many other factors involved in these success stories are intentionally ignored by the writers of the advertising.

Second, we are asked by implication to accept the cases cited as typical of results accruing to individuals taking this course of study. There is no evidence given to show that all of the graduates of this course had the increases in income mentioned as a typical increase. There remains the possibility that these cases are exceptional. The implication, however, is that this is the normal result of taking the course, and we are asked to view the examples cited as though they were ordinary, normal and typical. Third, we are provided evidence in the form of *percentages,* and as the next example of statistical argument points out, percentages are frequently "tricky." This Minnesota firm which increased its sales almost 400% in one year might possibly have been a new firm at the time records were first kept. Suppose the firm made one sale the first year and four sales the next year. We could claim that this Minnesota firm had increased sales 400%. The same possibility exists in the other percentages given. Increasing returns from advertising 800% per dollar and increasing mail returns 100% brings to our minds the questions, "What was the *base* of comparison?" and "What are the other circumstances necessary to an understanding of these percentages?" Remember that increasing sales from practically zero up to just a few may be an increase of several thousand per cent.

All these bits of information, even if we grant their truth, are given to us without accompanying information necessary to an understanding of them. They are *undocumented* and, because we are not supplied information which will enable us to interpret them, they must be classed as assertions. One type of undocumented evidence is found in the citing of nameless individuals and concerns which performed as indicated. Another and more abstract brand of undocumented statistical assertion is found in *prediction,* as in the last paragraph of the advertisement when we are told confidentially that supersalesmanship can add $2,000 to $20,000 a year to your income for the rest of your life. This prediction comes closer to pure speculation than the assertions about things which supposedly have happened.

Let us turn our attention to some applications of percentage argument in the fallacious use of statistics.

Tricky Percentages. In January of 1948 the Congress of the United States was debating income tax reduction. The proposal receiving most attention and one which ultimately became law was the Knutson Plan proposed by Representative Knutson of Minnesota. One of the major arguments for the adoption of the Knutson plan advanced by the author of the bill was that tax reduction would be greatest in low income groups, where such tax reduction was needed. In proof of that we have two bits of evidence taken from news stories appearing at that time. "Knutson said that 77% of the relief under his own bill goes to those with income under $4,000." This assertion was amplified when it was pointed out that the Knutson bill would "slash taxes from 30% in the lowest bracket to 10% in the higher brackets." [7] These percentages are undeniably convincing. It is probable that the casual reader noting these two items of evidence was willing to come to the conclusion that lower income groups would benefit more from Knutson's proposal for tax reduction than higher income groups. However, the

---

[7] A.P. News Story, *St. Paul Pioneer Press* (January 8, 1948), pp. 1, 2.

political opposition lost no time in reinterpreting the facts of this proposal.

Their line of attack was to substitute for "percentage of tax reduction" the concept of "percentage increase in income after taxes." In a table covering income from $2,400 they showed that the percentage income increase after taxes for the $2,400 salary was 3%. The percentage increase in income after taxes for the one million dollar income was 66%. There was a fairly steady progression from the 3% increase in spendable income for the lowest bracket cited up to the top bracket. For example, the $10,000 net income under the Knutson plan would receive an 8% increase, and the $50,000 spendable income would be increased 31% by the Knutson bill. A salary of $300,000 or $500,000 would be benefited the most by the percentage increase in income after taxes under the proposed legislation. Individuals receiving these astronomical salaries would, under the Knutson bill, have 67% increased spendable income. This argument was summarized as follows. "A good look at that last column will show how much relief the little fellow would get under this tax legislation. Is 3% more than 67%? Under this tax schedule who gets more relief?" [8]

Which of these interpretations the reader chooses to accept is dependent probably upon his income. The essential question to be answered is "Which is the better measure of benefit of tax reduction to different income groups, the percentage reduction in tax paid or the percentage increase in spendable income?" If you can answer that question to your satisfaction then you have a clear cut basis for choice and a good reason for preferring one statistical interpretation to the other.

The fact that opposite conclusions result from the same type of reasoning, argument from statistics using percentages, and the same set of facts, leads us to be suspicious of isolated percentage arguments. We can say that it is desirable always to secure supplementary information before accepting arguments limited to percentage interpretation of factual data. Only when we have many details of the existing circumstances can we decide whether percentage arguments are meaningful.

---

[8] "Everybody's Ideas," Letter to the Editor, *Minneapolis Star* (January 13, 1948).

Hypothetical Statistics. In our discussion of the "Iceboxes to Eskimos" advertisement we noted that the most ethereal of statistical arguments were predictions. You recall the assertion that supersalesmanship could increase your income from $2,000 to $20,000 a year. That type of statistical argument we may call "hypothetical" because it is based on little other than guess work. If a statistical argument is undocumented but deals with factual assertions about things which have happened, there is some possibility of securing related evidence helpful in establishing the probable truth of the figures cited. In hypothetical statistics the guesswork is not capable of substantial confirmation. There is just no *proof* that the course in supersalesmanship will or will not increase the income of a person from the suggested minimum of $2,000 to a suggested maximum of $20,000 a year. Doubt the statement as we may, we are unable to prove it impossible.

The best we can do is line up evidence from past experience which indicates the prediction to be improbable. But we must admit the possibility that it could come about.

Hypothetical statistics have served as convincing bases for many get-rich-quick schemes used to defraud. Some examples of these are found in a Public Affairs Pamphlet entitled "Gyps and Swindles." [9] Guaranteed gushers have been used to inspire tables of return on investments that have induced thousands of people to invest life savings in oil stock. There is a famous swindle called the Spanish Prisoner Fraud which is said to have been started in 1588. The writer calls himself a prisoner in Mexico and says he has a large amount of money which he will divide with you if you will go to Mexico and provide the money to buy his freedom. Sometimes the Spanish prisoner fraud is augmented by the lure of a beautiful senorita. The prospect of a lot of money for little investment has influenced many gullible people to part with hard-earned cash. A popular statistical hoax is the inducement to invest in a fur farm. It is easy (on paper) to compile statistics proving that *if* you buy a pair of silver foxes at a certain price, *if* offspring appear on schedule in probable numbers, and *if* the market stays up, profits will be huge. Many people have been induced by this

[9] W. T. Foster, *Gyps and Swindles,* Public Affairs Pamphlet #109. New York: 1945, pp. 12–15.

statistical computation to buy a pair of foxes and leave them on a fur farm while they stay at home and get rich. Many of these quick profit schemes are reinforced by money-back guarantees, by "back" contracts or unconditional guarantees of profit. People influenced by these assurances forget that a guarantee is only as reliable as the guarantor.

The "chain" letter is an interesting use of hypothetical statistics to defraud. It consists of circulating a form letter which requests that you send a sum of money, ranging popularly from ten cents to a dollar, to the person who sent the letter to you. You in turn are then privileged to send from five to ten or more copies of this letter to other people and keep the money they send to you. Thus the letter promises a return of something in the order of ten times your investment. To guarantee that the chain will not be broken a supplementary appeal to superstition is made, magic qualities are ascribed to the chain letter process, and the assertion is added that maintaining the chain unbroken will bring you, in addition to your profit, good fortune. The reader can speculate for himself on the reasons why this hypothetical statistic seldom works out and the real reasons why few people make their living writing chain letters.

Sound argument from statistics places great reliance on one consideration, the source. This occurs because statistics are commonly used to describe complex social phenomena. Very few people have enough information about social problems in general to detect misrepresentation in particular statistics. Consequently, if we are to use statistical argument we must first be sure that the source is so reliable that we can afford to assume that the figures are fair and representative. For example, if we are in search of statistical information on labor-management relations we could turn to the Federal Bureau of Labor Statistics for facts with considerable confidence. Or suppose that we are interested in learning the status of aircraft accidents resulting from private flying in the United States. The Civil Aeronautics Administration compiles such statistics and represents a reliable source of that information. Certainly the CAA would be more reliable as a source of information concerning private aviation accidents and their causes than would be a private manufacturer of aircraft for sale to civilian pilots.

Many considerations are involved in the use of statistics. To summarize the major tests of statistical argument, we suggest that in nearly all instances the following questions should be answered.

1. Precisely what is meant by the units which make up the totals?
2. To what extent is the quantity measured by the statistics an index of the thing concerning which we want knowledge?
3. Are the units compared really comparable?
4. Do the statistics cover a sufficient period of time?
5. Do the statistics cover a sufficient number of cases? [10]

ARGUMENT FROM CIRCUMSTANTIAL DETAIL

Circumstantial detail argument is that in which a number of items not intimately related to each other by cause to effect relationships combine to form a pattern. The conclusion in the circumstantial detail argument is the missing link completing the pattern. It has many applications and is one of the most flexible and useful forms of reasoned discourse.

This argumentative form is derived, obviously, from courtroom proceedings. Evidence in the traditional criminal trial is marshaled to show the existence of the pattern which may convict the defendant. This "circumstantial" array is a list of items such as (1) defendant was seen in the vicinity a short time before the commission of the crime, (2) fingerprints of the defendant were found on the doorknob of the room in which the murdered man was discovered, (3) a button torn from the coat of the defendant was found clutched in the hand of the corpse, and so on. Now, no *one* of these items is in and of itself conclusive and there is no causal linkage between individual items, but the cumulative effect of a list, such as the hypothetical one we just started, is great and the person occupying the role of defendant in such a situation may find himself truly a "victim of circumstances."

We should mention a weakness of circumstantial detail reasoning. Things are not always what they seem and this is doubly true because the lack of close connections among the items in circumstantial evidence causes frequent misinterpretation. Consequently, overlooking some one item in the pattern may change it completely. That is why one contradictory detail will totally annihilate a seem-

---

[10] W. T. Foster, *Argumentation and Debating.* New York: Houghton Mifflin Company, 1936, pp. 192–200.

ingly complete circumstantial detail pattern. In our hypothetical example the accused murderer, to free himself of the network of circumstantial evidence, need simply prove one thing: that he was visiting his Aunt Minnie on the night of the crime in a town twenty miles from the scene of violence.

Many simple circumstantial detail structures can be found. Oftentimes the qualifications of a candidate seeking election are presented in circumstantial detail. One candidate running for State Representative in Minnesota presented his qualifications in pamphlet form. Items are listed under two headings (1) "qualified" and (2) "experienced." Under the "qualified" heading we have items such as the fact that he is a life long resident of this particular district, is a taxpayer, is married, has a few children, had attended Minneapolis public schools, had graduated from the University of Minnesota, holding Liberal Arts and Law degrees, and that he is a practicing attorney and a member of the State Bar Association. Several other items of this nature are also listed. Under the category of "experienced" we are informed that the candidate has been a leading figure in the House of Representatives, he has served on tax judiciary and banking committees of the House, he is chairman of the Aviation Committee, he has authored a program termed progressive and forward looking for control of aviation in the state of Minnesota. He has supported measures beneficial to servicemen and has aided in "the enactment of legislation designed to assist the returning veteran." Other items such as these are included in the remainder of the experienced column. The summary of this circumstantial detail pattern is the slogan used by him in his campaign: "A record worthy of your support." Most of the items listed in this pamphlet are fact evidence. However, some opinion entered in as in the item concerning legislation to assist the returning veteran. That is generalized information subject to challenge, while the purely factual material stands and cannot be denied.

Circumstantial detail includes "argument from sign" and much that other authors might assign to "causal relation" argument. Since "causal relation" is difficult if not impossible to establish in the area of social problems, and since argument from sign is based on concurrence rather than a causal relation, we consider these forms as variations in the pattern of circumstantial detail. It is extremely difficult to prove that any single happening in the past can cause, in and of itself, any present circumstance. On the other hand, it is relatively easy to establish that a given event is followed frequently by the circumstance in question. Consequently, in the interest of practical argument we are substituting the notion of inevitable or probable concomittance for causal relations. Such concomittance is classified as circumstantial detail.

ARGUMENT FROM COMPARISON

Comparison in argument involves the examination of two cases. Their similarities are noted. The point of the argument is the establishment of the conclusion that what was true of one of the cases examined will be true, perhaps with modification, of the other. Just as you would suspect from the name of this category of support, it involves the comparison of similar or nearly identical sets of circumstances usually for purposes of prediction. The use of comparison is arbitrarily limited to *two* cases. Argument by comparison is sometimes called literal analogy. Reasoning from more than two cases will be considered under the heading "argument by generalization."

As an example of simple and direct argument by comparison, we present a portion of an editorial in a municipality considering ownership and operation of a liquor store. This editorial opposed the plan and within it we find comparison incorporating some argument from statistics.

> There can be no assurance that a municipal liquor store would yield sufficient revenue to solve even enough of our problem to merit its existence—if such existence can have merit at all. Fancy figures on liquor profits stem, for the most part, from "on sale" —by the drink—receipts. The proposal in question, however, is one for the establishment of "off sale" store only; a department of the business where the profit margin is slim.
>
> As a barometer of what the community might anticipate in "off sale" liquor sale during business years we might look to the financial statement of the Village of Excelsior, a community of comparable population that established a municipal "off sale" store in 1939. Taking the years 1939 through 1942 as normal business years we find the following startling and financially-disappointing net profit sheet: The Excelsior Liquor Store in 1939 made a net profit of $2,356.00; 1940—$3,581; 1941—$4,224; 1942—$2,806.
>
> We might point out that Excelsior is a marketing community

> whereas Wayzata is not. That municipal profits in Excelsior might be expected to be greater, yet, the average of slightly over $3,000 per year net profit falls into the category of "peanuts" in our city treasury where "acorns" must grow.[11]

The assumption that the communities of Excelsior and Wayzata are similar in business and other items affecting sales of liquor is essential to the acceptance of any or all of this argument by comparison. Note that the persuader stresses *one* difference between the communities—that Excelsior is a marketing community whereas Wayzata is not. This one difference he suggests causes us to expect less revenue from the projected liquor store in Wayzata than was realized in Excelsior. But the fact that this one difference is mentioned leads the reader to suspect that there might be other differences in the "makeup" of the communities which are not revealed in the argument. This editorial appeared in April 1947, and the statistics, serving as basis for comparison, stop in 1942. The discriminating reader will notice this fact and if he is interested probably he will investigate the revenue report of 1943–46 from the Excelsior Liquor Store. Omission of these recent years from the statistical evidence might be significant. By selecting the base of comparison the desired object can be made to seem relatively "good" or relatively "bad." The selection of the basis for comparison is a strategic item to the propagandist because he can, by careful selection, make "the worse appear the better." Those who are interested in maintenance of our status quo, through generally discouraging any tendencies toward change in our social or business structure, like to compare the abundance of American living with the status of day-to-day existence in a devastated country. We here paraphrase an argument popular when people in the United States were worrying about inflation as it affected a rapidly rising cost of living.

> Today Americans look at conditions in many other countries, where starvation, poverty and tyranny rule supreme, and they see nothing to be gained, much to be lost in changing to any other social doctrine. There are countries which call themselves democracies where a citizen may not own land or select his own job, he may not be tried by a jury of his peers, he may not stay away from work without good and sufficient reason, he may not employ

---

[11] Editorial, *The Minnetonka Herald* (Wayzata, Minn.), April 17, 1947.

> anyone to work for him, he does not have freedom of speech, freedom of assembly or freedom of religion, and his press and radio are censored by his government.
>
> The weekly wage of this same man will purchase 11 pounds of meat or 40 quarts of milk. An American worker, with his weekly income can buy 94 pounds of meat or 263 quarts of milk. Over there, it takes 104 hours of work to buy a pair of shoes, over here, it takes only 7 hours. Over there, it takes 250 hours of work to buy a wool dress, over here, it takes only 13 hours. Over here, one miner produces as much coal as 4 miners over there. With about the same number of acres under cultivation the average American farmer turns out four and a half times as much as a farmer over there. Certainly these contrasts speak for themselves!

In this sweeping and extremely general comparison there is an implication that the single factor accounting for these differences in standards of living is the difference in political and social organization. We cannot prove that such is or is not the case. However, we suggest a possibility that other factors are influential in lowering the standard of living in such countries as France, Britain, and Poland. Perhaps the influence of the war has been felt because these countries have suffered widespread devastation of their means of production and perhaps great loss of manpower might have adversely affected the efficiency of their industrial machines. Then there is the possibility that there are great differences in national resources available to these countries when compared to those that we have in the United States. It might be that the necessity for devoting a high percentage of available labor and industry to simple reconstruction of damaged means of transportation, industrial plants, living quarters and the rehabilitation of almost ruined farm land, lowers the production of refrigerators, automobiles, radios and possibly items of clothing and food. What we are doing in this analysis is searching for items of difference, because argument from comparison is only as good as the similarity you can establish between the two cases considered. For a comparison to be valid the items of similarity must clearly outweigh the items of difference.

There is an exception to this criterion, a type of comparison which relies not upon similarity but upon difference. We may call it comparison for purposes of contrast. In the case of this special type of comparison the point of the argument is found in differences which are highlighted by the comparison of the two cases considered. This type of argument occurs frequently in controversial journals representing labor, management, and industry. An example of comparison for purpose of contrast is found in the publication of a labor union. The argument they are supporting with the comparison, which occupies a major portion of one issue, is that wages are disproportionately low for their members and that they are justified in requesting increases in those wages. On the front page [12] we have a subheadline reading "How a U.E. Family Struggles to Get Along on $46.00 Per Week." There is a picture of Fred Piercefield of St. Louis reading the comics to his son. He is the head of an United Electrical Workers' family that is attempting to "get along" on his salary of $46.00 a week. At the bottom of the front page we have a headline taken from the Wall Street Journal which reads "Mr. X with $45,000 a Year can Barely Manage to Make Ends Meet." Carrying on the introduction to the comparison this quoted headline is labeled, "While the bosses can't live on $45,000 a year."

You begin to see the basis for the comparison. We have a picture story of the living problems of the Piercefield family. There are several children and many difficulties come about in securing minimum stands of nourishment, clothing, housing, and recreation for this family. Immediately following this pictorial story we have reprinted the story of Mr. X who can't make ends meet on $45,000 a year. It is photostated from the Wall Street Journal.

The Wall Street Journal story, presented in its entirety, is a sincere explanation by a Wall Street executive of his difficulties in getting along on his current salary of $45,000 a year. He cites items: That the operation of his household has increased from $700 a month to $1250 a month, that his club dues now amount to $1300 a year, and that his social and entertainment expenses have mounted to $4000 a year, and that he no longer can maintain two cars but is restricted to keeping but one Cadillac. The photostat of the Wall Street Journal article is accompanied by cartoon comment ridiculing the financial problems of the man with the $45,000 salary.

As is frequently done in arguments of comparison for purposes

---

[12] "How a U.E. Family Struggles to Get Along on $46.00 a Week," *U.E. News.* New York: December 28, 1946, pp. 1, 5–9.

of contrast no conclusion is stated. The persuader relies on obvious points of difference to establish the implied conclusion. In a little box on the page bearing the photostat of the article about Mr. X and his income difficulties there is a simple statement that the *U.E. News* is reprinting a "lead article" from the Wall Street Journal and that on other pages in this issue they "present the problems of a $46.00 a week U.E. family."

To test such "contrast" argument we can ask the question "Is there a legitimate basis for comparison of the two cases?" The use of the device of contrast implies that the two instances should be similar but are not. Are we willing, then, to accept that concealed assumption, that there should be a similarity of cases? If we are not willing to accept that assumption then there exists little basis for becoming perturbed about the differences stressed by the persuader.

Comparison and contrast arguments will be strengthened if they are so designed that the following questions can be answered satisfactorily:

1. Have the examples been chosen to support a preconceived conclusion?
2. Are the examples fair representatives of their class?
3. Are there contrary examples which have not been considered?
4. Do the examples represent a large enough portion of their class to justify a generalization?
5. Are the facts concerning the examples verifiable?
6. Is there other evidence to support probable validity of the generalization? [13]

ARGUMENT FROM ANALOGY

A popular and colorful way of strengthening contentions is the use of analogy. An analogy is the comparison of two cases which are fundamentally different in nature but which operate on common principles. Analogy, then, is comparison of unlike things for purposes of clarification and securing conviction. The process of argument by comparison is frequently termed argument by literal analogy. Our discussion of argument by analogy is limited to the category termed by some authors figurative analogy.

It happened that one of the authors, a subscriber to Blue Cross

---

[13] H. L. Ewbank and J. J. Auer, *Discussion and Debate.* New York: Appleton-Century-Crofts, Inc., 1951, pp. 124–126.

Hospitalization Insurance, fell behind in his dues. He received a reminder in the form of an analogy. At the top of the little reminder sheet was the picture of an ostrich with its head in the sand and the headline "Are You Burying Your Head?" The text below the picture and headline explained that ostriches are peculiar in that they believe that they can avoid danger by ignoring it, by hiding their heads in the sand. They suggest that Blue Cross subscribers who keep up their premiums are far wiser than the ostrich, because they know that one person in every ten becomes a hospital patient every year. A concluding argument is "don't be an ostrich, mail your remittance today."

It might have been impolite had the Blue Cross Organization called the author an ostrich in so many words. However they retained their reputation for politeness while implying that unmistakably. This analogy constitutes a dramatization of an argument. It has novelty and color, it gets and holds attention and reinforces the contention of the persuader with considerable effectiveness. Even admitting that certain ostrich characteristics can be attributed to the author, there will be agreement that the two subjects compared are considerably dissimilar. The basis for validity of the argument, if any, is identity of principle. In neglecting his premium payments, the author is said to be ignoring risk in the hope of avoiding it, as the ostrich does traditionally by refusing to see approaching danger. To the extent that the reader is willing to accept this identity of principle, this illustration is valid as well as appealing.

The analogy, by reducing complicated human problems to a principle or two, represents oversimplification. A good example of an analogy which reduces tremendous complexity to a simple figure of speech is the following argument designed to show that high prices do not cause inflation.

> Do wet streets cause rain? Do high prices cause inflation? Wet streets no more cause rain than high prices cause inflation. Wet streets are the result of rain. High prices are the disastrous result of inflation.[14]

Accepting the analogy as proof that inflationary causes are to be found outside of high prices, the remainder of the argument estab-

[14] Advertisement of National Association of Manufacturers. *Minneapolis Star* (December 4, 1947), p. 14.

lishes futility of price control measures in attempting to control inflation. Once you concede that the analogy is sound, it is a comparatively simple process to show that curtailing prices is a basically wrong attack on the problem of inflation. Key questions in evaluating this argument are: "What is the value of the comparison of wet streets and high prices and rain and inflation?" and "What weight can we assign to the similarity of principle underlying operation of these two patterns of circumstances?"

The reader will probably defend his own analysis, but the authors can discover only one principle common to the two cases compared. That principle is that events come about from causes. The cause to effect relationship stated in the advertisement is an asserted relationship saying one thing is the cause of another, hence in another and unrelated area one thing is the cause of another. This principle of identity is so general that little specific weight can be assigned to it. The strength of this argument appears to be psychological and involves the attraction of oversimplification which *apparently* enables us to understand things so complicated that they are difficult to grasp. Equally indefinite are many analogies in political oratory. They neglect to establish fundamental principles of identity in any serious sense. These analogies probably represent transition forms between logical reasoning and metaphorical language. Take, for example, one used by Franklin D. Roosevelt in his Teamster's Union speech. He said "No elephant can turn handsprings without falling flat on its back." The context of the speech makes the implication of the analogy clear. President Roosevelt was contending that the Republican Party had shifted position on certain basic issues and was arguing that they would not be successful in this temporary shift of allegiance. But any serious analysis of the relation of elephantine acrobatics to politics is impossible. Even an attempt to word such principles would destroy the elusive whimsy and humor which made the argument effective. Logical analysis, then, in some cases of analogical argument, is ridiculous. We consider such analogies as resourceful dramatics used for psychological effect and we deny that they can be profitably treated as examples of logical reasoning.

Can an analogy ever be a sound logical argument? Technically, no. Why not? Because an analogy is a form of comparison involving dissimilar cases in which its validity is technically determined by the points of similarity outweighing the points of difference. Due to the fact that the two cases compared in analogy fall in different subject matter areas, the points of difference will always outweigh the points of similarity. Consequently, identity of principles is never enough to make an analogy a valid comparison. In this sense every analogy is a false comparison.

But we should recognize different degrees of weakness. Certainly we can identify principles which carry through particular analogies more appropriately than the principles which are evident in other analogies. The ostrich analogy is based on a principle which is more readily identifiable and which seems more reasonable than the principle connecting wet streets with inflation. But judgment on appropriate and meaningful common principle is subjective. We can place only limited trust in analogical argument. There is no definite logical criterion that can be applied to answer the question "How valid is it?"

Analogies are favorite devices of commentators and columnists to put zip and pep into their utterances and writings. We suggest that in this context they should be viewed as devices for enlivening composition for popular consumption. Here is one introduced to support the argument that President Truman's proposed tax reduction of $40.00 per person is not a sound plan.

> A humpty dumpty proposal to give everybody $40.00 if they voted for you at the next election. It was like telling a man with cancer that he ought to take an aspirin tablet every wet Tuesday.[15]

Readings

1. Beardsley, M. C., *Practical Logic.* New York: Prentice-Hall, Inc., 1950, Chaps. 12, 13, 14.
2. Castell, Albury, *A College Logic.* New York: The Macmillan Company, 1935, Topic 8.
3. Ewbank, H. L., and Auer, J. J., *Discussion and Debate.* New York: Appleton-Century-Crofts, Inc., 1951, pp. 146–149.
4. Foster, W. T., *Argumentation and Debating.* New York: Houghton Mifflin Company, 1936, Chaps. 5, 7, 8.
5. Larrabee, Harold A., *Reliable Knowledge.* New York: Houghton Mifflin Company, 1945, Chaps. 10, 11.

---

[15] Billy Rose, "Pitching Horseshoes," *Minneapolis Star* (January 28, 1948), p. 25.

Exercises

1. Examine critically the evidence offered by Billy Rose in his article "A Wise Guy Goes to School and Learns Shocking Facts." What items are vital to the argument and which ones are incidental?

2. Which is the better measure of benefit of tax reduction to different income groups, the percentage reduction of tax paid, or the percentage increase in spendable income? Select one or the other and defend it, using data from the discussion of the Knutson tax plan in this chapter.

3. Prepare and present a five minute persuasive speech, supporting your proposition by a carefully developed pattern of circumstantial detail.

4. Locate an argument by comparison in newspaper or magazine advertising. Analyze similarities and differences in the cases being compared.

5. What are strengths and weaknesses of "comparison for purposes of contrast" argument? Do these apply to the Wall Street-U.E. family illustration given in this chapter?

Chapter XII

THE LOGICAL TECHNIQUES OF PERSUASION

Part II: Argument by Generalization, Authority, Condition, Alternation, and Category; Levels of Argument

I. The Methods of Supporting a Contention (Continued)

- A. Argument by Generalization
- B. Argument by Authority
  1. Prestige Authority
     - a. Expert Authority
     - b. Non-expert Prestige Authority
  2. Lay Authority
     - a. Individual Lay Authority
     - b. Grouped Lay Authority
- C. Argument by Condition ("If-then" Argument)
- D. Argument by Alternation ("Either-or" Argument)
- E. Argument by Category

II. The Levels of Argument

III. Summary

Readings and Exercises

Chapter XII

THE LOGICAL TECHNIQUES OF PERSUASION—PART II

The Methods of Supporting a Contention (Continued)

ARGUMENT BY GENERALIZATION

> History fails to record an instance of governmental operation of a business that could not be performed more efficiently and, when all factors are given honest consideration, more economically, by a privately owned enterprise. These facts are so well known as to be well nigh axiomatic among folk who really want to know the score. There is no exception whether the field be merchandising, manufacturing, transportation or public utility service.[1]

Argument by generalization inductively formulates a conclusion of a somewhat sweeping and general nature. The quoted generalization related to an issue in one of our previous illustrations, the ownership of a municipal liquor store by the city of Wayzata.

In making generalizations, varying amounts of evidence may be cited. At first glance the above illustration would seem to be based on evidence, but we find that no specific items are indicated and that what we really have is an assertion about events which supposedly have happened and which would be, according to the persuader, available for our study if we were able to unearth them. Nothing of a *factual* nature is given as support. We will term this type of generalization, one which has no visible means of support, an "asserted generalization." We have only the word of the person making the statement that the evidence exists.

A second type of generalization is that in which we have some

[1] Editorial, *Edina Free Enterprise* (Minn.), February, 1948, p. 2.

support in the form of evidence but not quite enough to justify the conclusion. Such partially supported forms are "hasty generalizations." Off-hand these seem to be much stronger than asserted generalizations because some evidence, often in itself quite impressive, is present and we are led to believe that a conclusion is based solidly on that evidence. Actually many times a little evidence is no better than no evidence at all. Consequently a hasty generalization may or may not be of greater logical worth than an asserted generalization.

Hasty generalizations are easy to find. Here is one used to establish the desirability of taking a course in public speaking to learn to influence others.

> An exhaustive study was made by the Carnegie Foundation for the advancement of teaching to determine the cause of business success. As a result it was determined that about 85% of success in business is due not to superior knowledge but to superior ability to influence others.[2]

Here is another quoted argument utilizing a different type of evidence.

> The Soviets appear to have launched a large scale campaign to win-over—or compromise—key American officials abroad by the use of sex as an implement of Russian Policy.
>
> The campaign already has won brilliant success, reports reaching Washington indicate.
>
> Three Americans in the United States Embassy in Moscow alone have fallen victims to the charms of Russians of the opposite sex in the last two years.[3]

Some time ago citizens of Minneapolis, Minnesota were discussing proposed legislation for a city-wide housing program. A pamphlet presented this argument from generalization in support of suggested legislation.

> "43 states have housing and redevelopment authority legislation. Our state has none! That's why Minneapolis needs Amendment No. 11. Vote—yes!"

Now, let's examine each of these arguments from the point of view of adequacy of supporting evidence. The study made by the

---

[2] Pamphlet, "Dale Carnegie Course" (p. 1), Minneapolis School of Business.

[3] Wallace R. Deuel, "Russ Aim Mata Hari Drive at U. S.," *Minneapolis Star* (June 17, 1948), p. 15.

Carnegie Foundation culminated in an 85% figure, but we know nothing of their method of measurement of business success or the avenues used to discover factors causing this undefined success. We might even doubt that superior knowledge and superior ability to influence others are different things. Those quantities might well be closely related and so contribute to each other. As we take this statement apart we see that it is largely meaningless. Instead of a clear cut boundary between two quantities being measured, we have an indefinite overlapping area which confuses rendering a conclusion concerning their relative proportions.

The second hasty generalization asserts that the Soviets have launched a large scale and successful campaign to use sex as an implement of Russian policy. The conclusion is somewhat alarming until we read that it is based on the fact that three Americans have fallen in love with Russian girls in 1946 and 1947. Perhaps this is not an unusually large number of young American men to desire brides in the countries in which they happen to be quartered. Certainly, before we become alarmed about these three American boys "falling for" Russian girls over a period of two years we should like to know comparative statistics from the forces of occupation in other countries over corresponding periods of time. Only then can we tell if this evidence is sufficient to justify the asserted "large scale campaign" to use sex as an implement of foreign policy.

The third hasty generalization is typical of many based on the reasoning that if a lot of people do something, or if the act is widely accepted, then it must be good and should be imitated. Here we have submitted the asserted evidence that 43 of 48 *states* have a housing program of a certain type. That is said to justify the conclusion that the *city* of Minneapolis should enact similar housing legislation. Many complicating factors make the situation of Minneapolis unique, and these would have to be known before we could conclude that we do need any *particular* housing program.

A third type of generalization, one seldom mentioned, is the "sound generalization." It consists of formulating a conclusion from the examination of evidence which seems to be adequately supported by that evidence. It is characterized by two identifying features. First, its wording is usually conspicuous for its conservatism, and second, the greater portion of the argumentative unit of sound generalization is devoted to the citation of specific evidence.

Examine the evidence in this following quotation supporting the generalization that the National Association of Manufacturers lobby has been effective in determining legislation passed by the 80th Congress.

> In this box score the "educational" organization claims 21 victories and only 6 defeats in its efforts to educate Congress with respect to legislation of top national importance. Of 14 bills the NAM endorsed, 11 became law. Of 13 that it opposed only 3 were passed.
>
> And that score even gives the Democratic Administration the benefit of the doubt with respect to the new price control law. NAM stood squarely against any extension of Office of Price Administration Controls over manufactured items. The resulting compromise legislation though listed in the NAM box score as a defeat for the organization is described in the same paragraph as "One of the Administration's major defeats."
>
> The tabulation showed only one instance in which the NAM and the labor lines ran parallel, that was when the President's Emergency Strike Control Bill was defeated.
>
> One of NAM's outstanding flash achievements in the lobbying field last session was the successful support of the revision of tax laws.
>
> This included repeal of the Excess Profits Tax and the general shake-up of corporation income taxes that will save the corporations about three billion one hundred million dollars this year in addition to two billion six hundred million dollars that was sliced off the individual income tax.
>
> Another achievement of the business lobby was the freezing of the Social Security Old Age Payroll tax at one percent each on employer and employee through 1947 instead of the scheduled increase to 2½ percent on January 1st. Tax money involved there amounted to an estimated one billion eight hundred fifty million dollars a year.
>
> It was in the field of labor legislation that NAM and the labor lobbies naturally collided most often and with the loudest shouting on both sides. Among its relatively few defeats NAM lists as number one the President's veto of the Case Anti-Strike bill and the House support of that veto. However, besides defeat of the generally unpopular emergency strike control bill NAM scored two flat victories in the labor-legislation field. It successfully backed enactment of the bill to curb the activities of President James C. Petrillo of the American Federation of Musicians. And it won passage of the Hobb Anti-racketeering bill.[4]

---

[4] Jack Wilson and Marr McGaffin, "Critics Rap 'Selfish' Lobby Role," *Minneapolis Sunday Tribune* (October 13, 1946), p. 6.

We are not absolutely sure that the evidence provided in support of the contention that the NAM has an efficient lobby is conclusive. We recognize that there may be facts not recorded here which would weaken that conclusion. But it seems *probable* in light of the variety of information of NAM policy and activities correlated with emerging legislation that the lobby of the NAM has produced significant results. Hence we might consider this to be a sound generalization.

A generalization is simply an hypothesis used to account for a series of events, the more the specific instances conform to the hypothesis the more probable the conclusion. If we grant that there are only a limited number of instances covered, thus the more cases that we know about and understand the more certain we are that our hypothesis is correct. If there is a limited number of cases and we have observed them all, then we can complete a perfect generalization. But since, in social argument, we can never account for all instances of a given phenomenon, we can never be absolutely sure that our hypothesis is correct. Again we are forced to accept some degree of probable truth.

Castell expresses this relation of the concept of probability to the hypothesis in generalization. "That is, granted the principle of limited variety, there is some point to the argument, if P happens M times, it will probably happen M plus N times, the probability increasing as M increases." [5]

In this simple equation the letter N represents the difference between the number of cases about which we know (M) and the number of cases which are possible. The equation says that the greater the percentage of possible cases for which we can account, the greater is the probable truth of an hypothesis stating what we can expect of all the cases.

ARGUMENT BY AUTHORITY

In matters concerning which we lack evidence or about which evidence would be difficult to obtain we often rely upon the opinions of others. We use these opinions in making our decisions because the people who hold them happen to be in a better position

---

[5] Albury Castell, *A College Logic.* New York: The Macmillan Company, 1935, p. 275.

to know the facts involved than we are. Or, possibly, their judgment in the problem area may be admittedly better than ours because of special training and experience. Regardless of special qualification and great knowledge on the part of the authority, we must always remind ourselves that his value judgment is *opinion evidence.* Authoritative statement is an interpretation of information which may or may not be mentioned and constitutes an opinion in which there is always possibility for error. Parenthetically, we remind the reader that an authoritative opinion appearing in print is not necessarily of any more significance than one which is spoken. We need to guard against our tendency to believe what we read, a tendency possibly resulting from "school-conditioned" attitudes.

Argument by authority may be classified according to source. Sources of authoritative statements run the gamut from hearsay authority, exemplified by the statement in cigarette advertising that "medical authorities agree," to the opinion of a recognized expert with name, date, and context given.

A common misconception is the notion that authoritative statements come only from experts or specialists. A popular and powerful brand of authoritative argument comes from people who are recommended to us because they are folks just like ourselves. They are specialists only in the sense that they are allegedly typical of the "man in the street," and consequently their actions and opinions are suggested to us as representative of great numbers of people. Such inexpert authority seems to be used increasingly in current persuasion.

The process of argument by authority is usually the simplest of our nine methods of strengthening a contention. Frequently the authoritative statement is in the form of a contention advocated by the persuader. In such cases the logical structure of argument by authority consists of repeating the contention in the words of the expert, which is not a difficult process. In other cases of argument by authority we have the authoritative statement serving as a premise for subsequent deductive forms of reasoning. Such usage would be a combination of argument by authority and the deductive form used in a particular instance.

Prestige Authority. A prestige authority is a person who is known to the audience. Some of the fame of such an authority is transferred to his judgment and, as a result, the significance of that judgment seems greater (or less) to them than it would when coming from a less noteworthy source. The prestige source may be expert or non-expert. But whether his qualifications are related or unrelated to the subject of his judgment, a prestige authority always has some characteristic which sets him apart from ordinary mortals. Conversely, almost any circumstances which do set an individual apart from the group enhance his prestige as an authority.

Expert Authority. We encounter expert authorities frequently at an informal level. Suppose that one of our male readers goes to buy a new suit and the clerk who is helping him make his choice in the clothing store calls in the tailor. The tailor remarks about the excellent fit of the coat. That has some impact on the young man and may be an influential force in determining his decision to buy or not to buy the suit. The advice of a plumber on comparative merits of different makes of bathroom fixtures, the advice of a mechanic on structural comparison of different makes of automobiles, the counsel of a minister on moral choices, and the admonitions of the doctor on diet are all examples of expert authoritative opinions. Experts giving these opinions may not be famous, but by reason of experience and study occupy positions of considerable prestige. Consequently, we accord weight to their statements.

Expert authorities frequently disagree. It has been said that any statement by an expert may be neutralized by a directly opposing statement taken from another equally qualified expert. We would say that this statement is too sweeping a generalization, but we would suggest in controversial issues such as are found in morals, religion, and politics that it is probably true.

Non-expert Prestige Authority. Prominent people frequently issue judgments on subjects in which they are obviously not qualified. Those of you who have studied the history of the United States prior to World War II recall Colonel Charles A. Lindbergh's well-publicized persuasion directed toward keeping this country out of war. Lindbergh was an undoubted expert in matters of aviation, and perhaps, too, in other related areas of scientific research. His qualifications in international politics were less definite and probably less genuine. Yet Lindbergh, because he was a famous individual, was able to speak seemingly with great authority on matters of international relations. Many people were willing to assign significance to his ideas concerning the diplomatic course which should be pursued by the United States. Colonel Lindbergh was an example of non-expert prestige authority, who speaks about items in which he is interested even though they lie outside his legitimate realm of specialized knowledge.

The movie star or the athlete who endorses liquor or cigarettes is a non-expert prestige authority. Here is an example of a non-expert testimonial by a United States Senator.

> Outside of a good environment and classroom studies there can be no better training for youth in his teens than the responsibility of a paper route. There is a feeling of self-confidence and self-reliance which comes through earning money . . . with this there follows a definite planning for the future.
>
> Many times while visiting with people who have been successful I have found that they assumed responsibilities early in life and developed the habit of saving. It was this early training which assisted them in becoming important people.

We have no knowledge of the senator's qualifications as an expert in newspaper carrier salesmanship. He may or may not have had a paper route as a boy. We suspect that he did not have such a youthful occupation because usually a non-expert prestige authority will mention personal experience. But his prominence and his reputation in government, his achievements as a former governor of a great state and in the United States Congress, transfer to his judgment the values of delivering newspapers.

Lay Authority. Lay authorities are folks who have no claims to fame. They are the anonymous consumers and producers of goods and services who constitute the great majority of our population. However, because such individuals are not widely known their opinions do not lack argumentative force. Quite to the contrary, statements of "the common man" are respected. Public opinion polls frequently give national publicity to statements of ordinary individuals. Groups of individuals pass resolutions representing their collective opinions. These group judgments have been most effective in motivating change and bringing about the realization of persuasive goals. Lay and unskilled, unsung authority is worthy of study.

Individual Lay Authority. Individual lay authority evidence is usually a statement by a person who has had first-hand association with the subject being considered. John Jones has "switched to Calvert," the advertisement says, because he "prefers that mellow flavor." The Home Loan company informs us that Mr. Brown of 227 Breeze Terrace made this statement about their company: "The Home Loan Company is a fine concern. I borrow on my signature only whenever I need ready cash, and they arrange payments so I can meet them easily. I don't know what I would do without the Home Loan Company."

Letters of endorsement are used by the persuader to build a favorable attitude. For example: "The course taught me how to overcome fear when speaking before a group by properly organizing my thoughts and presenting them in a logical order. It taught me the proper attitude toward the audience and incidentally improved my stance, gestures, and audience communication, all of which were vitally important."

Grouped Lay Authority. In grouped lay authority we have two predominating patterns. In one a group of people act together, as in passing a resolution or signing a petition. This represents a unified and concerted group action. In another grouped authority we have a collection of individual opinions, the grouping of which increases persuasive impact. For example, a pamphlet advertising the Dale Carnegie course in personality development lists the names, addresses, and telephone numbers of a large number of graduates of the course. The reader of the pamphlet is invited to call any of these people about the course. The politician returning from his cross country speaking tour may use grouped lay authority when he tells about the opinions he encountered in different sections of the country.

This miscellaneous grouping of opinions is convincing, but they cannot meet any logical test of argument because the sampling of opinion is certainly, by any accepted standard, inadequate.

By now the reader probably has concluded that argument by authority as logical proof leaves much to be desired. This is true, because, by its nature, argument by authority is limited to human judgments. Judgments emerge from underlying factual materials via a subjective process. There is no pattern of reasoning backing up a judgment which we can check for validity. In a sense, acceptance of argument from authority is making a jump in the dark. Yet we must recognize that sometimes argument from authority is valuable because other, more reliable, evidence on that issue may not exist. Here is a balanced point of view on the use of authority argument.

> Use authority only where facts are not available or where they need to be interpreted or supplemented. Do not ask others to believe a thing simply because some expert believes it. When facts are available, give the facts. No authority can be quite so persuasive as the power of facts well selected and arranged. The chief value of authority is to interpret complex facts or to supplement accepted ones.[6]

Obviously, authorities differ in qualification and, consequently, in weight we can assign to them. It is important that we study authorities analytically to determine the degree of expertness which entitles them to express their opinions. Common sense helps in determining the qualifications of an authority by indicating such questions as "What is the individual's training in this field in which he is making a statement?" and "What first hand experience has the authority had to increase his knowledge concerning this problem?" The following standard tests of authority argument will encourage the reader to be comprehensive in evaluation of his own and others' uses of authoritative judgments.

> (1) Is the authority competent? (2) Is the authority prejudiced? (3) Is the authority reliable? (4) Is the authority definite? (5) Is the authority supported by other sources? (6) Is the authority supported by argument from specific instances, causal relation, and analogy? [7]

ARGUMENT BY CONDITION ("IF-THEN" ARGUMENT)

The condition argument is a unit of deductive reasoning. It is deductive because like the alternation and the syllogism, it rests totally upon a foundation of assumption which must be granted before the argument itself is meaningful. An assumption is commonly a proposition of more or less comprehensive nature. Our basis for deciding whether or not we want to accept assumptions in conditional or other deductive argument is the test of reasonableness

---

[6] W. N. Brigance, *Speech Composition.* New York: Appleton-Century-Crofts, Inc., 1937, p. 164.

[7] A. C. Baird, *Argumentation, Discussion, and Debate.* New York: McGraw-Hill Book Co., Inc., 1950, p. 149.

discussed under "argument by generalization." A vital step in evaluating deductive forms of argument is location and explicit wording of assumptions and making the decisions as to whether or not they should be accepted.

Two separate items are related in a conditional argument by an if-then sequence. This demonstrates that, should one specified circumstance come about, another necessarily follows. Everyday examples come to mind, such as "If it rains we won't have a picnic," or "If he gets the majority of votes he will be elected."

The if-then relationship in logical argument is found to be important and widely used. Indeed, some philosophers suggest that all argument proceeding from the known into the unknown can be stated in the conditional form. For examples of serious conditional argument we turn to a speech by Senator Joseph H. Ball of Minnesota. Concerning labor relations and legislation dealing with that problem he uses this double if-then argument.

> Most major disputes are over wages which are the price of labor services in a reasonably free market. I do not see how it would be possible to fix wages whether by executive or judicial decree and avoid also fixing prices. If government does that our free competitive economy is finished.[8]

The first of these conditional arguments is thought provoking. If you fix wages then it would seem you would need also to fix prices, an argument of considerable reasonableness. Compared to it, his second conditional contention, "If government does that our free competitive economy is finished," probably represents "strawman" argument with negligible connection between antecedent and consequent. The absolute and all inclusive nature of the generalization in this second argument causes us to be suspicious of it.

Later in this same speech Senator Ball presents a chain of two if-then arguments which are effective in advancing the thinking of his hearers.

> If free collective bargaining is to be our policy, as I believe it should, then the great bulk of disputes should be settled by bargaining with both parties free to strike if they cannot agree. If government is too ready to intervene in disputes, as it has been for some years now, then one party or the other, believing he can

---

[8] Joseph H. Ball, "Extension of Remarks," *Congressional Record, Appendix* (January 22, 1947), 93: Part 10, p. 225.

> gain something by such intervention, will be sure to insist on it and the whole collective bargaining process is weakened and tends to break down. That is what happened under the war-labor board.[9]

This typical and rather complex political argument can be "taken apart" by breaking it down into (1) assumption and (2) the smallest steps that we can isolate leading to the conclusion. The assumption is stated first in the form of a conditional relationship with which few or any of us disagree; we might reword that to read "If we want collective bargaining then dispute should be settled by bargaining." That becomes the assumption that underlies the remainder of the argument. Now the steps in the argument seem to be:

1. If government is "too ready" to intervene then either labor or management will insist on government intervention.
2. If either labor or management insist on government intervention then the collective bargaining process is weakened.
3. But we do not want collective bargaining process weakened (our assumption), therefore, the conclusion:
4. We do not want government to be too ready to intervene in labor management disputes.

Some study of the quoted passage is necessary if you are to see the source of each of the steps in the argument. Some of the analysis involves implication. For example, the conclusion we reached is not stated by Senator Ball in so many words, but it is so clearly implied that a complete analysis of the argument demands that we put it into words. This illustration demonstrates the difficulty of breaking down living arguments into logical patterns, a process essential to evaluation of that persuasion.

The key to evaluating the if-then argument lies in two operations. The first operation involves locating the steps in the argument including conclusions and premises implied, rearranging them if necessary, because the arguments as given may not be in logical order. Second, locate and word the underlying assumptions with the greatest possible accuracy. Are these truths of a degree of probability you are willing to accept? If the assumptions are sat-

---

[9] *Ibid.*, p. 226.

isfactory, if the chain of if-then arguments leads apparently to the conclusion with close relationship between each antecedent and consequent, you will have reason to accept the conditional reasoning unit.

Analysis of if-then argument is a major task confronting the student of persuasion. Because this form is so popular and frequent, as well as difficult to reconstruct, we now consider a few more examples and their analyses. The first is a simple and frequent argument: "The public is satisfied with radio because it listens to it." This is a "one step" argument. First, we word the argument in strict if-then form: "If the public listens to the radio then it is satisfied with radio." What is the assumption? "If the public were not satisfied it would stop listening to the radio." We have here something suspiciously resembling "straw-man" argument because the condition part of our statement is undeniable. People do listen to the radio. The key in this case to our acceptance is found in our willingness to accept the assumption. At this point we must suspend our analysis, and we can either accept or reject the assumption. By so doing we accept or reject the entire argument.

A series of conditional arguments is seen in the following excerpt from a speech made at the time President Franklin D. Roosevelt was proposing to enlarge the Supreme Court.

> If a group of men can seize Chrysler's plant, they can likewise seize his home; if they can seize his home and take him out of it, they can do the same to you and anyone else and if the law—the officers of the law, the government—cannot protect property our human rights cannot be protected, our government fails and the door is open to mob rule.[10]

In this rapid-fire reasoning the if-thens come thick and fast. Let us attack the argument by breaking it down first into small steps, then wording the underlying assumption. Here are the steps:

1. If a group of men can seize Chrysler's plant then they can seize Chrysler's home.

2. If a group of men can seize Chrysler's home then groups of men could seize all homes.

---

[10] Radio Speech by Frank E. Gannett, Program No. 6, *The People's Fight.* Recorded and distributed by Committee for Constitutional Government, Inc., 205 E. 42nd St., New York City.

3. If groups of men could seize all homes then the law could no longer protect property rights.
4. If the law could no longer protect property rights then human rights could no longer be protected.
5. If human rights could no longer be protected then government would fail.
6. If government failed then we would have anarchy (mob rule).

This is a good example of *chain argument* in which the consequent of an if-then statement becomes the antecedent or condition for the following statement. What is the underlying assumption which we must accept before we can proceed along the links of the chain? A clue to it is found, as it frequently is, in the first link. Before we can accept the first conditional statement we must assume that legally and reasonably a group of workers striking an industrial plant is the same thing as a group of men seizing a private home and taking it from the owner. This identity is conveyed to us by the word seize. We are asked to accept that seizing, when used to pertain to strikers taking over a plant, is substantially identical to the meaning of seize when it refers to taking over a private home. To make this clear it would probably be well to avoid the use of the word seize in the wording of our assumption: "In the United States today immobilizing an industrial plant by a sit-down strike is comparable, legally and practically, to theft of private property!" This assumption we can check by referring to legal precedent. Making up our minds about that assumption is highly important because, once we grant it, the long chain of argument leads inflexibly to the conclusion, a startling one, that of anarchy and mob rule.

Detecting, formulating and evaluating conditional arguments in current persuasion is challenging intellectual exercise. Here is a concealed example taken from a popular columnist, included to give the reader an example for practice analysis. It was used to prove that General Dwight Eisenhower should be drafted to run for President of the United States and that there is a moral justification for the demand that Eisenhower undertake such a campaign: "On the battlefront he told our young men what to do with their lives. It follows that they have a right to tell him what to do with his. It's as simple as that."

Remember, begin by putting the argument in if-then form, then locate and word the underlying assumption.

ARGUMENT BY ALTERNATION ("EITHER-OR" ARGUMENT)

Argument by alternative involves first the limiting of possibilities in the argument to a small number, usually two, then determining a choice of one of the alternatives. Typically, the persuader says, "Now we are confronted by two possibilities; if we select number one this will happen—if we select number two that will happen, hence our choice." Assuming the speaker has not overlooked any possibilities, and assuming his predictions of what may happen are accurate, the choice frequently *is* clear-cut.

There is a type of either-or argument which presents two alternatives, allegedly the only possible courses of action. The persuader demonstrates that if either of these is adopted, unpleasant results will follow. Consequently, the choice becomes unimportant, since neither of the alternatives represents a usable course of action. The persuader alleges that the people making the choice face a *dilemma.*

In June of 1947 the foreign policy of the United States toward the then current issue of Palestine independence underwent some fluctuations. It happened that public statements on this issue by President Truman were contradicted by State Department actions and further statements issued a few weeks later. This justified the accusation that while the President was telling the people one thing his State Department was planning and executing something else. Critics of the administration attempted to crystallize their objections in a dilemma. Either President Truman had been guilty of "doubletalk" concerning the conduct of our government in the Palestine crisis or else the State Department had been carrying on a program without his knowledge. Those, they said, were the only two possibilities, and if Mr. Truman admitted to either one publicly he would certainly suffer considerable loss of face. He could not afford to admit that he did not know what was going on in his State Department and he certainly could not afford to admit that he had been intentionally misleading the home folks. This was a rather effective dilemma. President Truman responded as many public figures do when confronted with a tight dilemma. He ignored it.

The dilemma might be said to be the "black or black" type of alternation. Another popular use of either-or argument might be called the "black or white" variety. In the black or white alternation we have the alternatives again reduced to two, one of which is highly desirable and the other is most undesirable. This alternation is similar in some ways to the "straw-man" conditional argument. It is usually colorful in the rhetorical sense but it is not realistic. It commonly deals in generalities predicting doom or disaster on the one hand and Utopia on the other. It can be dramatic and assume the nature of a figure of speech. It is widely used in advertising and political argument. Consider the following black or white alternation, a composite of the conclusion of many a political speech: "The chips are down more than ever in America, and we stand on the threshold of an era which has in it either the miseries of depression or the fulfillment of decent living with full production and full employment and decent wages."

Candidates who use black or white alternations repeat them many times and in many forms in their persuasion. Apparently they hope that they can fool their listeners or readers into believing that they actually are voting for prosperity or depression. "But," you might comment, "two alternatives are suggested and we are given a chance to make our choice!" We contend that in general statements such as the above, *no alternatives actually are suggested at all!* Conditions described are so general and abstract that there is nothing in reality corresponding to them. There are many possibilities, which are more probable than either of the two extremes between extreme depression and Utopian full employment with high wages. There is no real statement of the problem. Here is simply a rhetorical device setting up a "straw-man" and pushing it over in the direction the persuader wants it to fall. The persuader never attempts to prove that the alternative he advocates can, in and of itself, produce magnificent results; and on the other hand, he does not attempt to prove that the other choice would produce the horrible results that he asserts. The lack of connection between asserted cause and effect is characteristic of the black or white alternation.

Another form of argument by alternation is one which in a realistic way attempts to enumerate possible courses of action and examine the results of each. Alternatives in this case are not limited to two as they were in the dilemma and the black or white alternations. Consequently, it is more comprehensive than either of the other forms of alternation. The possibility of more than two alternatives is a guarantee that we can recognize some of the varying shades of grey which may occur between two extreme possibilities. That is an advantage if we are interested in having our argument correspond to fact.

In 1940 Colonel Charles A. Lindberg made recommendations concerning our foreign policy, based upon the exploration of three alternatives which he asserted to represent the entire range of choice open to the United States. The first of his three suggested alternatives was open participation in the European war. His second alternative was to continue the then present policy described in the Roosevelt phrase "all aid short of war." The third possibility was to withdraw totally from the European conflict, including withdrawing aid to the Allies, and to build ourselves a maximum amount of security in the Western hemisphere.

Lindbergh examined each in turn. Concerning the first alternative, that of moving to open participation in the European war, he said: ". . . arming to attack the continent of Europe would necessitate that the lives and thoughts of every man, woman and child in this country be directed toward war for the next generation, probably for the next several generations." [11]

In examining the second alternative, that of continuing the present policy, he said:

> We cannot continue for long to follow the course our government has taken without becoming involved in war with Germany. There are some who already advocate our entry into such a war. There are many perfectly sincere men and women who believe that we can send weapons to kill people in Europe without becoming involved in war with these people. Still others believe that by just gestures and applause we can assist France and England to win without danger to our own country. . . . There is a saying that grew in the old West to the effect that a man who enjoys life should never touch his gun unless he means business; that he should never draw unless he is ready to shoot, and that he should never shoot unless he is ready to kill. These old pioneers of ours knew from long experience that there can be no successful dabbling with death.[12]

---

[11] Col. Chas. A. Lindbergh, Radio Address, June 15, 1940. *Vital Speeches of the Day*, VI: 18, p. 549.

[12] *Ibid.*, p. 549, 550.

The second alternative is dealt with by demonstrating that it will lead in time to the first alternative, already shown to be undesirable. We call your attention to the argument by analogy used in support of the contention that the second alternative, "all aid short of war," will lead, inevitably, to the first alternative, a shooting war. Although the analogy differs almost totally in subject matter, there is some identity of principle involved, verified perhaps by events following Lindbergh's speech.

Here is Lindbergh's statement about his third alternative, retiring from the European scene and building our security at home.

> With an adequate defense no foreign army can invade us. Our advantage in defending America is as great as our disadvantage would be in attacking Europe. From a military, geographical standpoint we are the most fortunate country in the world. There is no other nation in this hemisphere strong enough to even consider attacking us, and the Atlantic and Pacific oceans separate us from the warring armies of Europe and Asia. . . . With our geographical position nothing but the gross neglect of our military forces, or quarreling between American countries themselves, could make possible an invasion by foreign armies. America stands today where the road divides at the signpost of war and peace.[13]

A large proportion of this radio speech was devoted to the demonstration of the practicality of the third alternative. It could isolate us from the European conflict and would in the long run prove much more desirable than war for the American people, Lindbergh claimed.

Such argument by alternation, if it is carefully constructed, has the advantage of seeming to be comprehensive. It is possible to convey the impression that all possibilities have been considered, their relative advantages and disadvantages carefully weighed, and the conclusion made in the light of all available evidence. Consequently, it has a strong appeal. Evaluation of the argument involves answering these questions: (1) Are all possible alternatives presented and fairly stated? (2) Are the alternatives mutually exclusive? and (3) Are we willing to accept the evidence and reasoning submitted in support of the various alternatives or to break them down? For example, in Lindbergh's argument we might

---

[13] *Ibid.*, p. 550, 551.

question his proof that we could set up an isolated area of security in the Western hemisphere, one which would be impregnable to attack by modern implements of war. This illustrates a danger of argument by alternation. Since Lindbergh destroyed all other possible alternatives he was in a position of having all his eggs in one basket. If we do not accept his third alternative there is nothing left and his entire argument fails. When you say, "Here are a limited number of possibilities," and then you proceed to destroy all of them except one, your proof for that one must be convincing. Otherwise, you will find yourself arguing that nothing can be done.

ARGUMENT BY CATEGORY

The categorical argument is a deductive form of reasoning based upon two assumptions (propositions or premises) from which a conclusion can be derived. The purpose is to gain acceptance of the conclusion by securing agreement on the truth of the premises. The structure of the valid argument is such that, if the premises are true, the conclusion must necessarily be true also. Hence, when an audience accepts the premises they are bound logically to acceptance of the conclusion of any sound syllogism.

Categorical arguments occur frequently in current persuasion but seldom are they in full, expanded form. Either of the premises or the conclusion may be suppressed, i.e., these may not be stated completely, but they are clearly or not-so-clearly implied. Analysis usually involves the wording of the suppressed element and the reconstruction of the complete argument.

The theory of categorical reasoning is somewhat complex, but, basically, it involves classes of "things" (people, laws, political parties, vegetables, and so on). These categories are shown to overlap or fit into each other in patterns that lead to discovery of new knowledge, i.e., the conclusion. Remember that only similar categories can overlap; for example, a class of horses cannot be fitted into a category of people.[14]

The idea of fitting classes of things into one another seems abstract until we try a few examples. In the Dewey-Stassen debate, Portland, Oregon, May 17, 1948, Mr. Stassen used categorical rea-

---

[14] Max Black, *Critical Thinking.* New York: Prentice-Hall, Inc., 1952, Chaps. 7, 8.

soning to summarize his attack in order to clinch the argument (he hoped) that the Communist Party should be outlawed.

> All attempts to overthrow the government of the United States by force directed by a foreign power should be outlawed. The Communist Party is one attempt to overthrow the government of the United States by force under the direction of a foreign power. Therefore the Communist Party should be outlawed.

Mr. Stassen's strategy was to secure Mr. Dewey's agreement on the first statement, the major premise, and the second statement, the minor premise. Once this agreement was secured Mr. Stassen could force Mr. Dewey to agree with his conclusion. The first step in testing the validity of this argument is to adapt it to the standard form of two premises (worded according to a set pattern) and a conclusion.

Major Premise:	*All* attempts to overthrow the government of the United States directed by a foreign power *are included in* things which should be outlawed.
Minor Premise:	*All* Communist Party memberships *are included in* attempts to overthrow the government of the United States directed by a foreign power.
Conclusion:	*All* Communist Party memberships *are included in* things which should be outlawed.

Mr. Stassen had completed a VALID unit of categorical reasoning. *If we grant the truth of his premises then we must accept his conclusion as true.*

To illustrate various condensed forms in which categorical argument occurs, we will convert the following argument into three abbreviated examples.

All absent-minded people *are included in* brilliant people.

All professors *are included in* absent-minded people.

Therefore, *all* professors *are included in* brilliant people.

Suppressing the major premise, it is: "Professors, being absent-minded, are brilliant."

Suppressing the minor premise, we have: "Absent-minded people are brilliant, hence, professors are brilliant."

Suppressing the conclusion, it evolves: "All absent-minded people are brilliant, and professors are known to be absent-minded!"

Examine the above condensed arguments carefully. They represent the possible truncated forms in which universal categorical arguments occur in persuasion. Further reading will be needed to achieve an understanding of the theory of argument by categories. Suitable references are listed at the end of this chapter.

The Levels of Argument

A prerequisite to logical analysis is the stripping away of "nonessentials" and the consideration of an argument in its simplest form. We find a need for a supplementary system of classification that will deal with over-all argumentative units including innuendo, "loaded" language, and assertions that might not appear at all in a study of the basic reasoning structure of the argument. A system for accomplishing that purpose is suggested here. It is presented in the belief that, used in conjunction with the nine methods of supporting a contention, it will provide a rather complete description of any persuasive use of reasoned discourse.

The five levels of argument are found in the congressional reaction to a speech by the President of the United States. It was in January of 1948 that President Truman delivered this particular message concerning the state of the nation. A barrage of words was directed at us over radio and through the press to influence our reactions to that speech. The forces battling for acceptance, and those dedicated to rejection, competed for public favor.

A few statements from Minnesota legislators were strikingly similar.[15]

> Rep. O'Hara: I noted that the President read from the right and turned to the left.
>
> Rep. Judd: I was disappointed. It was a message loaded with vague shotgun proposals without a concrete plan. It was unrealistic and wishful thinking. The world will be disappointed because it was not the inspiring hard-headed leadership that the world needs to have at this time.

A favorable comment came from a non-Minnesotan.

> Sen. Bloom (N.Y.): It was a wise and farseeing address.

The outstanding characteristic that these arguments seem to have in common is this: they do not mention *what* the President said.

---

[15] All statements of legislators are taken from the *St. Paul Pioneer Press,* The *Minneapolis Star,* and the *Minneapolis Times* news stories, January 8, 1948.

Speaking figuratively, they sit back and call his message names *without explaining what they did not like about it.* A name that fits such sweeping and unsupported opinions is "generalized judgment."

Another group of comments proved to be homogeneous. Here are a few of them.

> Republican House Floor Leader Halleck: The message drips with demagoguery and special interest appeal—bait for radical votes.
>
> Sen. Brewster (Maine): It was a good acceptance speech.
>
> Rep. Miller (Conn.): The Pendergast machine used to get votes for two bucks, now Truman is offering $40.
>
> Rep. Arends (Ill.): This was not a speech on the state of the Union but a speech on the state of affairs of Candidate Truman appealing for votes in November, 1948. Candidate Truman has tried, in this speech, to be everything to everybody. I never saw a speech cover the waterfront like that one did.

Inspection of each statement in this second group reveals again a generalized judgment; however, a new element has been added. That vitalizing ingredient is an attempt to discredit the speech by asserting that it had an unacceptable motive. Note that nothing is said concerning the merit of the message itself! Our commentators ignore *what* Truman said and pounce on *why* he said it.

A name for this type of argument that discredits or endorses a cause by side-stepping the issue and asserting motives is "motivational judgment"—judgment because it represents opinion, motivational because it centers attention on *motives* for actions, and thereby draws us away from consideration of a vitally important item, the substance of the speech.

Thus far the statements analyzed have condemned or praised without mention of the object of condemnation or approval. Fortunately, some comments directed to the general public are more specific, and hence, more meaningful. Let us continue with commentary on the President's State of the Union Address. Some press releases centered attention on the Truman plan for cutting taxes.

> Rep. Knutson (Minn.): The President's Tax Plan is dead as a mackerel; the President's proposal is inflationary and would immediately start another spiral in prices.
>
> Sen. Taylor (Idaho): I will fight tooth and toe-nail to obtain congressional enactment of the President's excellent domestic program.

> Sen. Byrd (Virginia): The President did not offer a single suggestion to eliminate at least some of the waste and extravagance that permeates nearly every activity of the government.
>
> Rep. Gore (Texas): The President's tax proposal has social fairness and is economically sound.

This group of comments is less confusing to the citizen because he is given some orientation; he is told *what* the speaker likes or dislikes. It is true that the argument rests upon the assertion of the speaker. However, a real, live issue is in the center of the stage. Our reader has at least a chance to weigh the opinion accompanying the citation of the problem, comparing his belief with the persuader's in light of his knowledge of the particular topic. There is a real advantage in knowing *what* an arguer is talking about. A name for this category of statements is "unsupported, specific contention."

Still more informative to the citizen than unsupported, specific contentions was the next group of arguments. Here is a sample.

> Sen. Ball (Minn.): In one breath, the President said farm income is too low and should be increased and in the next he decried high food prices and demanded Congress grant him power to reduce them. That sort of political chicanery is unworthy of grave issues facing the people of America.

If we make allowance for flag-waving and name-calling in the last sentence, we must admit that here we have a specific criticism of the Truman address in the form of a charged inconsistency. The Senator presents some analysis for us to test. He does not stop with saying "I do not like this"; he says in effect, "Let me cite an example of poor reasoning in the President's speech and we shall see what you think of it." Possibly his entire comment is more of a challenge to the intellect than a stimulus to the emotions.

Several other comments were specific in nature and were amplified by explanation.

> Sen. Connally (Texas): I advocate the reimposition of excess profit taxes to as much as 80% of the former rates. If progressive taxation on individuals is justified, progressive taxation on corporations is justified.
>
> Sen. Tobey (N.H.): He (the President) talks of taking $40 off a John D. Rockefeller's tax and the same amount off a John Murphy's.

Senator Tobey's conclusion is implied and thus vague, but we have no difficulty in grasping the basis of his criticism of the President's system of tax reduction. As such, we have again a definite analysis of a specific proposal to examine.

This fourth class of arguments, that puts a finger squarely upon an issue and supplies some reasoning concerning it, is "specific contention plus analysis." The fifth and final type of argument, by incorporating *evidence,* goes the one remaining step of making the analysis constructive. Lest we fall into the popular error of linking one person with one type of argument, let us take an example from Representative Knutson, who contributed one of our finest unsupported specific assertions. Perhaps regrettably, we cannot count on any persuader to be uniformly and unfailingly illogical—or logical!

This condensation of Representative Knutson's argument is from a *Minneapolis Star* editorial.

> —600,000 additional workers must be put to work each year to keep our growing population employed. Technological improvements make it necessary to find new places for another 400,000.
>
> Average investment per industrial worker today is almost $7,000. So, $7 billion of new investment would be needed each year if the new workers went into factory jobs. That is an addition to the $8 billion expenditures needed each year to renew and replace factories and machinery.
>
> If tax rates go higher, corporations might decide NOT to make that annual investment after the present boom is over. When those investments aren't made, workers are made idle.[16]

There are "handles" to grasp on an argument like this. Are the statistics accurate and complete? Do the new workers go into factory jobs? The argument depends upon the condition that they do. If tax rates are increased as Truman proposes, will corporations be *unable* to make needed investments? Is the assertion that they "might decide not" to make new investments after the present boom sufficient reason not to increase corporation taxes now? These questions and others come to mind, leading intelligent citizens to the reading of other sources and the accumulation of more information.

If you do not like Mr. Knutson's conclusion, then you have to analyze his evidence and his reasoning, and find some thing to

[16] Editorial, *Minneapolis Star* (January 8, 1948), p. 16.

challenge. Such critical scrutiny is the duty of citizenship, and our public officials, by supplying facts instead of fiction, make the discharge of that duty possible.

Contrast this example of "revealed argument" with an example of generalized judgment wherein Senator McGrath (R.I.) told the press that the President has offered a "businesslike, practical program of progressive liberalism," or with an example of motivational judgment such as the statement of Carroll Reece, Chairman of the Republican National Committee: "This obvious attempt of the Pendergast wing of the Democratic party to make peace with the Moscow wing, is additional proof that this administration is unwilling to attempt to solve American domestic problems by American methods."

The most complete argumentative units are termed "specific contention with analysis and evidence." An argument cannot be classified in this category unless it is *specific,* unless it incorporates analysis revealing reasoning involved, and unless evidence is provided to support it.

The continuum nature of the five "levels of argument" can be made clear by relating them to the thought-response associated with each.

Argument	Generalized Judgment	Motivational Judgment	Unsupported Specific Contention	Specific Contention plus Analysis	Specific Contention with Analysis and Evidence
Thought Responses	Vague Emotion-alized Thinking		Mixed Emotion-alized and Reflective Thinking		Analytical Critical Thinking

We see in this relationship some implications of the choice of "level" made by the persuader.

One way to improve in critical thinking is to classify your arguments, and those directed to you, in these five categories.

1. Generalized Judgment
2. Motivational Judgment
3. Unsupported, Specific Contention
4. Specific Contention plus Analysis
5. Specific Contention with Analysis and Evidence.[17]

---

[17] William S. Howell, "Critical Thinking and Persuasion," The Gavel of *Delta Sigma Rho* (May, 1948), 30: 4, pp. 68–70. Much of the material on "Levels of Argument" is adapted from this article.

Another improvement comes when you succeed in increasing your use of categories 4 and 5. You are probably justified in heavily discounting the generalized, motivational and unsupported arguments. A motivational judgment is not much better than a generalized judgment, although an unsupported specific contention at least locates the issue. Specific contention plus analysis is much stronger, so that when you and others set up specific contentions with both analysis and supporting evidence, then the thinking process has optimum opportunity to advance.

Summary

These chapters on logical techniques of persuasion began by noting that reasoned discourse had two major parts, evidence and the logical interpretation of that evidence. The objective of reasoned discourse was to shed a maximum amount of light on a problem through a reasonable interpretation of available information.

The objective of reasoned discourse dictated the requirement of systematic patterns of interpreting evidence. There was a need, we found, for "rules of the game" that would guide us in arranging the evidence we have selected and lead the thinking process to sound conclusions. Logic was our source of these tested, verifiable rules.

We noted the close interaction of evidence and reasoning. Facts in argument were found to be of significance only as they are used by the persuader. As they are put to use they become parts of a logical reasoning structure. The *form* of this reasoning is dictated by the facts available, and the particular form in turn imposes certain criteria upon the factual information needed to support it. Hence, we concluded that reasoning and evidence are inseparable. In the forms of reasoned discourse presented, evidence and reasoning were considered jointly.

Two systems of analysis were suggested for examining and planning reasoned discourse. The methods of strengthening a contention represented the direct application of those principles of logic most helpful in analyzing and formulating practical argument. The five levels of argument are a classification upon a different base involving first, the division of a persuasive structure into its sequential steps, and then the classification of each of these units into one of the five categories. The five levels of argument furnish a survey technique for achieving a rough evaluation of the reasoned content of a persuasive appeal, and they suggest direct means of increasing the soundness of our own persuasion.

Readings

1. Beardsley, M. C., *Practical Logic.* New York: Prentice-Hall, Inc., 1950, Ch. 11.
2. Black, Max, *Critical Thinking.* New York: Prentice-Hall, Inc., 1952, Chaps. 3, 4, 6, 7, 8.
3. Castell, Albury, *A College Logic.* New York: The Macmillan Company, 1935, Topic 5.
4. Ewbank, H. L. and Auer, J. J., *Discussion and Debate.* New York: Appleton-Century-Crofts, Inc., 1951, pp. 149–154.
5. Searles, H. L., *Logic and Scientific Methods.* New York: The Ronald Press Company, 1948, Chaps. 7, 16.

Exercises

1. Bring to class an example of each of the five levels of argument.

2. Explain the relationship between the concept "probability" and the soundness of a generalization. Illustrate with examples.

3. Find three arguments by authority and classify them according to the categories given in this chapter.

4. Prepare a five minute speech based upon (a) an alternation and (b) a conditional argument. Be sure they are valid.

5. Collect several implied or openly stated conditional arguments from advertising. Which, if any, are "straw-man" arguments?

Part V

APPLYING PERSUASION TO SPEAKING

A knowledge of the bases and the tools of persuasion does not guarantee the successful oral presentation of a unit of persuasion. The persuasive speaker needs to know the principles and methods of effective public speaking if he is to lodge his appeals effectively in the minds of an audience.

Before a speaker prepares a specific speech, he should know what persuasiveness lies within himself, and he should know how to gain and maintain the attention of an audience. These topics are discussed in Chapters XIII and XIV. With these basic facts in mind, the speaker is ready to take the steps in preparing a speech. Chapters XV to XXI discuss these steps in their proper order.

Chapter XIII

FINDING THE AVAILABLE MEANS OF PERSUASION WITHIN THE SPEAKER

Chapter XIII

FINDING THE AVAILABLE MEANS OF PERSUASION WITHIN THE SPEAKER

Introduction

From our study of the persuasion process we turn to the individual persuasive speaker. What do we know about that part of persuasion originating in the personality of the speaker? What are his internal sources of persuasive power? What advice can be given to help the speaker utilize his full potential to persuade? It is the business of this chapter to locate and analyze the available means of persuasion *within the speaker.*

We can talk more meaningfully about the power of the personality to persuade if we introduce a generally accepted term, perhaps strange to some readers, *ethos.* This word may be broadly translated as "character." In the context of persuasive speech it includes two elements: (1) The reputation or prestige enjoyed by the speaker with respect to his particular audience and subject at the moment he begins to speak, and (2) the increasing or diminishing of that prestige as a result of what he says and does during the speech.

To say that the character of the speaker influences the outcome of his persuasion to some extent is clear and meaningful, but deceptive in its simplicity. A complex interaction involving topic, knowledge of topic material, opinions of speaker and audience, general sensitivity of the speaker, mechanics of his speech delivery and many other diverse factors, influences the ethos status of the speaker. Some insight into this phenomenon can be gained through examination of the comments on ethos made by qualified observers.

The term ethos, as we use it, is comprehensive with respect to manifest character traits. Sattler describes this usage.

> One interpretation of ethos is that the speaker exhibits qualities of a personal nature—intrinsic goodness and honesty, sound

> judgment, an interest in the well-being of the audience, together with respected traits of a non-ethical nature—which induce listeners to approve the arguments given in a speech.[1]

Certainly the aptitudes and knowledge essential to an analysis of the audience and the preparation of a speech might be considered as available means of persuasion within the speaker. However, we class the use of speech materials and aids to persuasion, found in audience and occasion, as *external* to the speaker. In this chapter we choose to study ethos, the extent and limits of which will become apparent as we see its various facets through the eyes of classical and contemporary authorities.

Classical Theories of Ethos

Aristotle supplies a definition of the role of ethos in persuasive speaking.

> The character (ethos) of the speaker is a cause of persuasion when the speech is so uttered as to make him worthy of belief; for as a rule we trust men of probity more, and more quickly about things in general, while on points outside the realm of exact knowledge, where opinion is divided, we trust them absolutely. This trust, however, should be created by the speech itself, and not left to depend upon an antecedent impression that the speaker is this or that kind of man. It is not true, as some writers on the art maintain, that the probity of the speaker contributes nothing to his persuasiveness; on the contrary, we might almost affirm that his character (ethos) is the most potent of all the means to persuasion.[2]

Reputation is thus conceded to be important, but Aristotle stresses that the conduct of the speaker, and the speech itself, can do much to communicate the "probity" of the speaker to the audience. We might conclude that Aristotle recommends calculated action on the part of the speaker to build his prestige, and warns the speaker not to rely solely on a previously established virtuous record.

Quintilian agrees with Aristotle in substance, asserting that public speaking demands first of all that the speaker possess, "or be thought to possess," praiseworthy virtues. To be thought a "bad" man, he

---

[1] William M. Sattler, "Conceptions of Ethos in Ancient Rhetoric," *Speech Monographs* (1947), XIV: 55, 56.

[2] Lane Cooper (trans.), *The Rhetoric of Aristotle.* New York: Appleton-Century-Crofts, Inc., 1932, pp. 8, 9.

notes, is a severe handicap, for such a person will not be given credit for speaking sincerely. In elaborating upon characteristics of speaking useful to the building of ethos he contends that, in order to move the feelings of others, the speaker himself must be moved; in other words, he must be actually emotionally aroused in order to appear thus, and so produce this response in others. Although he considers use of humor an asset, excessive joking, he fears, damages dignity. Possibly Quintilian more than Aristotle stresses the desirability of a speaker's *being* sincere in order to *appear* sincere. Also, he, more than Aristotle, seems to assign greater weight to the speaker's character being established *before* his speaking appearance.

Writers dealing with ethos usually specify its components. Aristotle says that the "sources of personal credibility" are three in number—sagacity, high character and good will. Means to establish and enhance a speaker's ethos are included in advice of classical writers. Aristotle recommends the use of "virtuous maxims" because they give the impression of virtuous character to the speaker. Cicero advises the speaker to select speech content carefully with an eye to building ethos, as illustrated by the praising of particular virtues that leads the audience to assume that the speaker possesses them. Cicero warns against overdoing the effort to build ethos, for it may become apparent or it may result in "pleading your own cause instead of that of your client." Quintilian calls attention to the positive ethos-building effect of being obviously humble, and representing oneself as weak, inferior, and a prey to human weaknesses. Conversely, ethos may be destroyed, says Quintilian, by a speaker's appearance of being "insolent, malignant, overbearing, or reproachful."

More modern classical writers on rhetoric frequently discussed elements of ethos in persuasive speaking. In the sixteenth century Thomas Wilson advised the advocate modestly to call attention to his qualifications and accomplishments, particularly to his good deeds, and especially to those affecting his audience. John Ward, writing in the seventeenth century, defined the four qualities of an orator as "wisdom, integrity, benevolence, and modesty," all of which we would consider as contributing to ethos. Some years later George Campbell provided a list of factors that increased and decreased sympathy for the speaker in an audience. On the positive side he mentioned "connective circumstances," including consanguinity, acquaintance, common citizenship, common religion, and, greatest of all, common interest. A lively and expressive delivery is useful in strengthening the bond of sympathy between speaker and audience. Campbell phrased a warning concerning listeners' prejudices in respect to the speaker's ethos.

> Sympathy in the hearers to the speaker may be lessened several ways, chiefly by these two: by a low opinion of his intellectual abilities and by a bad opinion of his morals. The latter is the more prejudicial of the two. . . .
>
> As to personal prejudices in general, I shall conclude with two remarks. The first is, the more gross the hearers are so much the more susceptible they are of such prejudices. Nothing exposes the mind more to all their baneful influences than ignorance and rudeness; the rabble chiefly consider who speaks, men of sense and education, what is spoken.[3]

Writing in the early nineteenth century, Campbell emphasized as did Gilbert Austin the role of delivery in communicating ethos to the audience. Austin somewhat cynically contended that since the majority of one's listeners are incapable of reaction to the matter of the speech, as separate from the manner of the speaker, delivery considerations become supremely important. If the speaker's manner outweighs what he says, then delivery becomes a means of conveying to the audience the impression of the speaker's personal worth—the item that amounts to the principal power of his persuasion. A large share of the effectiveness of delivery is to be found in bodily action, said Austin, whereupon he supplied detailed advice on the kinds and uses of gestures.

This brief sampling of ideas of some classical writers concerning ethos suggests thought-provoking applications to the rhetoric of modern persuasion. Let us see now what contemporary writers have to say on the subject.

Modern Ideas on Ethos

Contemporary writers deal extensively with the role of ethos in persuasive speech, although they seldom use the term. Thonssen and Gilkinson call it "ethical proof" and define current usage.

---

[3] Lester Thonssen, *Selected Readings in Rhetoric and Public Speaking.* New York: The H. W. Wilson Company, 1942, p. 241.

> Ethical proof derives from the speaker himself—from his personality, from his attitude toward his hearers, and from the way he approaches his subject. It is a broad, almost omnibus, term. It embraces such characteristics as the speaker's manifest intelligence, good will toward the listeners, tactfulness, sincerity, honesty, and general agreeableness.[4]

Sandford and Yeager discuss "personal persuasiveness" in some detail, listing qualifications of the speaker under this heading as: "character; popularity; appearance and bearing; fund of knowledge; self-confidence; clear thinking; tact; enthusiasm; age; intelligence; experience; opinions; activity level; and past successes and failures." [5]

This is a rather comprehensive list of ethos factors, although the individual categories may not be mutually exclusive. Improving one's personal persuasiveness, say these authors, is a matter of improving the personality itself, which is a job of considerable magnitude. Yet, because "for most of us it is more important even than the ideas which we seek to communicate," personality retooling may be worth the time and effort involved. Sandford and Yeager supply a list of desirable "habits" [6] that serves a dual function, that of check list for rating our own speech personalities, and that of selecting particular specific traits to guide efforts of personality improvement.

Personality is given a broad definition by Oliver, including all the elements of ethos. His four divisions of the speaker's personality, and the analysis of each division, are helpful to the student of persuasion.[7] In brief summary, the divisions of speaker personality and their elements are: (1) his qualities (character, reputation, appearance, social ease, sincerity); (2) his attitudes (toward his subject, toward his audience, toward himself); (3) his abilities (general intelligence, general knowledge); and (4) his mechanisms (voice, bodily action).

In Oliver's list, "social ease is an inclusive item, embracing poise,

---

[4] L. Thonssen and H. Gilkinson, *Basic Training in Speech.* Boston: D. C. Heath and Company, 1947, p. 330.

[5] W. P. Sandford and W. H. Yeager, *Principles of Effective Speaking.* New York: The Ronald Press Company, 1950, p. 118.

[6] *Ibid.*, p. 130.

[7] Robert T. Oliver, *The Psychology of Persuasive Speech.* New York: Longmans, Green and Co., Inc., 1942, pp. 94–104.

self-confidence and a social 'know-how' " that seems to be of practical importance. It connotes, also, an absence of tension and a relaxation of mind and body that we associate with well-adjusted and competent people. Qualities, attitudes, and abilities are closely related and all become apparent via mechanism, but each of these categories is identifiable. Criticism of elements of ethos in a speech may be sharpened by use of this or a similar system of categories.

The concepts of ethos have been adapted to fit the circumstances of mass communication. Doob speaks in psychological terms of the role of ethos in propaganda.

> A stimulus with prestige prevents the arousal of or weakens critical or incompatible responses that otherwise might block the learning of pre-action responses.
>
> The propagandist himself may possess prestige because of the position he occupies or because of his past successes.
>
> The propagandist may include among his propaganda stimuli persons other than himself and objects which have prestige.
>
> The past is always assumed by propagandists to have prestige and so they are always eager to demonstrate that their cause has the sanctity of antiquity.
>
> Sometimes the part of the propaganda stimulus with prestige has little or no logical connection with the preaction response and hence serves merely to produce submission without evoking related responses.[8]

Ethos of a "source" in a large system of propaganda differs from that of the single persuasive speaker, yet reactions to remote or present ethos elements are similar. For example, the source is usually impersonal, but is consciously or unconsciously invested with all the speaker personality traits listed by Oliver. The propagandee comes to have respect or lack of respect for a regular source of propaganda; he personifies its qualities, attitudes, and abilities. The radio station, the hostile foreign government, the large corporation attain varying degrees of ethos with respect to the regular recipients of their communications. Effects of their messages are selectively enhanced or diminished correspondingly.

Printed mass communications carry relatively few ethos-determining elements in the mechanisms of transmission. Quality of paper, type used, illustrations in color, artistry—all contribute to ethos.

---

[8] Leonard W. Doob, *Public Opinion and Propaganda.* New York: Henry Holt and Company, 1948, pp. 371–373.

Radio speech has many more ethos-determiners; a speech personality is conveyed with some completeness by the faithful reproduction of the voice. Now with television adding the visible code to the voice, we have all the delivery considerations and their impacts upon ethos in the large scale telecast that are found in the small, present, face-to-face, speaker-audience relationship. Not only does the radio speaker making the transition to television of necessity worry about his appearance, but his studio accessories should create an ethos-building setting for his particular speech performance. For example, to read obviously from a script might be damaging to his ethos, and to avoid doing just that demands painful alterations in his presentation pattern.

Yet, the more complete communication of the speech personality via television repays the radio speaker for his efforts in adaptation. Listen to a radio speaker who performs on both radio and television and compare your reactions to his speaking in the two media. Your feelings of like or dislike, acceptance or rejection, will probably be more intense from the viewing experience. The difference is most striking in programs of an "ad lib" format where the speaker's physical reactions to unexpected questions and unrehearsed circumstances may be as significant as, or even more revealing than, his planned responses. In a program like "Meet the Press," the viewer gets not only the reply to a question, with visible responses of the person being interviewed, but also the reactions of the panel-questioners who show their approval or disapproval by facial expression and small but definite body movements. The result is a more dramatic, more highly personalized communication. The essential ingredient in the apparent advantage of the TV speaker over the radio speaker is a more complete transmission of speech personality; all of us are interested in *people*.

In the fall of 1951, Secretary of State Dean Acheson presided at the San Francisco Peace Conference for the signing of a treaty of peace with Japan. The conference was telecast as the first nationwide television network presentation in the United States. For the first time the citizens of this country could study Dean Acheson at close range. He was a controversial political figure, and the people who were curious as to "what kind of person he really was" were able to observe his chairmanship of the conference as though they had invisible seats within ten feet of the rostrum. Concerning the impact of the Acheson speech personality, news commentator Edward R. Murrow said:

> It would be my guess that Mr. Acheson—a remote, aloof, and intellectually arrogant man—has done himself some good with the American public in the last two days. He suddenly became the visual symbol of American opposition to world communism. The minute-and-a-half well mannered brawl with the Polish delegate yesterday probably helped him more than a half-a-dozen of his closely written, rather dull policy speeches would have done. Some at least of the millions who witnessed that exchange, and the proceedings that followed, may have come to doubt, as they have been told, that this man is a communist sympathizer surrounded by men of like mind.[9]

A state department official summarized what occurred: "A lot of people expected to see a shifty-eyed ogre. Instead, they saw a man who could walk firmly across a heap of eggs without breaking any shells. They said, 'Hey, this man is good—what's the gripe?' "[10]

The fact that Dean Acheson is a large and handsome man suggests that personal appearance is a significant contributor to ethos. There is some experimental evidence to suggest that physical size correlates with vocational success to a significant degree. Men holding executive positions, for example, tend to be taller and heavier than clerks. This seems to be true of a wide variety of occupations. "Imposing stature" appears to be just that.

In our society physical beauty and attractive dress are powerful ethos factors. In college classes, or elsewhere, one needs not to look far to find examples of well endowed girls and boys who are accorded a prestige and have an influence beyond their intellectual capabilities. The very pretty girl in our culture finds many doors open to her, while her unattractive but more capable sister faces a stiff, continuous battle for favorable recognition.

Probably every speaker ought to remind himself frequently that he must do all that he can to enhance the impact of his physical appearance. A poised, dignified personality is in part a result of physical attributes, but presumably, in larger part, it is derived from such controllable items as dress, make-up, posture, and the

---

[9] Edward R. Murrow, "Edward R. Murrow with the News," CBS Broadcast, September 6, 1951.

[10] Peter Lisagor, "GOP Praise of Acheson Stuns Critics," *Minneapolis Tribune* (September 13, 1951), p. 6.

complex patterns of acquired habitual physical actions (facial expressions, tics, gestures, and so on).

Little is known concerning the *amount* of persuasive effectiveness attributed to ethos. In a study reported in Chapter XXII,[11] Haiman concluded that "variations in the prestige of a speaker" influenced attitude changes resulting from his speech significantly, that for his expert judges important ingredients of ethos were "competence," "likeableness," "sincerity," and "physical attractiveness," that original opinions of listeners on the speaker's topic influenced their reactions to his ethos, and that expert judges considered ethos and success in persuasion on the part of prominent public speakers to be rather highly correlated. Henrikson[12] found that with students in college speech classes (a) better known students are better liked, (b) better known students are judged to be better speakers, and (c) the most liked students are rated as better speakers. Apparently, an audience's "liking and knowing" a speaker increase his potential persuasive effectiveness, but to what degree we have no clue. Experimental evidence confirms that ethos is a significant factor in persuasion, and it locates some personality characteristics that people agree are thought to be important in determining ethos of the speaker, but quantitative measurement of its effectiveness in shifting attitudes or teaching facts remains to be done.

We can summarize the opinions of contemporary writers concerning the role of ethos in persuasion by saying that however much they may differ in subdividing it, they concur in asserting that it is one of the vital factors in determining responses to persuasive stimuli. In accord with the classical writers, some of our contemporaries stress the reputation built before the speech; others stress ethos-creating factors within the speech itself. Some authors write that ethos is an important ingredient; others write, as do Gilman, Aly, and Reid, that ethos of the persuasive speaker is the most important element contributing to his success.

> Of the three means of persuading—reasoning, disposing, and accrediting—probably the most powerful is the one associated

[11] Franklyn S. Haiman, "An Experimental Study of the Effects of Ethos in Public Speaking," *Speech Monographs* (1949), XVI: 2, pp. 190–202.

[12] E. H. Henrikson, "The Relation Among Knowing a Person, Liking a Person, and Judging Him as a Speaker," *Speech Monographs* (1940), VII: 22–25.

with the personality of the speaker himself. Day after day more changes are effected by request or direction based on faith in the speaker than by any argument advanced for a proposition.[13]

The Application of Elements of Ethos to Persuasive Speaking

Available means of persuasion within the speaker embrace his capabilities of preparation. These include skills in audience analysis, evaluation of evidence, planning of reasoned discourse and other motive appeals, plus his willingness to expend time and energy in the process of developing the speech to a state of readiness. These factors are treated in detail elsewhere in this and other books. Here we would like to know what a speaker's manifest speech personality (ethos) can contribute to his persuasive efforts. We wish to see as clearly as possible the personal dynamics of the interaction of a speaker and members of his audience because the speaker's ethos is a frame of reference for his message. Given the speech, the occasion, and the audience, the speaker must realize that every stimulus he originates is slanted by his ethos. Significance is added to, or subtracted from, everything he says and does, to correspond to *what the audience thinks of him at the moment.* His problem is to conduct himself before and during the speech so that the audience reactions to him as an individual inspire confidence in his particular message. The acceptance he wins as a person he hopes to transfer to the contentions he wishes his listeners to accept. Speech materials will have been selected, arranged, and worded with ethos in mind. This is the linkage between content and ethos, something to be carefully planned and never to be left to chance.

Reputation, that part of ethos in effect when the speaker begins to speak, is ordinarily established by many incidents over a period of time. We spend our lives trying to earn the trust and respect of other people. If we are personally well known to our audiences then our message will either benefit from, or suffer from, the sum total of their many impressions of us. There can be little immediate control over ethos, and only small changes in attitude toward the speaker can be expected from a single speech. The speaker's obligation to himself is to speak and act consistent with the best of the previously acquired audience ideas about him. Stereotypes of per-

---

[13] Wilbur E. Gilman, Bower Aly, and Loren D. Reid, *The Fundamentals of Speaking.* New York: The Macmillan Company, 1951, pp. 334, 335.

sonalities quickly become "set." One's close associates have fairly fixed opinions of one's essential trustworthiness.

The speaker who is prominent, who is not known intimately, and who is highly controversial, has great opportunities for ethos-building during a speech. Uncertainty cries out for guidance to a more comfortable positive belief. The case of Dean Acheson illustrates the possibilities of building ethos in the undecided, but much interested, audience.

Because people want to think well of other people, the speaker who is a stranger has the greatest opportunity of all, and his warmth and friendliness can easily evoke a similar response. Aside from the possibility that the audience may be hostile to the speaker because of a dislike for his topic, the unknown speaker has excellent chances of advancing a uniform image of his personality, cut according to the pattern he chooses.

Now let us turn to the *means* by which the speaker builds ethos during his speech. We must mention good delivery, frankness, friendliness, knowledge, rhetorical skill, in fact, all the elements of ethos supplied by classical and modern analysts. References that humbly call attention to his unusual experiences and qualifications probably help. However, the basis of a powerful aspect of ethos is more subtle. Contemporary writers call it *sincerity* of the speaker. This trait or characteristic is worthy of closer examination.

PRIMARY VS. SECONDARY AND TERTIARY SINCERITY

That most authorities advise the speaker to be sincere is evident, although what they mean by sincerity is not always clear. "Dedication to a cause" and "profound intellectual conviction" are listed frequently as characteristics of the sincere speaker. Oliver explains this concept in discussing sincerity.

> Great earnestness generates real power behind an idea. If we don't like the idea, we are apt to term the power fanaticism; if we do, we call it sincerity. In either case it might be described as a sense of mission. No real leadership is possible without it. We recognize it in the Minister's "call," in the reformer's zeal.[14]

Two aspects of speaker sincerity are evident—the personal commitment of the speaker to what he is doing (a "cause") and his

---

[14] Robert T. Oliver, *The Psychology of Persuasive Speech.* New York: Longmans, Green and Co., Inc., 1942, p. 100.

intellectual conviction. This leads to a follow-up question: "What is the *object* of his self dedication and in what must he believe so profoundly?" Here our authorities are in less agreement. Some assert that the profound conviction must of necessity be in the central proposition of his persuasive speech. Others admit that this source of sincerity may be centered in the belief that the persuasion *must* be done. In the second instance, the belief in an *objective* of his persuasion may or may not be accompanied by the speaker's acceptance of his specific persuasive proposition. We can identify three orders of sincerity: *Primary sincerity,* consisting of unreserved belief in the persuasive proposition; *secondary sincerity,* stemming from a conviction that securing acceptance of the persuasive proposition is socially desirable, regardless of the persuader's personal feelings toward the specific proposition; and *tertiary sincerity,* resting on the persuader's personal reward from the act of persuasion, but being disinterested in truth of the proposition and its social consequences. Examples may serve to clarify the differences in these levels or orders of sincerity.

John Foster Dulles, speaking before the Japanese Peace Treaty Conference in San Francisco in the summer of 1951, impressed television viewers as possessing a profound conviction, a complete faith in the treaty. When he answered Gromyko's complaint that the Russian-suggested changes had not received a fair hearing, he told of eleven months of negotiations over the Russian proposals, and, using a map of Japan, he showed the complete impossibility of two of the Soviet provisions. This was powerful speaking, and the power seemed to originate in Dulles' absolute conviction, developed painstakingly and deliberately, that the treaty was the best possible. If this impression is accurate, and if John Foster Dulles really had great faith in the wisdom of the treaty, then he gained ethos from his belief in his central persuasive proposition and developed a primary sincerity.

Let our second example be that of a patriotic citizen speaking on behalf of a drive to collect scrap aluminum during World War II. The persuasive proposition was, "If everyone contributes his unneeded aluminum, the war effort will benefit." Our speaker had reason for doubting that enough aluminum could be collected to do any real good, hence he had only a tentative faith in the central proposition. Yet he believed profoundly that "drives" and movements of this nature are needed to keep the people unified in times of stress. Consequently, he enthusiastically furthered the aluminum drive by speaking earnestly on its behalf on every available occasion. He doubted his proposition, yet he had complete faith in the desirability of persuading others to accept it. His ethos status was enhanced by a secondary sincerity.

A third example is a speaker hired by an advertising agency that in turn has been retained by the American Medical Association to stage a publicity campaign opposing socialized medicine. Our speaker favors the socialization of medical care, but he is convinced that the United States at the present time is not ready for it and that Congress could not possibly pass such a measure in the foreseeable future. Thus, his speaking against the cause of socialized medicine will lend little real or immediate damage to it; and further, he needs money and the salary is high. It is an offer on a trial basis, so he knows that unless he does an impassioned and eloquent job of advocacy he will be released and another speaker will be hired. The result is that he becomes a veritable firebrand of opposition to socialized medicine, impressing listeners by his "tremendous conviction." He is sincere because of his personal stake in the performance; his is definitely a tertiary sincerity, quite unrelated to the persuasive proposition and its social utility.

Two comments may be made concerning persuasive speaking that rests on secondary or tertiary sincerity. Rationalization is always involved, enabling the speaker to live comfortably with himself, as we note in the case of the aluminum drive advocate, and prominently so, in the instance of the opponent of socialized medicine. As the high correlation of belief and desire would lead us to expect, the persuasive speaker tends, over a period of time, to increase his belief in his central proposition. Writers on mass communication note the tendency of propagandists to believe their own propaganda. The paid advocate may develop a "profound conviction"!

From the viewpoint of the audience, it may be difficult or impossible to discriminate among primary, secondary, and tertiary sincerity of the persuasive speaker.

From the viewpoint of the speaker, primary sincerity is to be preferred. If he is unskilled, he will be unable to say something he does not believe with conviction, while great confidence in his message may help him in overcoming deficiencies in rhetoric and delivery. But the skilled persuader can probably weave as durable a fabric of ethos with the coarse fibers of secondary or tertiary sincerity as he can with the finer thread of a genuine faith in the action he advocates.

THE "GOOD" VS. THE "ABLE" SPEAKER

Less frequent than the advice to be sincere, but quite often noted, is some mention of a relationship between a man's morality and his potential power as a persuasive speaker.

> The old principle handed down from ancient times that an orator is a good man skilled in speaking is sound from both the ethical and psychological points of view.[15]

> People will believe a good man more quickly than a man whose motives are questionable.
>
> . . . Generosity, kindness, sympathy, hopefulness, cheerfulness, in fact all the virtues which we usually associate with a gentleman will aid a public speaker to understand and persuade his fellow men.[16]

What Crocker, Gray and Braden are talking about seems to be the possession by the speaker of *virtues respected by society*. Other writers deny any close relationship between conventional moral goodness and persuasive power. Compare the following description of the qualities of the effective leader of a mass movement to the specifications of the "good man" above.

> Exceptional intelligence, noble character, and originality seem neither indispensable nor perhaps desirable. The main requirements seem to be: audacity and a joy in defiance; an iron will; a fanatical conviction that he is in possession of the one and only truth; faith in his destiny and luck; a capacity for passionate hatred; contempt for the present; a cunning estimate of human nature; a delight in symbols (spectacles and ceremonials); unbounded brazenness which finds expression in a disregard of consistency and firmness; a recognition that the innermost craving of a following is for communion and that there can never be too much of it; a capacity for winning and holding the utmost loyalty of a group of able lieutenants.[17]

---

[15] G. W. Gray and W. W. Braden, *Public Speaking.* New York: Harper and Brothers, 1951, p. 545.

[16] Lionel Crocker, *Public Speaking for College Students.* New York: American Book Company, 1941, p. 31.

[17] Eric Hoffer, *The True Believer.* New York: Harper and Brothers, 1951, p. 112.

This is not a description of a "good man" in any conventional moral sense; yet Hoffer shows evidence indicating that these were characteristics of some of the most persuasive public speakers of recent times. We are led to call attention to the differences between the separate categories of morally good and the able speakers and to suggest that while our ideal persuader is both good and able, moral qualifications are an inadequate substitute for skill in speaking.

It is regrettable that some unscrupulous people are extraordinarily persuasive speakers. But it is important that we recognize this state of affairs and cease insisting that moral goodness is pre-requisite to effectiveness in persuasion. Sarett and Foster offer a balanced perspective:

> *A speaker may be an "able person" and yet not a "good man" in the popular sense.* It may be that his character liabilities are more than offset by his character assets. For example, he may be selfish, dishonest and cruel, yet may possess extraordinary mental powers, tenacity of purpose and courage. Or, again, he may possess such sheer brute vitality that despite his shortcomings he achieves power for the time being.[18]

Possession of the virtues generally respected by his social group is an asset to the persuader. When goodness is supplemented by the skills of an able speaker the upper reaches of effectiveness are attainable. The non-virtuous but otherwise capable speaker *may* be successful. But personal virtue cannot compensate in and of itself for the lack of any considerable number of concrete speech abilities.

Summary

Classical and modern writers agree that the power of the personality to persuade—ethos—is one of the most powerful elements in persuasive speaking.

In the speech situation two factors contribute to ethos—the reputation of the speaker with the particular audience when he begins to speak, and the changes in this initial prestige coming about in the minds of this audience as a result of the things he does and says.

---

[18] L. Sarett and W. T. Foster, *Basic Principles of Speech.* New York: Houghton Mifflin Company, 1946, pp. 29, 30.

Ethos is always in terms of a particular audience, occasion, topic, and speaker. Ethos of the same speaker changes with audience, occasion, and subject.

Sources of propaganda accumulate ethos as do individual speakers. Television, by restoring the visible code to spoken mass communication, creates new opportunities for the persuasive speaker in the building of ethos.

Important to ethos is the sincerity of the speaker. Three orders of sincerity are distinguishable; primary sincerity stemming from a "profound conviction" that the persuasive proposition is true; secondary sincerity, based upon the equally strong faith that securing acceptance of the persuasive proposition is socially desirable whether the persuasive speaker believes it or not; and tertiary sincerity, resting upon personal benefits to the speaker. Each adds power to the message.

The adage that the competent persuasive speaker is a "good man skilled in speaking" is socially desirable but not always true. Many less than moral men have been highly influential in determining the behavior of others through speech. While being able is enough to produce effective persuasion, goodness of character usually enhances the speaker's skills and makes possible the finest realization of his leadership capabilities. Only in rare and exceptional instances do anti-virtuous character traits seem to aid the persuader in reaching his goal.

The most stable and powerful ethos enjoyed by a speaker is that in the minds of his close associates. Here we have the closest relationship between goodness and persuasive effectiveness, for the people we live with come to know us as we are, and we would expect trusted personal acquaintances to be successful in persuading each other. It is interesting that in studies of factors causing people to change their political views, the main sources of influence were found in the small, permanent social groups. Since mutual trust over a long period of time produces predisposition to acceptance, even of ideas as drastic as those changing political affiliation, friends were found to be the best political persuaders. This is convincing evidence of the persuasive power of ethos among neighbors, relatives, fellow church members, and fellow workers, and something the persuader may well remember if he aspires to community leadership.

Readings

1. Haiman, Franklyn S., "An Experimental Study of the Effects of Ethos in Public Speaking," *Speech Monographs* (1949), XVI: 2, pp. 190–202.

2. Hoffer, Eric, *The True Believer.* New York, Harper and Brothers, 1951, pp. 3–20, 109–141.

3. Oliver, Robert T., *Persuasive Speaking.* New York, Longmans, Green and Co., Inc., 1950, Ch. II.

4. Sattler, William M., "Conceptions of Ethos in Ancient Rhetoric," *Speech Monographs* (1947), XIV: 55–65.

5. Thonssen, L., *Selected Readings in Rhetoric and Public Speaking.* New York, The H. W. Wilson Company, 1942, pp. 35–63.

Exercises

1. Report to the class upon your observation of a persuasive speech with a present audience. Comment upon (a) the speaker's ethos with this audience at the moment he began to speak, and (b) ethos building or destroying elements in the speech. How important was ethos in this instance?

2. Select a person of your acquaintance who is something of a leader and who is exceptionally well-liked. List what you consider to be significant ethos building factors contributing to his present prestige.

3. Select a person of your acquaintance who is unpopular. Analyze reasons for the lack of appreciation of his speech personality.

4. Locate examples of two speakers who appear to illustrate primary and secondary orders of sincerity. Assuming your examples to be good ones, does the difference in *kind* of sincerity seem to relate to their persuasive effectiveness?

5. Explain: "The effective persuader is a good man, skilled in speaking." Do you agree? State your reasons.

Chapter XIV

GAINING AND MAINTAINING ATTENTION

I. Introduction

II. The Nature of Attention

A. Fundamental Facts of the Act of Attention
1. Duration of Attention
2. Span of Attention
3. Selectivity of Attention
4. The Kinds of Attention
a. Involuntary
b. Voluntary
c. Non-voluntary

B. Attention from the Point of View of the Stimulus

1. The Natural or Unlearned Stimuli of Attention
a. Change or Variety
b. Intensity
c. Striking Quality
d. Repetition
e. Definiteness of Form
2. The Relation of Attention and Interest
3. The Conditioned or Learned Stimuli of Attention
a. Animation
b. The Vital
c. The Concrete
d. Suspense
e. Conflict
f. The Familiar
g. The Novel
h. Proximity
i. Humor

III. Applying the Principles of Attention to Persuasive Speaking

A. Respecting the Fundamental Facts of the Act of Attention

B. Applying the Natural Attention Values

C. Applying the Learned Attention Values

D. Overstreet's Principles of "Crossing the Interest Deadline"

1. Starting With Situations
2. Starting With Something that Makes a Difference
3. Beginning With an Effect Needing a Cause
4. Beginning With a Cause Implying an Effect
5. Using the Shock Technique

IV. Summary and Conclusions

Readings and Exercises

Chapter XIV

GAINING AND MAINTAINING ATTENTION

Introduction

The story is told that one Sunday morning Henry Ward Beecher prefaced his sermon by the remark: "If the sexton finds anyone asleep in my audience this morning, let him come up and wake me up." This places the responsibility squarely where it belongs. The speaker cannot escape it by such rationalizations as "my audience was an inattentive one," for there is no such audience. What the speaker really would have meant was the audience was not attending to him. In such a case, his speech must have been boring, trite, unclear, disorganized, lacking in vital materials, indirect or unanimated. So the audience attended to something else.

Without attention communication does not exist, and without it persuasion is impossible, for *attention is the first step in the persuasion process.*[1] This step is not always an easy one. It often is true that more formal audiences, out of their own courtesy and curiosity, will attend to the first few sentences uttered by a speaker. However, if this curiosity is not matched or surpassed by the speaker's own attention-gaining elements, the speech has, indeed, a weak start and a very uncertain future. If the street-corner advocate or the advertiser is to succeed, the attention devices must be effective from the start; the initial voluntary attention of the more formal audiences cannot be relied upon here.

The task of attention would be still relatively simple were it finished after the audience's initial attention is gained. But the

[1] This point is discussed also in Chapter II, *An Approach to the Study of Persuasion.*

job then has only begun. If after gaining the initial attention of the hearers, the persuader becomes anxious to continue with the matter of developing his many appeals, he should never forget that at all times he must keep his audience interested in what he has to offer. Truly here is a case with that "first, last, and always" quality about it.

Persuaders who have succeeded in keeping us attending to their ideas, their beliefs, their feelings, and their products are those who help us to formulate the self, for in a very real sense *what we attend to, makes us what we are.* If you would influence others, capture and maintain their attention. In this chapter we shall explore the nature of attention and suggest ways of applying the principles of attention to persuasive speaking.

The Nature of Attention

Man is an attending creature. With his sense organs—his seeing, hearing, smelling, touching, and tasting—he is constantly probing the world about him. When any of these sense organs are brought to bear on a stimulus, we have attention. In a definition helpful at this point, O'Neill and Weaver define attention as: ". . . a unified, coordinated muscular set, or attitude, which brings sense organs to bear with maximum effectiveness upon a source of stimulation and thus contributes to alertness and readiness of response." [2]

To understand this condition called attention, something must be known of its *span,* its *duration,* its *selectivity,* its *kinds,* and the *nature of the stimulus* which can create it.[3]

FUNDAMENTAL FACTS OF THE ACT OF ATTENTION

Duration of Attention. To know the length of time a stimulus can be attended is important to a speaker. It is often surprising to learn that the duration of absolute attention has been found to be only a few seconds. Pillsbury's[4] studies revealed the duration of a single act of attention to be from three to twenty-four seconds, with most acts falling within the five to eight second range.

---

[2] James M. O'Neill and A. T. Weaver, *The Elements of Speech* (Rev. ed.). New York: Longmans, Green and Co., Inc., 1933, p. 249.

[3] We are indebted to the work of Jon Eisenson in his *Psychology of Speech.* New York: Appleton-Century-Crofts, Inc., 1938.

[4] See W. B. Pillsbury, *Attention.* New York: The Macmillan Company, 1908.

Billings'[5] experimentation lead him to conclude that the average duration of attention is approximately two seconds. Walter Dill Scott makes the fact of the brevity of duration of attention meaningful to a speaker.

> All of our thinking is done in "spurts," which are uniformly followed by periods of inactivity. We can think of nothing consecutively for any great length of time. What we have called constant or fixed attention is simply spurts of attention and if we desire to hold it for a longer period of time on an unchangeable object, all we can do is to keep pulling ourselves together repeatedly, and avoid as far as possible all competing thoughts or counter attractions. A thought that will not develop . . . cannot be attended to for more than a few seconds, but thoughts which develop . . . may be attended to for a long period of time, although the attention will not be uniformly strong all the time.
>
> In a public address it is seldom that we are able to hold the full and undivided attention for more than a few seconds or a few minutes at best. The hearer's attention is constantly wandering or decreasing in force. He may renew it by personal effort, or else something we say or do may bring back the wandering or waning attention.[6]

This aspect of the nature of attention was summed up quite well by an electrical engineering student who was studying persuasion with the writer. After listening to a lecture on this point, this alert student remarked: "Well, then, what you are really saying is that my audience operates on AC, not DC." That is the precise point. And that persuader is wise who develops his speech in terms of it.

Span of Attention. To know how much, how many objects or ideas, can be attended at one time is equally important to the speaker. Strictly, this is a problem in perception. Through experimentation we know we can read two or three words at one glance. Some musicians group notes miraculously. In the psychological laboratory, subjects have been able to attend to around four or five objects visually, and five to eight auditorily.

The point to be remembered here is that attention span is not great, even though it does vary with the type of stimuli and the

---

[5] M. Billings, "Duration of Attention," *Psychological Review* (1914), XXI: 124–135.

[6] Walter Dill Scott, *Psychology of Public Speaking.* New York: Noble and Noble Publishers, Inc., 1926, pp. 112, 113.

individual. When a person is asked to attend to a number of objects simultaneously, the quality or intensity of the attention is reduced as one progresses to the edges of the focus of attention. There may be awareness of the stimuli along the margins of the field, but the stimuli are not definite or clear.[7]

Selectivity of Attention. Under most conditions our senses are confronted with a multitude of stimuli, and, as was mentioned earlier, attention tends to shift from one stimulus to another, exploring the value of each. In this process, however, attention will be found to dwell longer on stimuli that stand out from the others, be it some sort of odor, lights, shape, or sound. It is up to the speaker to direct this selectivity toward those stimuli upon which his speech rests.

The Kinds of Attention. It is to be expected that all acts of attention are not the same, for the process of attending has been subject to modification through learning, just as have many other aspects of human behavior. So it is that an individual may attend to some stimuli because he "just cannot help attending"; to others only as a result of effort; and to still other stimuli in an effortless, rather habituated manner. Ruch points out that the modification of attention goes through three stages: *involuntary, voluntary* and *non-voluntary.*[8]

Involuntary. There are some stimuli to which we must pay attention. They are so strong as to break in on attention already in progress. A few minutes ago the writer was concentrating on a point to be discussed in this chapter. That concentration was interrupted effectively, yet by no means willingly, by a pair of jet fighter planes swishing by overhead. There was no choice; attention was demanded and was paid. Loud sounds or other sudden changes in the environment will cause us to attend involuntarily. Every reader experiences this many times each day. Stimuli of this type are discussed below as the natural or unlearned stimuli of attention.

Voluntary. There are some situations which demand a definite effort to attend. If some school work is to be attended until it

---

[7] See D. W. Chapman and H. E. Brown, "The Reciprocity Between Clearness and Range of Attention," *Journal of General Psychology* (1935), XIII: 357–366.

[8] Floyd L. Ruch, *Psychology and Life.* New York: Scott, Foresman and Company, 1937, pp. 453, 454.

is completed, it may require a definite effort on your part. Your own interests may not yet be great enough to remove the effort, so it demands a definite voluntary type of attending. If we are to get the ideas of some speakers, we have to force ourselves to attend. Of course this does not speak well for the persuader's ability to make the speech so vital and interesting that to attend is no longer a chore.

Non-voluntary. When your interests are aroused, when stimuli are found to be linked with your desires, you find that the effort to attend seems to fade away and you attend with pleasure. The beginning of a speech or book may have required voluntary attention on your part, but if the speaker or writer was effective, he was able to shift your consciously directed attention to the involuntary plane by the arousal of your interests and motives. Suggestions for doing this are given below in the discussion of the learned or conditioned stimuli of attention.

ATTENTION FROM THE POINT OF VIEW OF THE STIMULUS

The Natural or Unlearned Stimuli of Attention

Change or Variety. Since, as was stated earlier, attention is mobile and exploratory, one would expect that varying stimuli would tend to gain attention. When once attention is gained, the stimulus or stimuli must be changing in nature to maintain attention. A monotonous stimulus means certain obliteration of attention. The "loud red" house next door draws intense attention when you first see it. Later, however, only your visitors remark about it; you now are "used to it." It is the movement of the rabbit or bird that attracts the eye of the hunter. The smart animal "freezes" or "plays 'possum" and escapes the attention of the nimrod.

The speaker's delivery and composition must be animated, alert, lively, and a changing, moving set of stimuli. Truly here is a case where "variety is the spice of life."

Intensity. All of us have found out that the shrill whistle, the brilliant light, the loud color, or the immense shape gains our attention naturally. Contrasts are usually necessary to produce the intensity. If, however, this intensity persists, then it can become monotonous, void of variety, and thus ineffective in maintaining our attention. The speaker must use this fundamental attention value judiciously, a point mentioned later in this chapter.

Striking Quality. Closely associated with intensity as an attention stimulus is striking quality. Stimuli which have a striking quality about them need not be intense. High pitched sounds are more striking than the low pitched ones. Itching and tickling stimuli generally have more attention value than broad and smooth pressures.

The speaker using only intensity in voice, thus gaining mostly involuntary attention, may soon exhaust his audience and lose them, but the speaker who cultivates finesse in the occasional use of a striking quality in voice may find it a useful device.

Repetition. Whereas a continuous light may not draw attention, a repeating or flickering light will. A single cry of "Help!" may not be enough to gain the attention of passers-by, but a repetition of this distress signal may bring the necessary assistance. Repetition will continue to be effective until its very repetition assumes a monotonous quality; when that occurs, it, too, can become ineffective.

Repetition has been, and is being, used quite effectively in all types of persuasion.

Definiteness of Form. The stimulus that is precise, clear-cut, or definite in form, is more likely to gain attention than the indefinite one.

> A small definitely shaped cloud is more attractive than a wide expanse of cloud without sharpness of outline. The arrangement of heavenly bodies into forms give us such constellations as the Big and Little Dippers, and Orion. These arrangements are attractive and win our attention when we gaze at the sky. The moon, having greater definiteness of shape, easily attracts our attention whenever it can be observed. Sounds assume definiteness of form when they are arranged into patterns which we call music. The simple tune or jingle represents an elementary type of well-defined sound. The motif of a symphony stands out, wins our attention, and is remembered.[9]

The Relation of Attention and Interest. Before we consider those types of stimuli to which an individual attends by virtue of past experiences or learning, it is necessary to consider the relation-

---

[9] Eisenson, *op. cit.*, p. 217.

ship of attention and interest. Every reader has had the experience of leafing through a new magazine with someone else. You probably wanted to observe something longer than your partner who urged you on. Later he or she may have wanted to linger on a page where you saw nothing interesting. The see-sawing nature of husband and wife window shopping has been the butt of many cartoons. She will stop where a new dress, a new curtain, or a new hat is on display and he where a new suit, a new gadget for the Ford, a boat, or a new automatic shotgun is in the window. We listen more intently when the radio announcer reads a news bulletin about a tornado hitting our home town or when he gives the score of a game played by our alma mater. In short, *what interests us gains our attention.*

Most of our interests have been a long time forming. The total of our experiences—our knowledge, wants, fears, motives, and so on—has left us with interests. These points of concern cause us to pay close attention to them because they are vital to us.

If the persuader is seeking attention, as indeed he must always be doing, he should look to the interests—the "learned attention stimuli"—of his audience or persuadees. He should not forget the use he can make of the natural stimuli, it is true, but the speaker will find more vital attention being paid to those stimuli which, through learning, have come to be interesting and therefore attention-gaining. Below we have surveyed some of the learned attention values which are sometimes called "factors of interestingness."

The Conditioned or Learned Stimuli of Attention

Animation. Actually this factor of attention has both learned and unlearned aspects. Earlier we discussed the naturally stimulative nature of movement and variety. Through learning we enjoy the satisfactions that come through change, movement, and variation. The alert, animated person often becomes looked upon as interesting, a person who has direction and purpose. We have learned that activities going on about us may hold something of concern to us. So, to learn "what is going on," we attend the moving object, the animated individual, or the cluster of moving people.

The speaker who "looks alive" and whose speech composition moves with interesting zest will arrest the attention of others.

The bore or the "dead beat" who mumbles monotonously along in voice, and moves sluggishly in body and in thought, soon loses his audience by the wayside; he travels alone.

The Vital. Those objects, persons, events, or conditions that bid fair to satisfy our desires and guard our interests, also gain our attention. The use of the vital simply means linking to the wants of the hearers that which the speaker wants. Our homes, our families, our means of livelihood, our health are *vital* to us. Speak in terms of these, and we will attend you.

The Concrete. Like animation, concreteness has learned and unlearned aspects. We learned earlier that definiteness of form tends to capture attention. Certainly concrete, specific, precise words present more clearly delineated stimuli than the more abstract and general words. But learning has been necessary for us to come to prefer and to respond more readily and completely to concrete words as stimuli. The specific, the concrete are more interesting than the abstract and general. Only those highly trained in the mental disciplines are able to find pleasure in dealing with the abstract.

Persuasive speakers, therefore, develop their persuasion in ways that give their ideas and appeals the vividness, the picturesqueness of concrete usages.

Suspense. Incomplete situations tug at us. We wonder: "Who was in the wreck?" "Will John, the AWOL soldier, be court-martialled?" "Who will play in the Rose Bowl this year?" "Will the Cleveland Indians win the pennant?" "Will John find out his wife is unfaithful?" "What is in that Christmas package?" Everyone knows the attention value of suspense. Whenever it is created, we attend. So we follow a serial running in a magazine, follow the news items about many incomplete stories or situations, or keep attending the play until the plot is worked out and the murderer is at last brought to justice.

The uncertain is so strong in its appeal that some of us complete the situations for our own peace of mind. As we shall see later, the speaker can make effective use of this factor of interestingness.

Conflict. Most people attend, yes enjoy, struggle in some form. This is not to say that we will enjoy the outcomes of conflict. It has action, suspense, color, drama, challenge; it often provides release from our pent-up emotions. To watch "Old Abe" battle "Little Doug" in their famous debates was an enjoyable grid-iron of argument for those of our predecessors who could not see a Big Ten football game. Today organized conflicts—be they in athletics, drama, politics, races, bull fights, or social reform—rely to a great extent on our love of the chase and hunt to keep us attending and participating. And we oblige.

The Familiar. Oftentimes the speaker uses points and references completely unfamiliar to his hearers, and they fail to respond. He wonders why. A moment's reflection would tell him that they can respond only in terms of what they know; in short, they need the new linked to something old or familiar. We interpret the unfamiliar in terms of the familiar. If we cannot, we are prone to reject it. Most readers have heard someone say he disliked a certain thing when, we know, he did not *know* the thing at all.

We like the familiar. It is our world; it holds our interests. We will pay attention to the persuader who develops what he wants in terms of our familiarities.

The Novel. We want the new related to the old and familiar, but we do not want the old and familiar always appearing in the same old garb. Then it becomes trite, "old stuff," monotonous, and loses much of its attention value. When the familiar can be put in a new or novel manner, giving it a fascinating newness and aptness, it can be a strong factor of attention. Most of us try to find a comfortable balance between the familiar and the novel.

He who cuts his language and ideas from the same old cloth may be doomed to failure, but he who tailors his thoughts in terms of the familiar, yet adds the challenge and vivacity that comes with the novel and new, will carry us with him.

A brief word of warning needs to be sounded regarding the use of the novel. Novelty can catch attention, but it cannot hold it long. Generally it is short-lived. If attention is to be maintained, the novel should be supplemented by other and more persistent stimuli of attention.

Proximity. Closely related to the use of the familiar is the use of proximity, or the use of references to persons, objects or events which are a part of the immediate speech situation. References to the history of the place of meeting, the lights, decorations, uncomfortable seats, or to some person in the audience or event on the program, usually gains some attention. Such devices are common and have been used with varying success throughout the history of persuasive speaking. Generally, the elements of any situation of which we are a part are of interest to us, and we tend to be alert to references to them.

Humor. Humor can release us, for a time, from our cares and anxieties; it can delight us by caricaturing those about us; it can disarm our personal enemies; it can bring gaiety into the somber concerns of daily living. In short, it has the ability to reduce many of our tensions, and therefore we find humor and its physiological manifestation, laughter, to be enjoyable. Thus it has attention value.

The humor industry is large in the United States. Annually we pay millions of dollars to our "humor hucksters" to help us avoid the pain of many realities and to keep us aware of this lighter component of living.

Like any spice, humor in a speech not designed primarily to entertain, must be used judiciously and sparingly. There are, of course, occasions where humor is completely in bad taste and would ruin all chances of success.

Humor should not be over-estimated in its ability to hold attention or to convince. In an extensive objective study, Lull found that humorous and non-humorous speeches were about equal in interestingness and convincingness.[10]

Applying the Principles of Attention to Persuasive Speaking

Thus far in this chapter our chief concern has been to develop understanding of the basic principles of attention. With this background, we are ready now to consider more specifically some of the ways in which a persuader may apply these principles to his ever-present task of gaining and maintaining attention.

RESPECTING THE FUNDAMENTAL FACTS OF THE ACT OF ATTENTION

We said earlier that the act of attention was characterized by brief duration, limited span, and selectivity, and that it can be of

---

[10] P. E. Lull, "The Effectiveness of Humor in Persuasive Speeches," *Speech Monographs* (1940), VII: 26–40.

an involuntary, voluntary, or non-voluntary type. How now can a persuader respect these basic facts and thus assure a greater measure of attention from his audience?

If the brief duration of attention is to be respected, if the speaker is to keep in mind that his hearers think "in spurts," then it is important to avoid getting into long, involved sentences. Repetition and restatement are helpful in gradually edging an idea into the mind of the hearer until, eventually, it dominates his thinking. Word-choice and delivery should keep the idea moving, alert, and apace with the rapid shifting of audience attention.

The span and selective nature of attention also must be respected. One or two clearly delineated ideas with attention focused on them persistently have a much better chance of survival than many ideas, each with but a few moments in the spotlight of attention and with insufficient time for adequate development. A few days ago the writer passed a hardware store which was advertising a general sale. Numerous stickers were pasted over the front window, each sticker advertising a separate article. Because there was no central focus of attention, the span of attention could not embrace all the items. As a result, I, along with other shoppers, hurried on to the next display window. This merchant had not given any article that quality which would make it "stand out" or give it "selectivity value." He had exceeded, too, the limits of the attention span. In short, he had violated two basic principles of attention.

Persuasion must respect these basic considerations if it is to succeed. One idea or point "filling the mind" at a given time is a wise procedure. The points being made here are summed up quite well in the following fable:

> A monkey (Aesop speaking) tried to take a handful of nuts from a small-necked jar, but he grabbed too large a handful and couldn't get his hand out, nor did he until he dropped some of the nuts.
>
> The attempt to grab too much of the public's attention often makes a monkey of what might be a good advertisement.
>
> A layout is made of a simple, strong, effective page. But the president wants another display line, the production manager wants the trade-mark larger, the secretary wants the package in, the sales manager wants a paragraph addressed to dealers, the advertising manager thinks the slogan should go at the top of the ad, the treasurer insists on smaller space and the branch managers want the addresses of all the branches.

A good handful.

Only the neck of the jar is exactly as large as the public's interest —and no larger.

To get your hand out, to get the public to look at and absorb any of the advertisement, you must drop a few nuts.[11]

In addition, the persuader should be aware of the kind or kinds of attention he is asking of his hearers: involuntary, voluntary, or non-voluntary. If he is asking them to give only the voluntary, effortful kind, disappointment likely is in store, for only under considerable social pressure do we force ourselves to attend for a prolonged period of time. Voluntary or forced attention not only may arouse resentment, but it results in fatigue. Some speakers, you have heard it said, "wear you out." Probably the cause is the forced or voluntary attention necessary to understand ill-worded and stringy sentences, unclear organization, uninteresting style, or weak or careless use of body and voice.

On occasion the voluntary kind of attention may be necessary, but in general, the persuader should strive to shift his audience to involuntary and non-voluntary attention. By a judicious blend of varied, strong stimuli of delivery and motivating subject matter, forced attention of the audience can be shifted to a level where it would take force of will power *not* to attend.

APPLYING THE NATURAL ATTENTION VALUES

Stimuli from the persuader must be *varied,* for it takes diversity of stimuli to keep attention focused on an idea or object. "Attention is like a bird," says Hollingworth. "Unless there are several branches to its perch, from which it can flit to and fro while yet remaining on that perch, it is likely instead to flit to some foreign object. Well organized diversity is, therefore, one of the conditions of sustained attention." [12]

This variety can be achieved in a number of ways. Certainly, as was mentioned earlier, the thought of the speech must be kept

---

[11] Published by Calkins and Holden, Advertising Agents, 247 Park Ave., New York.

Cited by H. A. Overstreet, *Influencing Human Behavior.* New York: W. W. Norton and Co., Inc., 1925, p. 25.

[12] H. L. Hollingworth, *The Psychology of the Audience.* New York: American Book Company, 1935, p. 59.

marching toward its goal by vivid, lively style of composition,[13] and by a development which provides "several branches" for the perch of attention. The following excerpt from a student oration indicates how movement can be given composition.

> War is not only man's costliest enemy, but his deadliest as well. Visualize a parade down Main Street, right here in Evanston. Stand on the curb; watch them file past! Remember, you are looking at dead men marching—soldiers who died in the world war—ten in a row, two seconds apart. Tramp . . . tramp, the Americans are passing. Not getting tired, are you? Stand up! This is only the first day. The French are still to come, then the English, the Belgians, the Italians, the Russians, the Germans . . . Tramp . . . tramp . . . Ten in a row, two seconds apart, for forty-six days and nights. These are the soldiers dead in the war! [14]

In the oral presentation of persuasion, the delivery also must provide a varied set of stimuli. This means a facile, animated body, and meaningful variations in the quality, pitch, force, and timing of the voice.[15]

Regardless of the means producing them, it should be remembered that the diversity of stimuli must be organized around a common purpose.

Sometimes persuaders depend too much on *intensity* of stimuli to gain attention, be it by loud voice, clapping the hands, banging the fists against the speaker's stand, or intense colors in advertising pages and billboards. The shouting lecturer may, by his constant use of this natural attention value, keep his hearers so attending his shouts that they miss the idea he assumes he is imparting. Intense stimuli of other types and appealing to other senses can produce the same result. The sophisticated individual often does not respond with any pleasure to the use of intense stimuli. The "high pressure" salesman who may surround his street-corner sales talk with blaring music, gaudy banners and dress, and who may present a rapid flow of words uttered with intense vocal force, is receiving less attention as the level of sophistication of the hearers

---

[13] See Chapter IX, *The Language of Persuasion.*

[14] Seymour Simon, "Mars and Wodan, Inc.," from Selections for use in Eleventh Annual Prince of Peace Declamation Contests, 1935–1936. Columbus: The Ohio Council of Churches, 1936, p. 20.

[15] See Chapter XXI, *Delivering the Persuasive Speech.*

continues to rise. The persuader who relies much on intense stimuli is often regarded with suspicion and disdain.

There are times, of course, when the use of some intense stimuli serves a very useful purpose. In general, however, they should find effective supplement in stimuli of striking quality and, together, these two attention values should be used only as help-mates to the many other methods of gaining and sustaining attention.

Mark Antony's repetition of "and Brutus is an honourable man" is the classic example of the use of repetition. *Repeated stimuli* tend to lodge within the fringes of our attention. Due either to the brief duration and mobility of attention or to poor audibility, a single presentation of an idea or point very often may not be received. When carried on with wise variation, repetition may be the means of impressing an idea indelibly in the mind. Commercial slogans of all sorts have this as a chief goal.

Jersild (1928)[16] and Ehrensberger (1945)[17] studied the effects of varying repetitions on listener retention and recall of information presented in a narrative speech. Jersild's experimental speech contained seventy statements, each being given a different type of emphasis. After testing the reactions of ten different audiences, repetition was found to be the most effective form of emphasis. Using a score of 100 to represent the recall value of a statement delivered once, the following comparative scores were obtained:

5 distributed repetitions	315
4 distributed repetitions	246
3 distributed repetitions	197
2 distributed repetitions	167
2 successive repetitions	139

Jersild concluded in part:

> The most effective, though not the most economical, form of emphasis is repetition to the extent of three or more presentations. The benefit arising from repetitions does not increase in proportion to the number of added repetitions.
>
> Repetition is most effective when the several presentations are separated by intervals of time. One of the least effective forms of

16 A. T. Jersild, "Modes of Emphasis in Public Speaking," *Journal of Applied Psychology* (1928), XII: 611–620. By permission of the American Psychological Association.

17 Ray Ehrensberger, "The Relative Effectiveness of Certain Forms of Emphasis in Public Speaking," *Speech Monographs* (1945), XII: 94–111.

emphasis is to repeat an item immediately following its first presentation.[18]

Ehrensberger found two successive repetitions to be more effective than two distributed restatements, and four repetitions with brief intervals between them less effective than three. Although the two researchers disagree on some points, there is general agreement on the value of repetition and the point that repetitions beyond three or four do not result in proportional increase in retention and recall. Further study in this area is to be desired.

Definiteness of form as a natural attention value can be utilized in several ways. A persuader can make a careful audit of each phrase and paragraph of his speech. Do they arouse definite, unmistakable images, or do they produce a blurred, uncertain reaction? Is the idea being presented so clearly hewn from our own experiences and hammered into such a vivid structure that we cannot help but attend it?

Audit should also be made of the use of the body and gestures in the delivery of a persuasive speech. Do the body and gestures impart definiteness and precise form to an idea or feeling? A limp, slouchy body, and gestures of face, arms and hands, which are nothing more than physical grimaces or pointless gyrations, do nothing toward giving definiteness of form to an idea or emotion. The definiteness that can come with direct eye contact should not be forgotten. Such direct, sincere contact tends to hold us in its grasp; it is not easy to break.

To achieve definiteness of form through the use of word choice, body, gestures, and voicc is not an casy task. Inability in the use of such means has caused many commercial persuaders to employ one of the most elementary examples of this type of basic attention stimuli: the jingle. In our day this type of well-defined sound keeps us attending to the merits of cigarettes, shampoos, soap-flakes, and of sending clothing to our fighting men.

Though not easy, the persuader should strive for definiteness of form in all the aspects of his presentation. This includes, also, the manner in which visual aids are prepared and used.

---

[18] Jersild, op. cit., p. 19.

APPLYING THE LEARNED ATTENTION VALUES [19]

The *vital* is a factor of interestingness that "makes a difference" to the hearer. It demands that the speaker know the vital problems, and the deep, abiding desires as well as any special, immediate wants of the audience members. In short, it is here that knowledge of all the bodily and social bases of persuasion comes into use. To tap these springs in the human wishing well is to use the vital as an attention-gaining device.

The instructor who opened his lecture by the remark, "One of you in this class will die within one year" gained immediate attention. The fire-truck headed in the direction of one's home gains one's undivided attention. The traffic officer who told a parent-teacher group, "If you have three children in your family, you can mark one of them off for eventual death or serious injury in a smash-up," had no trouble in holding attention.

Whenever the speaker strikes one of our vital interests, we will attend him absolutely. The vital is one of the chief attention-gaining tools for use by the persuader; it is, in fact, an indispensable tool.

The *concrete* brings vividness, simplicity and personal experience into the arena of the discussion. We may be listlessly sauntering along mentally, a pace or two behind the vague speaker until he states, "Now here is a concrete case," or "Let me give you an example." Then we catch up; we do not want to miss it. Actual people and places are involved now.

The concrete can be used in many ways. Individual words can have this quality. To use the word "house" arouses little attention. To say "bungalow" has more concrete value; and to say an English Tudor, a Dutch Colonial or a French Chateau helps still more in arousing a clear, precise mental image. Do not say a man "went" home when he "strolled," "staggered," or "hotfooted" it home. Use the precise, familiar word. In his often-quoted speech, "Who Knew Not Joseph," Bruce Barton demonstrated able use of specific words. The lines given below provide a sample.

> In the same brief interval, there have been born in this country several thousand lusty boys and girls to whom you gentlemen mean no more than the Einstein theory. They do not know the differ-

---

[19] Animation is not discussed here because of its treatment under the heading of *Change* and *Variety* above.

> ence between a Mazda lamp and a stick of Wrigley's chewing gum. Nobody has ever told them that Ivory soap floats or that children cry for Castoria, or what sort of soap you ought to use if you want to have a skin that people would like to touch. The whole job of giving them the information they are going to need in order to form an intelligent . . . influence in the community has to be started from the beginning and done over again.[20]

The speaker could have been content to say, "Each year are born many children who do not know the claims of advertisers, and so advertising must be a continuing process." Which statement is the more likely to hold attention and to lodge the point more vividly in the mind?

A New York department store showed the value of the specific and the concrete in its advertisement of types of perfume. It began:

> To the 19,312 men in New York who can't express themselves to her . . . to the 9,471 men who are tongue-tied, . . . the 5,208 who stammer . . . the 4,633 who blush uncontrollably . . . to the complete, unhappy 19,312 who can't tell her how uniquely charming, how devastatingly beautiful, how utterly queenly she is, we advise: say it with perfume. Come in and let us pick your mute, but eloquent tribute.

Examples and illustrations also are proven agents of vividness and attention. Like windows, they let light in on abstractions. In his famous lecture, *Acres of Diamonds,* delivered more than six thousand times, Russell H. Conwell used seventeen major illustrations and about as many lesser ones. No small part of Will Rogers' popularity was due to his ability to weave his points into interesting stories involving specific people and places. Every reader is aware of Lincoln's ability and success in doing the same thing.

There are times when abstract words seem unavoidable. In our day we speak of Americanism, fascism, communism, socialism, and many other vague terms. Whenever possible, the persuader should reduce these terms to concrete cases or usages.

The use of *suspense* is in evidence all about us; it is used by all types of dealers in influence. Our problem here is: How can it be used by persuasive speakers? As far as the composition of the speech is concerned, it may appear in single sentences, paragraphs, or entire speeches.

---

[20] W. N. Brigance, *Classified Speech Models.* New York: Appleton-Century-Crofts, Inc., 1928, p. 26.

The periodic sentence withholds its meaning until its end, thus keeping us curious and attending. "Until I was a grown man and only after fighting in Germany and Japan did I learn that (the meaning is still withheld) there are things in life far more precious (and still the meaning eludes us) than money." To prepare all sentences in this manner would, of course, violate the principle of variety. This type of sentence structure, however, does offer means of sustaining attention on vital points.

Sentences in question form also present incomplete situations; they tug at us, yearn for answers. Advertisers use this method often. "Do you have gingivitis?" "Do you know the thrill of feeling dressed like a king?" "Where will you spend eternity?" "What does the Bible teach about using the atom bomb?" "Do you know how to be able to retire at 50?" Every reader can add dozens more. Some of the popularity of the many radio quiz shows is directly due to the attention value of questions.

The speaker should not forget that this method is also available to him. Starting the development of an idea with a well phrased question may help considerably in keeping the audience in search of the answer he plans to provide. The interrogation was the late Senator William E. Borah's favorite means of direct discourse in his persuasive speeches. In a sample of seven of his major speeches, over eleven per cent of the sentences were of this type.[21]

A student orator used suspense by paragraph in the following manner:

> If my grandmother were here this afternoon, she wouldn't approve of my subject. My parents don't even know I am speaking on this topic, for they would be reluctant to sanction it. In fact, some of my professors and many of the students of the school I represent in this contest are censorious of my theme. The public has so condemned this issue that until two years ago a national chain would not permit the word to be broadcast. But regardless of this criticism, my subject affects every rank of society, the rich and the poor, youth and old age, every race and creed. It mocks the wedding tie, links arms with collegiate youth, hovers over beds of illness, escorts thousands into the visible presence of death . . . Yet condemnation and disapproval rest upon those who openly defy the virulent and ruinous social disease, syphilis.[22]

[21] Winston L. Brembeck, *William Edgar Borah's Speech Style and Motive Appeals.* Unpublished Master of Arts thesis, University of Wisconsin, 1938.

[22] Printed by permission of Velma Ebinger Goettel.

An entire speech may be organized in such a way as to create uncertainty of the outcome of situations developed throughout the speech. In his Cooper Union address, Lincoln held his audience in suspense as, step by step, he marched the points of his speech to a climax. The hearer could sense no completeness until the speech closed.

Whenever suspense is maintained for long periods, the speaker must be sure that the outcome justifies the prolonged attention. If it does not, the audience will feel "let down" and will tend to give less serious attention to its further use. It should be remembered, too, that one can suspend the hearers only up to a certain point. Thereafter, they will seek other sources of more immediate interest.

Every reader should be warned that the technique of suspense can be a vital part of persuasive trickery. As Gray and Braden point out:

> It is the familiar procedure of the unscrupulous door-to-door encyclopedia salesman who opens his sales campaign with an expression of deep solicitude over the educational welfare of your children, or the salesman who begins by apparently wanting to give you something for nothing. Like many other argumentative techniques, in the hands of a charlatan or a trickster it can be devastating in its potency. One's best defense is often a direct question which demands a direct answer, "Just what is your specific proposition?" The suspense in such situations may be intriguing, but if one is not careful, it may be quite expensive.[23]

As was stated earlier, all of us have the impulse of the chase or of the struggle which expresses itself in many ways. To use this impulse for attention-gaining purposes is to use *conflict.* Here, again, we see suspense also plays a part. If the speaker can present his points in terms of a struggle or contest, we are more likely to attend him. Political speakers in the United States frequently develop their speeches against communism, fascism, or socialism in the form of a struggle for survival. Religious speakers often speak in terms of the struggle between right and wrong, God and Satan. Educators may speak of life as a continuing struggle or race between ignorance and enlightenment.

---

[23] G. W. Gray and W. W. Braden, *Public Speaking: Principles and Practice.* New York: Harper and Brothers, 1951, p. 99.

On occasion, a speaker may use the principle of conflict to arouse a very indifferent audience by creating momentary conflict between the audience members and the speaker himself. A few antagonizing statements may bring bristling attention, but the speaker must be sure he can direct this antagonism away from himself to a target planned in advance. Great caution should be taken in using conflict in this manner.

Extended systems of promotion—propaganda campaigns—also find the chase technique useful in maintaining continued interest and attention. Great movements, therefore, have had their battle cries: the Battle against Booze; the Crusade for Freedom; Onward, Christian Soldiers, and so on.

When a speaker is determining the factors of attention he wishes to use in a given persuasive speech, he should consider the use of the *familiar,* and the *novel* as companion elements. William James showed how the two work together when he said: "It is an odd circumstance that neither the old nor the new, by itself, is interesting; the absolutely old is insipid; the absolutely new makes no appeal at all. The old *in* the new is what claims attention—the old with a slightly new turn." [24]

Again, these factors of interestingness may be used in small units of composition—words and phrases—and an entire speech may be written to make use of the familiar and/or the novel. The ineffective speaker uses the same old words and phrases; attention does not remain with him. As he rambles on, the audience seeks more interesting sources.

When a speaker developed his speech on traffic accidents in terms of a "piston paganism," it presented the hearers with an old topic in a setting they had not considered. The college orator whose discourse on the rapid, irresponsible living of youth in our modern age was developed as the Eleventh Commandment brought to our thinking a familiar Biblical code, but linked with it a new concept which we had not considered.

Throughout the persuasive speech the speaker should strive for an effective balance between the use of the old or familiar and the new or novel. Properly blended, these two factors play an important role in maintaining audience attention.

---

[24] William James, *Talks to Teachers.* New York: Henry Holt and Company, 1915, p. 108.

Proximity, or references to persons, objects, or other elements of the immediate speaking situation, can be used to supplement the work of the familiar. In his memorable speech to Congress on April 19, 1951, General Douglas MacArthur used an introduction characterized by proximity.

> Mr. President, Mr. Speaker, and Distinguished Members of the Congress: I stand on this rostrum with a sense of deep humility and great pride—humility in the wake of those great American architects of our history who had stood here before me, pride in the reflection that this forum of legislative debate represents human liberty in the purest form yet devised. Here are centered the hopes and aspirations and faiths of the entire human race.[25]

As it is no tool for the novice, great caution must be exercised in applying *humor* to persuasive speaking. Properly used, it can help much in the problem of attention; improperly used, it fails miserably. A few suggestions for its use are in order:

(1) *Humor should be in keeping with the mood of the audience and occasion.* The speaker's analysis of the audience and occasion should tell him what type of humor, if any, would be appropriate. Audiences sobered by tragedy or pending disaster are in no mood for humor. Audiences in a holiday mood will need some sprinkling of humor if they are to be kept attending to a basically serious subject.

Lincoln was a great story teller and renowned for his deep sense of humor, but in his Gettysburg Address and his first and second inaugural addresses there were no forms of humor; the moods and occasions were too sobering for such.

(2) *Humor should add to the purpose of the speech.* Every reader has heard anecdotes, stories, or humorous incidents used where they seemed "dragged in"; they did not serve the purpose of the speech. Such practice should be avoided, for it delays the goal of the speech and bids fair to bring disrepute to the speaker. If it is used, humor should contribute in some way to the idea being developed or to the goal being sought.

(3) *Humor should flow naturally, spontaneously.* To be effective, humor must be presented with such a delicate sense of timing and ease of presentation that it seems to flow naturally out of the discussion. This spontaneous quality of humor is its lifeblood.

---

[25] From the *Wisconsin State Journal* (April 20, 1951), Section 1, p. 3.

If the speaker cannot provide this, the humor is destined to die aborning.

(4) *Humor should not be trite.* Some bits of humor become so threadbare that they lose their vitality. The speaker should make certain his humor is not drawn from those common sources known to the many; he should have private sources also. Humor that has been through the mill of common usage has most of its substance gone.

(5) *Humor should be used sparingly.* Overused, humor will weaken the purposes of a serious speech. The humorous quality of the speech must be kept servant of the larger goals being sought.

On occasion a speaker succeeds so well in his wit and humor that, thereafter, no one will take him seriously.

Humor may appear anywhere in a speech. It may be useful in gaining initial attention at the beginning of a speech; it may serve to help keep attention focused on points during the development of the speech; or, it may help close the speech on a friendly, yet purposive note.

As was suggested earlier, the value of humor in speaking is still somewhat controversial. Humor does have value as an attention-getter, however. It has been useful in some of the great persuasive speeches of history, and so it can be for you.

OVERSTREET'S PRINCIPLES OF "CROSSING THE INTEREST DEADLINE"

In his interesting and very useful chapter, "Crossing the Interest Deadline," Overstreet points out that in all communication there is a certain deadline of interest which must be crossed early by a speaker or writer if the hearers or readers are to remain alert. To cross this interest deadline, Overstreet provides the following suggestions [26] which are discussed here. The reader will note that many of the points discussed earlier in this chapter are given application here. Overstreet's suggestion to "present a conflict" has been omitted because this point was discussed earlier in the chapter.

Starting With Situations. Mere abstract words have little lure; situations do. Successful plays, novels, and speeches frequently start

---

[26] Harry A. Overstreet, *Influencing Human Behavior.* New York: W. W. Norton and Co., Inc., 1925, ch. VI.

with a situation. The hero's boat may be leaking; the heroine may be trapped by villains; the rich dead uncle's will is being read to the greedy family members; the voter may be pictured in a quandary resulting from conflicting news reports, and so on. We attend to such situations because there can be movement, activity, interest, suspense, surprise, and others. To start with a well-chosen situation can help your speech leap over the interest deadline.

Starting With Something that Makes a Difference. Here the advice is for the speaker (or writer) to link immediately his opening remarks with the interests and wants of his audience. Often it is too risky to assume that they will attend the speaker as he gradually and boringly unfolds the data which, eventually, will show he is talking about something of concern to them. Overstreet treats this point in this manner.

> If one watches carefully, one notes that the usual dullness of a dull scientific lecture arises out of the fact that the lecturer describes one small fact after another. He knows that he is building up a structure of facts; *he* knows that if the audience will only manage to keep alive throughout the preliminaries, they will be in at the killing. But the audience, knowing not whither it is all tending; seeing no wider significance in the meticulously elaborated details, soon lose all hope, and sink, with a despairing gurgle, into the tides of slumber.[27]

Beginning With an Effect Needing a Cause. As causal-minded creatures, we want to know: Who committed the murder? Who was in my room while I was away? What caused the peculiar formations at the Wisconsin Dells? How did workers put the roof on the Empire State building? When something new enters our range of experience, almost at once we want to know the cause or causes of such an effect or situation. "Wherever . . . an effect is presented without its adequate cause, we have what might be called a dynamic form of vacuum. If we can induce such a dynamic vacuum, the mind of the reader or hearer is at once alert to fill the causal emptiness with adequate explanation." [28]

Beginning With a Cause Implying an Effect. The human mind not only proceeds backward in search of a cause for some known effect, but also moves ahead in exploration of effects when only a

---

[27] *Ibid.*, p. 118.
[28] *Ibid.*, p. 119.

cause has been given. Here again is an incomplete situation because there is suspense and it tugs at us. A student speaker once began his speech: "Have you ever killed a man? I have. And let me tell you this—it does something to you." The audience was alert as members asked: "What was the effect on you? Tell us!"

To tell a group of persons "I saw a horrible smash-up this morning" can demonstrate the two causal points we have been discussing. Viewing the accident as an effect, many will immediately inquire regarding its cause. Soon others, viewing the accident as a cause, will be eager to learn who, if anyone, was hurt or killed.

If you present an effect needing a cause or a cause needing an effect, you will get your hearers (or readers) to "leap on to the moving platform of cause-effect" and they will not rest at ease until a satisfactory explanation is given.

Using the Shock Technique. A shock, wisely administered, can shake hearers out of indifference and bring them into active concentration on a problem. On occasion this seems necessary. When used, its rather blunt technique should be justified by the urgency and accuracy of its message. The person using the shock technique is invariably engaging in a frontal assault on our comfortable complacency or on that which we have looked upon as desirable and respectable. Our initial reaction to such a shock, therefore, may well be antagonistic. In such an event, the persuader, now having our attention, must be prepared to proceed to grounds so vital that they automatically obtain our concession that the shock was justified. Winans reports a vivid example of the shock technique.

> Dr. Wiley tells a story of a member of a certain Middle West legislature who sought an appropriation of $100,000 for the protection of public health; but could secure only $5,000. One morning he put upon the desk of each legislator before the opening of the session, a fable which ran something like this: A sick mother with a baby is told by a physician that she has tuberculosis and that she should seek a higher altitude. Lack of means prevents her going. She applies to the government and is told that not a dollar is available to save the mother and her child from death. At the same time a farmer observes that one of his hogs has cholera symptoms. He sends a telegram, collect, to the government. An inspector comes next day, treats the hog with serum and cures it. Moral: Be a hog! The $100,000 appropriation was promptly granted. The legislators saw from this vivid presentation of the case that what they had variously called *economy, common-sense,*

business is business, etc., was really putting the hog above the child.[29]

Summary and Conclusions

Attention has been discussed as the first and continuing step in the process of persuasion and, as such, has been regarded as a topic of major concern to the persuader. Its importance demands the study of its basic nature and the types of stimuli which induce it. Suggestions for applying the principles of attention have been given only in an amount deemed necessary to provide the reader with ideas for further application.

One final suggestion is in order. Once gained, attention should be maintained without loss, because, once lost, attention is difficult to regain for two reasons: (1) the persuadee has lost the continuity of meaning and finds it difficult to recapture the flowing stream of thought; and (2) the listener or reader who has found other sources of attention more interesting is inclined to discredit the speaker or writer and to show no particular desire to reaffiliate with his thinking.

The battle for attention is a continuing struggle and is growing in intensity. The stimuli which succeed in capturing our attention from its many competitors must be carefully prepared, for without attention persuasion is impossible.

Readings

1. Eisenson, J., *Psychology of Speech.* New York: Appleton-Century-Crofts, Inc., 1938, Ch. XIV, "Attention."
2. Gilman, W. E., Aly, B., and L. D. Reid, *The Fundamentals of Speaking.* New York: The Macmillan Company, 1951, Ch. XX, "Holding the Attention of an Audience."
3. Hollingworth, H. L., *The Psychology of the Audience.* New York: American Book Company, 1935, Ch. V, "Securing an Audience" and Ch. VI, "Holding an Audience."
4. Jersild, A. T., "Modes of Emphasis in Public Speaking," *Journal of Applied Psychology* (December, 1928), XII: 611–620.
5. Overstreet, H. A., *Influencing Human Behavior.* New York: W. W. Norton and Co., Inc., 1925, Ch. VI, "Crossing the Interest Dead-Line."

---

[29] James A. Winans, *Public Speaking* (Rev. ed.). New York: Appleton-Century-Crofts, Inc., 1917, pp. 209, 210.

Exercises

1. Prepare and present a five-minute persuasive speech which depends essentially on one of the natural attention values or *one* of the learned attention values to maintain audience attention.

2. Clip from a newspaper or magazine three full-page advertisements which gained your attention. Present to your class an oral analysis of their methods of gaining attention.

3. Write a 600 word paper on: "The Factors of Attention Used in the Lectures of My Favorite Professor."

4. Prepare and present a five-minute persuasive speech, using as many of the principles of attention as you can.

5. Read A. T. Jersild's "Modes of Emphasis in Public Speaking" cited in reading reference number 4 above. Report this study to your class.

Chapter XV

THE PROCESS OF PREPARING THE PERSUASIVE SPEECH

Chapter XV

THE PROCESS OF PREPARING THE PERSUASIVE SPEECH

Introduction

In the preceding chapters we have attempted to provide an adequate understanding of the many elements of persuasion. We come now to the vital problem of compounding these into an effective discourse. This chapter presents only briefly the steps in the process of preparing the speech; succeeding chapters treat each of these steps in detail.

Successful persuasive speeches are not accidents but the reward of thoughtful and careful planning of a very high order—planning based on a knowledge of the basic principles of persuasion and skills in applying these principles. If the reader is to become not only an analyst of persuasion but also a practitioner, he must be concerned with ways and means of employing persuasive appeals in effective speech practices. The process of persuasion, as discussed in Chapter II, now must be adapted to the medium of speech.

The job of preparing the persuasive speech is eased if some useful method is developed and used. Below we present a sequence of steps in the preparation of such a speech.

Steps in Preparing the Persuasive Speech

These steps should not be taken independently of each other, but rather in relation to the others. On occasion it may be wise to change their order. The order given, however, is used most generally. The important point to note is that each step *must* be taken if the speech is to be adequately prepared.

DETERMINING THE GENERAL AND SPECIFIC PURPOSES OF THE SPEECH

Before the persuader can speak, he must have a purpose in mind. He cannot get up just "to say a few words" and expect to achieve anything. Does he wish to *stimulate,* to *convince,* or to *actuate* his audience? If he wishes to use stimulation (to arouse or deepen feeling and thought on some topic) as his general purpose, he must then determine his specific purpose. What specific stimulation does he seek? If he wishes to employ conviction (to gain conviction, or to induce or dislodge belief) as his *general* purpose, what specific point or proposition does he hope to have accepted? If he wishes to actuate (produce some overt action), what specific overt act does he desire of his audience? Without clear, precise answers to these questions the speaker is not ready to proceed further in preparing a speech. When the general and specific purposes are decided, all further preparation should serve these goals.

ANALYZING THE OCCASION AND AUDIENCE

After a definite purpose is determined, a clear picture of the conditions of occasion and audience must be gained. The goal of the speech can be reached only to the degree that the speaker recognizes and utilizes the motives, desires, prejudices, special interests, and general experiences of his audience, and the purposes, conventions and setting of the occasion of the speech. Knowing these factors, the speaker can proceed to the next step in his preparation.

GATHERING THE MATERIALS FOR THE PERSUASIVE SPEECH

Keeping in mind the purpose for which he speaks and the information gained from an analysis of the occasion and audience, the speaker is ready to gather those materials necessary to develop and support his proposition and to motivate its acceptance. The speaker should start with an inventory of his own information about the subject, occasion, and audience. Then he should proceed to a systematic investigation of such sources as books, magazines, newspapers, interviews, examples, and so on. The materials gathered should be carefully classified and filed to insure greatest efficiency in their use.

No matter what purpose is being pursued, that speaker usually has the advantage who advances in support of his contentions an ample amount of pertinent evidence vitalized by genuinely presented motive appeals suited to his audience.

ORGANIZING THE PERSUASIVE SPEECH

The human mind is ill-equipped to take care of a hodge-podge of information. To be comprehended, material must first of all be orderly, clear, unified, making the first step of a speech outline a provision for basic clarity to the materials of a speech.

In addition to providing this basic clarity, the organization of a speech should (1) outline the materials in such a manner as to help the speaker to provide the relative balance he desires between the logical and non-logical materials and (2) to place the materials in the most effective sequence for the specific audience.

COMPOSING THE PERSUASIVE SPEECH

After the speech is outlined, there remains the matter of writing all the materials of the speech and the outline into an effective discourse. Given the over-all framework, the specific materials now must give flesh and blood to the skeletal outline. This involves the selection of (1) the right amount of materials, if the time limit of the speech is to be observed; (2) the logical or psychological forms to give to the materials; and (3) the words that will clothe all the ideas and feelings of the speech in clear, vivid, and motivating dress.

All these tasks should be performed in terms of the analysis of occasion, audience, and the general and specific purposes of the speech.

PRACTICING AND DELIVERING THE SPEECH

Without an effective presentation of the speech all the work of the preparation of its content may be for naught. As the lives of the great persuaders of the past testify, practice must be diligent. It must also be in accord with proper principles because practice itself will not guarantee perfection. Practice makes permanent rather than perfect.

The final delivery of the speech should utilize the speaker's most effective vocal and visual communication to make the points of the speech understandable and vital to the audience.

Summary

In this brief chapter we have outlined the steps in the preparation of a persuasive speech, steps which are discussed in detail in the succeeding chapters. The reader should keep in mind this basic continuity of speech preparation as he studies each step.

Readings

1. Bryant, D. C., and Wallace, K. R., *Fundamentals of Public Speaking.* New York: D. Appleton-Century Co., Inc., 1947, Ch. X, "Analysis and Outlining."
2. Monroe, A. H., *Principles and Types of Speech* (3rd ed.). New York: Scott, Foresman and Company, 1949, Ch. VII, "The Process of Preparing a Speech."
3. Oliver, R. T., Dickey, D. C., and H. P. Zelko, *Essentials of Communicative Speech.* New York: The Dryden Press, 1949, Ch. II, "Planning a Speech."
4. Oliver, R. T., *Persuasive Speaking.* New York: Longmans, Green and Co., Inc., 1950, Ch. X, "Organizing the Persuasive Speech."
5. Soper, P. L., *Basic Public Speaking.* New York: Oxford University Press, 1949, Ch. IV, "Finding and Recording Materials."

Exercises

1. Recall your first public speech. Compare your preparation of it with the steps outlined above. Would these steps have helped you prepare the speech? Where was your preparation weak? strong?

2. Make a study of the methods of speech preparation practiced by some well-known speaker in American history. Report the results of your study in a five-minute speech to the class.

3. Assume you have to make a six-minute persuasive speech to your class ten days from now. Draw up a schedule of the time you think you should spend on each of the steps in preparing the speech.

4. How would you recommend going about preparing a ten-minute persuasive speech for which you are given only a five-hour advance notice?

5. Criticize the speeches of your classmates in terms of the steps mentioned above. What steps seem strong? What steps appear weak and in need of greater attention?

Chapter XVI

THE PURPOSES OF PERSUASIVE SPEECHES

Chapter XVI

THE PURPOSES OF PERSUASIVE SPEECHES

Introduction

One of the prime requisites for all successful speaking is that the speaker have in mind a clearly defined purpose and that his speech march interestingly, impellingly, and everlastingly toward this goal. Many speakers fail because of neglect of this fundamental point. They seem to aim at nothing and hit it. In this chapter we shall explore the ends persuasive speakers seek.

Thus far we have been speaking of persuasion as seeking to change beliefs, to arouse feelings or emotions, and to affect human action by the use of various appeals. Persuasion was defined as "the conscious attempt to modify human thought and action by manipulating the motives of men toward predetermined ends." The reader undoubtedly has noticed that the development of our subject has carried with it this implication that persuasion may serve more than one general purpose or end. We turn now to a discussion of these general purposes and to some special purposes of persuasive speeches.

In Chapter XX specific suggestions are given for the preparation of speeches having stimulation, conviction, or action as their purpose.

The General Purposes of Persuasive Speeches

THE SPEECH TO STIMULATE

On Mother's Day a speaker recounts the many sacrifices and other virtues of our mothers. We already know these and believe them, at least mildly. But the speaker wants to revitalize our appreciations. To arouse us, to deepen our concern, to sharpen our feelings is his purpose. The Memorial Day orator seeks to arouse greater concern and a more genuine gratitude toward those who gave their lives that we might live and live as we choose. The naturalist may exhort us on the beauty of nature, our wonder-garden of trees, of grass, of flowers, of birds, and of streams. The preacher may seek to stir the soul by discussing the exemplary life of Christ.

The commencement speaker, the anniversary orator, the speakers at inaugurals, reunions, patriotic conventions, pep rallies, and memorials generally have stimulation as their goal. The speakers at such occasions know we at least give lip service or hold in mild form the appreciations of which they speak, but they believe the audience should not be content with such apathy. They seek to make our sluggish appreciations, weak emotions, and beliefs a more vital part of our living.

The office of the speech to stimulate, therefore, is an important one. It has to do with ideals, appreciations, duties, sentiments, aspirations, desires, affections, moods, courage, endurance, faith, loyalty, and other values that make for the enduring satisfactions of life. The response it seeks is not as narrowly and precisely defined as those of the speech to convince and to actuate. The speech to stimulate, as Oliver points out:

> . . . aims at a much more generalized response. Its goal is not to win agreement that a certain proposal is just, but to induce its hearers to love justice; not to have them give ten dollars to the Red Cross, but to deepen their sympathetic and philanthropic dispositions. It asks its auditors not to *believe* or to *do* but to *become*. The goal of the speech to stimulate is broad and inclusive. It seeks not to change minds or actions, but lives. It recreates the emotional power of its listeners to the end that they will have the will to self-generation of such thoughts and deeds as the speaker favors.[1]

In gaining its goal the speech to stimulate relies essentially on nonlogical proofs in the form of appeals to emotions, desires, and motives. It may arouse some new emotional reaction to the topic being discussed; it may need only to vitalize some existing but mild emotional response; or it may need to substitute one emotion for

---

[1] Robert T. Oliver, *Persuasive Speaking*. New York: Longmans, Green and Co., Inc., 1950, p. 199.

another. Reliance on the nonlogical supports for the speech may not be enough, however; the use of some logical forms of proof is usually necessary to gain the response being sought.

THE SPEECH TO CONVINCE

Persuaders often deal (1) with propositions that are not now accepted and for which they seek acceptance, (2) with propositions now held but which they wish dislodged, or (3) with propositions which are being held in abeyance (neutrally) by the audience and which are in great dispute.

President Truman defending his foreign policy, Secretary Acheson under the Truman Administration trying to convince the people that the State Department is not infested with Communists, the American Medical Association attempting to prove socialized medicine is un-American, General MacArthur justifying his policy in the Far East, the college debater arguing the advantages of wage and price control, the chairman of the Board of Directors of United States Steel Corporation trying to convince the board that their present labor policy is wise, the salesman trying to convince his superior that a bonus should be paid to all salesmen are all cases in point. Our society is organized so highly that there are numerous occasions when decisions must be made and when beliefs must be created, modified or completely displaced. In short, convictions are being manipulated. The speech to convince, therefore, chiefly has to do with beliefs; it deals primarily with intellectual rather than emotional commitments. This means a reliance on the use of adequate evidence and clear, logical reasoning.

To convince an audience of the logic of your proposal may not be enough to produce acceptance; the speaker usually needs to provide the listeners with a motive for believing the proposition.

The speech to convince frequently does not call for any immediate or specific overt action. Future behavior is, of course, usually modified as a result of the change in beliefs.

THE SPEECH TO ACTUATE

After Demosthenes spoke, the crowd cried, "Let's go fight Philip!" A speech to actuate had succeeded. There are many occasions when the persuader seeks not the general or delayed type of response that may result from the speech to stimulate or the speech to convince, but a more immediate, definite, overt response on the part of the listeners. This is the purpose of the speech to actuate. Emotions may and certainly will be aroused, beliefs or convictions may well be created, strengthened, or displaced, but *explicit action must result.*

Every day we are asked to do a hundred things: "Vote for Congressman Alibi," "Go to the Senior Prom," "Give to the Cancer Fund," "Join the Marines," "Go to Church Sunday," "Take Political Science 7," "Be Safe, Use Lifebuoy," "Use Gillette Blue Blades," "Support the Red Cross," and ad infinitum. Successful persuaders keep us buying, voting, joining, refusing, seeing, enjoying, reading, working, vacationing, worshipping; in short, they keep us *acting.* The numerous appeals and media of persuasion help give our society a dynamic nature.

A speech designed to convince may try to convince an audience that there is a need for more strict laws regarding the moral conduct of public officials; the speech of actuation presses for adoption of a specific piece of legislation prepared to meet such a need. A speech designed to stimulate may try to deepen our concern for the plight of the aged; the speech of actuation may press for the passage of a bill to increase old age pensions. Usually the speech to actuate will employ many of the logical and nonlogical proofs used in the speeches to convince and to stimulate, but the persuasion will be directed and extended to produce overt action.

Some Special Purposes of Persuasive Speeches

In our day we have seen persuaders who are not willing to attempt to win their case by using the more legitimate appeals and purposes outlined above. They rely on the creation or existence of frustrations, disillusionments, anxieties, and fears to gain their ends. Used usually by the charlatan, the sophist, the demagogue and agitator, *this questionable procedure is discussed here to alert the reader to such tactics, not to encourage their use.*

The practitioners of such policies in persuasion seldom will admit their devious purposes, the ends of which are to serve very selfish and often anti-social goals. These goals are not designed to foster critical attitudes of an existing program or regime, or yet to present moderate and reasonable reform, but to uproot the old and to create a confusion and frustration amenable to their ambitions and often autocratic leadership. Their true purposes frequently are veiled behind patriotic, religious, economic, or political stereotypes known to be held in public favor. In speaking of one such practitioner, the rabble-rouser, Smith observes that:

> . . . The politician who resorts to rabble-rousing tactics is working for his own advancement, but he never admits it if he follows the generally accepted technique. He should not even admit it to his most intimate associates. He must say always and everywhere that he is the servant of the people and sacrificing himself for their welfare. The late Senator Huey Long illustrated the proper approach when he said "The poor people of the country have someone to guide them—old Huey P. Long, the champion of the people." [2]

To satisfy the ulterior motives of such promoters, the purposes of their single persuasive speeches often must differ from those discussed earlier. Their goals are sometimes served better by *confusing,* by *intimidating,* or by *irritating* their audiences.

THE SPEECH TO CONFUSE

It may seem incredible that a speech may actually seek to leave an audience confused. We are not used to thinking in such terms. Does not such a speech violate some of the basic rhetorical principles? Yet this is precisely what has been and is being practiced by some unprincipled men. It is done in two ways: (1) by displacement of the rational bases of belief and (2) by intentional creation or appropriation of frustrations. Let us look at these in the same order.

When the audience has a known belief on a proposition, the demagogue in the guise of a rational approach may present a maze of conflicting "facts" germane to the question at hand. At first the hearers are able to classify and evaluate the "facts" and keep a mental tally of them, but, as the speaker pyramids more data—many of these conflicting in nature but presented as true "pros" and "cons"—the audience gradually becomes slightly, and later badly, confused because their original beliefs now begin to be held in doubt. Soon a kind of desperation wells up in the hearers as they attempt vainly to find some reasonable basis for decision. At

---

[2] Charles W. Smith, Jr., *Public Opinion in a Democracy.* New York: Prentice-Hall, Inc., 1942, pp. 211, 212.

the close of such a speech the audience is saying to itself, "I see no answer to the complex problem," or, "The problem is too complicated for me to solve." Soon they are saying, "We must look to someone else to lead us out of this awful dilemma." The speaker has succeeded. The confusion will sooner or later be useful to his schemes.

This purpose to confuse can be used by the single propagandist or by the propaganda of a group desiring to rule a nation. The Nazis used atrocity propaganda as a part of their strategy of confusion.

> "This 'strategy of confusion,'" says Jacob, "opens to its users a wide variety of situations in which atrocity propaganda can be used effectively, even in the face of contemporary public skepticism. The propagandist, not having to establish conviction to accomplish his purpose, need only give enough impression of truth to his material to raise doubts and muddy the clearcut conceptions of his audience. The 'unstructured' audience then becomes more or less amenable to his own will, or at least sufficiently unnerved to offer but feeble resistance to the pursuit of his objectives. In a world where the line between peace and war becomes increasingly obscured and nations which are technically neutral are nevertheless viewed as potential enemies, this strategy can be applied to advantage at any time, and against all nations, not only an immediate enemy." [3]

Sometimes, and perhaps unwittingly, a series of speeches by officials on such topics as price control, taxes, or foreign policy may have the same effect. After hearing a number of speeches, many with conflicting views and data, the voter may cease all attempts at seeking or even maintaining a rational solution to the problem and, turning off his radio, may mumble, "Okay, you know more about it than I, go ahead; I'll accept whatever comes." Whether by design or not, a speech or series of speeches of this sort leaves the hearer confused, bewildered, and suggestible to the type of leadership the persuader or persuaders may see fit to offer.

The second type of the speech to confuse makes use of the audience's predisposition in a confused world. The agitators and other peddlers of discontent appropriate such common conditions

---

[3] E. Philip Jacob, in Harwood L. Childs and John B. Whitton, *Propaganda by Short Wave.* Princeton: Princeton University Press, 1943, p. 219.

of modern life as the anxieties, the distrust, the injustices, the hardships and disillusionments and weave them into a fabric of frustration. Such speakers frequently have no reasonable solution to existing problems. Nonetheless they often appear to be proper fellows who seem to be sensitive to our social conditions and to speak our inner thoughts. Their chief purpose, however, is to confuse issues by the use of words which clarify and intensify our frustrations, the net effect of which is to make hearers subservient to the leadership of the persuader.

Audiences (fortunately often small) still are held by such tactics. The names of Huey P. Long, Theodore Bilbo, Charles E. Coughlin, Gerald L. K. Smith, William Dudley Pelley, Joseph P. Kamp, and others are not forgotten. New ones are arising and will continue to do so.

The recipe for such persuasion was summarized quite well by Hitler's propaganda minister, Josef Goebbels, in an interview with the Rexist leader, Leon Degrelle, who was reported at one time to have had the ambition to become the dictator of Belgium.

> Work exclusively by parliamentary methods. Fascinate and terrify the crowds by painting Communist peril in darkest colors. Keep the ball rolling by resounding polemics. Send back every reproach like a boomerang at the head of your opponent . . . Above all, know how to arouse and delight the crowd. Be more lively than the others; everything depends on that.[4]

THE SPEECH TO INTIMIDATE

The word intimidate is used in the usual sense here. The speech designed to intimidate seeks to gain its goal by the use of fear based on appeals to existing fears or by the creation of fear through threats of one kind or another. Fear has great motivational power; it has led many men to nets laid by clever practitioners of such tactics.

Persuasion by intimidation takes place on varying levels. In its everyday, mild form we think little of it, but in its larger and more devastating applications it is a purpose of great danger. Let us look at several examples which will demonstrate the degrees of application of this type of speech. Listen in on a small, informal speech being given by a mother to her children who had been

---

[4] Quoted in *The Nation* (November 28, 1936), CXLIII: 619.

playing in the busy street. "You'll get hit just like Johnny Smith, the neighbor boy; you probably will be killed and you can't see any of us anymore. If you aren't killed, you probably will lose a leg and you won't be able to play anymore. Just sit inside and watch the others play." Such little lectures based on fear also have persuaded children to brush their teeth and eat big breakfasts. These are mild forms of this type of persuasion.

Now take the example of an evangelist preaching on hell. In vivid colors he paints word pictures of the "fires of hell, a burning caldron like Dante's Inferno, consuming the shrieking, writhing, gasping sinners who failed to repent before it was too late." He admonishes his congregation to seek forgiveness, for tomorrow they may die.

Notice that the above illustrations differ in scope, but they have one thing in common: the persuasion is based on nothing more than the normal trend of circumstances. Children do get hurt in the street; people do die. The persuader, however, has not been responsible for the accidents and the deaths. Now let us take some further examples.

A dictator has his henchmen "liquidate" certain uncooperative citizens and arouse certain tragic incidents. While these are still vivid recollections, the dictator makes a speech or series of speeches pointing out the danger of living uncooperative, unpatriotic lives. Or, again, take the example of the racial bigot who promotes a lynching or two, and stages secret, "hooded" threat-demonstrations while he campaigns for votes. Such examples show the more dangerous and represensible applications of the speech to intimidate. Their form or method of persuasion is clearly the strategy of terror, and their immediate speech purpose is intimidation. When intimidation is sufficiently in evidence, the demagogue is then ready to sue for the action he wants from his hearers or readers.

The milder, more common varieties of persuasion by intimidation do not alarm us much, nor do we condemn them greatly, even though some child psychologists warn of such method. The preacher depicting religion as a "fire-escape," the insurance agent dwelling unduly on the possibility of death, and the senator attempting to gain acceptance for a course of action by appeals to the fear of some "ism" are cases to be judged carefully. In the hands of dictators and demagogues, however, persuasion seeking the goal of intimidation has all the hazards and horrors of any terrorism.

THE SPEECH TO IRRITATE

For writers in the field of speech to suggest that irritation is an ultimate object of speech is indeed unorthodox. Examples tend to indicate, however, that the immediate goal of some persuasive speeches is to irritate. This irritation, it is hoped, will eventually produce some desired action. A simple example of this type of speech is its occasional use by children on their parents. When other methods fail, the youngster may deliberately seek to irritate, by a series of disconcerting comments, whines, and actions to disturb the indifferent or adamant parent. After a series of such irritations, the parent may, in the hope of relief, assent to the child's wishes. Wives have been accused of using the same persuasion on their husbands.

In at least one city news boys were advised by their employer to solicit subscriptions to newspapers by going to the homes just before dinner time, not so much for the reason that the potential customers were at home then, but because at that time the husband and wife are concerned with proceeding with the evening meal and perhaps preparing for guests or a night out. They did not wish to be bothered by a sales talk yet they did not desire to slam the door in a young face, so after having received repeated calls on other days at the same hour of the day, many parents decided that to buy was the only graceful way out.

Some adult salesmen use this same speech purpose to advantage. They find or create a tender spot in the potential customer's make-up and then persist in abusing this in repeated calls until a sale is made. Such a practitioner develops a clever balance in his use of favorable techniques and irritating devices. Some radio commercials seem to follow this pattern of persuasion, too.

Speech Purposes in a Propaganda Campaign

Changes come slowly. A persuader does not "move the world" in a single speech. To change long-existing beliefs or social customs, to promote the sale of a new product, or to build a strong political candidate generally requires considerable time and an extended system of persuasion. Such a plan of propaganda usually employs all the possible vehicles of persuasion and is extended over a period of many weeks, months, or years.

When persuasive speeches are used in such a campaign, their purposes will not always be the same. Some will seek to stimulate, others to convince, and still others to actuate. (And, of course, we must admit that some use the questionable practices discussed above as special purposes). The analyses of the occasion and audience, the scope of the end being sought, the ethical code of the promoters, and the over-all organization of the campaign will dictate the speech purpose to be used at a given time and place. The methods of occasion and audience analysis must be used in preparation for each specific speech of the campaign. If the end being sought by the campaign is one of considerable significance, i.e., one requiring a great change in personal conduct, one requesting an outlay of much money, one asking for a major change in policies of government, education, religion, and so on, then it may be wise not to attempt to gain the entire goal in one or two speeches. Secondary goals may be the necessary steps leading to the ultimate goal. One of these minor goals may require stimulation of the audience on a particular aspect of the larger purpose. Another such goal may be served by some speeches designed to build very convincing, logical cases in support of the lesser propositions upon which the larger propositions of the campaign rest.

Often later in a campaign, after ascertaining the tenor of the crowd, speeches of actuation are employed to bring about the ultimate action desired to put the whole program into operation.

Propaganda campaigns must be carefully worked out if they are to succeed. They require planning of great skill and cannot be discussed in detail here. Interested students should read the volumes now available on the topic.

Summary and Conclusions

In this chapter we have surveyed the chief general purposes and some special purposes of persuasive speeches. Our main concern has been with the speeches prepared to stimulate, to convince, and to actuate. It was pointed out that the speech to stimulate tends to rely predominately on the nonlogical appeals to gain its end, that the speech to convince rests essentially on the logical appeals, and that the speech to actuate will use varying combinations of the two broad categories of proofs to accomplish its goal. At this point it is well to note that these are only broad and general considerations and are not meant as invariable rules or regulations. The means of achieving the ends of speaking are numerous and often varied. The point to keep in mind is that every speech is a "special" case and the means of achieving its purpose must be decided in terms of the topic itself, the audience, the occasion, and the speaker.

The special purposes of persuasive speeches were presented in the hope of sensitizing the readers to the dangers of such purposes. Although this is not a textbook in promotion by extended systems of propaganda, the reader was presented with certain basic facts regarding the planning of the purposes of the speeches to be used in such a campaign. For speaking to be persuasive, it must be prepared in terms of clearly defined goals. This chapter has surveyed the chief purposes of persuasive speeches.

Readings

1. Brigance, W. N., *Speech Composition.* New York: F. S. Crofts and Company, 1939, Ch. III, "The Speech Purpose."
2. Lowenthal, L., and N. Guterman, *Prophets of Deceit.* New York: Harper and Brothers, 1949, Ch. I, "Themes of Agitation."
3. Monroe, Alan H., *Principles and Types of Speech* (3rd ed.). New York: Scott, Foresman and Company, 1949, pp. 167–177.
4. Oliver, Robert T., *Persuasive Speaking.* New York: Longmans, Green and Co., Inc., 1950, Ch. XIV, "The Sustained Campaign."
5. Weaver, Andrew T., *Speech: Forms and Principles.* New York: Longmans, Green and Co., Inc., 1943, pp. 80–84.

Exercises

1. Prepare and present a five-minute informative speech on one of the following topics:
   a. The Speech to Stimulate
   b. The Speech to Convince
   c. The Speech to Actuate

2. Report to the class an example of the use of one of the special purposes of persuasive speeches which you experienced. What attitude do you think your class should take toward such practices?

3. Prepare and deliver a five-minute persuasive speech having one of the following purposes:

a. to stimulate
b. to convince
c. to actuate

4. Assume you wish to conduct on your campus a propaganda campaign designed to create greater participation in student government. You have decided to use the public speech as your vehicle of persuasion. Outline a series of speeches and their purposes you would use in this campaign.

5. Attend a major persuasive speech given on your campus. What was the general and specific purposes of the speech? Did the speaker achieve his goal? If so, what did he do to achieve it? If not, what kept the speech from gaining its purpose? Write up your analysis of the speech in a 500-word paper.

Chapter XVII

FINDING THE AVAILABLE MEANS OF PERSUASION WITHIN THE OCCASION AND THE AUDIENCE

I. Introduction

II. Finding the Available Means of Persuasion Within the Occasion

A. Factors in Occasion Analysis

1. What is the Purpose of the Occasion?
2. Who are the Sponsors of the Occasion?
3. What is the Nature of the Place in Which the Speech is to be Held?
4. What is the Personal-Psychological Setting of the Speech?
5. Where Does Your Speech Fit into the Program?
6. What is the Larger Significance of the Occasion?

B. Methods of Occasion Analysis

III. Finding the Available Means of Persuasion Within the Audience

A. Factors in Audience Analysis

1. What is the Size of the Audience?
2. What Ages are Represented?
3. What is the Sex of the Audience?
4. What Races and Nationalities are Represented?
5. What Religious Beliefs are Held by the Audience?
6. What is the Occupation of the Audience?
7. What is the Educational and Cultural Status of the Audience?
8. With What Organizations are the Audience Members Affiliated?
9. What is the Attitude of the Audience Toward You?
10. What Does the Audience Know About Your Topic?
11. What is the Attitude of the Audience Toward the Response You Seek?
12. What Larger Influences May be Affecting the Audience?

B. Methods of Audience Analysis

1. Opinion Polls
2. The Panel
3. The Open Interview
4. The Prolonged Interview
5. The Coincidental Interview
6. Systematic Observation
7. Attitude Scales
8. News-Clipping Services
9. Statistical Information
10. Correspondence
11. Conversation
12. The "Show of Hands" Method

IV. Summary

Readings and Exercises

Chapter XVII

FINDING THE AVAILABLE MEANS OF PERSUASION WITHIN THE OCCASION AND THE AUDIENCE

Introduction

Any speech must be centered on the audience and occasion. It must be developed and presented in terms of the experiences, attitudes, sentiments, emotions, and desires of the audience and with full regard for the conventions, purposes, and physical setting of the speech occasion. Analyses of these factors are prerequisite to the selection of the attention elements, basic appeals, and type of organization to be used in the speech. In short, a speech must be tailored specifically in order to fit the peculiar demands of each occasion and audience.

This chapter presents many of the questions to be considered in occasion and audience analysis, and it suggests methods for finding answers to these questions.

Finding the Available Means of Persuasion Within the Speech Occasion

FACTORS IN OCCASION ANALYSIS

1. What is the Purpose of the Occasion?
   a. Is it a memorial occasion?
   b. Is it specifically designed to start a campaign?
   c. Will your speech purpose fit the purpose of the occasion or are you violating its basic purpose?
2. Who are the Sponsors of the Occasion?
   a. What is the relationship between the sponsors and the purpose of your speech?
   b. Does the sponsorship of the occasion give it prestige or a questionable character?

3. What is the Nature of the Place in Which the Speech is to be Given?

a. Is it a large auditorium, small room or out-of-doors? Will the audience fill the room or will audience members be scattered?

b. Of what significance is this building to the listeners? Is it a venerated public building or a private building with which there is a sentimental attachment?

c. Is the seating comfortable?

d. Is the lighting adequate? Is the lighting capable of producing any special effects?

e. Will the temperature assure comfort?

f. Are the appointments of the room favorable to the response you seek? What symbols will be affecting the audience? Will these be helpful or detrimental to your purposes?

g. What is the shape of the room? What will be the physical relationship of the speaker to the audience while sitting? While standing during the speech?

h. Are the acoustics satisfactory? Can all hear you easily?

i. Will weather conditions affect your approach?

4. What is the Personal-Psychological Setting of the Speech?

a. What audience attitudes does the occasion elicit?

b. What responsibilities does this occasion place on all members present?

c. Are rituals and other customs to be followed?

d. Do the above factors give a certain mood to the occasion? What is the nature of this mood? Will your speech fit it? Or go contrary to it? Does this mood narrow or broaden the channel through which you can gain the desired response?

5. Where Does Your Speech Fit into the Chronology of the Program?

a. What precedes your speech? If there are other speeches, what is their significance? Will there be music? In what mood will the events preceding your speech leave the audience? If others are on the program, do they have more or less prestige on this occasion?

b. What is the relationship of your speech to the entire program? Is it the chief attraction, or is it merely auxiliary?

6. What is the Larger Significance of the Speech Occasion?

a. Does this occasion have a significant relationship to any larger body, movement, or campaign?

b. Are others not in attendance interested in this occasion?

c. Is the larger significance of the occasion sensed by the immediate audience?

METHODS OF OCCASION ANALYSIS

The methods necessary to gain answers to the questions raised regarding a speech occasion are not difficult. Usually the necessary information can be obtained by correspondence and a few interviews with people who are in a position to know the facts you desire. The speaker's own observations should help considerably. These methods are discussed later in the chapter.

Finding the Available Means of Persuasion Within the Audience

After the speaker has analyzed the occasion of his speech, he must turn next to a diagnosis of the audience. Too often speakers neglect this important part of preparation. Probably more persuasion fails because of faulty or no audience analysis than for any other single reason! Students of the 1948 presidential campaign say Truman "out-analyzed" Dewey in the matter of diagnosing the American audience. In this competitive era persuaders must be more audience conscious than ever before. Increasingly audiences are becoming more informed, more analytical, more sophisticated. As the level of audience criticalness rises, persuaders must be able to meet the situation by a more complete and accurate audience analysis.

To analyze an audience accurately is a very difficult if not impossible task. Nonetheless, every persuader should persevere in this matter until all possible methods of analysis are exhausted. Only then should he risk inferring the attitudes, beliefs, desires, and sentiments of an audience. We turn now to some of the questions in audience analysis for which the speaker should find adequate answers.

FACTORS IN AUDIENCE ANALYSIS

What is the Size of the Audience? The size of the audience can make a great difference in the content and delivery of a speech. If the audience is small, there is not the possibility for the creation of an effective psychological crowd which will respond more as a unit. A larger audience is usually characterized by more suggestibility than a small group. The "together devices," discussed in Chapter X, should be used all the more in a small audience if a unity is to be created and maintained. If the small audience is scattered in a large auditorium, it is wise to assemble them shoulder-to-shoulder and nearer the speaker. The size of the audience also will indicate what visual and vocal usages will be necessary to deliver the speech effectively.

What Ages are Represented? If the speaker is to talk to his audience in terms of their wants and experiences, he must analyze carefully the members with respect to age. If the audience is composed of people sixty and over, his problem differs considerably from that of speaking to a group of college students or to an audience of all ages. Although it is very difficult to generalize in respect to the desires and interests of those of differing ages, some generalizations may be hazarded. Being more energetic and less inhibited than older people, youths usually need a speech developed and presented in a rather animated manner with the choice of words and appeals suited to their vocabulary, interests, and attitudes. Challenges and appeals to courage and adventure usually are successful, for, as Hazlitt once observed, "No young man believes that he will ever die."

By the time people reach middle age they tend to become more cautious. The pyramiding responsibilities of family, home, professional, and community life make of the middle-aged man or woman a more inhibited, more conservative, and more reasonable person than he or she was fifteen to twenty years earlier.

And as old age is achieved there generally is less physical and mental vigor. Reflectiveness is increased and philosophical attitudes are more in evidence. What once were the challenges of the future have now become the memories of the past. Security rather than adventure rules the day. Health, infirmities, and unemployability often are the major concerns.

What is the Sex of the Audience? It is important to know if the audience will be all men, all women, or a mixed group. The sexes have many interests in common, it is true, but they also have many separate interests. Men talk of business, industry, politics, and sports; women chat more about clothing, food, children, art, and music. In college, men tend to elect courses in economics, political science, engineering, chemistry, and so on, whereas college women tend to elect sociology, English, art, music, and home economics. The persuader must be able to adapt his points to audiences of men, women, or both.

What Races and Nationalities are Represented? If those of other races are to be persuaded, their culture, thinking habits, special problems, and attitudes must be understood. Without a demonstration of genuine appreciation and understanding of these factors, the persuader's appeals probably will fail.

This same advice applies to all persuaders who would motivate people of different nationalities. In the United States our various nationality groups have fused to a remarkable degree in a common culture. In some areas, however, national traditions survive to a considerable degree and play an important role in the conduct and thinking patterns of the people. There are the Irish in Massachusetts, the French in Louisiana, the Chinese in California, the Germans in Missouri, Pennsylvania and Wisconsin, the Italians in New York, the Norwegians and Swedes in Minnesota and Wisconsin. In addition to the general areas where one or two nationality groups may predominate, there are some states where many nationalities are present. Take Wisconsin as a case in point. Here are found concentrations of Germans, Cornish, Swiss, Russian, Dutch, Danish, Welsh, and Finnish. Each group contributes notably to the common welfare while retaining many of its cherished living patterns.

To gain a common ground and then to motivate people of varying races and nationalities, the persuader *must* know their customs, conventions, mores, art, music, special interests, and habits of doing things.

What Religious Beliefs are Held by the Audience? One of the basic foundations of American democracy is freedom of religion. Many of our forefathers came here seeking chiefly this important freedom, and it was to be expected that there would be many and divergent religious faiths existing in the United States. So it is that we have Methodists, Catholics, Jews, Presbyterians, Baptists, Quakers, Congregationalists, and many others worshiping side by side in their respective houses of worship. Each sect has its own creed, but it respects the right of the others to hold different creeds and forms of worship.

Many of our codes of conduct, attitudes, sentiments, and beliefs, are conditioned by religious concepts. There are few topics, therefore, that are not directly or indirectly related to religious beliefs. He who would persuade others must know and demonstrate respect for their religious beliefs and practices.

What are the Occupations of the Audience Members? For most of us a large part of our time and energy is directed to earning a living, so it should not be surprising that our occupations should have considerable influence on our behavior. The industrialist develops attitudes about labor problems; the laborer develops attitudes about management; the doctor's medical practice leads him to certain social roles and attitudes; the lawyer, teacher, preacher, journalist, farmer, engineer, grocer, and others see life from still other vantage points and develop attitudes, beliefs, and codes of conduct based on their experiences and information. While each occupational group is gaining behavior and attitudes toward its own work and problems, it is also acquiring attitudes regarding the other fellow and his "easy," "questionable," or "admirable" vocation.

With differences in occupation often go differences in economic status. The "haves" and "have nots" appear. Federal tax returns usually reveal that industrial executives, large bankers, movie stars, and large investors make more than teachers, preachers, farmers, and clerical employees.

The speaker must be able to fit what he wants into the often intricate fabric of the desires of those of differing occupations. Here, again, is an important part of audience analysis.

What is the Educational and Cultural Status of the Audience? The persuader's choice of logical and emotional appeals and his choice of words and presentation will be dictated to a considerable extent by the educational and cultural levels of his audience. If the audience members have had considerable formal education and adhere to a sophisticated culture, the speaker's approach necessarily will differ from his approach to an audience with little formal education and whose cultural tastes may be (though not necessarily) more simple and less fastidious. The persuader should not make the mistake, however, of assuming formal education is the *only* education. Some people have had little formal education, yet must be ranked among the most educated and cultured.

The magazines and books read by an audience offer a helpful clue to the cultural and educational level. Do they read *Harpers, The Atlantic Monthly, The Nation, The Saturday Review of Literature,* and other such periodicals, or do they read only newspapers and "quick" news magazines and digests? Are they members of book clubs? If so, what type? What are their tastes in music, art, entertainment?

Educational and cultural status are also manifest in types of conduct, thinking habits, attitudes, social practices, and so on. It is up to the speaker to be alert to these and other cues and to prepare his persuasion accordingly.

With What Organizations are the Audience Members Affiliated? As was stated earlier, we are a nation of "joiners." We are organized in more ways than the people of any other nation. Our religious, political, economic, educational, and social beliefs in conjunction with our interests in hobbies, sports, and so on have caused us to join numerous organizations. Organizations give strength to our beliefs and zest to our special interests or hobbies, prompting us to belong to the Republican or Democratic party, the Methodist church, a labor union, the Women's Christian Temperance Union, the National Student Association, the International Club, the Organization for United Nations Reform, the Rod and Gun Club, the Ceramic Society, the Audubon Society, the Boy Scouts of America, ad infinitum.

Study the affiliations of individuals if you wish to learn something of their beliefs and special interests. If you are speaking to a gathering of members of a particular organization, it is important to know the specific objectives and customs of the organization. When speaking to people of varying affiliations, you should seek out first the common denominators and then proceed into the development of your persuasive appeals.

What is the Attitude of the Audience Toward You? This point is discussed at length in Chapter XIII. Suffice it to say here, the regard in which the audience holds you is of great importance. Their attitude toward you can make a major difference in the outcome of your speech. A "favorite son" may have a ready following, but an unknown speaker or one held in question will have to earn every inch of the ground he gains.

What Does the Audience Know About Your Topic? If the material you plan to present is entirely new to the audience, you will need to beware of assuming knowledge that is not present, causing you to lose your chance of success. On the other hand, if you assume that little or no knowledge exists, when actually your hearers know much about your topic, they will accuse you of insulting their intelligence and they will label you naive and unworthy of leadership and trust in the matter at hand. In either event, you have alienated your audience, the result of which will most assuredly be failure to persuade.

The persuader must determine as accurately as possible the degree of audience information on his topic in order to proceed with the remaining preparation of his speech.

What is the Attitude of the Audience Toward the Response You Seek? This is a question of extreme importance because without an adequate answer to this question the persuader is drifting in uncharted seas. He knows only his destination, but how far he is from it, or the course he should follow, are enigmas. This means probable failure.

Commercial organizations constantly are attempting to know people's attitudes toward their product, their radio program, their motion pictures, and their services by means of polls and other interviews, or by contests requesting customers to explain ("in 25 words or less") why they like the product. Political persuaders watch for editorials and "voice of the people" letters in the newspapers. Movie and stage producers and directors and actors rush to buy copies of the critics' reactions to "opening night." In order to learn the attitude of the people toward their product or the service that they are selling, most large businesses hire public relations agents.

In an attempt to sense public opinion regarding a proposed piece of legislation, Congressmen may send out "trial balloon" statements. In short, all alert persuaders are diligent in learning the persuadees' opinions of the response that is being sought. Is it favorable? Opposed? Indifferent?

When once the attitudes are known, the persuader is then ready to develop his speech in terms of them. If a part or all of the audience is clearly partisan to his cause, the persuader should be concerned with directing this favorable attitude into useful channels of action. By pointing out additional justifications for their faith, the partisans should be made to feel a new fervor. On occasion, persuaders have lost or alienated partisans in their audiences by assuming they could be neglected while the neutrals and opponents were challenged. This is a serious mistake.

Ordinarily public speeches are aimed primarily at the neutrals—those undecided on the problem at hand. Here the speaker should attempt to dislodge those objections which have prevented favorable decision. Often this means a practical illustration of how the speaker's proposal can and does work, how it can be financed, how it has integrity, how it can give lasting satisfaction, and so on. If the speaker believes the neutral's indecision is based on a considered balance of the pros and cons of the case, it is up to the persuader to prove that his side of the case is actually the stronger. To persuade those neutrals who find it difficult to make a decision, some effective challenge or series of basic emotional appeals may do the job.

To deal with those who are actively opposed to a proposition presents a challenge of the highest order. Certainly it is necessary to establish rapport, and then proceed, because jumping at once into the argument would probably result in failure. For the speaker to demonstrate impatience or disregard toward those who do not share his views and who are reluctant to accept them guarantees failure.

The audience Henry Ward Beecher faced at Liverpool, England, during the Civil War was one of the most hostile audiences ever experienced by a public speaker. Beecher had gone to England to persuade her to keep out of our Civil War. At Liverpool, his audience was constituted largely of industrial workers who had been thrown out of employment because of a cotton shortage caused by the Union blockade of the Confederate states. Beecher's life had been threatened, the streets were placarded with derisive statements about him, and riots were caused by his presence. In this hostile situation, this brave persuader made his famous Liverpool Address. A portion of the introduction to his speech is given below. Note what he did to reduce the hostility and to establish a common ground.

> I have always held it to be an unfailing truth that where a man had a cause that would bear examination he was perfectly willing to have it spoken about. (applause.) And when in Manchester I saw those huge placards, "Who is Henry Ward Beecher?" (laughter, cries of "quite right," and applause)—and when in Liverpool I was told that there were those blood-red placards purporting to say what Henry Ward Beecher had said, and calling upon Englishmen to suppress free speech—I tell you what I thought. I thought simply this—"I am glad of it." (Laughter.) Why? Because if they had felt perfectly secure, that you are the minions of the South and the slaves of slavery, they would have been perfectly still. (Applause and uproar.) And, therefore, when I saw so much nervous apprehension that, if I were permitted to speak (hisses and applause)—when I found they were afraid to have me speak (hisses, and laughter and "No, No,")—when I found they considered my speaking damaging to their cause (applause)—when I found that they appealed from facts and

> reasonings to mob law (applause and uproar), I said: No man need tell me what the heart and secret counsel of these men are. They tremble and are afraid. (Applause, laughter, hisses, "No, no" and a voice: "New York mob.") Now, personally, it is a matter of very little consequence to me whether I speak here tonight or not. (Laughter and cheers.) But, one thing is certain—if you do permit me to speak here tonight you will hear very plain talking. (Applause and hisses.) You will not find a man (interruption) you will not find me to be a man that dared to speak about Great Britain three thousand miles off, and then is afraid to speak to Great Britain when he stands on her own shores. (Immense applause and hisses.) And if I do not mistake the tone and temper of Englishmen, they had rather have a man who opposes them in a manly way (applause from all parts of the hall) than a sneak who agrees with them in an unmanly way. (Applause and "Bravo.") If I can carry you with me by sound convictions, I shall be immensely glad (applause), but if I cannot carry you with me by facts and sound arguments, I do not wish you to go with me at all; and all that I ask is simply *fair play*. (Applause and a voice "You shall have it, too.") [1]

What Larger Influences May be Affecting the Audience? The usual motivational patterns of people may be upset or distorted when the society of which they are a part is being affected abnormally. The increased anxieties and insecurities of war or pending war, of depression, of disease, of epidemics, of flood, of drought, or, on the other hand, the exhilaration resulting from unusual prosperity or the release from war or other crises, may have considerable effect upon our normal response tendencies. We may not respond at all in the usual, predictable ways.

The Communists' post-World War II use of peace petitions of all sorts coupled with the anxieties of the "cold war" and "Red hunt" in the United States during the same period, upset our normal reaction to what were originally normal democratic techniques. The petition device came into great disrepute, and mass protest meetings were readily linked to some Communist tendency. Finally, one Independence Day, a reporter for *The Capital Times*, Madison, Wisconsin, went out to a local park to see how many people would sign a petition that was actually a portion of the Declaration of Independence and the Bill of Rights. The reporter

---

[1] Henry Ward Beecher, *Patriotic Addresses*. New York: Fords, Howard, and Hulbert, 1891, pp. 517, 518.

got one signer out of 112 interviews. In spite of the fact that people are not inclined to consider seriously petitions which are circulated during holiday activities, the survey does provide some support of the point being made here. The persuader must be aware of, and subsequently assess, any of the larger influences that may be affecting his audience.

METHODS OF AUDIENCE ANALYSIS

In the above paragraphs we have raised questions regarding the nature of the occasion and audience. We turn now to methods which may be used in seeking answers to these questions.

There are many methods of analysis available. Each persuader must select those methods which fit his particular needs and which he can afford to use. A complete study of these methods would demand a volume of its own. Here, we are surveying the methods only briefly in the hope that the reader will consult the more complete sources for detailed information.[2]

Opinion Polls. Before World War I certain newspapers began, in a rather crude way, to conduct straw polls. In 1916 *The Literary Digest,* a news magazine, discovered that straw polls could be used to boost circulation, so it took samples of opinions on prohibition, the presidential primary, presidential candidates, and so on. A lack of statistical training and refinements of methods and techniques made these early polls quite unreliable.

In 1935, Dr. George Gallup founded the American Institute of Public Opinion. In the same year Paul T. Cherington and Elmo B. Roper, Jr., began the *Fortune* polls. The Crossley poll started during the 1936 presidential campaign, and other polls followed. These polls, conceived with more care and knowledge than the earlier polls, continued to refine their techniques until today they are considered quite reliable in sampling public opinion on various topics.

General polls on many controversial topics are taken by these nationally known bureaus and they constitute a helpful source of opinion analysis for many persuaders. In addition, the *International Journal of Opinion and Attitude Research* carries the results of polls taken on various topics, not only in the United States but in

---

[2] See the reading references at the close of the chapter.

many foreign nations as well. This journal and the *Public Opinion Quarterly* are excellent sources on polling methods.

The services of pollsters can be hired to survey particular fields. Franklin Delano Roosevelt was said to have used a private poll, and at least one Congressman has used a poll in helping him conduct his own campaign for re-election.

The techniques of polling are intricate and they demand detailed study by anyone interested in understanding and developing such a method. The public opinion poll is more *extensive* than *intensive* in the data it gathers. Some more intensive measures of public opinion follow.

The Panel. Whereas interviewers used by public opinion polling agencies are encouraged not to interview the same persons more than once or twice yearly, the panel technique uses a constant group of people. Here the interviewer may meet with the group at scheduled dates and secure more intimate information regarding a product, an institution, a political campaign, and other things of interest. The panel, composed of individuals who are exposed to the same persuasion, can render valuable evaluations of the persuasion and information in terms of their own attitudes, beliefs, and interests, making this information available for future promotion.

The Open Interview. By using interviews a persuader can learn much regarding a future audience. The interviews can be used by an individual interviewing only a few people in a small community, or it can be used by professional interviewers as a part of some large public opinion survey. There are several different types of interviews. One type is used in taking the polls discussed above. The critics of such polls point out that the interviewing situation can be artificial because of the interviewee's self-consciousness, and because the interviewer asks him to accept only one of several standardized replies to questions. To eliminate this artificiality, Likert and his associates developed the open interview, using it from 1939 until 1946 in the Division of Program Surveys in the Department of Agriculture.

The method of the open interview simply uses questions which are open-ended; that is, they allow the interviewee to set the limits of his answer to such a question as: "What do you think of the Truman Administration?" This method allows the interviewer to reveal or conceal his real purposes, and it promotes informality. The skilled interviewer on occasion allows his informant to select topics for discussion and then gradually nudges these in the desired direction.

The chief disadvantages to this type of interview are the time involved and the difficulty in tabulating the results. Nonetheless, it does have the strong points suggested above. Any persuader can develop skill in this method and can find it very useful in gathering information regarding his audience.

The Prolonged Interview. Sometimes it may be more fruitful to engage in only a few but prolonged interviews (perhaps using the open-ended technique) than to interview briefly a larger sample of a group. A few intensive interviews sometimes provide adequate data and a helpful supplement to other types of analysis.

The Coincidental Interview. The coincidental interview is used for the sponsors of radio programs to check the radio listening habits of people. This type of interview is made in the United States by C. E. Hooper, Inc. A rival concern, the Cooperative Analysis of Broadcasting, Inc., used the same method until its recent dissolution. By telephone, the method takes a random twice-a-month sample of listeners in over thirty cities where the programs of all four networks (NBC, CBS, MBC, and ABC) can be heard. The popularity of any program may be judged in competition with the other network programs.

Briefly, the person answering the telephone is asked if the radio is turned on and to what station, what product is being advertised, and the number of men, women, and children in the household who are listening. Out of the data collected, the company compiles a Hooperating for each program. Sponsors and performers alike watch the ratings closely, for it reflects responses to their persuasion and provides clues for improvement.

Systematic Observation.[3] Many speakers and other persuaders have relied carelessly on their own casual and too often hasty observation of people and, as a result, the conclusions drawn regarding others' opinions are often inaccurate and quite incomplete. Many persuaders cannot conduct their own polls or interviews, nor can they hire the services of professionals. Everyone, however, can

---

[3] The reader should review the suggestions given in Chapter III.

develop systematic ways of observing people and gain data of some validity. The social scientist does this when he lives among peoples of other races for a time, watching their customs, mores, conventions, rituals, and so on, and then reporting on their social habits, attitudes, and culture. Ministers going into new communities must learn to become systematic observers of the people they are to serve. Professional speakers sometimes send, in advance of a speaking engagement, observer teams who report their observations to the speaker who, in turn, prepares his speech to fit the analysis given him.

Systematic observation of the newspapers and of radio programs' effect on their audience may also be made. During World War II a number of government agencies profited by careful analyses of every newspaper and domestic broadcast. Study of attendance at various types of meetings (political, religious, and others) and the study of the prevailing attitudes in a community often are helpful. In the community in which he is working, the alert salesman also makes a careful observation by attention to the number of home-owners, the prevailing religious faiths, the political beliefs of the people. If he is perceptive he can notice, when in a private home, many cues that can tell him of the economic and social status, the tastes, and dominant interests of the household.

All such systematic observations should provide an index into those things that make a difference to the people. In using this method of audience analysis the word to remember is systematic. This implies carefully executed observations—observations that are accurate, complete, and carefully tabulated. This method is reliable in direct proportion to the capabilities of the observer.

Attitude Scales.[4] The attitude scale uses the most refined method yet devised for measuring attitudes. This method employs many questions that have been pre-tested and scaled and are germane to the topic under consideration. Answers to these questions provide the tester with a quantitative measure of the degree to which a person holds a given attitude. There are various types of attitude scales and all involve some statistical complexity. The Likert and Thurstone scales should be studied by the interested reader.

Because of the time involved in their administration and their

---

[4] Attitude scales are complex and cannot be discussed in detail here. For an excellent yet brief discussion of them see Leonard W. Doob, *Public Opinion and Propaganda.* New York: Henry Holt and Company, 1948, pp. 182–191.

statistical nature, the attitude scales are impractical tools of analysis for the average persuader. He can, however, discern whether attitude scales of people present in his audience have been compiled on the subject of his concern. It may prove helpful to know the results of such measurements. These are generally found in journals in the fields of sociology, psychology, economics, political science, and public opinion.

News-Clipping Services. News-clipping services are used by clients interested in different phases of public opinion because these clipping services make a constant survey of many newspapers and magazines. For a fee they will clip those items of special concern to a client and mail them to him at prearranged periods, enabling the client to keep in touch with the attitudes of his customers and potential customers. Such news items aid in appraising the status of the public relations of large corporations. In all parts of the country the people's thinking and activities relative to a given topic can be ascertained by keeping in close touch with all news releases.

Statistical Information.[5] Every student of persuasion should keep in mind that much information about a prospective audience in a given community or area can be had from statistical sources, most of which are available to every citizen. Usually at the City Hall or local Chamber of Commerce are facts regarding the percentage of the population owning homes, telephones, television sets, and radios. The average income, the percentage of workers in this or that occupation, the number of church-goers, and other information can be learned with little investigation.

The *World Almanac* and the *Statistical Abstract* are in almost every library and are excellent sources of information regarding such larger statistical considerations as the number of Catholics or Protestants in a given area, the average income in the state or nation, the number of schools of this or that type, and the political dominance in an area. Much statistical information is available to the resourceful persuader and will provide him with a profile of the people he wishes to motivate.

Correspondence. Correspondence is such a simple and obvious method that it often escapes our attention and use, yet it can provide much valuable information. The personal nature of a sincere

---

[5] See also Chapter XVIII.

and well-written letter may gain information regarding an audience's attitude and an occasion not otherwise disclosed. It is an inexpensive and relatively quick way to tap sources that can give you information regarding individuals, communities, churches, secular societies, government bureaus, and many other items. Of course, the correspondence should be conducted in accordance with the rules of reliable sampling, and the information obtained should be assessed critically and tabulated accurately.

Conversation. The intimate conversation through its informality remains one of the most effective means of learning the attitudes and interests of others. Visiting with townspeople and farm folk in surroundings familiar to them will often reveal possible bases of persuasion which no other method can disclose. Christ talked with men in their shops, in the fields, and along the dusty roads, and He ascertained their innermost thoughts and desires. Many students of Lincoln have attributed much of his "knowing the people" and his "common touch" to the information he gathered by his many conversations with all whom he passed. Theodore Roosevelt made it a practice to converse whenever possible. Many and varied conversations keep the persuader in touch with the "pulse of the people."

The "Show of Hands" Method. The "show of hands" technique has been useful to gain desired information, that could not be had earlier, from an audience already assembled. "How many have been here before? Let's see your hands," the late Billy Sunday used to ask before beginning an evangelistic sermon. How many are farmers? business men? teachers? How many belong to some church now? How many do not belong to any church? These and other questions provide the speaker with valuable data at the beginning of the speech and help dictate the direction it should follow.

Most of us have been in meetings where this device served a very real need. If you should need such a method to help you in a given speech, prepare the questions well and be certain you can use profitably the information you receive.

Summary

The available means of persuasion are to be found largely in the occasion and audience, for here lie the mainsprings of human motivation. All that was said in Part III of this book will, in varying degrees, be found in the audience and occasion of each speech, and it is the persuader's task to discover these mainsprings. In this chapter we have raised a number of questions which should point the way, and we have offered methods which can be used as implements in making such discoveries possible.

Readings

1. Crocker, Lionel, *Public Speaking for College Students* (2nd ed.). New York: American Book Company, 1950, Ch. XXI, "Analysis of the Audience."
2. Gilman, W. E., Aly, B. and L. D. Reid, *The Fundamentals of Speaking*. New York: The Macmillan Company, 1951, Ch. XIX, "Understanding the Audience."
3. Monroe, A. H., *Principles and Types of Speech* (3rd ed.). New York: Scott, Foresman and Company, 1949, Ch. IX, "Analyzing the Occasion and the Audience."
4. Smith, Charles W., Jr., *Public Opinion in a Democracy*. New York: Prentice-Hall, Inc., 1942, Ch. XVIII, "Straw Votes and the Measurement of Public Opinion."
5. Young, Kimball, *Social Psychology*. New York: F. S. Crofts and Company, 1945, pp. 442–459.

Exercises

1. Prepare and present a five-minute informative speech on one of the factors of occasion analysis. Use the reading references above to help you prepare your speech.

2. Prepare and present a five-minute informative speech on one of the factors of audience analysis. Use the reading references above to help you prepare your speech.

3. Prepare and present a five-minute informative speech on one of the methods of audience analysis. Use the reading references above to help you prepare the speech.

4. Prepare and deliver a six-minute persuasive speech to be given in class. As part of your preparation for the speech, turn in to your instructor an analysis of this audience in terms of the purpose of the speech.

5. Through correspondence, interview and reading, study the methods of occasion and audience analysis of a noted public speaker. Write up your findings in a 600–800 word paper.

Chapter XVIII

GATHERING MATERIALS FOR THE PERSUASIVE SPEECH

I. Introduction

II. Gathering Information

A. Surveying Sources, Building a Bibliography, and Recording Selectively

B. Using Main Points as Guides for Selection and Grouping of Evidence

III. Evaluating Evidence

A. Classifying Your Evidence

B. Testing Your Evidence

IV. Summary

Readings and Exercises

Chapter XVIII

GATHERING MATERIALS FOR THE PERSUASIVE SPEECH

Introduction

This chapter is concerned with the problems of collecting two kinds of raw materials to be used in supporting and making vivid the arguments in a persuasive speech. We need pertinent information in the form of facts and authoritative opinions to serve the reasoning process that propels the critical listener toward our conclusion. Equally important are illustrations that bring human interest and visual imagery into our discourse and translate our contentions into concrete human terms. The materials essential to reasoning lend soundness to the argument; the other motive appeals dramatize the points of an argument so that they fire our imaginations. These are two kinds of evidence, one for logical support, the other for control of attention. The good speech blends them so that attending is effortless and following the course of the argument is easy.

Because you may have restricted the meaning of the term evidence to "materials for logical support," we ask you to remember that what is said in this chapter applies to the collection of material for use in logical and all other forms of motive appeals.

Before beginning to collect facts, study critically the wording of your specific speech purpose—the central proposition of your persuasion. Can it be improved? Review your assets and liabilities as a speaker, your analysis of the audience, and the special considerations of gaining and maintaining the attention of those particular people on this particular topic. When you are satisfied that the persuasive proposition is a clear, compact statement of precisely what you intend to accomplish by speaking, you are ready to set about the systematic accumulation of basic speech materials.

Gathering Information

SURVEYING SOURCES, BUILDING A BIBLIOGRAPHY, AND RECORDING SELECTIVELY

The process of sharpening your persuasive proposition will leave you with some concrete ideas of problem areas where information is needed. The library will be the principal and most comprehensive source, but you should investigate also items available in all of the mass media, including programming on radio and television.[1]

If you make the building of a bibliography for later intensive study a main objective of the first exploration, time will be saved in over-all speech preparation. There is always a limited time to be spent on the speech, and sources that might seem at first productive are found later to be less sound than others or to be on topics related to, but not precisely identified with, your problem. The only way to avoid wasting time on inferior sources is to first survey the possibilities, then select the ones that look best for careful investigation.

The speech with predominantly logical appeals can only be as good as its evidence. Poor reasoning can spoil the potential persuasive power of well-selected facts, but the best reasoning cannot fill a gap in essential information. Getting the facts, then, becomes of prime importance.

Recording the facts is equally important. Be reluctant to trust your memory; making methodical notes may seem tedious, but it is easier and more pleasant than returning to an original source to verify some half-forgotten information.

The most flexible system for keeping the records of either a bibliography or of subject matter from specific sources is based on note-cards. Three- by five-inch cards are suitable for bibliography uses, whereas four- by six- or five- by seven-inch cards are recommended for recording of actual data to be used as support in the

---

[1] H. L. Ewbank and J. J. Auer, *Discussion and Debate.* New York: Appleton-Century-Crofts, Inc., 1951, pp. 80–93. This reference includes much specific advice on the gathering of materials.

speech. Using one size for bibliography and another for data has the advantage of preventing their being inadvertently mixed. Here are samples of bibliography and evidence cards. Adaptations for particular purposes are desirable but it pays to be consistent, because only if you stay with one system will cards be interchangeable and suited to filing in the larger card index covering many topics that you may wish to establish. Such a file has many uses in and out of school.

Bibliography Card, Book

Topic	Radio and television in U. S. today
Source	Siepmann, Chas. A., *Radio, Television and Society.* New York: Oxford University Press, 1950.
Comment	An up-to-date comprehensive book, giving pertinent history as well as excellent coverage of the current problems of radio and television.

Bibliography Card, Magazine Article

Topic	Responsibility of the broadcaster to the public
Source	Chester, Giraud, "What Constitutes Irresponsibility on the Air?" *The Public Opinion Quarterly* (Spring 1949), 13:1, pp. 73–82.
Comment	A case study of a radio commentator undertaken to investigate ethical standards of current news commentary broadcasting.

Evidence Card, Book

Topic	Radio in World War II
Evidence	"The Second World War saw the full flowering of broadcasting, both domestic and international, as a vehicle for propaganda. The objectives of each belligerent were the same: (1) to demoralize enemies by confusing, terrifying, and dividing them; (2) to maintain the friendships of neutral countries by broadcasts justifying war aims and inviting cultural exchanges; (3) to stimulate the morale of its own fighting forces and civilian populace."
Source	Chester, G., and Garrison, G. R., *Radio and Television.* New York: Appleton-Century-Crofts, Inc., 1950, p. 159.

Evidence Card, Magazine Article

Topic	Growth of television (recent)
Evidence	Over 2 billion invested in TV since V-J Day. "A California bank estimates that we have recently been buying $40 worth of television for every $100 worth of new automobiles."

	In first half of 1950, over 3 million sets were sold, average cost in excess of $300. New Yorkers are "dirtying up" 40 per cent fewer dress shirts. Children "in the past year have cajoled their parents into buying some $200,000,000 worth of boots, hats, guns, and other gear as specified by their favorite TV horse opera heroes."
Source	Faught, Millard C., "TV: An Interim Summing-Up," *Saturday Review of Literature* (August 26, 1950), 33:34, p. 7.

In evidence cards several methods of recording selected materials are possible—direct quotations in full, direct quotation with omissions, mixed direct quotations and paraphrased material, and paraphrased in toto by summarizing content of source passages in your own words. Commonly an increase in note-taking efficiency results from reducing directly quoted material through use of omissions (indicated conventionally by three dots, thus, . . .) and by summarizing content in your own words where a particular wording is not likely to be needed later. Take pains to be accurate in your summations and be alert to avoid the omissions that change the meanings of your quotations. Taking quotations out of context is somewhat dangerous but unavoidable. Reasonable care in preserving the author's meaning will serve to prevent damage to his intended message.

Note that all cards have the topic at the top. A topical filing, probably alphabetical, will be used, so be certain in your wording of each topic that a significant word appears first, for it determines location of the card in your file. A limited number of topics can be selected and these can be listed in the cover of your card file or on a first card. It is wise to remember that the use of ink or typewriter in making bibliography and evidence cards is preferable, and that the back of the card is just as usable as the front. A series of cards can be kept together by consecutive numbering in the upper right hand corner, e.g., "Card 1 of 3."

USING MAIN POINTS AS GUIDES FOR SELECTION AND GROUPING OF EVIDENCE

When a survey of the extent you consider reasonable for the task at hand has been completed, you will have a number of bibliography cards, a few selected evidence cards, and a new point of view on your persuasive speaking problem. This is the time to select and group your evidence in terms of the main points of your speech.

The following chapter presents various patterns of persuasive speeches to help you plan your final outline. This choice need not be made as yet. Without worrying about final order or relative emphasis, you should word a few tentative arguments or points which will be important to the establishing of your proposition. An inspection of bibliography and evidence cards will aid you in determining what the probable main issues will be. Write down a list of all the major arguments you can think of, then compare and combine them so that they are mutually exclusive, and you will evolve a few main points. The obvious next step is to assemble, systematically, the strongest possible assortment of information to support each. You already have a few evidence cards which will fall under particular points, although some may be impertinent to the extent that the maturation of your topic has rendered them unusable.

Working from main points and bibliography cards plan your further reading. Investigate the sources which would seem to be potentially the most productive first, and select them so that a variety of sources and different kinds of evidence will be covered. Collect more evidence cards carefully, labeling each to indicate the point it supports. Resist any temptation to cut short the process by omitting any detail of documentation. Every bit of evidence must be so completely documented that any normal freshman could, without undue effort, locate the general source and particular item.

There will come a moment in the process of research when you know that you have enough pertinent information to permit the construction of a good, sound speech. You will have a balance of the two kinds of evidence, one essential to the logical structure of the speech and the other necessary to make your arguments vivid and appealing. There will be evidence cards not only from library sources but from interviews, your own first-hand observations, and, possibly, correspondence. You will feel prepared not only to prove your persuasive proposition but also to motivate your audience toward giving it fair and favorable consideration.

At this stage it is wise to read a half dozen more references and collect a few more highly selected cards of evidence to supplement the amount that you thought adequate. Assessing the relative worth of your items of information will leave you in readiness to proceed with the building of the speech.

Evaluating Evidence

CLASSIFYING YOUR EVIDENCE

In Chapter XI the intimate relationship between evidence and reasoning in the structure of proof is explained and illustrated. You will recall how the nature of the information to which you have access dictates the forms of argument you can use with optimum effect. Similarly, the particular forms of argument impose their own requirements upon the evidence offered in their support. We suggest that you classify your evidence in terms of the argumentative forms they serve the best. It will guarantee also that you overlook none of the major means of converting evidence into argument that produce more interesting and convincing speaking.

TESTING YOUR EVIDENCE

When the argumentative forms to support your main points have been selected you can judge the adequacy of the evidence for each. While you view each point in context you should assume the attitude of a rather critical member of your audience and answer this question, "Does the evidence support the reasoning well enough to establish a substantial probability that the conclusion (the point to be proved) is true?" A part of the answer to the test question will be found in the *Levels of Argument* section of Chapter XII. Much of this judgment is essentially subjective. You are unable to estimate the audience reaction to an item of evidence with any degree of precision. Much of the information needed to complete many of the stock tests of evidence is inaccessible, and concerning these matters you must speculate with as much fair-mindedness as possible. If it seems to you that the support for a given point does the job, assume faith in it and move ahead. In all probability, you will be a severe critic of your own evidence.

Summary

Every step in the process of readying a persuasive message is ideally done in context; i.e., it is oriented to a specific persuasion problem. For the particular persuader and his proposition, preparation as well as presentation is audience-centered. Research is no exception to this principle. Facts and opinions are accumulated to serve the purposes of advancing to real, live people certain arguments of special convictions and abilities under a predictable set of circumstances. You listen and read and you interview people to fulfill carefully delimited needs that can be met only by selected information bearing upon specific points of argument. Aimless research to provide a "general background" on your topic is usually inefficient expenditure of valuable energy. The search for specific materials will provide incidentally all required "general" information.

If your persuasion problem is at all large and complicated, the best beginning for research is the building of a bibliography. Cards offer the most flexible means of recording both bibliographical information and evidence. A standard and complete documentation format should be followed rigidly. It is convenient to use small cards for the bibliography file (three by five inches) and larger cards for evidence (four by six or five by seven inches). Suggested patterns for cards and advice for note taking were given.

Accumulation of evidence is ideally done systematically, usually according to arbitrarily selected argumentative points. Every item can then be chosen to serve a specific purpose, keying evidence cards to the points they support.

Evaluation of evidence is in terms of the forms of argument in which it will be incorporated. Stock tests of evidence and argument plus your own subjective judgment of how the audience will evaluate the support of each point will lead to necessary further collection of data and revision of argument.

Readings

1. Baird, A. Craig, *Argumentation, Discussion and Debate.* New York, McGraw-Hill Book Company, Inc., 1950, Ch. 3.
2. Courtney, L. W., and G. R. Capp, *Practical Debating.* New York, J. B. Lippincott Company, 1949, Chaps. 5, 6.
3. Ewbank, H. L., and J. J. Auer, *Discussion and Debate.* New York, Appleton-Century-Crofts, Inc., 1951, Ch. 5.
4. Gilman, W. E., Aly, B., and L. D. Reid, *The Fundamentals of Speaking.* New York, The Macmillan Company, 1951, Chaps. 3, 4.

5. McBurney, J. H., O'Neill, J. M., and G. E. Mills, *Argumentation and Debate.* New York, The Macmillan Company, 1951, Chaps. III, V, VII.

Exercises

1. Using the proposition of a persuasive speech to be given to the class, collect ten bibliography cards covering a variety of sources.

2. Using the proposition of Exercise #1, follow the advice of this chapter in making out ten evidence cards from varied sources, each keyed to an argumentative point.

3. Select the forms of argument from Chapters XI and XII which represent the best application of your evidence cards. Explain the reasons for your choices.

4. Write out one argumentative point as it might be delivered in a speech, including all evidence.

5. Present the "point" written up for Exercise #4 to the class from manuscript. Discuss each other's selection and application of evidence.

Chapter XIX

ORGANIZING THE PERSUASIVE SPEECH

I. Introduction

II. Organizing the Speech Based upon Logical Analysis

A. The Inductive Pattern

B. The Deductive Pattern

C. The Combined Inductive-Deductive Pattern

III. Organizing the Speech Based upon Psychological Analysis

IV. Organizing the Speech Which Integrates the Logical and Psychological Approaches

V. Summary and Conclusion

Readings and Exercises

Chapter XIX

ORGANIZING THE PERSUASIVE SPEECH

Introduction

Over the years many writers, applying the principles of persuasion to public speaking, have tried to devise organizational aids for the speech maker. This chapter selects a sampling of speech patterns that illustrate different approaches to the problems of persuasive speech planning.

Organizing the Speech Based upon Logical Analysis

THE INDUCTIVE PATTERN

Publishing in 1910 his analysis of reflective thinking, John Dewey provided a cornerstone for many inductive development patterns. He specified five distinct steps to be used in the solution of a problem. These were: "(1) a felt difficulty—the initial awareness of a problem; (2) location and definition of the problem; (3) suggestion of solutions to the problem; (4) rational elaboration of the suggested solutions; (5) observation and experiment leading to acceptance or rejection of the suggested solutions." [1]

One application of Dewey's analysis to speech preparation reduces his five steps to four: "(1) locating and defining the problem; (2) exploring the problem; (3) examining suggested solutions; (4) choosing the best solution." [2]

Ewbank and Auer suggest the four steps for those who are to participate in discussion and debate. The chief value they ascribe to utilization of this pattern is that tendencies to emotionality in thinking and speaking are reduced. As a guide for preparing many

---

[1] H. L. Ewbank and J. Auer, *Discussion and Debate.* New York: F. S. Crofts, 1941, p. 67.

[2] *Ibid.*, p. 70.

persuasive speeches, particularly those in which considerable exposition is necessary, this pattern of organization has many advantages. Its strength rests upon a resemblance to the natural pattern of human thought, and the persuasive speaker can lead his audience through a thinking process similar to the attempts it might make to solve the problem independently. Because it appears, and is, inherently reasonable, this kind of speaking is easy to follow.

A detailed organizational outline including items of support is often called a "brief." Here is the brief of a persuasive speech developed according to the Ewbank and Auer inductive pattern.

Brief

Speech Following Inductive Pattern

The following speech was prepared during a charter amendment campaign in St. Paul in 1947.

Locating and Defining the Problem

I. The present condition of St. Paul's public elementary and secondary schools is unsatisfactory.

A. These schools are now sub-standard.

1. Nationally known educators rated thirty-one St. Paul elementary schools as "poor."

2. The same educators classed thirteen below their rating scale as "worse than poor."

B. St. Paul spends less on its schools than do cities with better systems.

1. St. Paul's 1947 school budget is $3,826,000; other cities of St. Paul's size average nearly $7,000,000.

2. The St. Paul salary schedule for teachers is known as "lowest in the nation."

3. Lack of textbooks and equipment and old buildings in need of repair are evidence of too little money available for essential ingredients for education.

Exploring the Problem

II. The source of difficulties in the St. Paul school financing is found in present charter limitations and regulations on taxing and spending.

A. The ancient limitation of $30.00 per capita revenue from property taxes is completely out-of-step with current costs and incomes.

1. Minneapolis revenue from property taxes is $46.05 per capita.

2. Duluth raises $40.05 per capita from property taxation.

B. Schools must fight for the little money they receive.

1. At present, school money is lumped in the other funds.

2. Because not enough money is provided, political pressure determines which departments suffer greatest deprivation.

III. The result of this financial starvation of St. Paul schools makes imperative immediate action to relieve the situation.

A. Teachers are leaving, and qualified new ones can not be hired.

1. Comparison of beginning teacher salaries reveals why St. Paul is credited with "lowest in the nation" schedule.

Starting Public School Salaries

City	*Annual Salary*
Minneapolis	$2000
Oakland	2460
Seattle	2400
Denver	2280
St. Paul	1500

2. *Maximum* teacher salaries show the same discouraging comparison.

City	*Annual Salary*
Minneapolis	$4200
Denver	3650
Oakland	3660
Rochester	3550
St. Paul	2600

(after 13 years of service)

B. Minnesota State school inspectors listed physical deficiencies in their report on September 30, 1946.

1. "Textbooks, instructional supplies and equipment are sub-standard, both in quality and quantity."

2. "Library service is meager and inadequate."

3. "Many classes at all levels are too large."

4. "Many buildings are poorly lighted and ventilated, toilet facilities are very unsatisfactory."

Examining Suggested Solutions

IV. Municipal borrowing will not correct the fundamental inadequacies of our school financing system.

A. It is a temporary expedient where St. Paul needs a long-term solution.

B. Money borrowed must eventually be repaid with interest.

C. The school system would still be forced to compete with other city departments for funds.

D. It is unlikely that the city government would or could borrow enough money to effect substantial improvements.

V. The proposed charter amendment will effect several basic reforms.

A. It provides yearly expenditures for schools up to $18.00 per capita, of which at least $2.50 is used for supplies, equipment, and maintenance.

B. It provides funds for other city services up to $24.00 per capita.

C. Of the aggregate limitation of $42.00 per capita not more than $30.00 shall be levied on personal property.

D. Sales taxes on clothing, food, rent, fuel, income, or payroll taxes need not be enacted in St. Paul.

Choosing the Best Solution

VI. Charter reform appears to be wiser solution to the problem of school improvement than increased deficit spending.

A. The alternative of borrowing in increasing amounts without increasing city revenue is such an unsound financial procedure that it should be accepted only as a last resort.

B. The proposed charter amendment faces squarely the necessity of raising more money for schools and other city services and of distributing it equitably.

1. Property taxes would be kept at the present moderate level.

2. New taxes would be levied upon nonessentials and would be graduated according to ability to pay.

3. Additional revenue of $3,000,000 a year for schools would be available almost immediately.

4. Fixed amounts allotted to schools would permit long-term budgetary planning.

5. Buildings could be modernized and up-to-date books and instructional aids could be purchased.

6. More and better teachers could be hired at fair salaries.

7. The steady increase in grade school attendance over the next few years could be handled adequately within the proposed increase in school expenditures.

Final Appeal

VII. Since education is prerequisite to intelligent citizenship, we can help not only our children but also St. Paul and the nation by voting ourselves and by convincing our friends to vote for the charter amendment in the special election next week.

THE DEDUCTIVE PATTERN

When Aristotle indicated that the task of the persuasive speaker was twofold, saying that first you must state your case and then prove it, he summarized the deductive method of speech construction. The deductive pattern simply consists of stating your conclusions first and then supporting them as convincingly as knowledge and rhetorical skill permit. Usually the central proposition and two or three sub-contentions constitute the material which is presented first to the audience and then is later supported. For example a persuasive speech following the deductive pattern might begin like this.

> Should our University establish a rule prohibiting racial and religious discrimination among student organizations? I contend that it should for three reasons. First, student organizations are now publicly talking against such discrimination while they are practicing it in private. Second, the majority of our students are willing to conform to an anti-discrimination rule. Finally, only a University rule can make possible wide campus reform in the foreseeable future in this matter of discrimination.

This introductory paragraph to the speech dictates the structure of the remainder of the speech. Our speaker will undoubtedly take up his reasons in the order named, supporting each in turn. The speech will probably conclude with a summary of the contentions and a reiteration of the proposition stated in the first sentence. Here is a brief illustrating the deductive method applied in a persuasive speech.

BRIEF

Speech Following Deductive Pattern

Proposition: The University should establish a rule prohibiting racial and religious discrimination among student organizations.

Contention Number One — I. Student organizations are now publicly talking against racial and religious discrimination while they are practicing it in private.

A. Many fraternities and sororities have discriminatory sections in their constitutions.

1. Forty per cent of fraternities at the University of Minnesota have discrimination provisions in their national charters.

2. These fraternities threaten to drop from the national organization any chapter which violates a discrimination clause.

3. Yet many members of these fraternities verbalize opposition to the principles of discrimination in selecting members.

B. A confidential "gentlemen's agreement" often operates in the absence of open discriminatory provisions.

1. Secret discrimination clauses exist in some national offices and local chapters.

2. Students testify that secret informal agreements frequently take the place of clauses in a constitution.

Contention Number Two

II. Most students will obey an anti-discrimination regulation without protest.

A. Many students have learned in their courses that there are no physically or mentally superior or inferior races or religious groups.

B. A large number have had close friends among a variety of nationalities, races, and religions.

C. Since all of us admit that there is no *logical* basis for discrimination we will tend to accept a rule eliminating it.

D. Students will be eager to help their school lead in the crusade against discrimination.

Contention Number Three

III. A university regulation is needed to eliminate the practice of discrimination from our campus in the near future.

A. The present two-faced attitude tends to perpetuate itself.

1. It increases the "superiority" feelings of "exclusive" groups.

2. Competition among rival organizations extends to the practice of discrimination.

a. Prestige is accorded to groups which deny memberships to the largest number.

b. A desirable goal is to be recognized as the most "discriminating" student society.

B. A relatively small minority who actively desire discrimination can continue to lead the majority to accept it as long as our university administration tolerates its practice.

C. A clear-cut rule unconditionally forbidding practice of discrimination in student organizations is just what the majority of their members need to encourage them to stand by their convictions.

1. They will insist on abandoning the "double standard."

2. Organizations now selecting members on racial or religious grounds will immediately "put their house in order" in order to remain in good standing with the University authorities.

Summary and Conclusion — IV. Repetition of the three contentions with summary of support for each. Conclusion: The University of Minnesota should establish a rule prohibiting racial and religious discrimination among student organizations on its campus.

THE COMBINED INDUCTIVE-DEDUCTIVE PATTERN

Frequently induction and deduction are supplementary forms of argumentative support. It is not surprising that we find a popular speech pattern based upon their combination. This particular pattern is one which serves as a basis for construction of many debate speeches. It is predominantly logical in its approach and it represents, in the early steps, primarily inductive development and in the later steps, deductive method: " (1) the immediate cause for discussion (2) the origin and history of the question (3) the definition of terms (4) the restatement of the question as defined (5) the exclusion of irrelevant matter (6) the statement of admitted matter (7) the main contentions on the affirmative contrasted with those on the negative, and the main issues, reached through the clash of opinion thus revealed." [3]

The above steps are those of analysis. We must add two more steps, implied unmistakably by Foster because much of his book deals with them: (8) presentation, analysis, and support of each of the issues in turn, and (9) summary of contentions and restatement of proposition.

Not all these steps are used, necessarily, in any one speech. Occasionally in a particular speech, some may be only touched upon, while one of the steps is stressed. For example, in discussing some questions the definition of terms becomes highly important. Then the speaker should be willing to develop that step in detail, presenting much evidence and reasoning in support of his particular definitions.

---

[3] W. T. Foster, *Argumentation and Debating*. New York: Houghton Mifflin Co., 1936, p. 20.

As the student who has not had debate experience looks over this list of steps, some terms, like "admitted matter," may be confusing. The following brief is of a speech which incorporates all these steps so concretely that uncertainty of the meaning of any one of them should be resolved.

Brief

Speech Following Combined Inductive-Deductive Pattern

Proposition: Congress should adopt a national program of compulsory health insurance.

Immediate Cause for Discussion

I. Dissatisfaction with medical care exists.

A. Some people in need of medical care are not getting it.

B. Some sections of the country are better supplied with doctors and hospitals than are other sections.

C. Cost of adequate medical care is more than some people can afford to pay.

Origin and History of the Question

II. New medical plans have helped correct the maldistribution of medical facilities and services.

A. Private insurance plans partially covering costs of medical care, such as Blue Cross and Blue Shield, have flourished in recent years.

B. Community-wide cooperative medicine has been tried, as in Elk City, Oklahoma.

C. Henry Kaiser provided complete medical care for his employees during World War II for seven cents a day and gave impetus to industrial medicine systems.

D. Experiences of other countries in socializing medicine have led us to consider national plans to guarantee a basic minimum of medical care for all.

E. Federal, state, and local assistance to those unable to pay for their needed medical services has been rather widely granted.

F. Governmental medicine for veterans has become a large-scale operation.

G. The Hill-Burton Act makes federal funds available for hospital construction.

Definition of Terms

III. Terms upon which we must agree in discussing this problem are "national program" and "compulsory" and "health insurance."

A. A national program is a uniform system established throughout the 48 states and the territories of the United States.

B. Compulsory means that all wage earners and self-employed persons would contribute an assessed amount to the national plan, while utilizing its services would be entirely voluntary.

C. Health insurance is a system whereby fixed regular payments protect the contributor from costs of medical care by guaranteeing payment of specified expenses when they occur.

Restatement of Question as Defined

IV. We contend that Congress should enact legislation establishing a system of fixed regular payments from gainfully employed persons in all states and United States territories, in return for which the contributors can, if they wish, receive the medical services and materials they require without further cost to themselves.

Exclusion of Irrelevant Matter

V. This problem should be discussed from the point of view of the medical profession and its patients.

A. Socialism, communism, and fascism are not central issues in improving medical care.

B. We will limit our examination of the proposed plan to its effects upon the medical care afforded our citizens and upon the medical profession.

C. The fact that the United States has better medical care than less fortunate countries, we contend, is no reason for rejecting improvement of our present standards, and this fact ought not to enter into our discussion.

1. If China has fewer doctors than we have, it does not follow that we have enough.

2. If Russian peasants do not take advantage of free clinics, that does not prove that American citizens, better educated in the need for medical care, would not patronize cost-free hospitals and doctors.

D. The contention that sickness is desirable as population control, is not in harmony with our democratic ideals and cannot be considered as a serious objection to improvement of medical care.

Statement of Admitted Matter

VI. We grant that any national system of health insurance, even if administered locally, must provide federal supervision and national standards to be met by local units.

A. Some bureaucracy and red tape are inevitable, but these can be kept to a minimum.

B. Supervision involves some standardization.

Contrasting Affirmative and Negative Contentions

VII. There are four major clashes of opinion in the discussion of compulsory health insurance.

A. Present medical care is considered to be inadequate by some; others, however, contend that it is all that reasonably can be expected.

B. Some contend that maximum improvement in present levels of medical care can be achieved only through a federal program, while others believe that the greatest advances can be made under the present "free enterprise" system.

C. It is believed by many that a federal system of health insurance would produce desirable changes within the medical profession, whereas others believe that irreparable damage would be done to the profession by government supervision and direction.

D. There is disagreement as to whether or not the American people want compulsory health insurance.

Each Issue Answered and Supported

VIII. Present medical care is very inadequate.

A. The health of the people of this nation is unsatisfactory.

B. Medical services are supplied on a basis of ability to pay rather than on the basis of need.

C. Improvement in equalizing our badly distributed medical facilities and services is slow and haphazard.

D. Paying for medical care often causes financial hardship.

IX. Only a federal system of compulsory health insurance can bring medical care to those who need it rather than to those who can afford it.

A. Bad distribution of medical facilities is inherent in the present system.

1. It is impossible to coordinate a private system for all types of communities at all economic levels.
2. Doctors will continue to prefer to practice in centers of population where money is concentrated.
3. The differences in medical care available to population centers and to sparsely settled areas will continue to increase under the present system.

B. No non-federal plan has been found to overcome the twin obstacles of financing and coordinating a general nation-wide improvement of medical services.

C. Federal health insurance could provide the solution to these problems.

1. The Social Security structure already exists, and compulsory health insurance could be added to its services.

2. Other federal agencies could cooperate in collecting information on medical needs and available services in every community in the United States.

3. Federal taxation is an established mechanism of proven efficiency and health insurance payments could be collected by the existing personnel with but few added employees.

4. Minimum standards in medical care, like the pure food and drug regulations and the requirements for interstate commerce, could be enforced everywhere in the nation.

X. The medical profession would benefit from compulsory health insurance.

A. The patient-doctor relationship would be improved.

1. The patient's free choice of doctor would be preserved.

2. The doctor-patient relationship would not be changed except that neither would need to worry about payment for the doctor's services.

3. Patients would not be forced to use their health insurance.

4. Doctors could practice privately if they chose to do so.

5. Doctors cooperating with the plan would be well paid and be assured of a fixed, regular income.

B. Government sponsored medical research would make possible greater progress than the isolated, ill-financed projects under way today.

C. Physical facilities such as hospitals and surgical equipment would be increased tremendously.

D. Medical schools would be expanded with government aid to train the thousands of doctors needed to provide adequate care to all our citizens.

E. Dictation of government to doctors would be avoided.

1. All decisions on medical matters would be made by medical men.

2. Local administration under medical leadership would guarantee efficiency and adaptation to community needs.

3. Federal standards would be determined by a committee of top physicians who would revise them as often as they saw fit.

4. The government's tasks would be the collection and disbursement of funds and the enforcement of standards set by the medical profession.

XI. The people of this nation want prepaid medical care.

A. A large majority want some system by which they can pay their doctor bills through small regular payments.

B. A smaller majority wishes the government to organize and operate a nation-wide system of compulsory health insurance.

Summary and Restatement of Proposition

XII. Because our medical care in this country is far from adequate; because only a federal health insurance program can bring better care to those who need it; because compulsory health insurance would benefit the medical profession; and because the people favor such a plan, we conclude that Congress should adopt a national program of compulsory health insurance.

Organizing the Speech Based upon Psychological Analysis

Just as speech patterns have been based upon logic, other approaches to building the speech emerge from psychological principles. Oliver gives suggestions for the persuasive speaker that serve as a basis for the "Technique of Rationalization."

> That human thinking is subjective and predominantly selfish is a well established fact. There is no sounder method of winning support for a proposal than by identifying it with the self interest of the auditors so that they will want to accept it. The will to believe is a powerful factor in any persuasive situation. But the persuasive speaker should keep in mind the fact that many human desires are far from being narrowly selfish. Idealism and sentiment are forces strong enough to transmute much human action from a plane of gross materialism to one of lofty altruism.[4]

In brief, the persuader using the technique of rationalization first induces his audience to desire his proposal by the mention of selfish benefits (the real reasons). For accepting the proposal he then supplies "good" reasons with which members of the audience can reassure themselves and others in explaining their acceptance of his message. To be sure that they understand the point he hints at the selfish benefits, but by emphasis, he suggests that the main reasons for action are those which are socially approved. The substitution of "good" reasons for "real" reasons leads us to term it "rationalization."

An example will help to make clear the building of a speech utilizing the rationalization technique. Here is a description of a

---

[4] Robert T. Oliver, *The Psychology of Persuasive Speech.* New York: Longmans. Green & Co., Inc., 1942, pp. 55, 56.

persuasive speech situation and the brief of a speech based on this psychological approach.

Brief

Speech Based Upon a Pattern of Rationalization

Proposition: This university should adopt a system of student ratings of faculty teaching ability. (This speech is directed to student members of the All-University Congress. The persuasive purpose is to induce this organization to recommend to the University Administration the adoption of a system of student ratings of teaching ability.)

Introduction

I. Certain questions vital to students remain unanswered at this university.

A. Can students tell the difference between good and poor teaching?

B. Is good teaching important?

C. Is there a relationship between the quality of instruction and the realization of full satisfaction in the money spent for college?

II. Although these questions are vital to students, they apparently are of no concern at present to the university administration.

Appeal to Selfish Interest

III. Suppose students rated the teaching efficiency of their instructors; would the results benefit the students directly?

A. Student ratings would enable their teachers to improve in a short time.

1. Often teachers are unconscious of specific inadequacies.

2. Small deficiencies are easily corrected if the instructor knows what they are and how students react to them.

3. All teachers want to be good teachers in the eyes of their students; hence, they would be motivated to work hard to correct their faults.

B. Student ratings would encourage teachers to make more concrete applications of what they teach.

1. Courses would be kept up-to-date.

2. Courses would be a more direct preparation for life.

C. Better teachers mean better adjusted and happier students.

1. Students like good teachers, and, in their classes they would study more and thus benefit directly.

you can place members of the audience in appealing circumstances in their imaginations, you have taken a direct path to their motives. Visual imagery is most useful. The car salesman, for example, tries to help the persuadee see himself in a particular automobile in an attractive setting. He knows that the need for transportation satisfied by buying a car is not enough. He knows that action will be taken in a larger number of cases if the person contemplating purchase has vivid images of pleasant circumstances resulting from the purchase. One caution to the speaker using Monroe's pattern might be put simply: ". . . not only do not neglect the Visualization Step, but also recognize in it opportunity for great accomplishments in persuasion."

In the following sample brief the steps of the motivated sequence are labeled. Try to imagine (visualize) audience response to each of the steps and compare your imagined reaction with the audience response ideally resulting as noted in Monroe's table.

Brief

Speech Following Monroe's Five Step Motivated Sequence

Proposition: A liberal arts education should precede professional training. (The purpose of this speech, presented before an audience of college students and teachers, is to establish an attitude favorable to this proposal; it is a speech to convince.)

Attention Step

I. Have we "gone overboard" in educating people to make money?

A. Training in human relations may be just as important as learning how to earn an honest dollar.

B. "Man does not live by bread alone. Physiologically, biologically, psychologically, and socially, he can retain his health and flourish only in love of and cooperation with his fellow man." [6]

Need Step

II. Although knowledge of human relations never was needed as much as now, higher education subordinates it to vocational training.

A. "Professional" education does not meet the needs of our high school graduates.

1. Educators agree that students entering college are deficient in these characteristics:

---

[6] M. F. Ashley Montagu, "The Improvement of Human Relations Through Education," *School and Society* (June 28, 1947), 65:1696, p. 468.

a. They have no definite motivation for further education; they are "drifters" rather than purposeful students.

b. Their skills of communication are undeveloped.

c. They have few intellectual interests and few ideas.

d. They are unfamiliar with the methods of logical, scientific problem solving.

e. They do not know how to study.

2. The vocation curriculum offers little to correct these major inadequacies.

a. The professional school classes training in these items as a "non-essential frill."

b. Professional students are on their own to manage without help where they need it most.

B. But our increasingly complex society makes even the earning of a living *cooperative*.

1. Professional skills are of little value if personal characteristics prevent holding a job.

2. The citizen skilled in human relations has a great vocational advantage.

3. Organizations in industry (e.g. unions and corporations) are dominant, and it is essential that their members be able to contribute successfully to their group activities.

C. Perhaps our conspicuous failures to cooperate in groups are due partially to sacrificing study of the humanities on the altar of technology.

1. Sociologically, the greatest single cultural alteration brought about by the machine age is the increased interdependence of man.

2. It is ironical that while interaction of people is increasing faster than ever before, we should be busily de-emphasizing the analysis and study of that interaction.

3. Ignorance of the principles of human behavior is certainly no help in dealing with people.

Satisfaction Step

III. A direct attempt to restore balance to higher education has been made in the Boston University General College Program.

A. Here a two-year fixed liberal arts program precedes professional education.

1. The subjects studied are science, social science, English and literature, guidance, history and government.

2. Departmental lines have been broken down in order to emphasize the interrelationships among these subjects.

3. Emphasis in all courses is on clear and logical thinking.

4. Classes are small, discussion replaces lecture teaching, and there is much group and individual guidance.

B. After two years the student transfers to his chosen professional school for specialization.

Visualization Step

IV. The Boston University General College seems to be a reasonable plan with many advantages.

A. A plan like this could meet the present needs of our high school graduates.

B. Perhaps, over the years, it could render extinct the picturesque stereotypes of "engineers with hairy ears" and "barbarian chemists" and "uninformed electricians."

C. It would guarantee that *all* people experiencing education beyond high school would have a basic training in human relations.

1. Benefits to our necessarily cooperative enterprises would be direct and real.

2. Benefits to the individual would flow from his happier, more successful contacts with others.

D. Perhaps what is most important is that such a program would help place emphasis on human values rather than money values.

1. Motives are *human,* not economic.

2. Man is not a commodity, and attempts to deal with him as such are doomed to failure.

Action Step

V. If the main purpose of liberal arts education is to help the student learn how to think, why not make such training prerequisite to his vocational preparation?

A. Think about this question and discuss it with your friends.

B. You may discover that you agree that working and living in groups as we do today makes a liberal arts education essential as never before.

Summary and Conclusion

We have reviewed five basic approaches to the problem of organizing the persuasive speech. Yet, we have not answered the practical question, "Which pattern do I use, when, and where?"

The answer cannot be given in this or any book because it depends on at least four variables: analysis of audience, occasion, topic, and speaker. In general terms some advice can be tentatively submitted with the recognition that adaptation is the rule rather than the exception.

The Inductive Pattern is well suited to introducing a new subject to an audience. The Deductive Pattern is comprehensive with respect to a few issues, and if you have a limited number of clearly stated contentions, it might be a best choice. The Combined Inductive-Deductive Pattern often is best where much backgrounding and careful setting of the stage for argument is needed. The Technique of Rationalization probably is best when logical supports are scarce and strong desires related to the topic can be found in the audience. When logical development of reasoning leading to a course of action must be presented to an initially disinterested and possibly heterogeneous audience, the Monroe Motivated Sequence is excellently suited.

We urge the reader to experiment with these varied patterns for organizing persuasive speeches. The good speaker will come to prefer two or three, but, more important, he will also work out new combinations of these structures to fit particular circumstances.

Readings

1. Brigance, W. N., *Speech Composition.* New York: F. S. Crofts and Company, 1937, Chaps. 1, 3, 4.
2. Bryant, D. C. and Wallace, K. R., *Fundamentals of Public Speaking.* New York: D. Appleton-Century Co., Inc., 1947, Chaps. 20, 21.
3. Ewbank, H. L. and Auer, J. J., *Discussion and Debate.* New York: Appleton-Century-Crofts, Inc., 1951, Chaps. 25, 26.
4. Monroe, A. H., *Principles and Types of Speech.* New York: Scott, Foresman and Company, 1949, Chaps. 16, 17.
5. Oliver, Robert T., *The Psychology of Persuasive Speech.* New York: Longmans, Green and Co., Inc., 1942, Ch. 2.

Exercises

1. Give a five-minute oral report to the class on one of the above readings.

2. Prepare the brief of a persuasive speech using one of three Logical Analysis patterns.

3. Prepare the brief of a persuasive speech using the Technique of Rationalization.

4. Prepare the brief of a persuasive speech based upon Monroe's Five Step Motivated Sequence.

5. Select one of the sample briefs in this chapter and use it as an outline for a persuasive speech. Adapt it to your audience, add your own evidence and illustrations, but do not change the basic structure of the brief.

Chapter XX

COMPOSING THE PERSUASIVE SPEECH

Chapter XX

COMPOSING THE PERSUASIVE SPEECH

Introduction

After the purpose of the speech has been decided, its occasion and audience analyzed, its support materials gathered, and an outline of the speech constructed, there comes the vital step of selecting, fitting, and wording the specific materials in such a way as to achieve the goal being sought. Since most of the points pertinent here have been discussed separately and in detail in earlier chapters, our purpose in this chapter is to help the reader synthesize these materials into this specific step in the process of preparing a speech; therefore, only certain chief points are highlighted.

Respecting the Time Limits of the Speech

Many speeches have a definite time limit. When a speaker is invited to speak on a given occasion, the time limit usually is stated, and not to fulfill this request would not be wise or in good taste. Such a breach of courtesy has been known to cancel much of the effect of an otherwise persuasive speech. The salesman calling on a busy farmer, housewife, teacher, or business man can reduce his chances of a sale by spending too much of the other fellow's time. Radio and television speaking, of course, have very definite limits of time, but in most persuasive situations the speaker himself can decide the exact time to be used and whether or not he will respect a requested limit.

If a time limit is to be observed without impairing the speech, the speech must be composed with this limitation always in mind. The speaker must determine how many main arguments and how much support material can be developed clearly and adequately in the allotted time. He must decide what chief appeals must be included for the particular audience. Starting with a set of minimum essentials, the speaker can add whatever materials are next in line of importance until the time limit is reached. By the close of the speech the speaker must be certain that all the steps of the process of persuasion (see Chapter XV) have been served.

Beginning persuaders often attempt to do too much in a speech, and as a result, their appeals are numerous but weak and ineffective. It is wiser to impress one or two strong, well-motivated arguments in our thinking than to leave a number of weakly developed points which soon succumb to competing persuasions.

Selecting the Logical and Nonlogical Supporting Materials

Here we assume your speech preparation has arrived at the place of selecting and ordering your supporting materials in such a manner as to respect and utilize the audience's desires, motives, attitudes, sentiments, and stereotypes, and to fit the plan of organization that you have used in making an over-all outline of the speech. Let us look now at some points to keep in mind in selecting the supporting materials for the chief types of persuasive speeches. The reader will note that many of the points discussed in Chapters V, VI, VII, and VIII find application here.

FOR THE SPEECH TO STIMULATE

As we discussed earlier, the speech to stimulate seeks to arouse or deepen an emotional response toward some object, a person, group of persons, policy, or program. To gain this type of response the speaker will need to rely chiefly on nonlogical materials. He will need to include appeals to emotions, motives, attitudes, and sentiments. Many speeches to stimulate, therefore, appeal to fear, love, sympathy, grief, benevolence, pity, pride, patriotism, rivalry, mastery, and so on. In short, the response is gained essentially through motivation.

In selecting the nonlogical materials for such a speech, the chief appeal should be determined first. The speaker should ask himself: What strong motive, attitude, or sentiment within my audience can be sufficiently aroused to result in a deeper concern toward my topic? What basic appeal can be relied upon to take the audience members out of their apathy or opposition and kindle within them a burning fire of interest? Audience analysis must provide the answer.

During the early months of World War II some citizens needed to be aroused to appreciate the sacrifice of our men in uniform and to see their own duty more clearly. Note the chief appeal used by Roe Fulkerson in an editorial in *The Kiwanis Magazine* for October, 1942.

> Bill Jones is dead.
>
> He was a soda jerker in a small town, and when the bands blared and the flags fluttered, he signed up for the Navy. They put him on a torpedo boat. He learned to wear his hat on the corner of his head, and to roll when he walked. Then his boat got into a scrap down in the South Seas. Bill stood by his gun and laughed as he fired it, but a shell hit the deck beside Bill. When he tried to pull himself to his feet, he saw that his right arm was in the scuppers five feet away. He reached for his gun with his left hand, and then things went black. The list of the ship rolled a dead sailor into the scuppers where his dismembered arm lay. Its extended thumb touched the tip of his nose, so that, in death as in life, Bill was thumbing his nose at the Jap ship that got him.
>
> This was just the same day that you were raising hell because they were rationing gasoline, and for fear you couldn't drive up to the lake to go fishing every week-end this summer, you hid four cans of gasoline in your garage. . . .
>
> Bill Jones is dead.
>
> Bill was a boy who had inclinations for the ministry, but when the call came, Bill laid aside his Bible and joined the Marine Corps. Bill wasn't much fun around the blanket where they were shooting craps, and he wasn't so hot at the beer drinking contests in the jukes, but he earned his sergeant's stripes before they sent his gang ashore in one of those new boats which land through the surf.
>
> The fistful of fighting fools charged a machine-gun nest, and Bill had just taken careful aim and let go with a hand grenade when another machine gun caught him. Four bullets hit his head, but a Marine has four speeds forward and no reverse, and Bill fell toward the enemy.
>
> That was the afternoon when you were sitting at the golf club with a highball in your hand, telling the other three fellows in your foursome that if income taxes were not reduced they were going to kill initiative in this country.
>
> Bill Jones is dead.
>
> Bill was an uneducated clam digger on the New England coast, but he knew about boats. He had only one eye and the uniformed ranks would not take him, so he shipped on a tanker. His ship was bringing oil up the coast when a German pig boat came up out of the slime and sent a torpedo into the hull amid-

ships. The freighter burst into flames and Bill went over the side into the burning oil.

When he came to the surface, a machine gun was practicing on the bobbing heads. When the bullets hit Bill's head, it burst open like a dropped egg. His charred bullet-riddled body sank beneath the surface.

That was the time you were telling the boys at the poker game that the union racketeers and the munition manufacturers were making fortunes out of this war, when we had no business getting into it in the first place.

Bill Jones is dead. When God in His infinite kindness meets Bill Jones at Heaven's gate, He is going to say,

"Well done, thou good and faithful servant!"

What He is going to say to you, God alone knows.[1]

Note how Eric Johnston, then President of the United States Chamber of Commerce, appealed chiefly to the emotion of fear in his stimulative speech on "Intolerance" to the Writers' War Board during World War II.

. . . The obstreperous hate-mongers and their foolish or frivolous fellow-travelers who think it is smart to rock the American boat may drown with the other passengers.

If they achieve the calamity of race persecutions, they will drag our beloved America down to the barbarian level of Nazi Germany and we will pay for it in death and suffering and national degeneration, precisely as the Germans are doing today. We need to emphasize, day in and day out, that the spread of intolerance is not primarily a threat to the intended victims but to the whole country. Once the poison enters a nation's blood-stream, the entire population is doomed. Only six hundred thousand German Jews suffered through the triumph of Nazi barbarism—but the non-Jews who suffered from it include the more than eighty million Germans!

If the day ever comes in this country when tolerance gives way to internal enmities and persecutions and discriminations, it will be the end of American civilization. Remember this: the dictates of intolerance cannot be enforced finally without the connivance of government. Should intolerance triumph, it will mean, as a matter of course, that free government is stamped out. Racial persecutions—whether in the old Russia or the present day Germany—have always been conducted under the protection of a tyrannical governmental regime.[2]

---

1 Roe Fulkerson, editorial in *The Kiwanis Magazine,* October, 1942.

2 From an address by Eric Johnston, then President of the United States Chamber of Commerce, on January 11, 1945. Mr. Johnston is now President of the Motion Picture Association of America, Inc.

After selecting the basic or chief appeal, the contributing appeals should be determined. These should be able teammates of the chief appeal, so that, together, the appeals present a reasonable guarantee of arousing the desired response.

The reader should not think that the more logical materials, those materials of fact and reasoning, have no place in a speech to stimulate, for they often play an important role. The whole speech may need to rest on a rather broad base of factual evidence, be it statistics, examples, comparisons and contrasts, or testimony. These factual materials may in themselves produce a considerable emotional response. While this was being written the National Safety Council announced that 999,750 of our citizens have been killed in car smash-ups and that the *one-millionth* fatality would occur at the end of that year. Such data are crowded with emotion!

The materials supporting the speech to stimulate should be woven almost inextricably together, but selected and developed in such a way as to produce the type of emotional response demanded by the speech purpose.

FOR THE SPEECH TO CONVINCE

The speech to convince, you will recall, seeks to create, change, or dislodge belief or conviction. A particular overt action usually is not desired at the time. However, the changed beliefs undoubtedly will affect in some way the persuadee's action or conduct in the months and years ahead. In order to modify beliefs and to affect human thought in such a permanent manner, the contentions of the speech must rest on something more lasting than emotional excitation. It must be based upon strong evidence and logical reasoning that can withstand any critical analysis that may be made at the time of the speech or in the future. Some beliefs are based on flimsy evidence, fallacious reasoning, and prejudice, but if the speaker seriously desires to address his appeals to the intellect and to create such a case for his proposition that it can withstand refutative attacks, he must marshal in support of his contentions all the strong evidence he can (see Chapter XVIII) and reason so clearly and logically from this evidence that the argument stands of its own strength.

Before selecting the logical materials to be used, the speaker must make certain that he has defined the precise goal of the speech, the goal being stated usually in the form of a proposition. The burden of proof the proposition places on the speaker should be clear also. The speaker must know what changes in belief he is seeking and he should have an idea of what response he can reasonably expect from the particular audience. He should not attempt to accomplish too much nor should he be too easy on himself.

After the proposition is clearly defined, the speaker should make certain he knows the main issues involved, those basic questions which must be answered if the proposition is to be supported successfully. These issues—such as, "Is there a need for a change?" "Is the change practical or desirable?"—provide natural sub-divisions for outlining the speech.

After the proposition is clearly in mind, the issues thought out, and the chief contentions of the speech formulated in terms of the issues and of the audience analysis, the matter of selecting the supporting materials is placed on a clear basis. In beginning the selection of evidence, the speaker should ask himself two questions: (1) What facts and opinions are necessary to create a belief in the probability that each of my contentions is true? (2) Will my audience accept the evidence as good and sufficient? Keeping these questions in mind, the persuader should proceed to select the evidence which meets these demands.

Next the speaker should formulate lines of reasoning from the evidence which clearly and logically usher the hearers into the establishment of tenable grounds for belief. But is the logical structure of the speech enough to guarantee adoption of the proposition? Oftentimes logical proofs are not enough to produce conviction. There may be a need for appropriate emotional appeals to supplement the logical appeals. The speaker may need to show that certain personal interests, desires, or motives are served by the proposition he is advancing. So, like the speech to stimulate, the speech to convince usually is a mixture of logical and non-logical materials, but in the present case the logical proofs or appeals to the intellect generally play the dominant role.

In 1872 Susan B. Anthony was arrested for voting in the presidential election. After her arrest she made her well known speech on woman's right to the suffrage. A part of this speech is given below. Note her statement of the proposition, her use of evidence, reasoning, and certain emotional appeals.

Friends and Fellow Citizens: I stand before you to-night under indictment for the alleged crime of having voted at the last presidential election, without having a lawful right to vote. It shall be my work this evening to prove to you that in thus voting, I not only committed no crime, but, instead, simply exercised my *citizen's rights,* guaranteed to me and all United States citizens by the National Constitution, beyond the power of any State to deny. . . .

The preamble of the Federal Constitution says:

"We, the people of the United States, in order to form a more perfect union, establish justice, insure domestic tranquillity, provide for the common defense, promote the general welfare, and secure the blessings of liberty to ourselves and our posterity, do ordain and establish this Constitution for the United States of America."

It was we, the people; not we, the white male citizens; nor yet we, the male citizens; but we, the whole people, who formed the Union. And we formed it, not to give the blessings of liberty, but to secure them; not to the half of ourselves and the half of our posterity, but to the whole people—women as well as men. And it is a downright mockery to talk to women of their enjoyment of the blessings of liberty while they are denied the use of the only means of securing them provided by this democratic-republican government—the ballot.

For any State to make sex a qualification that must ever result in the disfranchisement of one entire half of the people is to pass a bill of attainder, or an *ex post facto* law, and is therefore a violation of the supreme law of the land. By it the blessings of liberty are for ever withheld from women and their female posterity. To them this government has no just powers derived from the consent of the governed. To them this government is not a democracy. It is not a republic. It is an odious aristocracy; a hateful oligarchy of sex; the most hateful aristocracy ever established on the face of the globe; an oligarchy of wealth, where the rich govern the poor. An oligarchy of learning, where the educated govern the ignorant, or even an oligarchy of race, where the Saxon rules African, might be endured; but this oligarchy of sex, which makes father, brothers, husband, sons, the oligarchs over the mother and sisters, the wife and daughters of every household—which ordains all men sovereigns, all women subjects, carries dissension, discord and rebellion into every home of the nation.

Webster, Worcester and Bouvier all define a citizen to be a person in the United States, entitled to vote and hold office.

The only question left to be settled now is: Are women persons? And I hardly believe any of our opponents will have the hardihood to say they are not. Being persons, then, women are citizens; and no State has a right to make any law, or to enforce any old

> law, that shall abridge their privileges or immunities. Hence, every discrimination against women in the constitutions and laws of the several States is to-day null and void, precisely as in every one against negroes.[3]

FOR THE SPEECH TO ACTUATE

In Chapter XVI we noted that the speech to actuate seeks some definite, overt act on the part of the hearers. Here the listener is asked to do more than agree or believe that a course of action is desirable; he is asked to do something about it in the form of some explicit action.

In such a speech the speaker's proposition should be phrased in terms of the action desired. His purpose and his audience analysis should indicate the proportions of logical and nonlogical proofs to be used. Some speeches of actuation will need a predominance of the logical materials, others will need a predominance of the nonlogical, while still others will require a near balance of the two categories of support materials. Thus it can be said that many of the materials for the speech to actuate may be like those used in a speech to stimulate or to convince. However, there is one big difference. The speech hoping to actuate needs to go beyond stimulation or conviction into action, and its materials must provide this extra requirement. Here the third step, producing the desired response, in the process of persuasion often must be worked out at greater length and in more detail. The action must be motivated and specifically directed.

In motivating the desired action the persuader may need to supplement his logical reasons for the action with a series of appeals to emotion and motives that are so impelling they overcome all conservatism and produce action. Notice how the state's attorney in a famous murder trial ends his summation speech to the jury. How many appeals can you identify? Do they press for action?

> Gentlemen, yours is the most serious task of any who are connected with this important trial. You have been selected with much care, and to you are intrusted far more than the ordinary responsibilities of citizenship. The people of the state feel that the honor of the commonwealth, the very sovereignty of the State,

[3] Susan B. Anthony, "On Woman's Right to the Suffrage," in William Jennings Bryan (ed.), *The World's Famous Orations.* New York: Funk and Wagnalls Company, 1906, X: 58–60.

are upon trial. And it is true. We are practically testing the efficiency and strength of our State government. Will it protect property? Is life secure within the dominion? Is law its supreme and guiding force? Does justice reign within its temples? What is this splendid fabric which the restless energy and indomitable courage of the old pioneer has carved from the wild waste of the great Northwest and set as a gem in the crown of our common country? Is it, in fact and in truth, a commonwealth where men can dwell together in peace and safety and women and children rest in the sacred security of the home, where industry may secure its just reward and enterprise have its merited protection? Can the law-abiding and industrious and peace-loving citizen find shelter beneath its sovereign power? Has it power to punish crime?

Or is it but a miserable pretense; a shameless, deluding mockery, where anarchy rules with ruthless sway, and the most revolting of crimes go unwhipped before the altar, where murder walks the streets of your town, selects its victim with indifference and slays him with impunity, yes, more, in the very presence of death the officers of the law laugh hyena-like above the prostrate victim and dance above the bleeding form like spirits incarnate from the crypts of hell.

These are questions you must answer, matters upon which you must pass. It is for you to say what our young state shall do. Shall high-handed crime continue within her midst and ply its trade in open defiance of law? Is our young State to become the rendezvous for criminals, the by-word of sister States? Is our State's pride forfeited? Is our manhood dead? I appeal to you, as men and citizens, give back the reign of law; deal fairly but fearlessly with those who would continually trample all authority and the State's honor beneath the feet of lawless vengeance.

To you I now submit the whole cause, and may the power which works for the betterment of all give unto you the righteousness of judgment which will enable you to deal in justice and without fear of man or the dread of man between this defendant and your sovereign State.

I thank you again and again for your attention and the exercise of your patience and submit this matter for its final adjudication in the court of your own conscience.[4]

If the action-appeals are not strong or well chosen they can lead to failure. Customers have been unsold by poorly selected

[4] A part of the summation speech for the state by William E. Borah in the Coeur d'Alene Riot Murder trial, District Court, Wallace, Idaho, July 27, 1899. Recorded in Frederick C. Hicks, *Famous American Jury Speeches*. St. Paul: West Publishing Company, 1925, pp. 405–407.

or over-played appeals. A man and his wife, acquaintances of the writer, had decided to buy a new car and had made up their minds regarding the kind. They went to see the dealer about the transaction. During their discussion the salesman was showing the good points of the car and elaborating on them. In getting in and out of the back seat the wife noted that she had considerable difficulty but did not consider the matter of any great importance. Noticing the difficulty, the anxious but inept salesman proceeded to teach the lady how "to back into the back seat," a lesson which highlighted a negative appeal. Then, to make matters worse, he concluded with what he considered persuasion by mentioning that the lady was "the only person to complain," and "Let's face it, you are quite chubby." The unwise statements sent the couple out to buy another kind of car.

In directing the desired action there must be clear, easy-to-follow directions. If blood is to be donated, the hearer should be told exactly where the blood bank station is located, what hours are observed, how a person can get there, how long the trip will take, what the precise procedure is, and so on. The salesman soon learns that he must have the action step meticulously worked out. To know how to close a sale is indeed important. The client must be able to fill out the necessary papers, set up the system of payment, and execute other details, easily and without any hazard which would tend to weaken his will to act.

Selecting the Persuasive Techniques or Forms to Be Used

While the speaker is considering the selection of the materials for a particular speech, he should at the same time be thinking about what form or technique his supporting materials should use to be most effective. This involves application of the suggestions given in Chapters X, XI, and XII.

After the psychological materials have been selected, the speaker should answer such questions as the following in deciding how to use the materials: Should I use some materials to create direct or indirect suggestion? What materials can I use to create a "common ground" with this audience? Do I need to create an atmosphere effect? If so, what can I do to create it? Will the together device be useful? If so, what materials do I have to implement such a technique? Should I place my materials in the form of a rationalization for my audience? What points of my speech need to use the technique of repetition to become effective? What materials do I have that can create prestige for me and my cause? Such questions as these should constantly be in the mind of the speaker as he selects the techniques or forms for the nonlogical materials of the speech. If these forms are not remembered readily or clearly, the reader should review Chapter X.

Similarly, in dressing the logical materials for appearance in the speech, the speaker should determine, in the same careful manner, their forms or techniques. Thus he should ask such questions as: Can I support my proposition best by argument from statistics, circumstantial detail, or by comparison? Will argument by authority be useful in this speech? Will a well-drawn analogy do the job in establishing a given point? Does my material lend itself to a convincing generalization? To support my side of the basic issue will argument by alternation or by condition show the validity of my position? In answering these and other questions arising relative to the use of logical techniques, the reader should review Chapters XI and XII.

The selection of both the logical and psychological techniques should be made in terms of the speech purposes, the occasion and audience (partisan, neutral, or opposed), and the ethical standards of the speaker.

Wording the Persuasive Speech

All the materials and methods of a persuasive speech are dependent, of course, on words that clearly, accurately, and impellingly arouse within the hearer those meanings that will produce the desired response. The language of persuasion was discussed in Chapter IX and word manipulations was discussed in Chapter X. Our purpose here is to highlight a few additional points the speaker should keep in mind as he words his speech. Because this topic is an extended study in itself, the interested reader is encouraged to become familiar with the references given at the end of the chapter.

WRITTEN AND SPOKEN STYLE

Long ago Aristotle observed that each kind of rhetoric has its own appropriate style and that the style of written prose is not that of spoken oratory. Borchers and Wise [5] suggest some important points to be considered in the use of oral language. They remind the speaker of the effects of distractions on language and that the speaker, more than the writer, must counteract the distractions that can take away audience attention. Then, too, there is the effect of voice and action on language: the words must be coordinated with the expressions of voice and body. The speaker prepares for a specific audience whereas the writer arranges for a more general audience; therefore, the speaker's language must be adapted to a specific set of listeners in a visual and direct speaker-to-audience relationship. The reader can re-read written persuasion; the listener must comprehend immediately, thus instant intelligibility is required of the speaker's choice of words. This means simple, specific words should be used in addition to oral language which should be consistent with the speaker's personality. "The babyish or kittenish voice and manner which very tall, strong-looking women sometimes assume by way of compensation for their unusual size is a negative illustration of the point. Such women should speak like themselves, not like their opposites in type." [6]

Successful speakers show marked individuality in their speech style. Each speaker should develop those positive qualities of his own, and the language should be appropriate for the audience and occasion. The sentence length of oral style varies more than that of written style. There is a greater variety in the kinds of sentences used. Oral style is more personal, using more personal pronouns than the written style. The speaker says "I," "you," and "we" in his attempts to make his message personally vital to each hearer. The speaker finds repetition to be a valuable characteristic of oral style.

It might be added that a speaker should not forget Herbert Spencer's thesis that good style and economy of effort are indissolubly linked and that good style makes minimum demands upon the hearer's ability to comprehend. Meanings should come as directly and simply as possible. Exhausting, indeed, is the speaker whose expenditure of speech exceeds his income of ideas.

---

[5] Gladys L. Borchers and Claude M. Wise, *Modern Speech.* New York: Harcourt, Brace and Company, 1947, pp. 192–199.

[6] *Ibid.,* pp. 194, 195.

UNITY, EMPHASIS, AND COHERENCE

These are the three great rhetorical elements of oral and written composition. They should be familiar to every reader. The organization of the speech and the choice of words should assure unity of purpose and thought. Each addition to the growing speech should add to the essential unity of the argument.

The speaker must determine the relative importance of the points or ideas of his discourse. Emphases should be made to let the hearers know the intended relationships. Normally the points of a speech are not equally important. Their comparative value can only be known by the manner in which the speaker emphasizes each, whether by the amount of time given to it, by repetition, by restatement, or by vocal and visual emphases.

Orderliness of the material and clearly worded transitions from one point or part of the speech to the next can help assure the coherence of the composition. Transitions usually involve a summary of the point just concluded, a statement of what is to be considered next, or, better still, both a summary and a forecast. Lord Erskine, famed British advocate, provides an example of the latter type of transition in his speech on "The Rights of Juries."

> Having established this important right in the jury, beyond all possibility of cavil or controversy, I will now show your Lordships that its existence is not merely consistent with the theory of the law, but is illustrated and confirmed by the universal practice of all judges. . . .[7]

Summary and Conclusions

In this chapter we have discussed certain basic considerations in fitting materials to the speech and of wording these materials. We have noted that the time limit of a speech must be respected, that the logical and nonlogical materials must be selected in terms of the purpose and audience of the speech, that the persuasive forms or techniques to be used must be selected on the basis of their contribution to the speech purpose, and that the speech must be worded in such a way as to make for clarity, appropriateness, and impressiveness.

---

[7] Chauncey A. Goodrich (ed.), *Select British Eloquence.* New York: Harper and Brothers, 1852, p. 661.

As you proceed to the study and practice of delivering the persuasive speech, you will be testing its oral style. Perhaps practicing the speech out loud will reveal errors in the choice of words, and you will discover that they may not be suited to your own personality or to your vocal and visual action. Invariably you will make changes.

The problems regarding memorizing a speech, extemporizing one, and reading from manuscript are discussed in the following chapter.

Readings

1. Borchers, Gladys L., and Wise, Claude M., *Modern Speech.* New York: Harcourt, Brace and Company, 1947, Ch. VII, "Oral Language."
2. Baird, A. Craig, *Argumentation, Discussion, and Debate.* New York: McGraw-Hill Book Co., Inc., 1950, Ch. XVII, "Argumentative Composition: Language."
3. Brigance, W. N., *Speech Composition.* New York: F. S. Crofts and Company, 1939, Ch. VI, "The Use of Words."
4. Gray, Giles W., and Braden, Waldo W., *Public Speaking: Principles and Practice.* New York: Harper and Brothers, 1951, Ch. XVII, "Using Language for Vividness."
5. Hummel, W., and Huntress, K., *The Analysis of Propaganda.* New York: William Sloane Associates, Inc., 1949, Ch. IV, "Propaganda in Action."

Exercises

1. In preparation for a five-minute speech to stimulate, discuss in an interview with your instructor the types and proportions of logical and nonlogical materials you plan to use in seeking the desired response.

2. In preparation for an eight-minute speech to convince, discuss in an interview with your instructor the logical and psychological forms or techniques you plan to use in support of your proposition.

3. Write a 1000-word analysis of the composition of General MacArthur's speech to Congress, April 19, 1951.

4. Prepare and present a five-minute informative speech on "Written and Oral Style." Use the reading references above to help you prepare the speech.

5. Prepare and present a six-minute speech to actuate. Make certain the action you seek from your audience is particularly well motivated and directed.

Chapter XXI

DELIVERING THE PERSUASIVE SPEECH

I. Introduction

II. The Bases of Delivery

A. Vocal Elements

1. Intelligibility
2. Vocal Flexibility

B. Elements of Bodily Action

1. Animation and Coordination
2. Naturalness in Bodily Action

C. Delivery and Circular Response

III. The Modes of Delivery

A. Impromptu Delivery of the Persuasive Speech

B. Extemporaneous Delivery of the Persuasive Speech

C. Manuscript Delivery of the Persuasive Speech

D. Memorized Delivery of the Persuasive Speech

IV. Summary

Readings and Exercises

Chapter XXI

DELIVERING THE PERSUASIVE SPEECH

Introduction

In Chapter XIII, "Finding the Available Means of Persuasion Within the Speaker," we concentrated upon ethos but mentioned delivery as important in determining ethos and as a critical transmission link in oral communication. Obviously, many of the changes in attitude toward the speaker that come about during his speech are a function of audience response to his delivery. Equally apparent is the role played by delivery as a vehicle transporting ideas, attitudes, emotions, and facts from the mind of the speaker to the minds of his audience.

Delivery includes everything the speaker does physically to communicate his message. Visible and audible stimuli result, forming a complex code to be deciphered by the audience. This code is composed of intentional elements representing content deliberately projected by the speaker and unintended items revealing much about the speaker, e.g., further information concerning his purpose, his attitudes, his personality, and his message. All the resources of voice and bodily actions serve speech delivery.

In persuasive speaking, as in most other applications of speech, the best delivery is inconspicuous. Speech can be such an efficient conveyor of concepts that our preoccupation as audience can be totally with the ideas transmitted to the exclusion of the mechanisms of transmission. Do we become intrigued with the speaker's thinking to the point of forgetting how he communicates it? If so, the speaker has met the severest test of effective delivery. Any speech delivery that attracts attention to itself is to some degree less than ideally efficient. Exhibitionism of any sort is obsolete in purposeful speech. In persuasion any delivery detail which becomes conspicuous is especially damaging. Persuasion demands sustained attention to the logically and psychologically developing message, and breaks in that attention caused by delivery or anything else make the task of carrying the audience toward a new belief or course of action more difficult than it might have been otherwise.

Styles of delivery vary widely, but there is little experimental evidence of the inherent superiority of any style or mode. Dietrich found an apparent advantage for conversational delivery as compared to dynamic speaking over the radio. (See Chapter XXII on Studies in Persuasion.) But after the criteria of intelligibility have been met, we are speculating when we assert one type of delivery to be better than another. We need many objective experimental studies isolating factors of delivery and measuring their relative effectiveness in persuasive speaking.

The Bases of Delivery

VOCAL ELEMENTS

Intelligibility. One prerequisite to success in persuasive speaking is to be intelligible in order to permit understanding of the message. Rhetorical considerations affect intelligibility, but delivery adds to, or reduces the difficulty of, grasping meanings. Gesture and movement sometimes help clarify meanings to some degree; however, the main determiners of intelligibility in delivery are vocal.

Articulation contributes most directly to being heard and understood. Precise, vigorous movements of all speech organs involved in the production of words are necessary. Loudness appropriate to the speech environment is next in importance. It is desirable to speak loudly enough but not too loudly, and to project this level of vocal intensity toward the most remote auditors. Phrasing (the grouping of words and the location and duration of pauses) and inflection (the use of pitch changes) affect intelligibility. Generally, word groups are too long and pauses too infrequent for easy understanding. Short word groups and pauses of varying length create a changing stimulus to which it is easy to attend. Similarly, a wide range of appropriate but unpredictable inflection patterns conveys meanings by highlighting important words and phrases and by subordinating incidental elements.

Contributing least of any of the voice factors to intelligibility but still vital to communicating connotative overtones to language is *quality,* the characteristic of the voice that gives it timbre or tone and causes people to react to it as pleasant or unpleasant. A generally pleasant voice quality is an aid to intelligibility in that we find listening easy and possibly enjoyable. Strictly speaking, however, a nasal or hollow voice can be as intelligible as any other if given equivalent articulation, loudness, inflection, and phrasing.

Vocal Flexibility. A wealth of significance beyond simple intelligibility is carried by the skillfully spoken word. This results largely from controlled changes of loudness, pitch, rate, and quality produced by a coordinated animation of the voice mechanism we term vocal flexibility. Wide variations of all four elements are characteristic of the flexible voice. Continuous and integrated change involving all elements is also typical. Both abrupt and gradual changes are widely used for different effects.

A bodily state hostile to vocal flexibility is that of general tension. Relaxation of the whole physical mechanism, and particularly the throat, aids in producing optimum voice control. The speaker cannot control his tensions completely, but he can minimize them by regular practice and conscious effort. He can work toward the goal of greater flexibility and thereby increase his vocal skills. The guiding principle of such practice is "Maximum controlled variation consistent with the content of the speech." Exaggerated practice exercises in vocal flexibility are probably valuable.

ELEMENTS OF BODILY ACTION

Animation and Coordination. Highly successful persuasive speakers are animated through vigorous activity. Adolf Hitler, Franklin D. Roosevelt, Billy Sunday, and, more recently, Billy Graham are noted for the role played by extensive bodily action in their speaking. Analysis of the use of the physique by these and other speakers yields a few conclusions concerning the nature of appropriate animation for the persuasive speaker.

Good speaker animation is always total and never localized to parts of the body. Whether subtle or obvious, a gesture or movement involves the entire physical mechanism moving as a unit. Books on elocution used to say that a hand gesture starts at the center of the body and flows off the finger tips, a concept that probably helped students achieve integrated bodily action. When movement or gesture is used as a means of emphasizing particular words and phrases it is timed so that it coincides with or slightly precedes the utterance. Early timing of physical means of emphasis is apparently not critical; late timing is absurd and often intentionally or unintentionally humorous. A little experimenting with the timing of gestures will verify this; it will also develop a sense of the permissible leeway in the timing of various kinds of bodily action.

Physical activity of the speaker should always be energetic, but large or small in extent as the occasion demands. A lifted finger may emphasize for a small audience something which requires a full sweeping arm and hand gesture for a lecture hall. Action before intimate groups therefore tends to be suggestive and for the formal, extended public speaking situation it becomes more literal or complete. The speaker should never show that he is conscious of particular physical movements. An extreme violation of this principle is the speaker who carefully watches his own gesture. Physical action is convincing only when it preserves the illusion of complete spontaneity. Studied or practiced looking gestures are resented because they dispel this illusion.

A moving object is infinitely more attention-compelling than one that remains still. If animation is not completely denied by topic or circumstances it will usually contribute to the effectiveness of your speaking. The lively speaker is commonly thought to be an interesting speaker, and usually that is the case.

Naturalness in Bodily Action. There is no correct pattern for bodily action. The teaching of complete gestures as a part of the training of a public speaker is almost obsolete. At least two facts undermined the mechanical approaches to improving the speaker's visible code: memorized gestures seldom become inconspicuous, and a person's bodily activity in speech is highly individualistic. Better results come from efforts toward general animation than from the teaching of particular movements. Student speakers are encouraged to begin their practice by "doing what comes naturally" in gesture and movement, with refinements coming about through (1) suggestions for change by the instructor, (2) repeated practice to determine what "feels right," and (3) unconscious imitation of better speakers.

The interactions of integrated speech are so complicated that a delicate balance must be maintained. Concentration upon changing one detail of speech production, e.g., articulation of a particular consonant, may destroy the coordination necessary to smooth, effective speaking. Just as a golfer's swing can "go to pieces" when he begins to worry about the position of his right foot, a good speaker can become uncoordinated through concentration upon the process of gesture or an attempt to eliminate an annoying physical mannerism. Improving speech through correcting details of voice and action one by one and then putting them together again is practically impossible. It is also dangerous because the level of coordination existing in the speaker when training began may never be re-established.

A device for improving bodily action without upsetting coordination is the complete preoccupation of the speaker with his problem of transferring his ideas accurately to his audience. If he succeeds in becoming so involved in his message and its transmission that he forgets how he looks and sounds, his vocal and bodily elements will probably be well integrated. It is only the conscious gesture that is ill-timed, for example. Enthusiastic, energetic efforts to communicate lead almost spontaneously to abundant, motivated bodily activity. This type of training discourages any attempt to assume a new personality for certain speech purposes. It aims at freeing voice and body so the real personality the speaker has been accumulating all his life can exert all its potential charm. We want the speaker to be himself completely. We know that above all else people like and respect genuineness in others. A speaker's bodily action is ideally a symbolic presentation of himself, not an imitation of anyone else in a similar situation.

DELIVERY AND CIRCULAR RESPONSE

"Talk with, not at, your audience." This advice is both popular and sound. Effective delivery of a good speech creates a continuous round robin of interaction between speaker and audience. Speaker-originated stimuli produce in the listeners physical responses which are perceived by the speaker; and, in turn, these responses modify his behavior. This psychological teamwork termed "circular response" is a pleasant experience with esthetic qualities; only a polarized audience, however, is capable of a significant degree of circular response. A persuasive speaker naturally desires as much circular response as possible; hence, a large proportion of his preparation and delivery efforts is directed toward its achievement.

An avenue to the control of audience cooperation via delivery is found in the empathic nature of human behavior. Empathy is the tendency to imitate physically what we see and hear. In subtle forms, as in art and music appreciation, it is often termed "feeling in." Empathy guarantees that energetic, lively speaking will increase the physical alertness of the audience. The speaker's delivery can control audience tension over a wide range, relaxing his listeners by slowing his own delivery and reducing energy of his speaking and lifting them to a tense climax by increasing his own vigor, loudness, rate, and pitch variation. Some of this is independent of content. But much empathic effect comes from concrete word pictures so vivid that the audience imitates what they see in their own imaginations! Coordinating dramatic human interest images with delivery to produce maximum empathy effect often brings about a startling amount of circular response.

At its most literal level the speaker can use empathy to secure physical response through direct imitation. If he smiles at the audience in friendly fashion, they will smile back at him. If he frowns seriously and nods, a large proportion of his audience will similarly frown and nod. These automatic surface responses affect attitudes to some extent. The speaker who "beams" at his audience and gets them to "beam" back at him probably has made a significant step toward gaining acceptance of his proposition.

Empathic response explains the strong reactions of an audience when a speaker is ill at ease. The tensions that plague the speaker are communicated subliminally to the audience, causing them physical discomfort. In the case of severe stage fright of the speaker the audience's empathic response may reach the intensity of physical pain. By contrast, a well coordinated speaker produces pleasant harmonious tensions that actually make the audience feel good physically. You will remember hearing the comment, "He's comfortable to listen to."

Modes of Delivery

A persuasive appeal may be delivered without prior thought or with any amount of preparation up to and including writing it out and memorizing it. We will discuss four points along this continuum of preparation and discuss some problems of delivery associated with each. These "modes of delivery" are impromptu, extemporaneous, manuscript, and memorized.

IMPROMPTU DELIVERY OF THE PERSUASIVE SPEECH

The word "impromptu" conveys accurately the notion that a speech so described is an on-the-spot performance. This is true in the sense that there has been no prior planning of motive appeals and their sequence or of speech details. But a speech purpose may have been selected and precisely defined. A great amount of knowledge and many arguments may be available to the persuader from extensive previous experience; thus, the usual impromptu persuasive speech is impromptu only in content selection and wording.

Practically all impromptu persuasive speaking takes place in small, primary groups, and nearly all the persuasion in primary groups *is* impromptu. This mode of delivery is close to that of conversation because it is similarly flexible and cannot be held to rigorous standards of organization and progression.

Impromptu primary-group persuasion is relatively unpredictable. It places the greatest premium on the quick-wittedness of the persuader, who must adapt continually and instantaneously to responses of the persuadee. He cannot achieve the fine organization of the polished public speech, but he must still develop a coherent unit of argument. While busily cutting and fitting the parts of his speech together he must be a relaxed and alert conversationalist. Skill in impromptu persuasive speaking demands not only ad-lib ability but also such a knowledge of the topic that all needed information will leap to mind without notes or other reminders. Fortunately, we all spend a large part of our conversational lives in impromptu persuasive speaking. If we "hold our own" with family and friends that is good evidence that we are already reasonably proficient!

Impromptu speaking in a formal audience-speaker situation is rarely necessary. The circumstances demanding that a speech be delivered without specific preparation are improbable. Usually some advance notice is given the speaker, and if he has a few hours or days in which to prepare, there is little justification for relying upon the impromptu mode of delivery.

EXTEMPORANEOUS DELIVERY OF THE PERSUASIVE SPEECH

The extemporaneous mode of delivery implies a somewhat detailed preparation of a speech for a specific audience and occasion without the final step of wording the entire speech. All evidence, illustrations, and arguments can be selected and arranged in order. Some extemporaneous speakers prefer to write out their speeches, but do not memorize the words and do not read the speech from manuscript. At the time of delivery the speaker chooses words that seem at the moment best suited to conveying his facts and ideas to the audience. He may rearrange and edit subject matter on the spot. He is in an optimum position to meet audience needs in many ways. Certainly the extemporaneous delivery pattern has much to recommend it as a technique of adapting speech content to different audiences and situations.

The majority of direct speaker-audience persuasion is in the extemporaneous mode. The two-way communication that is so much a part of the direct speaker-audience relationship makes desirable a delivery pattern that can be varied more than can a speech from manuscript or memory. Thorough preparation of content guarantees that the extemporaneous speaker will not wander far afield, yet he can enjoy the advantages of freshly chosen language that sounds spontaneous and natural. Extemporaneous delivery demands that the speaker concentrate upon ideas rather than words. Extemporaneous speaking tends to be *with* rather than *at* the audience. Stage fright and self-consciousness are minimized because the speaker is busy with the wording of his argument and observing the audience to ascertain how the speech is being received.

Both impromptu and extemporaneous speaking tend to be inefficient because of poorly chosen and unnecessary words. However, most difficulties in extemporaneous speaking are caused by inadequate preparation, or, in other words, treating the problem in impromptu fashion. Speakers who have their content well in hand usually are efficient in extemporaneous use of language. There is no danger of over-preparing an extemporaneous speech as long as no final wording is attempted. Timing is admittedly difficult, but talking the speech aloud enables the speaker to estimate time closely and it results in a better word choice when the speech is delivered.

Extemporaneous speaking is often aided by notes or a delivery outline which should be brief and inconspicuous. Three by five or four by six cards are good for either notes or outline. Notes are often harmful because they are used when they are not needed at all, or they are overused. Many speakers look at and handle their notes to relieve their tensions rather than to aid their memories. A delivery outline should be a skeleton affair with the simple function of insuring that the speaker maintain the right order and forget no important points. Frequently the only notes needed are quotations and other bits of evidence that would be difficult to memorize. Notes are a potential hazard in that they may get in the speaker's way, but their proper use is learned easily, and they can make a contribution in saving time and energy in preparation and in offering security to the speaker. Sometimes reading source material from cards adds authenticity to the evidence and makes it more effective as persuasion. Documentation is simplified by appropriate notes.

MANUSCRIPT DELIVERY OF THE PERSUASIVE SPEECH

When precision in expression and timing becomes important, when the occasion is such that no chance of misspeaking can be tolerated, and when very large audiences such as those in radio or television are addressed, speaking from manuscript is usually the most suitable mode. Microphones are generally used.

The advantages of a manuscript are substantial. All the guesswork is absent from the final performance insofar as we are concerned with exact and polished rhetoric, perfect timing, and precise use of language to convey just the right shades of meaning. The speaker need not rely upon inspiration to give him the right word at the proper time.

The problem of bringing the typed page to life for an audience is a real challenge. Only a highly skilled interpretative reader can achieve an effect of spontaneity, and most able speakers fall far short of converting a manuscript into the equivalent of good extemporaneous speech. When delivered by at least nine out of ten speakers the manuscript speech sounds as though it were being read. Audiences recognize this fact, and although they do not like it they tend to accept it as inevitable. They are appreciative of good reading of a speech, possibly the more so because it is rare.

The speaker, then, should realize that he is paying a price for the advantages of the manuscript; he should practice reading it until he knows his speech so well that he can do a respectable job of interpretation. If possible, recording the speech and studying the record will help the speaker to develop a natural reading style.

Because electronic devices are almost always involved in manuscript speaking in this age of the media of mass communication, some details of microphone delivery should be noted. The manuscript should be easy to read and double or triple spaced in large type on one side only of a soft paper that does not rustle readily. A stable reader's stand located so that the speaker is properly positioned before the microphone is a practical necessity. As each page is completed, it is moved aside on the reader's stand or, in the case of radio studio speaking, it may be dropped to the floor. With an audience present the speaker should maintain eye contact with them. This will help him to concentrate on communication of ideas rather than just on reading words. A fairly constant distance from the microphone should be maintained unless intensity change is used, in which case the speaker steps back to shout and leans forward as he speaks softly. With an audience present one does not talk *at* the microphone. While maintaining the correct position with respect to it, the speaker apparently ignores it and talks *with* the people. A properly adjusted public address system does not tie the speaker closely to the microphone, twelve to twenty-four inches being a reasonable range of distance. Output volume should be such that the speaker's voice is reinforced rather than enlarged. The effect on the audience is ideally one of uncertainty as to whether the speaker is being heard directly or via the public address system. Although the microphone can amplify weak sounds, the speaker should be encouraged to speak vigorously, his speech gaining vitality thereby. A fairly rapid rate of delivery and a conversational manner are suited to radio speaking, but with a large present audience a slower rate with more and longer pauses and more decided vocal emphases are needed.

The manuscript becomes more obvious in television speaking than in any other speech situation. A variety of concealment devices have been used to make the typed copy disappear, but the searching eye of the TV camera leaves no doubt that the speaker is reading something, somewhere. One solution is to bring the manuscript out in the open and do a good job of reading it while maintaining eye contact with the camera. As the radio speaker chats intimately with a small hypothetical audience, so the television speaker can read to people in their living rooms. The script is conspicuous at first, but if it is handled honestly and well, it may come to be accepted.

MEMORIZED DELIVERY OF THE PERSUASIVE SPEECH

Practical considerations dictate that the memorized delivery of persuasive speeches occurs most often when the speeches are to be delivered repeatedly and intact. Popular lectures, sales talks, some sermons, and political "stumpspeaking" are examples. Occasionally a significant speech opportunity indicates the most thorough possible preparation of careful writing and a word-by-word memorization of the speech. Even though this is desirable, it is easy to see why the relatively easy manuscript delivery is more popular. A well-memorized speech has the precision of the manuscript without the inhibiting influences of reading. In capable hands this mode offers great possibilities. Bringing a memorized speech alive is difficult but much easier than accomplishing the same feat with a manuscript. When it is made to sound natural, the memorized speech creates the illusion of extremely polished and efficient extemporaneous delivery. This in itself can be profoundly persuasive.

Our greatest speakers have memorized their key speeches. The student of persuasion should consider giving himself sufficient experience in the memorized method to become familiar with this more precise and controlled type of speaking. Preparing a ten to twenty minute speech and refining and polishing it for an entire academic year is a worthwhile exercise. When a memorized speech is used repeatedly over a period of time, the objective of the speaker is not to settle upon a static pattern but to evolve a continuously improving rhetorical unit. Delivery is never twice the same, and with every repetition variations in content, arrangement, and wording are tried. The popular notion that the memorized speech is delivered always as a carbon copy of itself is not accurate, at least not according to practices of capable speakers.

Summary

Delivery (everything that the speaker does physically to communicate his message) is not only a major factor in conveying speech content to the audience but also is a factor determining ethos of the speaker. Much of the prestige of the speaker depends upon competence in delivery. Weak delivery handicaps the persuader as much as strong, powerful delivery aids him. The best delivery is so efficient that it becomes inconspicuous, focusing all attention upon the message.

The bases of delivery are voice, bodily action, and the psychological interaction of audience and speaker known as circular response. Vocal elements ideally are intelligible and flexible. Good bodily action is characterized by animation, coordination, and a naturalness of movement and gesture that harmonize with the personality of the speaker. Circular responses are possible with all present audiences and the role they play increases as the size of the audience decreases. Continuous circular response is desirable because it is usually evidence of genuine speaker-audience cooperation. Principles of empathy seem to govern circular response. An understanding of empathy helps the speaker to control behavior of his audience.

The persuasive speaker may choose among several modes of delivery. Impromptu speaking, without previous specific preparation other than possible definition of purpose, is best suited to primary group persuasion. More formal audience-speaker occasions are served best in the majority of instances by extemporaneous delivery, a mode permitting detailed speech preparation but requiring that the speaker clothe his ideas in language at the time of delivery. Extemporaneous speaking is a happy compromise that allows both careful preparation and great adaptability.

Speaking from manuscript provides opportunity for precision, polished rhetoric, and exact timing in the formal or large scale communication. Due to the difficulty of reading in a manner that sounds like extemporizing, most speeches from manuscript sound "read." Occasional deviations from the script help the speaker to sound more spontaneous. The manuscript is always a mechanical obstacle between speaker and audience, yet its advantages dictate its general use in our media of mass communication. Memorized delivery is the most time-consuming and difficult in preparation but it frees the speaker from his manuscript while retaining all the script advantages. The most polished and powerful speeches throughout history have been delivered from memory. The memorized method of speaking is difficult, but potentially highly productive.

Appropriate delivery makes possible the attainment of an important objective in spoken persuasion, the psychological teamwork of speaker and audience wherein the speaker converses *with* rather than talks *at* his auditors.

Readings

1. Chester, Giraud, and Garrison, G. R., *Radio and Television.* New York: Appleton-Century-Crofts, Inc., 1951, Ch. 17.
2. Gilman, Wilbur, Aly, Bower, and Loren Reid, *The Fundamentals of Speaking.* New York: The Macmillan Company, 1951, Chaps. 7, 21.
3. Monroe, Alan H., *Principles and Types of Speech.* New York: Scott, Foresman and Company, 1941, Chaps. 3, 4, 5, 6.
4. Oliver, Robert T., *Persuasive Speaking.* New York: Longmans, Green and Co., Inc., 1950, Ch. 4.
5. Thonssen, L., and Gilkinson, H., *Basic Training in Speech.* Boston: D. C. Heath and Company, 1947, Ch. 21.

Exercises

1. Record a speech delivered in part extemporaneously and in part from manuscript. Compare details of your vocal treatment of ad libbed and read material.

2. Memorize your next classroom speech. Compare extemporaneous and memorized delivery in this speaking situation

3. Deliver a speech in which you attempt to reach the limit of your effective range of vocal variation and vigorous bodily action. Note the empathic responses of the audience.

4. Observe several television speakers and compare their handling of manuscripts.

5. Describe from memory an occasion when an unusually great amount of speaker-audience circular response came about. What evidences indicated functioning circular response?

Part VI

EVALUATING PERSUASION

Any complete study of persuasion must include those evaluative materials, principles, and methods which have called, and can continue to call, the subject matter into strict account and thus help it to grow in usefulness and responsibility.

Chapter XXII makes a comprehensive survey of the studies that have been made in persuasion. Chapter XXIII suggests methods for assessing the effectiveness of persuasion, and Chapter XXIV poses a yardstick to be used in measuring the ethics of persuasion.

Chapter XXII

STUDIES IN PERSUASION

I. Introduction

II. Content Analysis Studies

III. Audience Analysis Studies

IV. Media Comparisons

V. Stimulus Studies

- A. Studies in the Arrangement of Materials
- B. Studies Measuring the Effects of Training the Persuadee
- C. Studies Measuring the Relative Effectiveness of Particular Methods of Persuasion

VI. Case Studies

VII. The Army's World War II Communication Research Project

- A. Evaluation Studies on Effects of Films
- B. Studies Employing Controlled Variation

VIII. Summary and Conclusions

Readings and Exercises

Chapter XXII

STUDIES IN PERSUASION

Introduction

For a great many years the answers to perplexing problems of human motivation were sought through casual observation, speculation, and moralizing. Results, though filled with errors, were helpful. Aristotle, for example, made many shrewd guesses concerning the means of influencing men's minds. The lack of certainty inherent in speculative methods of research foreshadowed a clash with the more precise techniques of scientific investigation. Our twentieth century has witnessed a steady growth of controlled and objective experimentation in the effort to increase our reliable knowledge concerning the process of persuasion.

This sector of investigation is only a small portion of the broad front of scientific research into the phenomena of human behavior. Chase calls this crusade for enlightenment the "Science of Human Relations." In a recent book [1] he surveys most interestingly our progress in finding facts about human behavior. His title comes from two lines of Alexander Pope's "Essay on Man":

> Know then thyself, presume not God to scan;
> The proper study of mankind is man.

Chase concludes that the scientific investigation of human relations has only begun. Certainly that is true in the research in persuasion. Many scholars have studied isolated instances of functioning of parts of the persuasion process, but to date no over-all comprehensive pattern has emerged. Our attempt to compartmentalize pertinent research yields five categories: content analysis, audience analysis, media comparisons, stimulus comparisons, and

---

[1] Stuart Chase, *The Proper Study of Mankind.* New York: Harper and Brothers, 1948.

case studies. This chapter surveys selected studies under these headings. In addition, several pages are devoted to a summary of studies done on military communication and orientation in World War II. Trends of specific agreement and disagreement among the studies are interpreted in the conclusions.

Content Analysis Studies

Since the process of persuasion is carried on by communication, one obvious means of increasing our understanding of it is systematic study of the content of a variety of persuasive communications.

> Content analysis provides a precise means of describing the contents of any sort of communication—newspapers, radio programs, films, every day conversations, verbalized free associations, etc. The operations of content analysis consist in classifying the signs occurring in a communication into a set of appropriate categories. The results state the frequency of occurrence, of signs for each category in the classification scheme.[2]

A simple and direct application of content analysis is found in Weingast's investigation of the bias of a popular columnist. This was a study to classify value judgments expressed by Walter Lippmann in his newspaper columns concerning selected controversial issues in the years 1932 through 1938.[3] The categories were: FDR, New Deal, first AAA, NRA, TVA, National Labor Relations Act, Social Security Program, and Wage and Hour Legislation.

Statements on each were grouped into "favorable," "unfavorable," and "neutral" categories. Only statements expressing a clear value judgment were counted. The experimenter selected and classified these statements. Totals were run for the eight categories and tables for each were converted into percentages, showing percentage of judgment statements favorable, percentage neutral, and percentage unfavorable. These were considered as measures of Lippmann's published opinion on the selected issues during the period studied.

Results showed Lippmann's columns to have been consistently anti-New Deal and decidedly "unfavorable" to all specific items of social legislation listed above, except Social Security and TVA.

---

[2] Lasswell, Leites and Associates, *Language of Politics.* Cornwall, N. Y.: George W. Stewart, Publisher, 1949, p. 55.

[3] David E. Weingast, "Walter Lippmann: A Content Analysis," *The Public Opinion Quarterly* (1950), 14: 2, pp. 296–302.

His judgment statements on Social Security were 45 per cent neutral, 30 per cent unfavorable, and 25 per cent favorable. On TVA the score was 50 per cent neutral, 12.5 per cent unfavorable, and 37.5 per cent favorable. A result surprising to many authorities who considered Lippmann to be "pro-labor" was his published opposition to the Wagner Act (NLRB); over the 1934 through 1938 period his value judgment statements concerning it were 100 per cent unfavorable. Consistent with this finding was his record toward wage and hour legislation, 94 per cent unfavorable and 6 per cent neutral.

The author makes no attempt to prove validity of his allocations of statements or to justify the necessary assumption that numbers and percentages of statements relate closely to strength of the attitudes held by the person who makes them. We can say only that he has measured something quantitatively which can be related to other research with interesting and probably profitable results. At least, a person who claimed Lippmann was decidedly "pro-labor" from 1934 through 1938 would be encouraged to re-examine his evidence when confronted with Weingast's table.

Bigman [4] studied the arguments in seven contemporary periodical publications which contend that the movement sponsoring World Federal Government is a Communist plot. Themes of reasoning were ascertained by reading through all publications and noting statements bearing on this issue. Dates and numbers of periodicals read were not specified, and numerical quantification was not reported. Some interesting agreements, apparently developed by collective subjective evaluation of the periodicals, appeared. For example, World Federal Government as a plan was asserted uniformly to have originated "in Moscow" and to have as its purpose surrendering the United States to Russia. The word "Communist" was considered synonymous, on frequent occasions, with "Socialist," "Zionist," and "Jew." Measures of international cooperation such as the Marshall Plan were strongly condemned, and all but one of the publications (*The Daughters of American Revolution Magazine*) disapproved of the United Nations.

> From all of this we conclude that the charge of "Communist" brought against the United World Federalists—as against the

[4] Stanley K. Bigman, "The 'New Internationalism' under Attack," *The Public Opinion Quarterly* (1950), 14: 2, pp. 235–261.

> United Nations, the Marshall Plan and so on—is not the main issue. The views rather consistently expressed in the writings discussed here are those which are called "isolationist" by their opponents and "nationalist" by their adherents. The issue seems in truth, to be between those views and those conceptions which conflict with them.[5]

Where Weingast classified, counted, and submitted totals, Bigman's study classified, subjectively interpreted, and presented a sampling of statements. Here quantification was minimized and consistency, uniformity, and freedom from serious exception were accorded prime significance.

Since radio has become a vital medium of persuasion, it is helpful to know the composition of domestic radio broadcasting. Baker[6] surveyed programs in a recent year and determined that our stations devoted almost one-half their time to music, and that over one-half of the music broadcast was dance music. Sixteen per cent of radio time was devoted to the drama, of which six per cent was the day time serial. One-eighth of the broadcast time went to newscasters, news broadcasts, and news commentators. Fourteen per cent of radio time consisted of messages and announcements, of which 90 per cent were commercial. One-third of broadcast programs were not sponsored. Of the sponsored programs, networks supplied 50 per cent. Networks provided well over 50 per cent of the unsponsored program material.

Inkeles[7] made an interesting report of a survey on broadcasting in the USSR, covering program content and audience analysis. We will mention certain of his audience findings below; here we note that Soviet broadcasting presented much good music, much literary reading, and that the whole system was "characterized by an education and 'uplift' quality."[8] Nothing was broadcast resembling our "soap opera" or radio comics. Political material was drawn from printed sources, and in a very real sense radio in USSR supplemented the press. There were highly developed and skilfully presented programs for children of all age groups. The tone of children's programs was "positive" and proper, with total

---

[5] *Ibid.*, p. 261.

[6] P. F. Lazarsfeld and F. Stanton, *Communications Research, 1948–1949.* New York: Harper and Brothers, 1949, pp. 57–72.

[7] *Ibid.*, pp. 223–293.

[8] *Ibid.*, p. 263.

omission of "hair-raising" or "scare" features. Advertising on the USSR radio was outlawed in 1935 and resumed in 1947.

> All of the commercials are grouped in a single program of 8 to 10 minutes duration, broadcast three times a day, and the announcements are read alternately by male and female announcers without interruption. There is no attempt at salesmanship, which would of course, be superfluous in a country of commodity and service scarcity. The commercial programs represent a type of shopper's service, or a form of radio "red book" in the absence of other advertising media resulting from the paper shortage.[9]

Inkeles mentioned that the major published objectives of broadcasting in the USSR were to provide "a pleasant, sensible recreation" and "cultural relaxation."

Mott[10] made an extensive investigation of persuasive content of newspapers in years of presidential elections from 1792 to 1944. He found no correlation of any significance between support of a majority of newspapers and success following the national presidential campaigns. He confirmed that in recent elections the press has endorsed losing candidates and suggested but has not explored the problem of the obligation, if any, a newspaper has to represent the majority interest of its reading public.

White[11] subjected twenty-one speeches by Hitler and seven speeches by Franklin Delano Roosevelt during the period 1935 through 1939 to value analysis statistical treatment in order to determine some similarities and differences in their propaganda methods. He tabulated 4077 value-judgments for Hitler and 1249 for Roosevelt, using their relative frequency as an indication of strength of appeal.

A striking similarity was found in the heavy reliance of both speakers on appeals favoring peace and conventional morality. Twenty-seven per cent of Hitler's emphasis-units embraced "peace, non-aggression, non-domination, friendship and tolerance" while Roosevelt's record in these categories was 22 per cent. White comments: "All propagandists must appeal—truly or falsely—to the

---

[9] *Ibid.*, p. 274–276.

[10] Frank Luther Mott, "Newspapers in Presidential Campaigns," *Public Opinion Quarterly* (1944), 18: 3, pp. 348–367.

[11] Ralph K. White, "Hitler, Roosevelt and the Nature of War Propaganda," *The Journal of Abnormal and Social Psychology* (April, 1949), 44: 2, pp. 157–174.

goals and values of men; and the goals and values of men are, to a remarkable extent, everywhere the same."[12]

A second similarity was reliance on the glorification of the home nation, F.D.R. devoting 11 per cent and Hitler 12 per cent of units to this category. The speaker's nation was seldom criticized. Both speakers were found to follow the black-white pattern, implemented with simple concepts, in which the speaker's group is the model of all that is good and the opposing nation's is entirely bad.

The most significant difference, and one which White believed may characterize a propaganda prelude to aggressive war, was Hitler's excessive emphasis on ideas of persecution. Explicit denunciation in this vein constituted 32 per cent of the Hitler speeches, of Roosevelt's, 10 per cent. Hitler created persecution stereotypes which made any military venture a necessary "first-blow," justified because it is in the cause of self-defense. White noted this tendency in contemporary propaganda of the USSR and suggested that a persecution delusion similar to that encouraged by Hitler may be growing in the Soviet Union today and that it may well lead to "defensive" measures.

Janowitz[13] analyzed the content of sixty-three radio speeches of Gerald L. K. Smith from December 14, 1941, to November 15, 1942, during which period Smith was a candidate for the U. S. Senate. He classified Smith's persuasion under fourteen "Major Radio Propaganda Themes" and tabulated their relative frequencies. He found major themes to be: the ability and Christianity of the speaker, the assertion that the speaker was personally being persecuted, and the assertion that only a return to religion could save America from bureaucrats, financiers, and monopolists.

A qualitative analysis of themes of contemporary American agitators was made by Lowenthal and Guterman.[14] Ten prominent persuasive writers were selected because pro-Fascist and anti-Semitic sentiments were emphasized in their speeches and publications. Twenty-one propaganda themes were found to be used by these

---

[12] *Ibid.*, p. 163.

[13] Morris Janowitz, "The Technique of Propaganda for Reaction: Gerald L. K. Smith's Radio Speeches," *The Public Opinion Quarterly* (1944), 8: 1, pp. 84–93.

[14] Leo Lowenthal and Norbert Guterman, *Prophets of Deceit: A Study of the Techniques of the American Agitator*. New York: Harper and Brothers, 1949.

persuaders. The authors interpret these themes psycho-analytically and explore the social and psychological significance of them. Outstanding was the agitators' tendency to present themselves as "Bullet Proof Martyrs," i.e., brave little men fighting against great odds for a good cause. Many quotations with helpful explanations give the reader insight into powerful, possibly dangerous, forms of persuasion. However, no measurement or estimate of the extent of the influence of the ten selected sources was attempted.

Audience Analysis Studies

Perhaps the most extensive attempts at audience analysis have studied the radio-audience. Lazarsfeld and Kendall[15] reported work done by the National Opinion Research Center, sponsored by the National Association of Broadcasters. Begun a few years ago, the project has become a series of surveys to continuously extend our knowledge of listening habits and preferences of the American radio public. This particular report resulted from 3,529 personal interviews of people carefully selected to constitute a cross section of the United States adult population.

The mass media of communication were found to supplement each other rather than to compete for audiences; for example, a radio fan tended to be a heavy movie-goer and a frequent magazine reader. Radio fans were found to listen whenever possible, as in the case of women who listen regularly to morning serials and who were found to listen more than an average amount to afternoon and evening radio as well.

Program preferences of listeners in a later survey agreed almost perfectly with those expressed in the earlier one. Most popular was the category of news broadcasts, followed by comedy, popular music, and talks or discussions on public issues. Less popular were religious broadcasts, serial dramas, and specialties such as homemaking and farm programs.

The more educated listeners expressed a preference for serious music and public discussions, while lower socio-economic groups had as their favorites hillbilly music, religious programs, and daytime serials. Quiz programs were liked most by a middle group.

---

15 Paul Lazarsfeld and Patricia L. Kendall, *Radio Listening in America.* New York: Prentice-Hall, Inc., 1948.

Young people liked dance music and comedy much more, and forums and serious music much less than did older people. More men than women liked discussions, news, sports and comedy programs, while more women than men preferred drama and semi-classical music. Of the characteristics of radio broadcasting the feature singled out for greatest criticism was advertising, mentioned by 26 percent of people interviewed. Fifteen percent, largely married women and housewives, objected to mystery and crime programs, suggesting that these not be broadcast until after 9:00 P.M. in order to prevent children's listening.

By and large, two-thirds of the listening public was satisfied with United States radio. But the critical one-third was almost entirely made up of our better educated, higher income people who have been, as Lazarsfeld and Kendall indicate, the source of most worthwhile social reforms. When you add to this picture the fact that more infrequent and nonlisteners are found among the highly educated than among the middle or lower educated groups, the probable significance of this dissatisfied minority increases.

Inkeles,[16] in a previously mentioned report on broadcasting in the USSR, noted a rather startling fact about Soviet broadcasting. It is accomplished principally through a network of wired loudspeakers, the "Radio Diffusion Exchange." One result is that listeners are largely urban; another is that the audience of some fifty million (approximately ten million speakers averaging five listeners each) can receive only approved programs; and, wired programs can be confined to the desired audience.

Audiences for printed communication have been analyzed, as in Mott's study of American book sales from colonial times to the present.[17] Books that have been regarded as poor literature always have sold well, but there has been an equally steady if somewhat smaller demand for the better and the "best" in current and reprint materials.

Wolf and Fiske [18] studied children who read comic books, inter-

---

[16] Inkeles, *op. cit.*, pp. 239–252.

[17] Frank L. Mott, *Golden Multitudes.* New York: The Macmillan Company, 1947.

[18] Katherine Wolf and Marjorie Fiske, "The Children Talk About Comics," in Lazarsfeld and Stanton, *Communications Research, 1948–49.* New York: Harper and Brothers, 1949, pp. 3–50.

viewing children from ages six through seventeen. They found that normal, well adjusted children passed through a fixed series of preferences as they grew older. First came funny animal stories (e.g., *Bugs Bunny*), then supernatural comics (e.g., *Superman*), then more realistic but still heroic comics (e.g., *Batman*), and finally, comics which tell true stories, these being gradually abandoned for the reading of books. Neurotic, maladjusted children did not follow this pattern, but tended to stop at one stage, frequently the supernatural comic level, and become an addict to the exclusion of other reading material.

Klapper summarizes effects of mass media on tastes of audiences, as revealed by the above and other researches into audience composition and behavior.

> Persons on various culture levels use each medium to satisfy their already established tastes. This mass media content largely selects its own audience. Good material is sought and consumed by persons of good taste, poor material by persons of poor taste. The most likely effect of mass media upon public taste thus seems to be to render the taste static. This has been demonstrated with regard to print and radio.[19]

Media Comparisons

Some investigators have attempted to measure relative effectiveness of the various media of communication. In the comparison of persuasive effectiveness measured by attitude change, Knower[20] found oral presentation superior to written presentation. Wilke[21] conducted a three-way experiment using a ten-minute persuasive speech which was delivered to one present audience, heard by another via loudspeaker, and read in mimeographed form by a third. The direct speech delivery proved most effective in bringing about attitude change, the loudspeaker presentation being somewhat less effective, and the printed presentation the least effective.

---

[19] J. T. Klapper, *The Effects of Mass Media: A Report to the Director of the Public Library Inquiry*. New York: Bureau of Applied Social Research, Columbia University, 1949, pp. I–43, I–44.

[20] F. H. Knower, "Experimental Studies of Changes of Attitude: II. A Study of the Effect of Printed Argument on Changes of Attitude," *Journal of Abnormal and Social Psychology* (1936) 30: 522–532.

[21] W. H. Wilke, "An Experimental Comparison of the Speech, the Radio, and the Printed Page as Propaganda Devices," *Archives of Psychology* (1934), 169.

Stouffer,[22] in interpreting a study of newspaper and radio preferences, said that radio listeners are more "suggestible" than newsprint consumers, hence we may expect radio to be more "persuasive." Holoday and Stoddard [23] found a marked tendency for both adults and children to accept as true all material presented as factual information in commercial motion pictures.

Parentesis [24] made a study of the effects of a motion picture trailer (movie short) in influencing votes in a race for a Common Pleas Court judgeship in Detroit. Familiarizing himself with the areas of the city which were exposed to the trailer, and making various comparisons of voting publics, he was able to estimate that 13 to 26 per cent of the registered voters who saw the thirty-second movie of the candidate and who voted were influenced by the trailer. He submitted some evidence which indicates that the influence of the trailer was greatest in low income groups.

Heron and Ziebarth [25] compared retention of material learned in a university General Psychology course by students in the lecture room and by students who listened to the lectures over the radio. At midterm the radio listeners became the classroom audience. There were no significant differences in amounts learned; the present and remote audience did equally well on the objective course examinations. Although the students found radio listening more convenient than going to class, a substantial majority preferred to learn in the classroom. Fifty-eight per cent said it was more difficult to concentrate on the radio lecture.

Stimulus Studies

The largest number of studies in any category of research in persuasion is found in attempts to measure effectiveness of alternative persuasive stimuli. Application to persuasion is direct; each study indicates one or more probable truths helpful in actual implementation of persuasive appeals.

---

[22] Samuel Stouffer, untitled report in Lazarsfeld, *Radio and the Printed Page.* New York: Duell, Sloan and Pearce, Inc., 1940, pp. 200–254, 258–276.

[23] P. W. Holoday and Leo D. Stoddard, *Getting Ideas From the Movies,* New York: The Macmillan Company, 1933.

[24] John L. Parentesis, "Effectiveness of a Motion Picture Trailer as Election Propaganda," *The Public Opinion Quarterly* (1948), 12: 3, pp. 465–469.

[25] W. T. Heron and E. W. Ziebarth, "A Preliminary Experimental Comparison of Radio and Classroom Lectures," *Speech Monographs* (1946), 13: 1, pp. 54–57.

STUDIES IN THE ARRANGEMENT OF MATERIALS

Different arrangements of persuasive materials have been studied to determine whether varying the time pattern changes their overall effectiveness. Jersild,[26] in a pioneering study, found distributed repetitions highly effective as emphasis. Somewhat less effective were pauses preceding the point to be emphasized and *primacy,* placing the point near the beginning of the appeal. Speaking very slowly for emphasis was found to have a negative effect.

Collins [27] found that listeners preferred, to speeches with sustained appeals, a speech in which a series of short logical arguments was followed by brief motive appeals, either logical or emotional. Ehrensperger [28] also investigated modes of emphasis in public speaking and secured results some of which agreed with and some of which contradicted Jersild's earlier findings. He found repetition to be effective emphasis, as did Jersild, but further discovered concentrated repetitions to be more effective than distributed repetitions. Ehrensperger agreed with Jersild that a pause preceding the element to be emphasized was effective in increasing retention. He differed with Jersild principally in two findings: slow speech is effective emphasis, and statements near the end of a speech are better remembered than those near the beginning ("Recency stands out as definitely superior to Primacy as an aid to recall.").

Further evidence on the effectiveness of slow speaking rates as emphasis is needed. However, a study by Sponberg [29] bears upon the primacy-recency controversy. He used a large argument, a medium, and a small argument which could be interchanged, and measured both immediate and delayed retention and attitude shift. "Climax order" was first small, then medium, then large, and "anticlimax order" was first large, then medium, then small arguments. In both retention and opinion change the large argument was found

[26] A. T. Jersild, "Modes of Emphasis in Public Speaking," *Journal of Applied Psychology* (1928), 12: 611–620.

[27] G. R. Collins, "The Relative Effectiveness of the Condensed and Extended Emotional Appeal," *Quarterly Journal of Speech* (1924), 10: 3, pp. 221–230.

[28] Ray Ehrensperger, "An Experimental Study of the Relative Effectiveness of Certain Forms of Emphasis in Public Speaking," *Speech Monographs* (1945), 12: pp. 94–111.

[29] Harold Sponberg, "A Study of the Relative Effectiveness of Climax and Anti-Climax Order in an Argumentative Speech," *Speech Monographs* (1946), 13: 1, pp. 35–44.

to be more effective when presented first in anti-climax order in the speech. Sponberg concludes: "The study revealed the operation of the law of primacy in the presentation of oral material, and, in general, favors the anti-climax order of speech composition." [30]

Cromwell [31] compared attitude shifts resulting from equally strong affirmative and negative speeches on the same proposition in affirmative-first and negative-first orders. He found that the speech in second position, whether affirmative or negative, produced the greater change in attitude. However, when he used two equally strong speeches on different topics, change of position did not affect attitude shift. This suggests that something other than primacy-recency position was operating to give the second speech in an affirmative-negative combination an advantage. This might have been a refutation effect, the answering of some of the arguments of the first speech directly or indirectly by the second speech. Significance of Cromwell's study in the primacy-recency dispute is doubtful, but it supports Ehrensperger rather than Jersild and Sponberg.

STUDIES MEASURING EFFECTS OF TRAINING THE PERSUADEE

A few studies have attempted to measure effects of educational experiences such as the resistance to persuasive appeals, the ability to recognize and analyze propaganda, and the ability to think critically. Research in this category promises to be of help to the educator in his task of producing a thinking citizen as well as to the persuader who should understand the discriminating powers of his audience.

Watson and Glaser [32] developed a battery of tests to measure the ability to think critically and used it to measure results from ten-week units designed to teach the principles of sound reasoning to twelfth grade high school students. Retesting was done after a six months interval. Their report incorporates other evaluations

---

[30] *Ibid.*, p. 44.

[31] Harvey Cromwell, "The Relative Effect on Audience Attitude of the First Versus the Second Argumentative Speech of a Series," *Speech Monographs* (1950), 17: 2, pp. 105–122.

[32] Edward M. Glaser, *An Experiment in the Development of Critical Thinking.* New York: Teachers College, Columbia University, 1941.

derived from pupil interviews, teacher and pupil reactions, and subjective judgments of the experimenters.

Experimental classes outgained control groups decisively in critical thinking scores over the ten-week period. Most closely related to achievement on these tests were intelligence, reading ability, and school marks. The correlation between composite Z-score on the critical thinking tests and the Otis intelligence test was found to be .46. Reading ability as measured by the Martin Reading Comprehension Test correlated .77 with critical thinking scores, leading to the conclusion that these particular tests of reading and thinking measured similar abilities. Retest after six months revealed significant retention of growth of critical thinking ability which took place during the experimental period. Transfer of abilities measured by the tests to the solving of problems of daily living is not established, but the reactions of teachers and pupils provide an indication that some significant carry-over occurs.

Collier[33] measured the effects of propaganda upon people who have made a critical study of propaganda methods and have analyzed the propaganda in question. Thirty-four students in his Applied Psychology class served as the experimental group, and the propaganda examined was that of the German Library of Information then being distributed widely in the United States. Attitude tests oriented around specific points of view in the propaganda were used as measures.

Differences between experimental and control groups indicated that the experimental group members, although they recognized the material read as propaganda and had experienced lectures and exercises in its analysis, were influenced by it in the direction desired by the propagandist. Collier concludes:

> 1. Attitudes of individuals who are well informed regarding the character and purpose of propaganda and who may at the same time approach it analytically can, nevertheless, be positively influenced by the materials studied.
>
> 2. The inhibitory quality of the kind of insight with which these subjects approached the propaganda has apparently been overrated in the past.[34]

---

[33] Rex Madison Collier, "The Effect of Propaganda Upon Attitude Following a Critical Examination of the Propaganda Itself," *The Journal of Social Psychology* (1944), 20: 3–17.

[34] *Ibid.*, p. 16.

The second conclusion above possibly refers to the Institute for Propaganda Analysis, which seemed to take for granted (at least to some extent) that the ability to *detect* propaganda carries with it the ability to *resist* the propaganda.

Howell[35] used the Watson-Glaser tests mentioned above in an attempt to measure the effects of high school debating on critical thinking ability. Two hundred eighteen debaters from twenty-four Wisconsin high schools were tested before and after the 1941 to 1942 interschool debating season, over a period of six months. A control group from each school was matched with the debater group on age, sex, and scholarship record. An item validation enabled the experimenter to increase somewhat the over-all reliability of the battery of tests. Debaters outgained non-debaters, the critical ratio of the difference in mean gains being 1.04. This means that there are approximately eighty-five chances in one hundred that the difference is real. Experience in debating correlated highly with critical thinking scores. Results from individual schools varied widely, some showing great debater gains, others no gain at all, and some actual losses in critical thinking scores. This suggests that the type of debating experience probably influenced growth in critical thinking.

Incidental findings showed a mean intelligence quotient (I.Q.) for the high school debaters of one hundred nineteen and a debater scholarship record in which 50 per cent were classified by their teachers as "A" students and 35.6 per cent as "B" students. Scholarship accomplishment was more directly related to critical thinking scores than was I.Q., debating skill, or amount of debate experience. "The evidence suggests that the abilities measured by the Watson-Glaser tests are essential to the getting of good grades in high school." Only a slight relationship was found between age and critical thinking scores, but "a uniform sex difference in critical thinking scores in favor of the males was found in all groups."

Brembeck[36] in a related study measured the effects on critical thinking ability of the one-semester college course in argumentation. He used the Watson-Glaser tests of critical thinking with Howell's

---

35 William S. Howell, "The Effects of High School Debating on Critical Thinking," *Speech Monographs* (1943), X: 96–103.

36 Winston L. Brembeck, "The Effects of a Course in Argumentation on Critical Thinking Ability," *Speech Monographs* (1949), XVI: 2, pp. 177–189.

minor revisions. Experimental classes were in eleven colleges and universities, totaled two hundred and two students, and control groups were equated with experimental groups by matching individual students in each of the participating institutions. Matching criteria were age, sex, educational background, and debating experience. Argumentation students outgained control students in critical thinking scores. The critical ratio of the difference in mean gains was 2.56, or ninety-nine chances of one hundred that the difference was real. In ten of eleven institutions the students of argumentation had higher pre-test scores than did the control groups.

"Argumentation students with high school and/or college debate training made significantly higher *pre-test* scores than those without debating experience." Critical thinking scores of men students were significantly higher than those of participating women, and the men outgained the women by a slight margin. Here, again, no significant relationship between age and gain in critical thinking scores was found.

Concerning the wide variations in critical thinking gains among the experimental classes of various institutions (which paralleled the variation in gains of debaters from various high schools noted by Howell) Brembeck comments: "The wide variation in individual school gains in critical thinking scores suggests that probably argumentation, like some of the other academic courses which have been tested, can be taught in a manner which makes for greater transfer of training in the area of critical thinking." [37]

The complex of attitudes toward a subject developed over a period of years seems to affect both what is remembered and the type of response toward particular persuasive materials. Edwards tested the hypothesis that ". . . experiences which are in harmony with an existing frame of reference will tend to be learned and remembered better than experiences which are in conflict with the same frame of reference." [38] A speech consisting of an equal number of pro-New Deal and anti-New Deal statements was presented to students who were pro-, neutral-, and anti-New Deal. Immediate and delayed (twenty-one days) recognition of material pre-

---

[37] *Ibid.*, p. 188.

[38] Allen L. Edwards, "Political Frames of References as a Factor Influencing Recognition," *The Journal of Abnormal and Social Psychology* (1941), 36: 1, p. 48.

sented was measured. Pro-New Deal subjects tended to label the speech and speakers pro-New Deal while anti-New Deal subjects thought the speech was unfavorable to the New Deal. The subjects tended to remember the arguments which harmonized with their frame of reference, i.e., agreed with their political predisposition, much better than they remembered opposing statements. This differential persisted over the twenty-one-day delay period. Apparently material conflicting with one's frame of reference tends to be forgotten.

In a later report, Edwards [39] submitted data from the same basic experiment relating to the tendency of the subject to *rationalize* the remembered statements which conflicted with their opinions. He found that the tendency to rationalize conflicting statements was directly proportional to the "degree of conflict" between the statement and the frame of reference of the subject.

STUDIES MEASURING THE RELATIVE EFFECTIVENESS OF PARTICULAR METHODS OF PERSUASION

Because of the obviously large number of possible forms for the presentation of a persuasive appeal, much experimentation has dealt with measurement of results from one method of persuasion as compared with results from another alternative structure.

Knower [40] measured the comparative effectiveness of logical-factual and emotional persuasive speeches in changing the attitudes of college students toward prohibition. He used six hundred and seven experimental and three hundred control subjects. Attitudes changed significantly in the desired direction after exposure to a single speech. Greatest attitude changes were found among those who were neutral in their opinion on prohibition before the speech. When a student heard an appeal *alone* (person to person persuasion) he was more heavily influenced than when he heard it as a member of a group. Emotional and factual-logical speeches were equally effective in securing attitude shift. Knower also arranged for subjects to read the speeches in mimeographed form, and discovered

---

[39] Allen L. Edwards, "Rationalization as a Result of a Political Frame of Reference," *The Journal of Abnormal and Social Psychology* (April, 1941), 36: 2.

[40] F. H. Knower, "A Study of the Effect of Oral Argument on Changes of Attitude," *Journal of Social Psychology* (1935), VI: 315–347. Also, *Journal of Abnormal and Social Psychology* (1936), XXX: 522–532.

that while some changes of attitude resulted, these were much smaller than the changes that came about from listening to the speeches.

Lull[41] in an effort to assess the persuasive effect of humor, compared attitude shifts resulting from humorous and non-humorous speeches on the topic "Socialized Medicine." Subjects were, again, college students, and the speeches, with exception of humor content, were judged to be comparable. Attitudes as measured immediately after the stimulus were shifted significantly. A delayed test three weeks later revealed a rather uniform regression toward the original attitude held, although one-third of the subjects at that time still retained an attitude change that was statistically significant. Humorous and nonhumorous speeches produced similar results and were rated by those who heard them as just about equally interesting and convincing.

Willis[42] measured attitude shifts resulting from different types of radio programs. He used the straight talk, the complete dramatization, and the talk with dramatized illustrations. His subjects were predominantly high school students ($n = 526$) with a supplementary group of eighty-nine college speech students. Programs were fifteen minutes in length. He found significant changes in attitude after all experimental programs, and by a delayed posttest found that the change persisted for at least two weeks. While talk, drama, and drama-illustrated talk were equally effective in changing the attitudes of college students, the dramatization proved to be most effective with the high school students and the illustrated talk was second in effectiveness. High school students preferred the dramatization with illustrated talk as second choice, but the college student subjects preferred the illustrated talk, with straight talk in second place and the dramatized program at the bottom of their list.

Dietrich[43] attempted to collect evidence bearing upon a current controversy concerning the mode of radio speaking: Is dynamic or

---

[41] P. E. Lull, "The Effectiveness of Humor in Persuasive Speeches," *Speech Monographs* (1940), VII: 26–40.

[42] Edgar E. Willis, "The Relative Effectiveness of Three Forms of Radio Presentation in Influencing Attitudes," *Speech Monographs* (1940), VII: 41–47.

[43] John E. Dietrich, "The Relative Effectiveness of Two Modes of Radio Delivery in Influencing Attitudes," *Speech Monographs* (1946), XIII: 58–65.

conversational delivery more convincing? An attitude scale (Likert type) was constructed to measure attitude toward Russia, and a fifteen-minute persuasive speech to influence attitudes in favor of Russia was written. Six competent male radio speakers delivered the speech, each recording a dynamic (dramatic, formal, enthusiastic, rapid) and a conversational (quiet, relaxed, informal) interpretation of the speech. Subjects were college students; seven hundred and sixty were in experimental and control groups.

A small but statistically significant difference in attitude shift resulted from the conversational mode of delivery. Attitude changes from both interpretations of the speech were large, and after two weeks, although considerable regression had taken place, remaining changes were still significant. The speech was of greatest influence among those students who indicated high interest in the program.

Preferences of the subjects for one of the two modes of delivery were decided but about equally divided. Free responses of the listeners revealed an interesting sidelight on the experiment—forty-one labeled the dynamic broadcasts "propaganda," but only two applied this term to the same speech when it was delivered conversationally. Dietrich suggests that although this research does not imply that a skilled dynamic radio speaker should change his delivery it does challenge the widely-held belief that radio speaking must be full of "punch"—loud, fast, and enthusiastic—to be effective.

Matthews [44] devised a means of identifying "loaded" language in a speech, and constructed six speeches on labor-management relations that were pro-labor, anti-labor, and neutral, "loaded" and free from "loaded" language. These were recorded by a professional newscaster and were played back to three hundred and fifty college speech students. "Loaded" and "unloaded" paired speeches had the same factual content. Only retention was measured, though it was correlated with admitted bias on the topic of the speeches. "Loaded" language neither helped nor hindered retention of the content of the speeches. Whether students agreed with a speech or disagreed with its point of view the emotive language used had no identifiable effect on their learning the factual content in the speech.

---

[44] Jack Matthews, "The Effect of Loaded Language on Audience Comprehension of Speeches," *Speech Monographs* (1947), XIV: 176–186.

Some aspects of ethos were tested for persuasive effectiveness by Haiman.[45] He used a Woodward ballot to measure shift of opinion and wrote a speech favoring compulsory health insurance (fifteen minutes) to be administered under variable ethos-climates. In one experiment he controlled the speaker's character and reputation by introducing the recorded speech as delivered by (1) a communist, (2) the Surgeon General of the United States, and (3) a college sophomore. In a second experiment he used four student speakers who appeared to differ significantly in such ethos factors as physical appearance, speech competence, and likeableness. Audience ratings of these and other personal characteristics were obtained to verify that these differences in ethos existed in the minds of the listeners. A third experiment attempted to vary only the speaker's likeableness and physical attractiveness. One speaker was used, and he attempted to deliver the speech with equal skill whether well-dressed, and well-mannered, or unshaven, surly, and ill-dressed.

Variations in prestige produced by altering the introduction of the recorded speaker did influence significantly changes of attitude resulting from the speech. Persons of different ethical appeal, delivering the same speech, produced different amounts of attitude change. General speech competence here seemed to increase persuasive influence, but changes in physical appearance and likeableness made little difference in persuasive effectiveness. Incidental findings included the discovery that the greatest opinion changes occurred in students originally opposing the proposition, that more females than males changed their opinions, and that females were more generous in their estimates of ethos factors of the speaker than were the males. Haiman concludes, on the basis of this and an associated questionnaire survey of speech teachers, that some factors of ethos are correlated positively with success in persuasive public speaking.

A unique and highly specialized analysis of wartime persuasion is presented by Herz,[46] who in World War II was Chief Leaflet Writer for the Psychological Warfare Division in the European Theatre, and "was in charge of leaflet writing and interrogation

---

[45] Franklyn S. Haiman, "An Experimental Study of the Effects of Ethos in Public Speaking," *Speech Monographs* (1949), XVI: 190–202.

[46] Martin F. Herz, "Some Psychological Lessons from Leaflet Propaganda in World War II," *Public Opinion Quarterly* (1949), 13: 3, 471–486.

of prisoners for the combat propaganda team of the Fifth Army in Italy." [47]

Certain measures of leaflet effectiveness enabled our propaganda sources to adapt to enemy responses to an unusual degree: "(a) quantity of leaflets found on the persons of prisoners; (b) recollection of leaflets by prisoners, and comments about them; (c) favorable mention and detailed discussion by soldiers behind the German lines, as reported by cooperative prisoners; (d) detailed description of their surrender by prisoners; (e) pre-occupation of German counter-propaganda with specific Allied leaflets, including plagiarism by German combat propagandists; (f) comments by the enemy command as learned from captured documents on troop morale." [48]

Several lessons learned by the leaflet writers have application to other propaganda, for example, "The insufficiency of truth." Leaflets telling the actual facts of life in an American prisoner of war camp could not be used, as details such as eggs for breakfast proved to be unbelievable to German soldiers. The revised leaflet said "It's no fun being a prisoner-of-war!" and "Better Free Than a Prisoner-of-War, Better a Prisoner-of-War than Dead!" Similarly, the fact that Henry Kaiser assembled ships in five days could not be used because the enemy could not be expected to believe it. Definite predictions about coming military events proved dangerous and unnecessary; a slight failure to live up to details predicted cast an aura of falsity over all our propaganda.

The most productive target for combat leaflets was the person Herz designated as the "potential waverer," the "marginal man." The firmly fanatical enemy patriot could not be moved by an appeal. Addressing appeals to the previously converted is likewise unproductive: "Too much out-put may be addressed to persons who already agree with us." [49] Using leaflets to answer enemy charges was unsuccessful. "In general, to deny a lie disseminated by the enemy is in most cases merely to give it added circulation. . . . Propaganda is essentially an offensive weapon." [50]

A few simple ideas, stressed repeatedly in leaflets, proved effective where more complicated efforts boomeranged. "Many men sur-

---

[47] *Ibid.,* p. 471.
[48] *Ibid.,* pp. 472, 473.
[49] *Ibid.,* p. 475.
[50] *Ibid.,* p. 475.

rendered during the last war who had been convinced by our combat propaganda that to fight on was hopeless and that they would be well treated if they gave up. To convince them of the falsity of Nazism and of Hitler's iniquity might have taken many months and perhaps years longer." [51]

Excessive demands in propaganda proved fruitless; for example, some Soviet leaflets suggested that Hitler be overthrown. The language used had to be that of the persuadee; unfamiliar wording negated any propaganda effect. "Generally speaking, it can be said that domestic propaganda and propaganda addressed to the enemy simply do not mix." [52] Points of common ground shared by persuader and persuadee must be established; in American combat leaflets two of these were "(a) the belief in the excellence of the soldierly qualities of the German infantryman; and (b) the belief that he was being crushed by Allied superiority of material, rather than out-fought man for man." [53]

"Black" propaganda—that supposedly from sources within enemy territory—proved difficult to execute because some slight slip usually caused its real source to be revealed, and complete concealment of the real source was essential for it to have any effect. Threats and toughness were ineffective. "There does not appear to be a single case on record in the last war when an ultimatum resulted in the surrender of a surrounded enemy unit." [54] The helpless civilian proved to be a good propaganda target, but the big difficulty was in specifying things that he, in his state of impotence, could do to help the Allied cause.

Although we tend to think of rumor as accidental and inconsequential we realize that it occasionally affects public opinion. Study of rumor as an intentional tool of the persuader as well as an accidental influence on human behavior is needed. Allport and Postman [55] presented an analysis of the normal "processes" of rumor spreading. These are patterns of distortion, principally leveling, sharpening, and assimilation, and secondarily, exaggeration, condensation and conventionalization.

---

51 *Ibid.*, pp. 474, 475.
52 *Ibid.*, p. 478.
53 *Ibid.*, p. 480.
54 *Ibid.*, p. 484.
55 Gordon W. Allport and Leo Postman, *The Psychology of Rumor.* New York: Henry Holt and Company, 1947.

Leveling is a process of omitting, systematically, details of the rumor that do not conform to the stereotypes of the person transmitting the rumor. Sharpening stresses the details that remain in the familiar pattern, and is partly a result of the leveling operation; since fewer details remain, those left are more prominent. Assimilation adapts the rumor to the most available frames of reference. It is given local and timely significance.

Exaggeration is evident in the imputation of motives, the tendency to increase numbers, and the emphasis upon an incidental item. Condensation reduces the rumor to a few easily remembered details. If the original rumor is complex a synopsis soon evolves. Conventionalization removes unfamiliar elements from the rumor, such as strange words, subtle shadings of meaning, and so on. "The story sinks in verbal simplicity to the level of the least educated, and verbally least gifted member in the chain of transmission." [56] Allport and Postman concluded that hearsay is an important social influence. Deliberate use of rumor spreading for social control is cited, and tribute is paid to its effectiveness.

Reduced emphasis on advocacy characterizes speaking in the various forms of public discussion; hence it is interesting to compare the opinion or attitude changes evolving from listening to, or taking part in, discussion to those resulting from debate or other forms of frankly persuasive discourse.

Millson [57] in 1935 reported results of an experiment measuring audience reaction to a symposium discussion presented by student speakers from several colleges and universities. One hundred twenty-two members of a student and townpeople audience were balloted before and after the symposium, using a simple ballot permitting the audience member to check one of four proposals he favored for solving the problem being discussed and a fifth category, "undecided," for those who had not approved a solution to the problem. Changes in opinion consisted of shifting allegiance to another solution, of choosing one after initial indecision, or becoming undecided during the course of the program. Millson compared the changes registered by this ballot with the pattern of

---

[56] *Ibid.*, p. 156.

[57] William A. D. Millson, "Audience Reaction to A Symposium," *The Quarterly Journal of Speech* (1935), XXI: 1, pp. 43–53.

opinion changes from debate as reported in 1928 by Woodward.[58] Where Woodward reported that debate practically eliminated the originally undecided category, Millson's discussion reduced the number of undecided only a slight amount. Actually, 84 per cent of the original undecided group made up their minds in favor of a proposal during the discussion, but enough others became undecided during the discussion to keep the number in the category relatively stable.

Woodward reported a strong tendency for original decided opinions to remain the same or to be strengthened after debate. Millson found this to be true to a lesser degree after discussion. Unlike debate, the symposium weakened many strong opinions and, apparently, did not further strengthen those that were strong to begin with. Millson infers that while debate tends to make people more fixed in their prejudices, discussion tends to produce a variety of opinion changes in many directions, possibly indicating more critical thinking.

Participants in an intercollegiate discussion conference were polled by Utterback [59] to ascertain their views on three controversial issues of the discussion before, in the middle of, and after the conference. A linear scale was used to register opinion, a continuum of nine divisions running from "no" to "yes" with "undecided" in the middle. Both discussion (of committee type) and debate were experienced in the three day conference, making it possible to assess some effects of each. Over the period of the conference more than half of the delegates registered a shift of opinion, and the shifts were about equally divided in direction. General movement of attitude change was away from the middle (undecided) section toward a positive decision.

More and greater opinion changes took place in committee sessions than in the debate that followed. The changes from debate were, as in Woodward's study, those of strengthening conviction rather than moderating existing opinions. Discussion, by contrast, seemed to weaken or reverse previously held convictions. However, those who were most certain in their initial judgments shifted least. Be-

---

[58] H. S. Woodward, "Measurement and Analysis of Audience Opinions," *The Quarterly Journal of Speech* (1928), XIV: 1, pp. 94–111.

[59] William E. Utterback, "The Influence of Conference on Group Opinion," *The Quarterly Journal of Speech* (1950), 36: 3, pp. 365–370.

cause of the nature of the individual attitude shifts, about equally divided in the two possible directions, the mean position of the group opinion on any of the three issues did not change appreciably.

Howell [60] used high school students as subjects in an experiment to measure retention of factual material and attitude change resulting from two kinds of radio discussion programs, the radio round table (for example, The University of Chicago Round Table) and the radio forum (for example, America's Town Meeting of the Air). The round table pattern proved to be somewhat more effective in teaching factual material than was the forum, but both were about equally effective in producing significant changes in attitudes as measured by previously validated attitude tests (Thurstone type) which were available for the topics used.

The two subjects of the experimental discussions were Socialized Medicine and Federal Aid to Education. Many of the audience of high school juniors and seniors had formed opinions pro or con on these familiar controversial issues, with the result that the initially undecided group was rather small. The outstanding fact about the many attitude shifts in both directions resulting from hearing the recorded discussion programs was that nearly two-thirds (61.5 percent) of the changes were from a more extreme to a more neutral position. Here, apparently, the discussions operated to moderate extreme, possibly hastily or irrationally formed, convictions.

A post-test administered five weeks after the programs were heard revealed that the students had forgotten about half the facts they had learned from them. Surprisingly, however, there was no comparable regression in changed attitudes. Total amount of attitude shift was just about the same after five weeks, and the individuals tested proved to have retained their original changes in the same direction to about the same amount as revealed by the immediate post-test. This stability of attitude change resulting from discussion is in marked contrast to the substantial regression toward the initial position found in many delayed post-tests of the attitude changes resulting from persuasive speaking. The persuasive talk produces a unidirectional change in attitude which seems to regress to some significant amount with the passage of time while the bi-directional

---

[60] Wm. S. Howell, *The Relative Effectiveness of the Radio Round Table and the Radio Forum.* Unpublished M.A. Thesis, University of Wisconsin, 1938.

changes coming about through discussion seem to be more stable and relatively permanent.

Case Studies

Cutting across our categories of investigation are comprehensive attempts to encompass the many pertinent facets of a complete case of actual persuasion. These are enlightening because they reveal interaction of many elements that laboratory-type experiments examine in isolation.

Merton[61] made an intensive analysis of persuasion in the Columbia Broadcasting System's War Bond Day, early in World War II. Kate Smith was on the air eighteen hours, from 8:00 A.M. to 2:00 A.M., making sixty-five separate appeals for listeners to buy bonds. Thirty-nine million dollars of bond pledges were made by phone calls to Columbia Broadcasting System stations during the day. Three sources of data contribute information: (1) content analysis of broadcasts, (2) intensive focused interviews with one hundred listeners, and (3) polling interviews, using certain specific questions, with nine hundred and seventy-eight listeners and nonlisteners, a selected cross section of Greater New York population. The intensive interviews were in homes of the subjects and each lasted three to four hours.

Merton concludes that many variables other than the content of the particular persuasion were influential in determining response to the Smith marathon. He explores the "Kate Smith symbol," the attitudes of predisposed and nonpredisposed bond buyers, the sentiments of listeners with and without close personal involvement in the war, and speculates reasonably as to the probable sources of revealed sentiments and stereotypes. Particularly interesting is the emergence of guilt-feelings as a strong source of motivation for bond purchase. "It is significant that, in contrast to the predisposed group, who characteristically explained their decision as a matter of convenience, the susceptible group phrased their "motivation" in terms of a renewed sense of guilt."

Program content omitted financial gain arguments for bond buying and relied upon emotive appeals. A percentage analysis yielded this division of themes: sacrifice, 51 per cent; participation, 16 per

---

61 Robert K. Merton, *Mass Persuasion.* New York: Harper and Brothers, 1946.

cent; familial, 6 per cent; competition, 12 per cent; facilitation, 7 per cent; personal, 6 per cent; miscellaneous, 2 per cent. A major premise was that buying bonds would "bring the boys home sooner." Buying bonds as a good investment was subtly ridiculed. The themes of patriotism and sacrifice shouldered aside considerations of practicality.

Merton summarized "tactics of the technicians in sentiment."

> Typically, they seek out sources of guilt and inner conflict among her listeners and direct their thrusts toward these areas of moral vulnerability. Having reinforced the conflict, they at once suggest a ready solution. To say, therefore, that they appeal to sentiment is to be something less than adequate. Their techniques can be more precisely defined. By utilizing the tensions between disinterested moral obligation and narrow self-interest, they motivate the listener to follow their suggestion. An immediate act promises surcease from moral conflict.
>
> And through the generous use of sacred symbols, invulnerable to attack, they ally Smith with national pieties.[62]

Ethical criticism was made of ". . . exploiting mass anxieties, . . . using sentimental appeals in place of information, and making private purpose in the guise of common purpose." [63]

Content of Communist Party propaganda in the city of Chicago for a five-year period, 1930 through 1934, inclusive, is carefully studied by Lasswell and Blumenstock.[64] During this depression period the party's efforts to spread the doctrines of communism were at a high point. The authors investigated its propaganda channels, techniques, volume, and influence. They studied demonstrations, regular and irregular publications, leaflets, songs, slogans, buttons and badges. After collecting extensive data and interpreting it intensively, the authors conclude:

> This case study of Communist propaganda in Chicago during the Great Depression has demonstrated the strength of the restrictive factors which prevent the universalizing of the USSR. Despite some favorable circumstances, Communist propaganda was blocked by American nationalism and individualism and thus contributed more to the catharsis of insecurities than to the readjustment of American symbols and practices.[65]

---

62 *Ibid.,* p. 184.

63 *Ibid.,* p. 187.

64 H. D. Lasswell and D. Blumenstock, *World Revolutionary Propaganda.* New York: Alfred A. Knopp, 1939.

65 *Ibid.,* p. 357.

Lazarsfeld, Berelson, and Gaudet[66] report an extensive study to determine ". . . how and why people decided to vote as they did," with reference to the 1940 presidential election. A representative community, Erie County, Ohio, was chosen, and, through careful sampling techniques, four matched groups of six hundred potential voters each were secured. Members of three groups experienced two personal interviews and the fourth group was individually interviewed once each month from May to November. Effects of many vote-determining influences were identifiable in the data resulting from the great number of personal interviews.

High socio-economic status, membership in a Protestant church, and rural residence tended to correlate with Republican voting. The people most interested in the election tended to be men, of above-average education and socio-economic status, living in urban areas and belonging to older age groups. People who did not vote apparently did not because of disinterest in the election. There were more women than men nonvoters. A large majority, three-fourths, of the voters knew in May how they would vote in November.

The people who shifted their party allegiance were generally disinterested and subjected to unusual cross-pressures. Election propaganda aroused interest, but people selected propaganda agreeing with their political predispositions. Propaganda apparently did not change votes; it may have reinforced earlier decisions since it was received mainly by already decided, concurring voters. The majority of voters attempted to ignore campaign propaganda.

Radio was more influential than the newspaper in general, though Republicans preferred newspaper sources of political material and Democrats preferred radio sources. Roosevelt's superior radio speaking (as compared to Willkie's) apparently won some votes. Political discussion (informal) reached and influenced more voters more often than did propaganda. The family and the small work or social group exerted strongest influences upon the voting decision. Personal influences rather than issues seemed to change votes.

> In the last analysis, more than anything else people can move other people. From an ethical point of view this is a hopeful aspect in the serious social problem of propaganda. The side which has the more enthusiastic supporters and which can mobilize grass-root support in an expert way has great chances of success.[67]

---

[66] Paul F. Lazarsfeld, Bernard Berelson, and Hazel Gaudet, *The People's Choice.* New York: Duell, Sloan and Pearce, Inc., 1944.

[67] *Ibid.*, p. 158.

The Army's World War II Communication Research Project[68]

The following multiple case study is in the authors' opinion a most significant contribution to communication research. Because of its many implications to persuasion we are devoting a separate section of this chapter to reporting and interpreting a small part of this excellent collection of related research.

During World War II the Research Branch of the Army's Information and Education Division conducted controlled experimentation in the effectiveness of films and other mass communication devices. Results of these rather extensive and well controlled projects, while not in themselves conclusive nor usually of a nature permitting wide generalization, suggest many implications of profound significance to the student of persuasion. These provide tantalizing glimpses into the interactions of the communication media and the nervous systems of people receiving their stimulation. Truly, these contributions push back the frontier of our knowledge concerning those factors which determine human response to modern mechanized messages. The two types of research reported are the general evaluation of army film materials and the studies employing controlled variation in measuring effects of films and other types of program material.

EVALUATION STUDIES ON EFFECTS OF FILMS

(1) Four major orientation films from the "Why We Fight" series, including "The Battle of Britain," "Prelude to War," "Divide and Conquer," and "The Nazis Strike," were investigated to determine their effectiveness in teaching factual information and in influencing opinions. Over two thousand men comprised control and experimental groups. The films proved highly effective in the teaching of factual material. "The fact that the upper limit of effects was so large—as for example in the cases where the correct answer was learned well enough to be remembered a week later by the *majority* of the men—indicates that highly effective presentation methods are possible with this type of film." (Page 64 of Hovland, Lumsdaine, and Sheffield.)

Specific opinions on factors covered by the films were affected "markedly," though these changes were less impressive than the

[68] Carl I. Hovland, Arthur A. Lumsdaine, and Fred D. Sheffield, *Experiments on Mass Communication*. Princeton: Princeton University Press, 1949.

increase of factual knowledge. Opinions (and attitudes) of a more general nature were, apparently, affected little. Test items designed to measure the soldier's willingness to serve showed little if any change.

Opinion tests revealed that the longer a man was in the army, the less he wanted to be a soldier; in other words, he became steadily "less-motivated" in terms of orientation objectives. The films apparently slowed the rate of "motivational deterioration" to some extent, since the men who showed opinion change in the direction advocated by the films did not lose their enthusiasm for soldiering as rapidly as did the others. All, however, became progressively less anxious to participate actively in the then current conflict. Men attempting to persuade American soldiers to *want* to fight and die in World War II had a heavy "burden of proof."

(2) Audience evaluation of these "Why We Fight" films was carefully assessed, although the authors' opinion is: "In the case of most educational films, however, the best criterion of success is not whether the audience *approves* of a film but rather whether the audience *learns* from it." (Page 80.) Group interviews and questionnaires proved that the movies were well-liked. The minority not liking the films, in the order of 10 per cent, tended to be "less well educated, to have foreign-born parents (particularly from Axis countries), to come from smaller cities and towns, and to have isolationist attitudes." (Page 86.)

Most of the men thought the films were fair and accurate. Only 27 per cent suggested that they recognized in the film any attempt to mold attitudes and guide their thinking. A "negligible proportion" used the word "propaganda" in their responses to the films. "The evidence in this study indicates that in terms of either the falsification connotation or the manipulative aspect of "propaganda" the film was not regarded as propagandistic by a great majority of the men." (Page 88.)

These results demonstrate that orientation movies *can* be made so that men like them. Probably the appreciation of these skillfully produced pictures prevented their being recognized as propaganda. This suggests that an artistic presentation which involves an audience emotionally may achieve its persuasive purpose with complete concealment; the auditor may never be conscious that he was intentionally and methodically influenced. Probably, too, we would tend to regard the movies we *like* as "fair and accurate."

Polygraph measurements, in which groups of twenty men registered instantaneous approval and disapproval throughout the films, were obtained by supplying each man with two push-buttons, one to register "like," and the other "dislike" responses. Short films from a series called "This War" were used. From the program-analyzer (Polygraph) records, graphs were drawn that showed the numbers of men liking and disliking each episode in each film. Results showed the greatest acceptance for cartoon material and vigorous action shots. The least liked was any close-up of a person speaking. Regardless of who did the talking, any prolonged utterance where the speaker appeared on the screen caused numbers of men to release the "like" button and, in many cases, register "dislike." Results from the Polygraph program-analyzer correlated well with interview and questionnaire findings.

Since this type of device will be used increasingly to measure effects of motivational rhetoric, the student of persuasion will be interested in two developments and two recommendations in the use of the audience analyzer. The men confused "liking" for the film with "liking" of *content.* For example, when Japanese soldiers were shown, some men pressed the "dislike" button, registering disapproval of the enemy rather than of the film. Furthermore, when an auditor became absorbed in the parts of the film that interested him, he tended to forget about the push-buttons! Instructions given before a film seemed to be critical, and extremely well planned instructions proved necessary to insure that all men would record judgments on the specific item the experimenter wished rated. It might be desirable to have a greater range of opinion than the three-step (two-button) scale of "like," "neutral," and "dislike."

(3) The sound motion picture, with its realistic movement, synchronized sound, and slow-motion animation, is often claimed to be uniquely effective in teaching information and in influencing opinions. Its rival in service schools in World War II was the film strip, a series of still pictures to be presented either with commentary and class participation or with a recorded explanation. Sound motion pictures were expensive to produce and took a long time in the making, whereas film strips were quickly and inexpensively made and were reproduced cheaply and easily. A study compared relative effectiveness of a movie and a film strip in teach-

ing factual information about map reading. The forty-three minute movie covered the same content as did the film strip that was taught, after typical preparation, to platoon-size groups by average-ability instructors in fifty-minute periods.

In over-all teaching effectiveness the film strip was slightly but not significantly better than the movie. The more intelligent men learned much more from both movie and film strip than did those in the lower intelligence group. On most items the men learned slightly better from the film strip, but on understanding what is represented by the space between contour lines on a map learning was definitely greater from the movie. The motion picture taught this item by using a roving viewpoint, from horizontal to vertical, something that was impossible in still pictures. This indicates that certain materials probably lend themselves to movie presentation for greatest effectiveness. The experimenters conclude that this comparison demonstrates only that movies are not *always* better than film strips for teaching purposes.

(4) Two types of radio programs were adapted to service education in World War II through transcription, the radio commentator, and the radio documentary. The commentator format is that of a single speaker whereas the documentary is a dramatic production. Shortly after victory in Europe, equivalent commentary and documentary programs (two of each) were transcribed with the intention to convince men in the army that the war with Japan would last a long time. Both veterans and new recruits heard the programs in regular orientation meetings in platoon-size groups.

Dramatic and commentator programs were equally well-liked by the listeners. With no appreciable difference in their effectiveness, both types of program were highly impressive in changing opinions of the men regarding the length of war with Japan. Commentator programs, inexpensive and easy to produce, were not only as effective as the documentaries in accomplishing their persuasive purpose, but also were judged by their listeners to be as interesting as the dramatic programs.

(5) Under number 2 above we mentioned the use of pre-discussion, post-discussion, and test-assignment motivation to increase the teaching effectiveness of movie and film strip. Men learned significantly more from the movie with either pre- or post-discussion than from the movie without either. Pre-discussion was slightly

more effective though the difference was not statistically significant.

(6) The effects of varying intellectual ability were explored, and some of these findings are of great interest to one who would understand persuasion or who himself would persuade. We commonly assume that varying backgrounds determine differences in knowledge, opinions, and attitudes. But, in these army studies:

> . . . analyses were undertaken in the expectation that men's knowledge and opinions would be significantly related to characteristics of their personal history. But the studies showed the surprising result that region of birth, religious affiliation, marital status, Army rank or grade, length of Army service, age (within the adult range represented by the Army population) and several other personal history items introduced in special studies showed few consistent or significant relationships to initial knowledge and opinion, and were almost uniformly unrelated to the effects of the films.
>
> The one relationship which emerged clearly and consistently was the relationship of both information and opinion to intellectual ability, as indicated by AGCT score or years of schooling completed. (Page 147.)

The concluding sentence of the above quotation suggests an interesting incidental finding in these film studies: the high correlation between intelligence scores and years of schooling. The two quantities varied together so consistently that they could be used almost interchangeably. To the student of persuasion this should be apparent: (1) intellectual abilities are closely related to knowledge and opinion but factors of home training, religion, and other personal background items seem to be only mildly influential; and (2) a surprisingly accurate index of the intellectual capabilities of an *adult* audience is found in the simple measure of years of school completed.

Intellectual ability affected the acquisition of knowledge from film sources: "the positive correlation between educational attainment and film effects on information items was a consistent phenomenon throughout the study." (Page 150.) A table gives the "Average Effectiveness Index for Factual Information Imparted by Orientation Films." (Page 153.)

Grade school men	16.3%
High school men	36.6%
College men	54.2%

The more intelligent subjects (generally those of greater amount of school experience) can apparently be expected to remember many more items of knowledge in any communication than will their less able associates. The persuader will adjust the "learning burden" of his message to the quantitative schooling of his audience accordingly.

STUDIES EMPLOYING CONTROLLED VARIATION

(1) One of the experimental details lending itself readily to controlled variation was the time between stimulus and post-test. Varying this quantity yielded a measure of retention of facts learned and opinion changes.

Factual knowledge learned from an orientation film showed a sharp "decrement"; retention was about 50 per cent after nine weeks. A similar regression in opinion changes did *not* occur. Some opinion items regressed but more continued to shift in the direction advocated by the film. The net result was a slight increase in opinion effect over the nine-week period! Explaining this is not easy. The experimenters hypothesize "sleeper" effects, coming about through "reminiscence" over a period of time. This seems reasonable, as basic opinions change slowly and fundamental attitudes have great inertia. It presents the person who would do research in persuasion with two real problems, *when* to measure opinion shift from a program and *how* to interpret early or delayed opinion tests.

(2) Persuasion experts since Aristotle have differed sharply on whether or not presentation of both sides of a question increases persuasive power of a message. Should a persuader suppress "opposing arguments" or give them a hearing? Radio transcriptions were prepared to measure comparative effectiveness of the two approaches to influencing opinions on a controversial matter—the probable length of the war with Japan after victory in Europe was a fact.

In preparing the commentator persuasion giving both sides, eight "rules" were, in general, observed. Because these are of interest to the persuasion student (although they are hypotheses without experimental verification) we quote them here.

> (1) All of the main arguments on the other side should be mentioned at the very outset. . . .

(2) Any appeals to the motives of the opposed audience members should be presented early. . . .
(3) Opposed arguments that cannot be refuted should be presented relatively early. . . .
(4) An attempt to refute arguments on the other side should be made only when an obviously compelling and strictly factual refutation is available. . . .
(5) An unrefuted opposed argument should be followed by an uncontroversial positive argument. . . .
(6) The timing in presenting counter arguments of the opposition should be: positive argument leading, objection raised by an opposed counter argument, and then positive argument off-setting the objection. . . .
(7) Any refutations, and those positive arguments which are potentially most antagonizing, should come late in the presentation. . . .
(8) Members of the opposition should not be given a choice to identify themselves as such. . . . (Pages 203–205.)

Both programs, the one which omitted opposing arguments and the one which mentioned them, took the identical stand that the war after victory in Europe would be difficult and would last at least two years. Program II mentioned the major arguments indicating a short, easy war but Program I ignored them. Effects of the recorded commentator programs was measured in terms of the increase in numbers of men who believed that the war with Japan would last longer than one and one-half years.

Both programs had nearly the same immediate over-all effect of a significant and substantial change of opinion. But men who were initially opposed to the point of view of the program were definitely influenced more by the presentation of both sides, while those who initially agreed were influenced more by the one-sided program. The "both-side" presentation was more effective with the higher education group whereas the "one-side" program changed opinions more effectively in the less educated. ". . . the argument giving both sides is more effective among the better educated regardless of initial position whereas the one-sided presentation is primarily effective with those who are already convinced among the less well educated group." (Pages 214–215.)

The presentation of both sides in persuasion would seem wise when facing a hostile audience regardless of educational level, or when the audience has more than average education regardless of its initial position on the opinion advanced.

Shifting opinions of those opposed is a key problem of persuasion, and many critics of propaganda say that it frequently not only does not achieve its purpose but also it reinforces the established contrary ideas. This experiment revealed no such tendency. Opposed or not, regardless of educational level, the direction of change of opinion was preponderantly that which was intended in either a one-sided or two-sided program. "This is definitely contrary to the contention that propaganda merely reinforces existing beliefs." (Page 221.)

(3) Involving the audience actively seems to increase effectiveness of both instruction and persuasion. Results from the teaching of a film strip with and without audience participation were compared.

A film strip on phonetic names to go with the alphabet ("Able" for "a," "Baker" for "b," and so on) with accompanying sound recording (narration plus effects) was used. The participation groups "shouted out" the key words for letters in the several review lists in the strip while the nonparticipation groups were asked to read them silently from the screen. Half of the participation and nonparticipation groups was told that a test would follow the filmstrip.

Participation increased the amount remembered and reduced the time necessary for recall of individual items. Recall of the more difficult names was helped more by participation than recall of the easy names. Assigning a test increased learning substantially. Participation produced the most striking advantage among learners who were not motivated by an assigned test. The less intelligent benefited more from participation than did the more intelligent. In short, the greatest gain from audience participation seems to be found among "unintelligent, unmotivated men with difficult material." With these men the comparison of amounts learned ranged from 44 per cent without participation to 66 per cent with participation.

Summary and Conclusions

From the preceding sampling of studies we can draw a few tentative conclusions.

A. Concerning content analysis studies in persuasion

(1) The content analysis methods currently employed are capable of rather precise description and quantification of persuasion materials.

(2) Content analysis can reveal significant writer or speaker bias.

(3) Thematic analysis is useful in locating the basic arguments of a persuader and in determining the degree of his reliance on each.

(4) Both qualitative and quantitative analyses are helpful in increasing understanding of a unit of persuasion; statistical measures and consistency arc to be considered as supplementary sources of information.

B. Concerning audience analysis studies in persuasion

(1) Extensive interviewing has established great differences in listener preference in radio programs; these are correlated with education and age.

(2) A majority of American listeners are satisfied with radio; the discontented minority, however, is largely made up of highly educated people.

(3) Tastes of people tend to determine what they hear and read rather than mass media of communication administering a change of the tastes of the people.

C. Concerning media comparison studies in persuasion

(1) Direct speech seems to be more persuasive than radio speech or printed materials.

(2) The motion picture audience appears to be more suggestible than newspaper or radio audiences.

(3) Learning by radio lecture seems to be approximately as efficient as learning by classroom lecture.

D. Concerning studies in methods of persuasion

(1) Listeners prefer a variety of brief motive and logical appeals intermixed to either extended logical or extended emotional appeals.

(2) Apparently material conflicting with one's frame of reference tends to be forgotten.

(3) Repetition is a strong means of emphasis. Factors of vocal and physical variety are also helpful.

(4) Both the beginning and ending of a speech are relatively well remembered; which one has the advantage is in dispute.

(5) Specific training in methods of problem solving, argumentation, and debate can increase critical thinking ability of a group.

(6) Recognizing propaganda methods does not render a persuadee immune to influence from that unit of propaganda.

(7) Logical-factual persuasion seems to change attitudes about as effectively as do more colorful and emotional appeals.

(8) Attitude changes from persuasion tend to regress more than do those resulting from discussion.

(9) Conversational radio delivery seems to be as effective persuasively as dynamic delivery.

(10) The status accorded the speaker by the audience is an important determinant of his persuasive effectiveness.

(11) Effective persuasion must be "set" within the experience of the persuadee and use his language.

(12) Threats are, generally, ineffective persuasion.

(13) Demands of propaganda must not be excessive as judged by reasonable expectations of probable outcomes. Conversely, attitude changes from persuasion are usually modification, seldom conversion.

(14) Debate tends to strengthen previous convictions whereas discussion apparently more often ameliorates them.

E. Concerning case studies in persuasion

(1) Feelings of guilt can be used by the persuader to motivate action. Interviewers in the Merton study found that bond purchase frequently relieved disagreeable tensions.

(2) Personal influences rather than issues seem to change votes.

(3) Audience response recorders fail when the audience becomes interested in the message and forgets the push button.

(4) Film strips are about as effective teaching devices as are sound motion pictures.

(5) Dramatic and commentator radio programs are about equally well-liked and equally effective in changing attitudes.

(6) Intellectual abilities are closely related to knowledge and opinion.

(7) The average number of years of school completed is an accurate index to the intelligence of an *adult* audience.

(8) Presenting both sides is effective with highly educated and/or initially opposed auditors.

(9) Presenting only one side is effective with the less educated and/or initially favorable auditors.

(10) Audience participation techniques help the persuader most with the less educated, less able, and unmotivated audience.

Vallance[69] reviews propaganda research to date and develops four classifications: (1) "linear conceptualizations"—a framework in which he groups studies of variables in the propaganda *materials,* as for example, the various forms of content analysis; (2) "psychological conceptualizations"—a category containing studies which emphasize personal characteristics of propagandees, such as attitudes and values, and the effects these forces have on determining responses to propaganda stimuli; (3) "situational conceptualizations"—inclusion of propaganda studies emphasizing variables in group organization and the effects these elements have in determining responses to propaganda; and (4) "structural conceptualizations"—a category of propaganda studies almost non-existent, the studies of which stress "interdependent functioning" of psychological, social, and propaganda content forces.

---

69 T. R. Vallance, "Methodology in Propaganda Research," *Psychological Bulletin* (January, 1951), 48: 1, pp. 32–61.

The fragmentary nature of linear, psychological, and situational propaganda studies reduces their significance, says Vallance, and only the admittedly complicated and expensive structural conceptualization of research can deal realistically with attempts to direct human behavior through propaganda.

While we admit the desirability of the large and comprehensive research study in persuasion, we suggest that piecing together the fragments of smaller studies yields much useful information. We seem to be making progress which, if continued, may some day make possible the prediction of outcomes of the efforts of men at a level such that this unhappy summation of our failures may no longer apply: "History reveals no society which has gained a consciousness of the mechanics and dynamics of its institutions sufficient to prevent their operation to ends quite different from those for which they were devised and quite alien to any comprehensible purpose." [70]

Readings

1. Chase, Stuart, *The Proper Study of Mankind.* New York: Harper and Brothers, 1948. Ch. 27.
2. Guetzkow, H. (ed.), *Groups, Leadership and Men.* Carnegie Institute of Technology: Carnegie Press, 1951, pp. 146–176.
3. Nafziger, R. O., and Wilkerson, M. M. (eds.), *An Introduction to Journalism Research.* Baton Rouge: Louisiana State University Press, 1949, pp. 103–125.
4. Rohrer, J. H., and Sherif, M. (eds.), *Social Psychology at the Crossroads.* New York: Harper and Brothers, 1951, Ch. 17.
5. Simon, Clarence T., "Speech as a Science," *The Quarterly Journal of Speech* (October, 1951), XXXVIII: 3, pp. 281–298.

Exercises

1. Prepare and present a five-minute speech illustrating the application to persuasive speaking of one or more of the conclusions at the end of this chapter.

2. Write a brief report on one of the suggested readings, including both your summary of main points made and how they relate to the process of persuasion.

3. Which of the studies reported in this chapter yielded the finding which seemed most surprising? Explain why you did not anticipate this result.

---

[70] Frank D. Graham, *Social Goals and Economic Institutions.* Princeton: Princeton University Press, 1942, p. 5.

4. Outline the procedure for an experiment designed to measure the effectiveness of some particular technique of persuasion. Explain it to the class and encourage criticism of your design.

5. What are some of the limits of "scientific" (objective) investigations of persuasion? Analyze the sources of obstacles to such experimental research.

Chapter XXIII

METHODS OF EVALUATING THE RESULTS OF PERSUASION

I. Introduction

II. Measuring the Results of Face-to-Face Persuasion

- A. The Direct Response
- B. The Simple Ballot
- C. The Linear Scale
- D. The Shift-of-Opinion Ballot
- E. Thc Rating Scale
- F. The Critic Judge's Ballot for Debate
- G. The Audience-Analyzer (Polygraph)

III. Measuring the Results of Extended Persuasion

IV. Summary

Readings and Exercises

Chapter XXIII

METHODS OF EVALUATING THE RESULTS OF PERSUASION

Introduction

In Chapter XXII we reviewed the studies that have been made in the various areas of persuasion. These studies provide helpful information regarding the analysis of the content of persuasion, of audiences, of media, and of certain stimulus and case studies. The individual persuader, however, needs also a few more simple methods to use in judging reactions to his persuasion.

Because the effectiveness of much persuasion is difficult to determine, many persuaders neglect this important step. They go to great lengths in preparing what they hope will be an effective unit of persuasion, present it, and then assume that it has produced the desired response; no attempt is made to assess the results critically. There is much *post hoc ergo propter hoc* thinking today regarding the results of persuasion, and this "after-this-therefore-because-of-this" type of reasoning has led some persuaders to think that when people buy more, give to the Red Cross, join the church, and so on, it is because of the persuasion presented. They forget that the responses they observe in others may not be *because of* but *in spite of* the persuasion. The point we are making is that a persuader must develop reliable methods of evaluating the results of his persuasion if he is to assess and improve his ability in moving men. Below we review some methods which may be used in evaluating face-to-face persuasion with emphasis upon methods useful in classroom training, and we suggest methods useful in checking persuasion directed at remote audiences. The methods of audience analysis discussed in Chapter XVII may be used also in checking the audience's reactions after the persuasion is presented.

Measuring the Results of Face-to-Face Persuasion

THE DIRECT RESPONSE

If in a face-to-face situation the speaker desires a direct sale of a subscription to a newspaper, a specified donation to the Red Cross, orders to the college yearbook, or new converts to a religious faith, the amount of actual responses (inside the classroom or elsewhere) provides a test of the total effectiveness of the persuasion. If the action gained is not close to what was reasonably expected from the audience, the speaker needs to rethink his approach.

THE SIMPLE BALLOT

If the speech does not press for a specific action, but, as in the speech to convince, seeks to modify belief in some way, the simplest ballot to use is one which provides opportunity for the members of the audience to check their support or disapproval of the speaker's proposition. The ballot needs only to include a simple question and provide a space for an affirmative or negative answer. An example would be: "Do you believe that every citizen should be conscripted for essential service in time of war? Check one: Yes ——. No ——."

This type of ballot does not show small changes in belief and, like any such ballot, it assumes that a person's check represents his actual belief.

THE LINEAR SCALE

The linear scale may be used when it is desirable to learn the movement of attitude change more precisely than does the simple ballot discussed above.

Speaker's Name ______________________ Date __________

Speaker's Purpose ______________________________

MY ATTITUDE TOWARD THE SPEAKER'S PURPOSE

Before the speech is given, indicate by a circle (○) that position on the scale below which represents your present attitude toward the speaker's purpose. *After* the speech is concluded, again indicate your attitude toward the speaker's purpose by placing a cross (X) on that position on the scale.

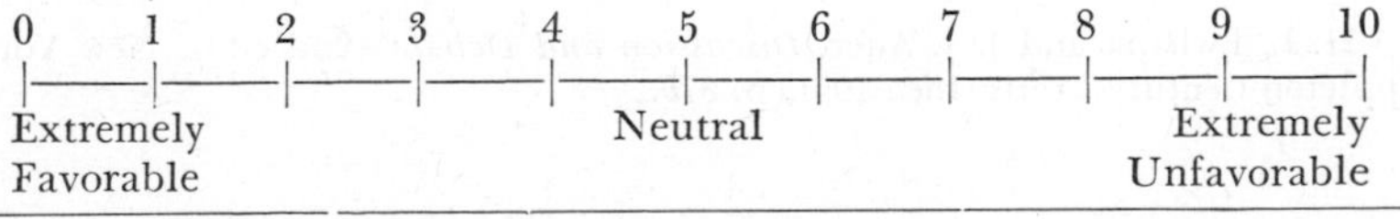

This ballot is easy to construct and it does afford opportunity for a type of check on persuasiveness. Like all such scales, it should be administered in such a way as to gain thoughtful evaluations.

THE SHIFT-OF-OPINION BALLOT

The late Professor H. S. Woodward of Western Reserve University developed the shift-of-opinion ballot. This is another method of measuring the shift of attitudes. It has been used extensively in evaluating collegiate debates. A standard example of the ballot is given below. You will note that information can be secured also regarding the person checking the ballot. By comparing the pre and post speech checks, the shift of attitude can be determined.

TO THE AUDIENCE

The debaters will appreciate your interest and help if you will, both *before* and *after* the debate, indicate on this sheet your personal opinion on the idea proposed for debate.

Please return your ballot to an usher at the close of the debate.

This ballot is filed by a man ____, woman ____, student ____, faculty member ____, lay citizen ____.

BEFORE THE DEBATE

____ I believe in the affirmative of the resolution to be debated.

____ I am undecided.

____ I believe in the negative of the resolution to be debated.

AFTER THE DEBATE

I have heard the entire discussion, and now

____ I believe more strongly in the affirmative of the resolution than I did.

____ I believe in the affirmative of the resolution.

____ I am undecided.

____ I believe in the negative of the resolution.

____ I believe more strongly in the negative of the resolution than I did.

THE RATING SCALE

When a series of proposals are presented, as in a symposium, the rating scale may be used to gain audience reaction to the proposals. It can be given before and after the speech (or speeches) to indicate shifts of opinion. A sample, used for a discussion on "The Right to Strike," is given below.[1]

[1] H. L. Ewbank and J. J. Auer, *Discussion and Debate* (2nd ed.). New York: Appleton-Century-Crofts, Inc., 1951, p. 370.

QUESTION: What About the "Right To Strike"?

Below are five possible solutions to this problem. Place a "1" before the solution you believe best, a "2" before the second best, etc.

_______ The right to strike is the union's only effective weapon.
_______ The right to strike should be limited only by making unions legally liable for losses to employers through unauthorized strikes.
_______ The right to strike should continue as at present.
_______ There is no right to strike when the public would be harmed thereby.
_______ Strikes should be forbidden by law.

THE CRITIC JUDGE'S BALLOT FOR DEBATE

The effectiveness of the various elements of a debate may be evaluated by the use of the ballot given below. It provides a useful breakdown of the important parts of this form of persuasion.[2]

BALLOT FOR JUDGING DEBATES

I. Quality of the Debating

Indicate the relative skill of each debater in each of the six phases of debating by placing numbers selected from the following scale (1, 2, 3, 4, 5, 6, 7) in the appropriate column. 1 *is poor;* 4 *is average;* 7 *is superior.*

	Affirmative		*Negative*	
	1	2	1	2
1. Analysis—plan of case	( )	( )	( )	( )
2. Knowledge, evidence	( )	( )	( )	( )
3. Reasoning, inferences	( )	( )	( )	( )
4. Adapting to opposing case	( )	( )	( )	( )
5. Skill in rebuttal	( )	( )	( )	( )
6. Speaking skill	( )	( )	( )	( )
Totals				

II. Rank of Debaters

Please rank the debaters in order of their excellence.

First _______________
Second _______________
Third _______________
Fourth _______________

III. Decision

I believe the better debating was done by the _______________ team.

(Signed) _______________

[2] *Ibid.*, p. 474.

THE AUDIENCE-ANALYZER (POLYGRAPH)

You will recall (Chapter XXII) that polygraph measurements were made by the Army's World War II Communication Research Project. This polygraph registered "like" and "dislike" on the part of certain audience members by pressing the appropriate buttons. A more elaborate polygraph has been used experimentally for a number of years. The desk of each student in the experimental classroom is equipped with a variable potentiometer which registers degrees of "like" and "dislike" on a ten point scale. The combined student reactions are electrically tabulated, and individual variations are noted on separate meters as the persuasive speech is given. After the speech is concluded, the speaker has a graph of audience reaction throughout all the parts of the speech. The audience-analyzer opens a challenging field for research and experimentation.

In addition to the methods cited above, such methods as the show-of-hands, the interview, correspondence, and conversation can be used to help measure the results of a persuasive effort. Certainly the attentiveness of the audience, applauses, hisses, boos, and other such types of audience reaction provide useful indices into the attitudes of the audience regarding your persuasion.

Measuring the Results of Extended Persuasion

Most of the methods discussed earlier (Chapter XVII) as methods for analyzing an audience before a speech is given can be also used to check their reactions after the speech. These include polls, the panel, the types of interviews, attitude scales, news-clipping services, statistical information, and so on.

Commercial organizations use various methods to observe sales trends after a new unit of promotion is launched. Two cities may be used experimentally, one city being given the persuasion, and the other carefully controlled in order not to be influenced. Then, after the experimental period, the sales of a product in the two cities are compared. All types of devices—such as the "box top" method, coupons, free samples, and others—are used to learn the places and amounts of consumer reaction to planned persuasion. Of course, the "Hooperating," discussed earlier, is relied upon to provide a measure of the effectiveness of radio programs. Letters (critic and fan mail), telegrams, newspaper and newsmagazine editorials, and telephone calls are analyzed and tabulated carefully by many professional persuaders.

It should be clear that the methods for evaluating extended systems of persuasion are many, varied, and often very complex. To discuss these here would be to go beyond our purposes. Readers interested in these methods should study the more complete treatments, some of which are cited in the reading references below.

Summary

In this chapter we have encouraged each student to develop means of evaluating his persuasion. Some methods of evaluation have been suggested. We have emphasized the methods which are useful in the classroom since our primary interest lies there. Comparisons of results gained from successive attempts at persuasion can be made, and these comparisons should be studied carefully with a view toward improvement. Only through carefully planning and controlling the cycle of preparation, presentation, and evaluation can any plan of persuasion be repaired and improved.

Readings

1. Ewbank, H. L., and Auer, J. J., *Discussion and Debate* (2nd ed.). New York: Appleton-Century-Crofts, Inc., 1951, Ch. XXII, "Evaluating Discussion" and Ch. XXVIII, "Evaluating Debate."
2. Gilman, W. E., Aly, B., and L. D. Reid, *The Fundamentals of Speaking*. New York: The Macmillan Company, 1951, Ch. XXII, "Listening to Speeches."
3. Hepner, H. W., *Effective Advertising*. New York: McGraw-Hill Book Co., Inc., 1949, Part VI, "Appraising and Coordinating Advertising."
4. Likert, Rensis, "A Technique for the Measurement of Attitude," *Archives of Psychology* (1932), XXII: No. 140.
5. Thurstone, L. L., and Chave, E. J., *The Measurement of Attitude*. Chicago: University of Chicago Press, 1929.

Exercises

1. For your next class in persuasive speech prepare copies of a linear scale for your classmates to use in evaluating your speech. Work out a system of tabulating and interpreting the results you receive. Prepare a five-minute report on your findings.

2. Perform the same exercise as no. 1, but use the shift-of-opinion ballot instead of the linear scale.

3. Put on a symposium in class. Have five speakers present separate solutions (speeches to convince) to some common problem. Prepare copies of the rating scale to be used by the audience members in evaluating the speeches. Have the scale checked before and after the speeches in order to observe shifts in opinion. On the basis of results, which speaker was most effective? least effective? What made the one speech stand out? What made the least effective speech so weak?

4. Prepare and present a class debate. Have each class member check a copy of the critic judge's ballot. Tabulate the results carefully. Observe points of weakness and strength.

5. Make a study of (a) a professional speaker's methods of evaluating the results of his persuasion or (b) a commercial organization's methods of evaluating the results of their system of advertising. Write up your findings in a 1,000-word paper.

Chapter XXIV

THE ETHICS OF PERSUASION

I. Introduction

II. Popular Approaches to Ethical Problems in Persuasion
- A. Forbidden Words
- B. Shameful Deceptions
- C. The Cult of Reason
- D. Ethical Motive Appeals
- E. Ethics of the "End That Justifies the Means"
- F. Ethics of "What You Can Get Away With"

III. The Social Context Theory of Ethics of Persuasion
- A. Social Utility
- B. Experimental and Nonexperimental Bases of Behavior
    1. Flexibility of Nonexperimental Beliefs
    2. Frequent Contradictions of Nonexperimental Beliefs
    3. Tendencies to Rationalize Our Nonexperimental Beliefs
    4. Resistance of Nonexperimental Beliefs to Change

IV. Applying Ethical Standards to Persuasion
- A. Prerequisites to Ethical Judgment
- B. Miscellaneous Misunderstandings in Ethics of Communications
    1. The Separability of Theory and Practice
    2. Advisability of Honesty
    3. Explanation as a Part of Description
    4. No Place for Tact in Ethics
    5. Resolution of All Ethical Disputes Through Reason
- C. The Role of the Persuader in Making Ethical Decisions

V. Summary and Conclusions

Readings and Exercises

Chapter XXIV

THE ETHICS OF PERSUASION

Introduction

Why should a discussion of ethics enter into a book on persuasion? A great number of the most troublesome problems in applied persuasion arise from ethical issues. What are ethical issues? At the risk of oversimplifying Stevenson's definition,[1] we will say that any (1) currently controversial concept involving (2) significant disagreement in both attitude and belief, amounts to an ethical issue. The layman's definition, i.e., "a troublesome problem to be decided on a moral basis of rightness and wrongness" is probably adequate as a tool for locating ethical issues in persuasion.

We have talked about many matters of theory and have mentioned illustrative incidents that may have caused our readers to react by thinking, "But is that right? or justifiable? or moral? or decent? or Christian? or legitimate?" Chances are that the stimulus triggering such a response was a revealed or implied ethical issue. It is no exaggeration to say that most persuasion is planned according to, modified by, or done in defiance of the answers to these questions.

The failure to resolve problems of ethics in persuasion as satisfactorily as we have made progress on some other related matters is due in large part to a misconception most of us share. We (students, teachers, and those who write articles and books) have searched for rules and principles to guide us. Think about this a moment and you will see that this implies that such rules and principles of a fixed and definite nature exist, or they can be formulated. Is this a true assumption? We are unable to judge its

1 Charles L. Stevenson, *Ethics and Language.* New Haven: Yale University Press, 1944, pp. 11–19.

truth categorically; instead we can only turn to inspection of the world around us to look for evidence of the operation of fixed ethical principles manifested in the behavior of people. Our quest is for absolutes that can be derived from the moral behavior of those who preceded us and of our contemporaries; only such evidence can establish the functioning of the general and universal moral rule.

As a test case, let us consider the most fixed, definite, carefully defined, and unchanging doctrine concerning ethical issues in our culture—the written law. Does it, in application, resemble in any sense the predictable exactness of a law in a physical science? Pareto analyzes some factors determining outcomes of one category of criminal law:

> Take, for example, a penal decision following the verdict of a jury. Distinguishable among the factors entering into such a sentence are the following: 1. Written law—the part it plays in criminal cases is often insignificant. 2. Political influences—in certain cases very important. 3. Humanitarian inclinations in judges and jurymen—these are knowable from humanitarian theory and literary sources. 4. Emotional, socialistic, social, political, and other inclinations on the part of jurymen—all knowable from theories and literary sources. 5. The general notion common to all despotisms, whether royal, oligarchical, or democratic, that the law does not bind the "sovereign," and that the "sovereign" may substitute personal whims for enacted law. This notion, too, is knowable through theories. In our day it is the fashion to say that "what we need is a 'living law,' a 'flexible' law, a law that 'adapts itself to the public conscience.'" Those are all euphemisms for the caprice of the individuals in power. 6. Numberless other inclinations, which are not perhaps generally operative, but which may chance to be preponderant in the minds of the twelve individuals —usually of no great intelligence, no serious education, no very high moral sense—who are called upon to serve on juries. 7. Private interests of the citizens in question. 8. The temporary impressions made upon them by some striking fact—so after a series of startling crimes juries are inclined to be severe for a time.
>
> In a word, it may be said that court decisions depend largely upon the interests and sentiments operative in a society at a given moment; and also upon individual whims and chance events; and but slightly, and sometimes not at all, upon codes or written law.[2]

---

[2] Vilfredo Pareto, *The Mind and Society* (edited by Arthur Livingston, translated by Borgiomo and Livingston). Copyright, 1935, by Harcourt, Brace and Company, Inc., New York.

It would be interesting to examine other instances in our experience which illustrate as does Pareto's example that a literal and uniform application of a moral rule is rare indeed. Even the most basic and generally accepted principles, thought of as absolutes, become in practice entirely dependent upon attendant circumstances. The commandment "Thou shalt not kill," for example, means that if conditions are thus and so you should refrain from taking the lives of other human beings, but in other situations it is of little consequence (bombing of civilians) and in still other times and places it is an act worthy of highest praise (law enforcement and killing the enemy soldier in war). Without attempting a large-scale survey (some ethical advices are examined below) we suggest that accepted moral (ethical) rules in application are characterized more by adaptation, reinterpretation and redefinition than by uniformity. This does not say they have no influence. It alleges that their influence is variable and is determined in great degree by other forces (see above list by Pareto). It suggests that any notions we have of exact, universal, and unchanging moral laws do not conform to reality. Possibly uniformity here is *desirable;* our point is that *it does not exist.*

To get back to persuasion, your own observation and study have undoubtedly convinced you that actual ethical standards of persuasion fluctuate. More than that, you probably feel that they *should,* that what is wrong in one instance may be highly moral in another. Many people feel that way without realizing that this conviction renounces the search for absolute rules to govern ethical decisions in persuasion. Another philosophical base is needed; the simple substitute we suggest might be worded: *ethics of persuasion is a function of context.*

Popular Approaches to Ethical Problems in Persuasion

While the ethical aspect of persuasion and propaganda has not been stressed by writers in these fields, each has usually had some contribution in offering at least an approach to the problem. Here we describe some of these attempts, with comments on their strengths and limitations, to supply ethical guidance to the student of persuasion.

FORBIDDEN WORDS

The simplest approach to improving the relative morality of an utterance is to specify words and phrases which are taboo. Polite social usage has resulted from a long history of conditioning by church, school, and other civilizing agencies. Euphemisms are one incidental result of the operation of the principle of forbidden symbols. Certainly persuasion which conforms carefully to a gentlemanly and polite vocabulary would be free from ethical criticism in one concrete and identifiable sense.

A fairly recent expansion of the censorship of certain symbols has become prominent under the label "name-calling." This was one of the seven propaganda devices specified by the Institute for Propaganda Analysis. Probably it was purely descriptive originally, but the term has come to have such a negative sanction that to use the technique of name-calling in persuasion is in itself often considered unethical.

Not as clearly negative as name-calling but a member of the same family is the concept of "loaded words." Here our current authors admit many degrees of "loading" (connotative meaning) and generally agree that extreme "loading" or relying on the emotional impact of words rather than their referential meanings smacks of the unethical in persuasion.

Forbidden symbols are aids to ethics, but they are only a fragment of our problem. By the devices of implication and suggestion an intelligent but unprincipled persuader can do very nicely without any particular terms or without name-calling or even without heavily "loaded words." Advertisers have seldom found the denial of use of a particular phrase a severe handicap in conveying it or its equivalent to the public. Control of symbols amounts to little or no control over goals and methods of the modern persuader. The heart of ethical decisions in question lies elsewhere.

SHAMEFUL DECEPTIONS

Attempts to deceive the persuadee have caught the attention of the careful observer of persuasion and some most helpful material ethics-wise is to be found in the description and classification of these "tricks of the trade." The Institute for Propaganda Analysis offers four borderline or outright unethical deceptions: (a) "glittering generality," the unsupported sweeping statement: (b) "the plain folks device," the attempt to appear as an ordinary person to disarm the persuadee; (c) "card-stacking," the selective distortion of an issue by presenting it in an unfair, one-sided fashion; and (d) "band-wagon," the technique of inducing people to go along, not because of the merits of your proposition but because you apply the social pressure resulting from adoption of your recommendation by many other people. A fifth instance from the Institute for Propaganda Analysis is that of "transfer," which may or may not be ethical depending on the nature of the transfer of qualities from one example or context to another. Certainly using the American flag and patriotic songs to enhance a fascist appeal by simply meshing them together could be a shameful deception.

A list of unethical deceptions which applies particularly well to political persuasive speaking is that of Ewbank and Auer.

> 1. It is, of course, unethical for a speaker to distort or falsify evidence.
> 2. It is unethical for a speaker to use emotional appeals when he lacks evidence to support them, or when he knows his listeners would not support his conclusion if they had the time and the opportunity to investigate the problem for themselves.
> 3. It is unethical for a speaker to divert attention from weaknesses in his argument by unsupported attacks on his opponent or by appeals to hatred, intolerance, bigotry and fear.
> 4. It is unethical for a speaker to conceal his real purpose, or the organization he represents, pretending to speak objectively when he is an advocate of one point of view.
> 5. It is unethical for a speaker to pose as an "authority" when he has only a layman's knowledge of the subject.[3]

This is good advice, but there may be exceptions as the authors undoubtedly would agree. We mention two possibilities: diplomats representing the United States abroad often pose as authorities in military and other matters when their knowledge is that of the layman in order to increase their prestige and influence, and the distortion or falsification of evidence is desirable when revelation of an actual state of affairs would precipitate disastrous mob action, for example, a lynching. Most of the time the advice to avoid

[3] H. L. Ewbank and J. J. Auer, *Discussion and Debate* (2nd ed.). New York: Appleton-Century-Crofts, Inc., 1951, p. 258.

these specified deceptions is good counsel, but careless application of these suggestions as *absolutes,* to test the ethical soundness of all instances of persuasion, is absurd. Just as telling the literal truth often amounts to extreme and unnecessary cruelty, belief that these practices are *bad* per se can lead to damaging and even unethical results. As is the case with some other approaches, it illustrates that the better rules can cover one type of persuasion in the aggregate, but are never adequate to all specific instances.

THE CULT OF REASON

A number of people have "gone overboard" for so-called "psychological techniques" of influencing people. What is not as generally recognized is the smaller but almost equally evangelical counter-movement we call the cult of reason. The hard core of solutions to ethical (and many other) problems of persuasion is to be found in a rigorous interpretation of the maxim, "stick to the facts." If we as persuaders limit our evidence to what we know for sure, and our rhetoric to reasoning according to strict logical forms, we will become ethical, according to the advocates of this approach. The zeal of the person dedicated to reason is often as irrational as are many of the targets of his criticism.

Primary in the cult of reason is complete honesty, including as its essential ingredient *revealed intent.* Concealed purpose is considered to be inherently unethical. Secondary characteristics include the elimination of emotional appeals, emotive language, and all communication that tends to stimulate the secretion of adrenalin rather than reflective thought. This approach assumes that the persuadee is capable of setting aside his prejudices and focusing his intellect on an issue. It tries to provide every incentive for him to do just that. There are obvious values in being factual and logical. A weakness rests in the fact that much human conduct is nonlogical. Choices are made frequently on bases other than those of evidence and reason, which, though involved, are not deciding factors.

The cult of reason evangelist fails to recognize the need for supplementing his scientific method with known behavior tendencies derived from psychology, sociology, philosophy, and other studies dealing with nonlogical conduct. A realistic middle-ground would be to increase the emphasis on facts and logic but to rely upon them only where they are clearly pertinent. For example, don't expect logical analysis to change religious convictions.

Since at least a great many decisions made by people are more nonlogical than logical, the voluntary self-limitation of the persuader to the tools of facts and reason may purify his ethics to some degree but do little for his effectiveness (which is also a matter of ethics, since he may not have the moral right to be ineffective in a crisis). Quite possibly he may misrepresent the facts of his case through attempting to reason logically about matters of nonlogical motivation.

The deception of pseudo-logic in persuasion, while not a part of the cult of reason, has prospered because of the prestige won by reasoned discourse. The speaker says, "Now let's be logical and look at the record," then presents a complicated pattern that confuses his audience. He later draws a conclusion with appropriate "therefores" and "because of's" which he asserts to be logically inevitable. This intentional trickery is only a small step from the persuasion of a person attempting to reason about nonlogical matters with too little information to satisfy the requirements of reason. He has his conclusion to begin with and the temptation is great to claim for it a purely logical development. Intentional and unintentional pseudo-logic grow out of extreme reliance upon evidence and its logically patterned manipulation. Increasing the reasoned discourse content of a communication has some bearing upon its ethical qualities, but the relationship is not close. Other factors that we can term nonlogical are of at least equal importance.

ETHICAL MOTIVE APPEALS

Ever since writers in the field of persuasion discovered the "motive appeal" concept, they have related ethics to appeals to different levels of motives. Appeals to "high" motives have achieved respectability and appeals to "low" motives have been frowned upon. Another dichotomy is the "selfish" vs. "altruistic" categories, with their obvious ethical overtones. Recently, selfishness as a motive has gained in respectability, and, as will be noted below, has achieved rather high standing when it meets certain requirements. There are several approaches, but they are alike in that they select some motives as more moral than others or certain appeals as relatively higher on the scale of legitimacy.

Gray and Braden offer ethical advice in a list of general principles in the use of motive appeals.[4] Three principles of the eight cited are:

> The motive itself must be "worthy of the deed." . . .
> Make your appeal to the highest motives to which your listeners are likely to respond. . . .
> Make your appeal, as a rule, to more than one motive, on the theory that if one will not have the desired effect perhaps another will![5]

One difficulty in applying this advice is the practical one of identifying "high" and "low" motives. Gray and Braden define these as "altruistic" and "selfish" respectively. But they add:

> It should be pointed out that there is in this distinction, or in the labels that have been attached to the two general types, no implication that the "lower" or "selfish" goals are in themselves always reprehensible, or that the "higher" or "altruistic" motives are necessarily always justifiable.[6]

So we see that it may be unethical to appeal to '"high" motives and high ethically to appeal to "low" motives. A sensible way of resolving our uncertainties is to admit that these suggestions are for motive appeals in the aggregate, and that the quotation immediately above is to center our attention on the fact that none of these rules are universals, that none of them *may* apply to a specific case. On the whole, these ideas are sound and helpful.

"High" and "low" motives, however, remain in a state of confusion. "Selfish" motives may, coincidentally or otherwise, serve the highest of purposes. "Altruistic" motives may cause much more harm than good. The selfish may appear to be altruistic, so convincingly that the owner of the motives may himself be fooled. An altruistic motivation is often cloaked under the guise of selfishness (frequently intentionally as in the case of some philanthropists) so effectively that it defies detection. And, finally, few of us are

---

[4] G. W. Gray and W. W. Braden, *Public Speaking.* New York: Harper and Brothers, 1951, pp. 72–75.

[5] *Ibid.,* pp. 72–74.

[6] *Ibid.,* p. 55.

willing to label even most selfishness as unethical, since we grant to each other liberal freedom of thought and action in providing for our own personal comfort and well-being.

While we are discussing "selfish" motives we should note the tendency to condemn as undesirable appeals to immediately personal, short-range selfishness, such as encouraging hoarding of scarce commodities in a time of inflation, that hurts other people. However, a broader base selfishness which does protect the person's "self" but is also compatible with interests of his group is something considered as quite ethical by many writers. An example of the latter might be to urge the citizen to eat plenty of good food, see his doctor regularly, and thereby maintain good health. Oliver[7] speaks of "enlightened selfishness" as involving intelligent estimation of ultimate goals. Merton explores the same concept from the viewpoint of the persuader who is "oriented toward democratic values":

> He would not only have asked which techniques of persuasion produce the *immediate result* of moving a given proportion of people to action, but also, what are the *further, more remote* but not necessarily less significant, effects of these techniques upon the individual personality and his society?[8]

Merton and Oliver openly defend the right of the persuader to be selfish and to appeal to selfishness in others in the process of attaining his goals, but they insist that this should be done in a framework of social consciousness. How many people will be helped or hurt by this persuasion, immediately and in the future? Answering this question is certainly ethically sound. It centers attention upon a concept vital to the persuader which we shall talk about later as *social utility,* and it illustrates that *ethics of persuasion is a function of context.*

ETHICS OF THE "END THAT JUSTIFIES THE MEANS"

A popular indictment of ethics in persuasion is found in the statement that "some unprincipled rascal is letting the end justify the means." In other words, the desirability of the goal is so

---

[7] Robert T. Oliver, *The Psychology of Persuasive Speech.* New York: Longmans, Green and Co., Inc., 1942, p. 48.

[8] Robert K. Merton, *Mass Persuasion.* New York: Harper and Brothers, 1946, p. 188.

great that the persuader considers the use of shady tactics, otherwise unethical, to be necessary and therefore ethical. A universal implication is that the end should *not* be used to justify the means.

Yet great students of human behavior, for example, Aristotle and John Dewey, have told us with devastating and simple proofs that the *purpose* of persuasion can be a sound justification of the techniques used to reach it. If the end does not justify the means, what can? Obviously total rejection of the principle that one should study his desired objective in judging the ethics of his method is absurd. Studied in context, the end can serve as a most excellent and meaningful check upon the ethical legitimacy of the means.

Evaluation of means of persuasion in terms of their goal is a first step in establishing an ethical base. This has gained an unsavory reputation probably because of partial and selfish estimation of end results. The end includes immediate and long term effects, from the persuader's viewpoint and from the point of view of all other people whose lives will be touched directly or indirectly by the persuasion. If we justify means *solely* by personal, immediate benefits, ignoring such items as injury to others, we are misapplying the perfectly good procedure of examining the end to determine (partially) the ethical quality of the means.

We say *partially,* because this good principle is far from the complete story. Highly moral, imperative purposes encourage laxity in choice of means, an extreme example being the willingness of some reformers to resort to physical force, torture, and execution. Methods in and of themselves must meet many ethical standards (for example, humanitarian and social). The zealous proponent of a good cause must continually review his methods to be sure that he is not slipping into short-cut practices he himself would condemn when used for a lesser purpose. Because of the intimate relationship between means and ends, borderline methods detract from moral worth of the goal. Inducing people to give to the Community Chest by publishing names of contributors and amounts given would cheapen the reputation of this praiseworthy agency.

To illustrate the fundamental nature of the ends-means relationship in persuasion we remind the reader that a persuader starts with his conclusion, and the means grow out of the predetermined end. Pareto calls the resultant thinking a "logic of sentiment": "In ordinary logic, the conclusion follows from the premises. In the logic of sentiment, the premises follow from the conclusion." [9]

ETHICS OF "WHAT YOU CAN GET AWAY WITH"

Although somewhat unsavory, this theory of the ethics of persuasion probably has more popular support than ends-means justification. A laissez-faire capitalist tradition has left us with a small, durable core of this philosophy, at least in the business world. Two powerful negative forces operate to control ethics of the persuader operating on the "what you can get away with" principle: (a) social sanctions (including business boycotts, and others) and (b) the law.

Rough, tough, and Machiavellian, this school of ethics has the great advantage of simplicity. Considerations of forbidden words, deceptions, rationality, pure motives, and worthy ends go out the window. Our persuader has only to worry about staying out of jail and avoiding ostracism and retaliation of a highly personal sort. All known tools for controlling people lie close at hand. Let the buyer beware, if you get hurt it is your own fault and you will (possibly) be more careful next time.

Mass communications increase the potential danger of this philosophy. For example, some giant corporation or combination of business interests could conceivably get a virtual monopoly of these channels for a particular kind of advertising. The natural exclusion of competition would leave us dependent upon the ethics of the advertiser. "What they could get away with" would increase, possibly to the point of real damage, if unrestrained by their own voluntary limitation of profits.

With its vindictive overtones of "getting even with the world," the principle of "what you can get away with" is probably the least defensible base for an ethics of persuasion. Yet we must recognize that it contributes direct and powerful controls; we have all become more ethical persuaders because of the long list of things we know we "cannot get away with!"

Our survey of some approaches to ethical problems of persuasion provides much helpful but fragmentary advice. These suggestions must be interpreted as comments on central tendencies. The better rules apply to the majority of one type of persuasion, but no rule

---

[9] Pareto, *op. cit.*, p. 310.

covers every specific case, and the frequent necessity to adapt advice to concrete circumstances leads us to repeat our topic sentence of this chapter: *ethics of persuasion is a function of context.*

The Social Context Theory of Ethics of Persuasion

We have rejected any single formula approach for judging ethical qualities of persuasion while admitting that each has positive values. To proceed constructively, we have selected for brief presentation several concepts useful in analyzing communication contexts from an ethical viewpoint. These are to a large extent adaptations of ideas of Vilfredo Pareto.

SOCIAL UTILITY

When we try to take the "long view," or estimate effects of our actions on other people, now and later, we are applying an ethical standard of great importance, a complicated one which might be termed "social utility." Will the social group concerned benefit? Is there a revealed or concealed penalty to be paid? Could injury to one or a few individuals outweigh the group gains? These are questions typical of those that must be answered in measuring the social utility of an act of persuasion.

A simple definition of social utility will serve our purposes, particularly since the term implies its meaning clearly: usefulness to the people affected. What do we mean by "useful" in this context? This becomes a bit more complex because it demands that we first define the group and develop a general understanding of its members' common objectives, and then estimate as well as we can the ways in which our contemplated action (utterance) will help or hinder their attainment. Ultimately the *survival potential* of the group is involved. But thorough understanding of all implications of the social utility concept is not necessary. A conscientious effort to understand (a) the group members and their common interests, (b) ways our persuasion may help or hurt the group, and (c) favorable and adverse effects upon individuals, will yield a rough estimate of probable social utility.

Because persuasion is, essentially, rearranging the lives of other people, we believe that the persuader's sincere effort to abide by some social utility principles is the first and perhaps most important step toward being ethical. Just the attempt helps, but the following concepts will add system and meaning to this process of estimating social consequences of a unit of communication.

EXPERIMENTAL AND NONEXPERIMENTAL BASES OF BEHAVIOR

Individuals living in groups have two clearly different sources of influence upon their decisions. Different principles operate in the functioning of the two types of influence and it is necessary to understand them in order that the principles of one not be applied inadvertently to the other.

Experimentally based behavior is derived from tested or verified data. The decision to add fresh vegetables to my diet may be made because of factual knowledge of what has happened to animals and people who lived without eating them. ("Fact" is used here in a narrow sense, meaning something inherently verifiable through receptor experience.) I stop at STOP signs because I know (from experience) what can happen when I do not. The school board buys a certain brand of paint on the simple evidence of a comparative weathering test. The experimental basis of choice is the fact, verifiable in a scientific sense. Experimental behavior is cool and intelligent, whether consciously so or not, and it is always in terms of a probability resting upon our own experience and the experience of others.

Behavior growing out of propositions accepted without proof, or even a quest for proof, is *nonexperimental.* Group traditions of long standing are powerful influences yet frequently are unverified and unquestioned. Is it best for a man to have one wife, or a woman one husband? Does joining a church improve one's chances of a happy life after death? Are fireworks the best means of celebrating the Fourth of July? Is Easter the best time for buying new clothes? Are three meals a day—morning, noon and early evening—the best pattern for feeding the human animal? Is honesty the best policy? Are all men created equal? Is it good that graduating seniors wear caps and gowns and that we have commencement speakers? Are there advantages to driving on the right, rather than the left, side of the street? Is it right that men wear suit coats and ties in summer?

Whether the affirmations of these questions make sense or not, great numbers of people behave as though they are proven fact. Some of them could be investigated, given extensive resources, whereas others by their nature are inaccessible to any scientific sort of study. The point is that we live by large numbers of customs, maxims, and so on, their lack of proof bothering us not a whit. Truth of an experimental claim is a laboratory-type probability. Truth of a nonexperimental basis of behavior is accord with our sentiments.

Much unethical persuasion takes nonexperimental propositions as premises and uses experimental forms of reasoning to get a conclusion. Unfortunately this illegitimate hybrid can be highly convincing. Nonexperimental beliefs often conflict—think of the flexibility of logical persuasion which can use as a premise either "A stitch in time saves nine" or "Haste makes waste"!

You can be ethical by keeping your experimental and nonexperimental categories straight, and refusing to yield to the temptation to reason with nonexperimental premises as though they were verified, i.e., rested on a respectably objective investigation.

The role of nonexperimental beliefs in determining behavior is not a simple one. We call attention here to some of their nonlogical characteristics. For further information see Pareto's *General Sociology,* mentioned earlier in this chapter.

Flexibility of Nonexperimental Beliefs. In sharp contrast to the theories of physical sciences many of our key traditional values and codes are in general terms that defy precise definition. The result is a long continuum of varying interpretations. Some cynical observers have contended that the vagueness of a moral rule correlates highly with its usefulness.

We noted some current considerations in interpreting the commandment "Thou shalt not kill." "Freedom of speech" is a firmly fixed value in our democratic society, but the list of things which can be said without penalty varies with national and international affairs. In the United States a man is considered innocent until proven guilty, and has the right to face his accuser in court, unless he happens to have been accused of disloyalty or subversive activities. We reject poison gas because we are committed to the use of only humane weapons of war, but we rely heavily upon Napalm and the flame thrower, which have not as yet been acted upon by any international convention. We believe in monogamy and permit polygamy via divorce in one of three marriages.

Our evolving patterns of behavior are affected by nonexperimental beliefs and, in turn, affect the beliefs themselves by redefinition of terms and imposing conditions under which the beliefs apply. Hence, the formally stated belief is an inaccurate guide to one who would locate the functioning rule. Behavior is the only reliable index of the extent to which a nonlogical belief corresponds to the conduct of people.

A rigid and unrealistic interpretation of a nonexperimental belief for purposes of persuasion is unethical. People tend to accept such premises because the words are in familiar patterns to which they have long subscribed. The ethical persuader who uses nonlogical precepts must do the best he can to indicate the range of current interpretations. He should make explicit any implied conditions and any notable exceptions. This is a severe requirement! Often the flexibility of the nonexperimental belief the persuader would like to use will flex his argument right out of existence!

Frequent Contradictions of Nonexperimental Beliefs. The contradictory nature of nonexperimental beliefs has already been presented in two forms, incompatible rules or maxims ("Haste makes waste," "he who hesitates is lost"), and elastic interpretations of certain generally accepted principles of conduct which to some degree deny apparent meaning. There is, however, another interesting, more subtle contradiction: people tend to hold opposing nonexperimental beliefs concurrently.

Moral rules, for example, supposedly cut across all areas of conduct, yet the failure of people to generalize from one area to another has been demonstrated. Hence an altruistic person may not be uniformly generous, in fact altruism and selfishness often go together, manifested under differing circumstances. Tenderness and cruelty may be found side by side in a single personality. Tolerance in the broad sense may be characteristic of a person's attitude toward Caucasian peoples, narrow prejudice descriptive of his attitude toward Negroes. Insistence upon strict scientific methods in his field may mark the same scholar who is nonscientific, prejudiced, even irrational in his politics.

Because a person is found to hold one nonexperimental conviction, we cannot assume that others logically consistent with it will be held also and that contradictory ones will not be just as firmly believed. Any persuasion resting upon the assumption that people are logical in their nonexperimental belief patterns is to some extent unethical. Because people like to think of themselves as consistent, this is an easy assumption to sell. It is as insidious as it is unrealistic.

Tendencies to Rationalize our Nonexperimental Beliefs. Much of man's mental energy has been directed toward self-justification, finding "good" reasons for what he wants to do or believe. Our nonexperimental premises come to us with high prestige, from parents, associates, respected institutions, and so on, so we *want* to believe them. When they conflict with our common sense—we are trained in reflective thinking to some extent—we can search only for reasoning in their support. Because many of these traditional advices work out quite well in practice some of this reasoning is sound enough to be termed experimental verification. Often it is specious for lack of data and is characterized by gaps and leaps in induction.

Where information is inadequate and rigid reasoning forms cannot be applied the ethical persuader will abandon the pretense of basing his claims on reason. Instead of saying, "These premises lead inevitably to this conclusion," let the speaker admit the lack of proof in any scientific sense but ask for acceptance of his proposition because it accords with experience, judgment, and sentiments of his audience. These, too, are well-established bases of decision.

Resistance of Nonexperimental Beliefs to Change. For a very good and simple reason we would expect nonexperimental beliefs to be more stable than those experimentally derived. Since they are not induced from facts, discoveries of new facts and new relationships among facts do not affect them in the way that new discoveries affect the premises of a science. "Honesty is the best policy" is in no danger of being categorically disproved tomorrow.

"Social equilibrium" is a label for the balance that results in a society from the interaction of stable forces. Fundamental behavior and belief patterns evolve gradually, and if sudden change is introduced, compensations often develop to restore something close to the original balance. For example, an increase in severity of penalty for a crime could be partially nullified by fewer verdicts of "guilty," and there is some evidence to indicate that such would be the case. Where large groups such as nations subscribe to the same basic nonexperimental beliefs, small groups within find marked deviation impractical. Nonviolent change of our traditional patterns is slow and irregular, a matter of breaking and re-establishing points of social equilibrium. The Eighteenth Amendment to the Constitution, the many compensating social forces which developed, and its ultimate repeal, amounts to a dramatic instance of the difficulties in bringing about abrupt changes in belief and behavior patterns.

Some persuaders would have us believe that basic nonexperimental behavior patterns and beliefs can be changed drastically in a short time. We have heard that the insidious influence of seventy thousand Communists might cause the majority of Americans to suddenly switch allegiance from democracy to Communism. Considering the fundamental differences in ideology involved, to say that this eventuality is highly improbable is an understatement. Other speakers scare us with threats that labor may rise at any moment and take over the properties of management, or that management may with equal suddenness enslave workers. Government may abolish private enterprise, or big business may, at one blow, install a fascist regime in Washington. Persuasion which represents fundamental tenets of our culture as threatened with imminent overthrow through inadequate forces and in opposition to the known facts of social change would seem to deserve ethical criticism.

Applying Ethical Standards to Persuasion

Ethical planning should be a vital part of the preparation of persuasion, as ethical analysis should be important to the examination of the persuasion of others. There is no fixed sequence of steps but the following considerations should be observed:

PREREQUISITES TO ETHICAL JUDGMENT

Social Utility Considerations of the Over-all Project. As soon as the purpose of persuasion is determined the analysis of its social utility can begin. Basically, it is a process of "end inspection" via study of the group. Location of central experimental and nonexperimental beliefs involved is helpful, for these contribute to quite different sorts of social utility.

Social utility analysis yields much information vital to many aspects of persuasion besides ethics. For example, whether your objective amounts to a reasonable burden of proof and should be restricted or extended will probably be decided. Simply examining both long-range and immediate probable consequences will increase your grasp of the problem and help you to develop an over-all consistent pattern.

Content Details. From experimental and nonexperimental beliefs motive appeals can be derived suited to the different behavior patterns of each type of belief. Then the role of reason, i.e., the extent of reliance upon reasoned discourse, can be ascertained. Good advice from the approaches discussed earlier in this chapter is now pertinent. Forbidden words, shameful deceptions, unethical motive appeals, legal limits, all figure in the detailed development or the detailed analysis of the persuasion. Again, ethical values exercise continuous pressure. Each decision on method is shaped in part by its contribution to the ethical unity of the communication.

MISCELLANEOUS MISUNDERSTANDINGS IN ETHICS OF COMMUNICATIONS

To supplement our major procedures above we note here a few fairly common erroneous ideas with ethical implications.

Separability of Theory and Practice. This notion is clearly stated in the saying "This is sound theory, but it won't work in practice." Obviously, a theory should be examined in a particular context, and the best test of a theory is whether or not it *will work* in a specific instance.

Advisability of Honesty. The student of persuasion learns early that the instances of suppression or avoidance of known facts are too frequent to be ignored. Some authorities lend legitimacy to certain deviations from the truth by arguing that the persuader has no obligation to present all the evidence he knows when it is in opposition to his purpose. The law does not demand that a defendant build a case against himself by supplying damaging factual information.

A few writers endorse suppression of certain facts but condemn distortion. This is an untenable distinction, since selection or censorship *is* distortion. Deviation from known facts is a serious matter. The decision to lie is a weighty one, a burden not to be taken lightly by the persuader. Is our government justified in concealing battle losses in wartime to safeguard domestic morale? Answers to questions like these are both vital and complicated. Probably ultimate judgment must come from considerations of social utility.

Explanation as a Part of Description. Description in persuasion is the process of citing factual patterns for purposes of information and later interpretation. Consciously or unconsciously we are tempted to "load" our descriptive passages by what Pareto terms "slipping explanation covertly into description." For example, in recounting the actions of another individual we will say, "He did this because—" and supply a motive from our imaginations that stands in the story with the stature of a fact.

When the persuader says, "Here are the facts, this is what happened," his first ethical obligation is to keep the description pure. Secondly, he should set apart his explanation by unmistakable signposts such as "Here is my interpretation of these events." Explanation has no place in description if it may be taken at face value as a part of the descriptive detail.

No Place for Tact. Tact is considered by many to be a part of pleasantness and politeness in persuasion, but too superficial to figure in basic ethics. We believe tact to be of ethical importance because people have no right to injure the feelings of others unnecessarily. When a message might have been implemented in an effective way that would have spared the prestige and ego of a minority group but it did not, it falls short of being moral.

Most untactful persuasion has become so through carelessness. Tact might well be made another test of ethics and applied continuously in planning or analyzing persuasion.

Resolution of All Ethical Disputes Through Reason. It is a popular contention that "if people with fundamental disagreements are willing to make the necessary efforts to teach each other the bases of their beliefs they can come to understand each other and the disputes will disappear." We contend that this is true only of disputes concerning experimental beliefs. The most resounding ideological clashes come from nonexperimental attitudes, and these by their nature are detached from the world of evidence and logic. As Stevenson puts it: "If any ethical dispute *is* rooted in disagreement in belief, it may be settled by reasoning and inquiry to whatever extent the beliefs may be so settled. But if any ethical dispute is *not* rooted in disagreement in belief, then no *reasoned* solution of any sort is possible." [10]

---

[10] Stevenson, *op. cit.*, p. 138.

The reasons advanced for this point of view on ethics in persuasion will do little to convert anyone who enjoyed contrary attitudes in the first place. If you contend that ethical principles are fixed, definite, and absolute you may understand the experimental basis of our concept of flexible ethics adapted to context, but you will not approve of it!

THE ROLE OF THE PERSUADER IN MAKING ETHICAL DECISIONS

Let us analyze the role of the individual persuader in making ethical decisions. As a man's knowledge limits his problem-solving ability so his habitual patterns of morality limit the ethical quality of his persuasion. He may not reach the upper limits of his ethical capabilities just as he, for want of particular skills in method, may not be able to solve certain problems. His ethical quotient (E.Q.) may be higher than the level of the ethical decisions he makes in the process of persuasion.

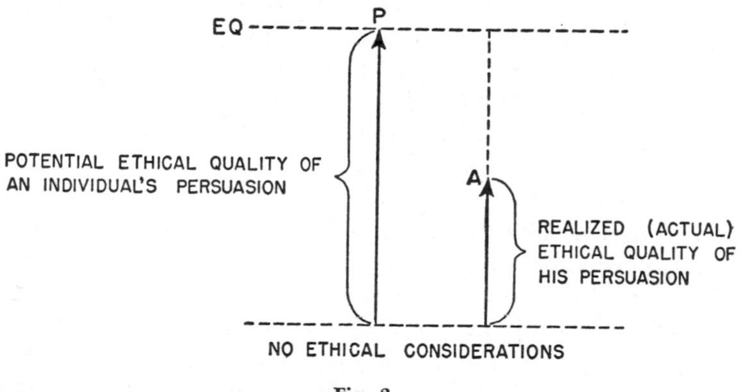

Fig. 3

Obviously, a person may not be able to solve a problem in algebra that falls within the powers indicated by his I.Q. if he knows nothing about algebra. Why does a persuader commonly fall short of his ethical potential? Two factors help account for a general failure of persuasion to measure up to the optimum ethical standards of the individual persuader: (a) the careless neglect of the ethical part of his persuasion, and (b) the lack of a system for "checking up" on his ethics. We omit consideration of the person who deliberately chooses to have a low ethical quotient in the belief that such an attitude serves him best.

Persuaders carelessly neglect ethical considerations because social events place emphasis elsewhere. Incidentally, or accidentally, we let the end become all-important. "Getting the job done" crowds out any worries that might arise over the rightness and wrongness of the act. Many persuaders consciously deal with ethical concepts but in the exceptional instance when unusually dramatic human problems emerge. We tend to forget, carelessly, that our acts of persuasion have ethical implications.

When we do think about being ethical, we frequently want to "do right" but do not know how. "Checking up" on the ethical quality of our persuasion demands specific criteria of ethical judgment. The desire to be moral persuaders is, in the opinion of the present writers, more prevalent than well-thought-out standards of ethics of persuasion. The study of persuasion can make a frontal attack on these twin deficiencies. The student can become so conscious of the ethical qualities of persuasion that he will be unable to neglect them. In addition, he should become familiar with criteria of the ethics of persuasion suggested by various authorities. The course in persuasion has a real responsibility and an opportunity to help the student-persuader climb from "A" to "P." (See Figure 3.)

But we suggest that the ethical quotient of the persuader is not fixed and that the study of persuasion may well increase it. Understanding persuasion in context cannot but impress the persuader with the social consequences of his acts. Clarification of the many aspects of social utility involved in influencing others in our present-day society helps him to redefine his responsibilities to himself and to all those affected by his persuasion. The realization that a person possesses power over people may occasionally intoxicate, but more often it sobers the intelligent adult. Hence many leaders, becoming conscious of determining destinies of their followers, have grown in moral stature. Responsibility for the well-being of others is implicit in all persuasion. It is a moral force of a high order. If the mantle of power happens to settle about our shoulders, most of us will respond by becoming better people.

Summary and Conclusions

Ethical issues seem to be both inherent in and important to the process of persuasion. Accepted standards of ethics not only are worded in general terms but vary with the times and with varying circumstances. This adaptability or flexibility is so impressive that we are forced to conclude: *ethics of persuasion is a function of context.*

Different approaches to the perplexing problem of how to be ethical in persuasion have yielded some excellent advices but each is found to have severe limitations. Rules regarding words to be used or not used, deceptions to be avoided, permissible motive appeals, legal limits to be respected, and cautions respecting the limitations of logic contribute to our formation of a sound concept of ethics. Yet a unified system in which to fit these assorted items is desirable.

Ethical standards for persuasion can be formulated through a context analysis using experimental and nonexperimental bases of behavior and the concept of social utility. With a list of common misunderstandings regarding ethics of communications and a discussion of how the individual persuader may become more ethical, we leave the reader with knowledge of many ways to attack his problems of ethics in persuasion.

The ability to persuade has always been a great power; today it is greater than ever before. In a world ruled by competing persuasions we cannot encourage persuaders who ignore the social utility of their deeds. Both producers and consumers of persuasion must work toward increasing the part played by the interests of people involved in acts of influence.

Readings

1. Merton, Robert K., *Mass Persuasion.* New York: Harper and Brothers, 1946, Ch. 7.
2. McBurney, J. H., O'Neill, J. M., and G. E. Mills, *Argumentation and Debate.* New York: The Macmillan Company, 1951, Ch. II.
3. Stevenson, Chas. L., *Ethics and Language.* New Haven, Conn.: Yale University Press, 1944, Ch. VI.
4. Thonssen, L., and Baird, A. C., *Speech Criticism.* New York: The Ronald Press Company, 1948, Ch. 18.
5. Tsanoff, Radoslav A., *Ethics.* New York: Harper and Brothers, 1947, Ch. XV.

Exercises

1. Find, and describe to the class, an example of a current and generally accepted moral "law" which is stated in absolute terms but is relative in application.

2. Report to the class on particular "forbidden words" and "shameful deceptions" which are often considered to be unethical in advertising.

3. Why is it difficult to separate "high" (worthy) and "low" (unworthy) motives? Give examples.

4. Write a case study of an instance of persuasion in which social utility considerations are important. Under "estimated response" analyze the probable social consequences of this persuasion.

5. Analyze two or three primary forces that have contributed to the building of your present E. Q. Has it changed recently? Why or why not?

Appendix

EXAMPLES OF PERSUASION AT WORK

1. Play golf
2. Join our fraternity
3. Work on our light crew
4. Permit a late audition
5. Clean up after a party
6. Patronize my store
7. Buy this suit
8. Buy this hat
9. Buy this brand of aspirin
10. Radio sales—buy our washing powder
11. Political speech—defeat Taft-Hartley law

Appendix

EXAMPLES OF PERSUASION AT WORK

The authors of this chapter are college students in a beginning class in Argumentation and Persuasion. They had studied materials similar to those presented in the first three chapters, and, at the beginning of the fourth week of school, were assigned projects in the observation and reporting of persuasion in action.

Each student turned in three reports. So that a variety of activities would be studied the assignment specified that one of the three cases should take place in a "primary group," one should deal with a direct speaker-to-audience relationship, and the third should examine an instance of speaker-remote audience persuasion.

This selection represents a cross section of the better case histories turned in by the class. However, these are first observations. It is suggested that the reader analyze each case critically in terms of the standards of observation and reporting set forth in Chapter III. In his own studies of "live" persuasion he may thus benefit from the imitation of good techniques used by these students, and avoid making the mistakes he has found in their work.

Case # 1. *John V. Jensen.*

I. Topic: Conversation between two students.

II. Specific purpose of persuader: To get a friend to go golfing.

III. Occasion: Eating dinner at the boarding house, Monday, October 13.

IV. Persuader (s): A student.

V. Persuadee (s): A friend of the persuader; a fellow student.

VI. Items of Persuasion: List elements of persuasion in the *setting* first, then significant details of what happened in *chronological* order. *Underline* items which seem to be of key significance.

A. Extremely beautiful day.
B. They were heartily enjoying their dinner.
C. The student began his persuasion by telling his friend that they ought

to go out golfing after dinner instead of studying. His persuasive points were as follows:

1. It was such a beautiful day; it would probably be the last nice day all fall.

2. It would probably be their last opportunity to play golf this year.

3. The exercise and sun would do them good.

4. *The day was supposed to have been a Holiday originally anyway.* (Monday, October 13) They might as well use it as a Holiday.

5. His friend had no classes the next day so he had no immediate preparation to worry about.

D. The persuader then filled up another glass of milk for his friend.

E. He then repeated the arguments in a sort of summary fashion, placing special emphasis on the nice weather.

F. *There was then a period of silence* as the persuader let his argument "soak in." The persuadee probably thought he was thinking it over objectively, but I rather suspect that he was only able to run over in his mind all of the arguments listed on the positive side of going golfing, and wasn't finding much to counteract them, except perhaps a faint glimmer of conscience which hinted to him that he should study.

G. After a few minutes of this decision-forming silence, a query from the persuader received an affirmative reply.

VII. Response to Persuasive Effort.

A. Observed: At the end of the meal the friend was thoroughly convinced that they should go golfing.

B. Estimated: They evidently went golfing.

Case # 2. *John N. Christianson.*

I. Topic: The advantages of belonging to a fraternity.

II. Specific purpose of persuader: To convince the group of prospective pledges that they should join Sigma Nu fraternity.

III. Occasion: Rushing dinner.

IV. Persuader (s): Single speaker—fraternity "active."

V. Persuadee (s): Group of prospective pledges, already approved by the fraternity chapter.

VI. Items of Persuasion: List elements of persuasion in the *setting* first, then significant details of what happened in *chronological* order. *Underline* items which seem to be of key significance.

A. Setting

1. The supposed Hollywood conception of the ideal way to live while attending college. The cozy fireplace, the massive easy chairs, the general, luxurious appointments of the room and, of course, the inevitable cigarette held so nonchalantly by a properly adjusted segment of college life.

2. The dapper or, at least, orderly manner of dress of the fraternity members.

3. Not really a physical setting, but certainly a psychological element —the feeling that one has gained admittance into one of those inner-sanctums of mystery, the fraternity house.

B. Elements of Persuasion.

1. All fraternities are good, otherwise they wouldn't be on campus. However, the prospective pledge should join where the members seem to be that type of men whose company he enjoys.

2. This fraternity has all sorts of men, as far as personality is concerned. Nevertheless, they are all of a certain standard with respect to character and the like. The prospective pledge has an opportunity to become acquainted with men in all walks of endeavor, from all walks of life.

3. The aid and assistance that might result from other members of the fraternity in making good grades, an academic success. The emphasis on the graduate counselor plan. Member of the faculty who will help you plan your college program.

4. The advantages that might result after you get out of college through various interested members of the alumni who are already established in that field in which you are working.

5. The great social advantages that a fraternity brings. Sorority girls, parties, etc.,—fraternity gives you a chance to be a campus leader—a BMOC, as it were.

6. The small cost that is incurred in joining a fraternity—small, that is, in comparison with the many advantages which the member will receive.

7. The many ways that the parents are included in the Fraternal life —such things as the Mother's Club, the Father's banquet.

VII. Response to Persuasive Effort.

A. Observed: As all the strong points of fraternity life are given a thorough airing, the persuadees become noticeably impressed with the whole set up. Seemingly, their only hesitance comes from points which have been carefully stated by parents and which the prospective member has been instructed to inquire about—such things as "Are fraternities still as wild as they used to be?" and "Is there great danger in Hell week?" . . . this is especially existent among those students who recently graduated from high school.

B. Estimated: I would say that the prospective pledges were very impressed. They are all men who wish to join some fraternity. Many of them harbor the fear of not being asked to join and believing that this would attach some social stigma to their names. They want to be impressed, to be persuaded—let a persuasive speaker at them and their resistance is at low ebb. This feeling is always there, regardless of the fraternity. There is a definite inclination towards fraternities as a whole.

Case #3. *Shirley Snackenberg.*

I. Topic: Stage work.

II. Specific purpose of persuader: To persuade a person to work on the light crew for a show.

III. Occasion. The show, *All the King's Men.*

IV. Persuader (s): The person in charge of the light crew.

V. Persuadee (s): Myself.

VI. Items of Persuasion: List elements of persuasion in the *setting* first, then significant details of what happened in *chronological* order. Use reverse side of sheet if more space is needed. Underline items which seem to be of key significance.

A. You can see the show for nothing.
B. It's fun working backstage.
C. You'll meet people.
D. It's good back stage experience.
E. *You'll learn how to operate the light board.*
F. *If you work hard backstage, you might get a part later in a show.*
G. You might get a walk-on in this show.
H. You'll learn how to act by watching the actors in the show.
I. *You'll be able to count your hours for Masquer points.*
J. The light crew will not take too much time.
K. You'll be able to go to the cast party after the show is over.
L. *We need more people to work backstage.*

VII. Response to Persuasive Effort.

A. Observed: I worked on the light crew for the show.
B. Estimated: None.

Case #4. *John S. Rogers.*

I. Topic: Advisability of allowing a student to audition for the Radio Guild after he had missed his original appointment.

II. Specific purpose of the persuader: To persuade the membership chairman to give the student a special audition.

III. Occasion: See below.

IV. Persuader (s): Myself.

V. Persuadee (s): Membership chairman.

VI. Items of persuasion: List elements of persuasion in the *setting* first, then significant details of what happened in *chronological* order. *Underline* items which seem to be of key significance.

A. Setting: The student had missed an audition and had been told he could not audition again until next quarter. He had a valid excuse: he had been called by the Navy to get a uniform fitting at the time of the audition and had called the radio station but all of the telephone lines were busy. The membership chairman preferred to disqualify anyone who missed an appointment. I had been asked to persuade the membership chairman to give the student a special audition.

1. I informed the membership chairman that I thought the student should be given a special audition, because radio was one of his main interests.
2. The chairman was convinced that the student could have telephoned the radio station if he had tried.
3. I explained that many times I have been unable to telephone the radio station because the lines were tied up. He admitted he had had the same experience.
4. I stressed the point that the student had no choice but to obey the orders of the Navy, since his schooling was being directed by the Navy.
5. I further stated that the student had had previous experience in radio at the University of Pennsylvania and *thus would likely be an asset to our organization.*
6. I finally pointed out that the student was especially desirous of having an audition and *extremely disappointed at not having been able to keep his original appointment.*
7. The membership chairman finally acquiesced, and the student was given an appointment.

VII. Response to Persuasive Effort.

A. Observed: Stoic acceptance of facts.

B. Estimated: The final response to my persuasive efforts was given rather grudgingly, but I felt that the appeal to "the good of the organization" as well as the student's disappointment were the items that changed the persuadee's mind.

Case #5. *Paul V. Webber.*

I. Topic: House clean up.

II. Specific purpose of persuader: To persuade men to clean up the house after a party.

III. Occasion: Sunday morning after the party.

IV. Persuader (s): House president.

V. Persuadee (s): Unfortunate members reclining around the house.

VI. Items of Persuasion: List elements of persuasion in the *setting* first, then significant details of what happened in *chronological* order. *Underline* items which seem to be of key significance.

A. Dirty dining room.
1. coke bottles lying around.
2. unclean drinking glasses.
3. torn house decorations.
4. popcorn and confetti on the floor.

B. What happened.

1. House president arrives, surveys the condition of the house and the men reading the Sunday newspaper.

2. He requests the attention of the men and makes the following explanation of the situation. "Men, we will all have to turn to and get this place cleaned up."

3. The persuader said it will only take a short time if we "all pitch in."

4. He then stated after no response that there would be no more parties if the clean up wasn't taken care of. This stirred a few of the men, but when he said, *"This place must be cleaned up before dinner will be served and I wish you men would help me,"* all the men moved to clean up the house.

VII. Response to Persuasive Effort.

A. Observed: One of the persuadees asked, "Where are the men who are supposed to clean up?" Another asked, "Where are the pledges?" Still another asked, "Where are the town men?" But they all helped.

B. Estimated: None of the men cared to do the cleaning up, especially those that did not attend the party.

Case #6. *Lucille J. Venetucci.*

I. Topic: Promotion of sales for Dayton's University store.

II. Specific purpose of persuader: To have girls buy from Dayton's through her representation.

III. Occasion: Evening dinner at the Women's Co-operative Village.

IV. Persuader (s): Miss E. W.

V. Persuadee (s): Audience of girls who live at the village.

VI. Items of Persuasion: List elements of persuasion in the *setting* first, then significant details of what happened in *chronological* order. Use reverse side of sheet if more space is needed. *Underline* items which seem to be of key significance.

A. *Dinner-time:* girls in a good, hungry mood, quiet enough to listen to a speaker.

B. *Speaker took the center of the room* to be sure of everyone's attention.

C. Girls could eat their dinners and listen to speaker at the same time; no break-up in the meal; *did not have to stop eating to listen.*

D. Speaker stated she was the *"Official Representative* of the Co-ops at Dayton's."

E. Inquired how many girls were interested in having a *style show:*

1. would be arranged to be given at the co-ops.
2. would use *co-op girls as models* for the show.

F. She had several free hours to give advice on the selection of clothes and would be glad to help anyone when thinking of buying.

1. gave telephone number and address.
2. stated free hours—would also be home in the evenings.
3. sincere offer to help on *planning a "clothes budget."*

G. Could give the girls a *"preview" of new stock coming in.*

H. Could arrange to have the articles from downtown Dayton's brought to the University Store if wanted:

1. *saves you the extra trip downtown and carfare.*

I. See her before buying—she had all the information.

VII. Response to Persuasive Effort.

A. Observed: Girls still in a good mood after the brief talk All said the style show would be a good idea. Seemed to like the speaker personally.

B. Estimated: Will be a good turn-out when the style show comes up. Don't think that many will actually buy new clothes soon. Girls feel that Dayton's is a quality high-prestige store, so if they have a chance to save some money through the "Official Representative" they'll be up to talk things over with her. The fact that she is "one of the girls" and easy to reach will help. The girls have little money to spend on new clothes but will probably keep her in mind and think of Dayton's.

Case #7. *Arley E. Hegne.*

I. Topic: Pre-war selling.

II. Specific purpose of persuader: To sell a suit.

III. Occasion: My regular fall visit to a men's clothing store.

IV. Persuader (s): Salesman.

V. Persuadee (s: Myself.

VI. Items of Persuasion: List elements of persuasion in the *setting* first, then significant details of what happened in *chronological* order. *Underline* items which seem to be of key significance.

A. Smiling floor manager meets you and asks your desires; then, with a flourish, *calls over a clerk thus giving you a feeling of importance.*

B. The clerk pleasantly asks what type of suit you had in mind. If you are in doubt as to material he may suggest something that he assures you would be flattering but which is probably a dead item in his stock.

C. He may be short on certain colors in your particular size so he convinces you that the color he has are the colors you should wear.

D. Then he'll begin fitting coats. He may try two or three in rapid succession but *then if you're still not interested he will slow up and begin emphasizing the details.* When he finds one that fits and pleases you he accelerates his flattery, and he holds the trousers up to you—if you are still interested he suggests you try on the trousers.

E. This last move is your downfall because in your absence he has called the tailor and *when you emerge from the dressing booth they will both begin giving you that critical approval and the tailor will begin chalking up your suit.*

F. When you emerge from the dressing booth the second time, dressed in your old clothes, the clerk hands you your bill along with effusive flattery and tells you your suit will be ready in one week.

VII. Response to persuasive effort.

A. Observed: Patience and pleasantness on the part of the salesman along with a glib tongue to inflate the customers' ego are the chief weapons in accomplishing this sale.

B. Estimated: The customer, when flattered enough is so glad he'll look like a page out of *Esquire* in his new suit he doesn't even think of the dent it will make in his budget.

Case #8. *Beverly Brown.*

I. Topic: Retail selling.

II. Specific purpose of persuader: Sell hat.

III. Occasion: This summer when new fall clothes were coming in—The Emporium.

IV. Persuader (s): Miss Swanson of millinery department.

V. Persuadee (s): Fairly well-dressed customer.

VI. Items of Persuasion: List elements of persuasion in the *setting* first, then significant details of what happened in *chronological* order. Use reverse side if more space is needed. *Underline* items which seems to be of key significance.

A. Customer is trying on jackets when Miss Swanson of the adjoining millinery department rushes up to her and says, "I just unpacked a hat which will be stunning on you, simply stunning. You must come right over and try it on before someone else sees it—then you can come back and look at the jackets."

B. Swanson helps customer take jacket off, gets her purse and packages for her, *takes her by the arm and leads her to the millinery department.*

C. Swanson seats the customer ahead of the mirror and tries the hat on her, saying, "It's stunning, simply stunning!" (Swanson's favorite phrase.)

D. *Swanson backs away from customer to get a better view. She clasps her hands and says, "You don't have to try on another hat,* not another hat—that hat was made for you." Pause as customer turns to get back view of hat. "The profile is excellent, look at that beautiful line—and the color is perfect on you."

E. Another pause, Swanson again, "Do you know what that hat reminds me of, a $45.00 John Fredrics that I saw in New York last week—and on you the hat looks like it was meant to look."

F. Customer finally says in a small voice, "But I wasn't looking for a hat today."

G. *Swanson gets another clerk to rave over the hat,* then she continues, "With your new fall ensemble, it'll be stunning. You know that hat definitely has the new look, it's fall, 1952—and it's the only hat we have like it."

H. Customer finally admits "It does look pretty good."

I. Swanson continues with her line. "You don't know how fortunate you are to find such a beautiful hat, to find 'your' hat—shall I charge it and send it out?"

VII. Response to Persuasive Effort.

A. Observed: The customer bought the hat.

B. Estimated: I do not know whether or not the hat came back. Swanson had a high percentage of returns as several women could not say "no" to her face, but took the hat home and then sent it back. (This actually happened. I was the clerk trying to sell the jackets.)

Case #9. *Gordon Owen.*

I. Topic: Retail selling.

II. Specific purpose of persuader: To sell the brand of aspirin which nets the greatest profit for his employer.

III. Occasion: A routine selling situation.

IV. Persuader (s): A fellow drug clerk.

V. Persuadee (s): Two middle-aged lady customers.

VI. Items of Persuasion: List elements of persuasion in the *setting* first, then significant details of what happened in *chronological* order. *Underline* items which seem to be of key significance.

A. Setting.

1. The ladies asked merely for aspirin without indicating a brand name.

2. A few bottles of each brand of aspirin are kept at the front of the counter with their prices plainly marked on each.

3. *The favored brand nets 50% profit to the retailer while the better known brands net only 33% profit.*

4. The favored brand sells for twenty cents less per hundred than the popularly advertised brands.

B. Chronological Details.

1. In response to the request for "aspirin" the clerk asked the customers if they would like the favored brand, quoting the price as he handed bottle to them for inspection.

2. In response to the customer's hesitation and remarks to the effect that they never heard of the favored brand, the clerk explained, in authoritative tones, that *all five-grain aspirin is alike. He cited United States Food and Drug Pharmaceutical laws requiring standardization as well as the well-known Reader's Digest article on aspirin.*

3. Still unconvinced, the ladies asked why the favored brand could sell for less. The clerk explained that this particular drug company spends nothing for advertising and depends on the local drug stores *to make the bargain known and available to their better, more particular customers, who know and appreciate a bargain.*

Thus by claiming practicality, citing the word of supposed authorities whose very names constitute persuasive power, and by flattering the persuadees the clerk made his sale.

VII. Response to Persuasive Effort.

A. Observed: The only observable reaction of the persuadees was an interest in the persuasion and the evidence of its success in their purchase of the product.

B. Estimated: The persuadees entered the situation with completely unprejudiced minds, and were willing to be persuaded. Early in the episode they were more curious than unconvinced. They left the situation feeling that they had not actually been persuaded, but had demonstrated their knowledge of wise buying.

Case #10. *Andrew M. Nelson.*

I. Topic: Radio Advertising.

II. Specific purpose of persuader: Advertise Dreft soap powder.

III. Occasion: Radio newscast.

IV. Persuader (s): Cedric Adams.

V. Persuadee (s): Radio public.

VI. Items of Persuasion:

List elements of persuasion in the *setting* first, then significant details of what happened in *chronological* order. *Underline* any items which seem to be of key significance.

Dreft is a new *wonder-working* washing powder; it leaves no greasy film; it makes dishes positively *sparkle.* Dishes *dry clean without wiping;* it *cuts grease.* Dreft is easy on the hands. Try it.

VII. Response to Persuasive Effort.

A. Observed: None.

B. Estimated: It keeps the name before the public and no doubt as a result many buy who otherwise would not. People are so used to exaggerated claims that the italicized words probably have little effect.

Case #11. *Geraldine O'Donnell.*

I. Topic: The Taft-Hartley Law.

II. Specific Purpose of Persuader: To persuade his audience to get out and vote at the next election for representatives who will vote for a repeal or amendment of the Taft-Hartley Law in Congress.

III. Occasion: A labor rally at the St. Paul Labor Temple.

IV. Persuader (s): James Shields.

V. Persuadee (s): Members of the A.F. of L., C.I.O., Railroad Brotherhood, and independent unions.

VI. Items of Persuasion: List elements of persuasion in the *setting* first, then significant details of what happened in *chronological* order. Use reverse side of sheet if more space is needed. *Underline* items which seem to be of key significance.

A. Setting.

1. Numerous posters are distributed about the room.

a. *Pictures of how conditions would be* should the Taft-Hartley Law be enforced in the near future.

b. Signs appealing to the whole group: "Labor Must Unite Against Capital."

2. Numerous *flags* were placed on the speakers' platform.

3. Every person present is informed that *Shields* who was the former regional director of the NLRB *resigned from his position when the Taft-Hartley Law went into effect.*

B. Chronological order.

1. City and state *dignitaries* were present in the audience.

2. Community singing preceded Shields' speech.

a. Patriotic songs.

b. Labor words written *to* the tune of *The Battle Hymn of the Republic.*

3. Mr. Shields is given a complimentary introduction in which all of his virtues and background are mentioned.

4. Shields then takes the floor, and appeals to his audience in the following manner.

a. *"You and I are here to represent the interests of the masses of American people—the laboring men."*

b. Shields explained that he resigned from his position because he was unable to tolerate the abuses that the Taft-Hartley Law would no doubt inflict on labor. (Personal sacrifice for a cause.)

c. He went on to describe the situation in which labor unions will be in about a year from now when this law really starts to operate.

d. He picked certain phases of the *law* to point out how it favored *capital's interests* and not those of the working man.

e. "This law is abusive *to all labor.* Labor must unite in its aims."

f. Shields pointed the way to prevent the threatening condition.

(1) Go out and register to vote.

(2) Vote. *"Elect our friends; defeat our enemies."*

VII. Response to Persuasive Effort.

A. Observed.

1. The audience responded by rising spontaneously at the end of his speech and clapping and cheering loudly for a number of minutes.

2. Many crowded around Shields to shake his hand.

3. Remarks could be heard as the crowd filed out of the auditorium:

"Shields knows what he's talking about!"

"I'll have to get my wife to register with me; she'll never do it on her own."

B. Estimated: Only the coming elections will show if Mr. Shields' speech had any effect.

AUTHOR INDEX

F

G

H

I

J

K

L

SUBJECT INDEX